Approaches to Social Inequality and Difference

Series Editors
Edvard Hviding
University of Bergen
Bergen, Norway

Synnøve Bendixsen
University of Bergen
Bergen, Norway

The book series contributes a wealth of new perspectives aiming to denaturalize ongoing social, economic and cultural trends such as the processes of 'crimigration' and racialization, fast-growing social-economic inequalities, depoliticization or technologization of policy, and simultaneously a politicization of difference. By treating naturalization simultaneously as a phenomenon in the world, and as a rudimentary analytical concept for further development and theoretical diversification, we identify a shared point of departure for all volumes in this series, in a search to analyze how difference is produced, governed and reconfigured in a rapidly changing world. By theorizing rich, globally comparative ethnographic materials on how racial/cultural/civilization differences are currently specified and naturalized, the series will throw new light on crucial links between differences, whether biologized and culturalized, and various forms of 'social inequality' that are produced in contemporary global social and political formations.

More information about this series at
http://www.springer.com/series/14775

Synnøve Bendixsen • Mary Bente Bringslid
Halvard Vike
Editors

Egalitarianism in Scandinavia

Historical and Contemporary Perspectives

Editors
Synnøve Bendixsen
Dept of Social Anthropology
University of Bergen
Bergen, Norway

Mary Bente Bringslid
University of Bergen
Bergen, Norway

Halvard Vike
University College Southeast Norway
Skien, Norway

Approaches to Social Inequality and Difference
ISBN 978-3-319-86702-1   ISBN 978-3-319-59791-1   (eBook)
DOI 10.1007/978-3-319-59791-1

© The Editor(s) (if applicable) and The Author(s) 2018
Softcover reprint of the hardcover 1st edition 2017
This book was advertised with a copyright holder in the name of the publisher in error, whereas the author(s)/editor(s) are holding the copyright.
This work is subject to copyright. All rights are solely and exclusively licensed by the Publisher, whether the whole or part of the material is concerned, specifically the rights of translation, reprinting, reuse of illustrations, recitation, broadcasting, reproduction on microfilms or in any other physical way, and transmission or information storage and retrieval, electronic adaptation, computer software, or by similar or dissimilar methodology now known or hereafter developed.
The use of general descriptive names, registered names, trademarks, service marks, etc. in this publication does not imply, even in the absence of a specific statement, that such names are exempt from the relevant protective laws and regulations and therefore free for general use.
The publisher, the authors and the editors are safe to assume that the advice and information in this book are believed to be true and accurate at the date of publication. Neither the publisher nor the authors or the editors give a warranty, express or implied, with respect to the material contained herein or for any errors or omissions that may have been made. The publisher remains neutral with regard to jurisdictional claims in published maps and institutional affiliations.

Cover illustration: © rudchenko/GettyImages

Printed on acid-free paper

This Palgrave Macmillan imprint is published by Springer Nature
The registered company is Springer International Publishing AG
The registered company address is: Gewerbestrasse 11, 6330 Cham, Switzerland

Preface

Seen from afar, Scandinavia is often perceived as a single society, differences between its constituent countries neglected or subtle. This is not consistent with the typical insider view, where differences tend to be emphasized and mutual national stereotypes, often expressed through joking relationships, abound.

Such contrasting exercises are not merely an outcome of the navel-gazing sometimes described as the narcissism of small differences. The three Scandinavian countries (Finland, part of Norden but not of Scandinavia, is bracketed here, justly or not) share many things, but they have distinct histories which have provided rather different raw material for contemporary arrangements and the current role of egalitarian ideologies and practices. Sweden, a regional power of significance for centuries, has a long history of mining and industrialism, economically powerful families, and an influential aristocracy. In Denmark, a fertile agricultural country with colonial ambitions and a rich merchant class, mansions and castles dot the landscape, witnessing deep-seated hierarchies and inequalities in a not-too-distant past. Norway is different and seems to fit the template of historically rooted egalitarianism more snugly than its neighbors. For centuries relatively poor, it failed to produce the kind of economic surplus that could support a substantial nobility; by geographical default, it was decentralized, and the independent Norwegian peasant has long been lionized as a heroic symbol of egalitarianism.

Yet hierarchies are by no means absent from recent Norwegian history either, although nation-builders have sought to obliterate them.

In Knut Hamsun's stories from coastal Northern Norway, the "village owner"—*væreieren*—looms large. He would typically be the owner of the pub, the store, houses, and many of the fishing boats, and ordinary fishermen would instinctively doff their cap to him. In the author and songwriter Alf Prøysen's (1914–1970) popular works from Hedmarken, the rich agricultural lands east of Lake Mjøsa, the major themes are inequality and the humiliation of ordinary folk at the hands of the people from the big houses. So, as many of the contributors to this wonderfully rich and insightful book point out, Scandinavian egalitarianism is neither eternal nor natural. Moreover, the three countries have distinct historical itineraries. A pressing question, to which the authors offer a range of mainly complementary answers, must therefore be how it could be that three countries with so different pasts have turned out so similar in the present.

Trust is a key term in many of the chapters that follow, some of which indicate that interpersonal trust is kept in check by a strong and relatively impartial state preventing the debilitating effects of nepotism and corruption from getting the upper hand. The prevalence of interpersonal trust and informality characterizing the Scandinavian societies, often cited by economists as a comparative advantage, require a certain capability for treating others as equals: they are like us, so we can trust them; or, they are like us, so we can address them by their first name. A simple answer as to the origin of this high level of trust would identify scale as a crucial factor. All other things being equal, the chance that you know someone who knows the Prime Minister is nine times higher in Denmark (pop. 5 million) than in Spain (pop. 46 million). Network structure, famously studied by John Barnes in the early 1950s and followed up in this book, is equally important by ensuring the cross-cutting ties, vertical links, and overlapping networks enable politicians to speak to their nations as family members without sounding overly hollow.

Another important aspect of social organization that the Scandinavian societies have in common concerns family organization. In spite of his background in lineage studies, Barnes did not study kinship and family, instead focusing on networks and committees in the local community after asserting that kinship-based corporate groups did not exist in Bremnes. Ironically, had he looked into family life rather than moving on to non-kinship-based networks, he might have discovered a different source for Scandinavian egalitarianism. Gullestad and Segalen's (1997) important volume about family and kinship in contemporary Europe demonstrates variations in the internal organization of the family as well as indicating connections between family and state. A far bolder, and accordingly more controversial, perspective is found in Emmanuel Todd's (1985) studies of family, kinship and politics. Todd argues that family organization fundamentally shapes political ideology in such a way that styles of political leadership are consistent with styles of family management. In other words, the centrality of the nuclear family as a corporate entity in its own right, characteristic of Scandinavian societies, generates a different set of parameters for political leadership to the hierarchical lineage system found elsewhere. While gender equality in the family, as ideal and practice, is often commented upon, it also deserves mentioning that Scandinavian social life often gravitates around the needs and requirements of children. Children are accorded rights, but they can only be vindicated within the broader compass of the egalitarian nuclear family. As a template for politics in societies of relatively small scale, the nuclear family emphasizes equity, reciprocity, and compromise. qualities associated with Scandinavian societies in general. Consistent with the claims of mid-twentieth-century culture and personality research, these claims deserve to be taken seriously and scrutinized critically.

The strength of the conjugal tie, and—more recently—the promotion of children to the status of full citizens of their families, schools and even kindergartens—represent a powerful expression of egalitarianism. In recent decades, this ideology has come under pressure from the potentially disruptive forces represented by immigration. Anthropologists, in particular, have shown that many migrants represent a view of personhood that contrasts with the predominant view in the majority population; individuality, autonomy, and equality enter into conflict with respect, loyalty, and hierarchy. In the current, historically unprecedented situation where ethnic minorities, including immigrants as well as indigenous groups and "national minorities", demand both equality and the right to difference, it has become evident time and time again that the welfare state is geared toward dealing with inequality, as regards gender, class and regional inequities, but has few tools available for handling cultural diversity as anything but a social problem to be resolved through a stronger emphasis on equality as well as equity. The complementary gender roles favored by many immigrants, for example, are generally perceived as a shortcoming, an evolutionary dead end, an indication that "the immigrants" have not yet quite achieved the high levels of cultural sophistication enjoyed by native Scandinavians. The lineage-based social organization represented by many immigrant groups, while leading to frictions between first and second generations, remains a challenge for societies taking the primacy of the nuclear family and the autonomy of the individual as foundational values. Finally, the culturalization of minority issues witnessed in recent years, where cultural values are discussed more intensively than social justice, may have shifted the point of gravity from a politics of redistribution toward a politics of recognition. Reconciling diversity with equality, and finding a workaround enabling well-established egalitarian ideologies to make peace with alternative kinship ideologies and notions of personhood, may well be among the greatest challenges for the Scandinavian societies in the years to come. For this reason alone, this book ought to be read thoroughly by decision-makers at every level.

Taking on the themes I have hinted at as well as much more, this book shines in its nimble shifts between the small and intimate, on the one hand, and large-scale historical and political processes on the other hand. The editors are to be commended especially for their emphasis on comparison and their willingness to dive fearlessly into the deep and sometimes murky waters of interdisciplinary dialogue. Far from being the last word on the subject, this book is doubtless a significant contribution to serious reflection on Scandinavian societies, and—at a loftier theoretical level—the conditions and possible implications of egalitarian ideologies. Not least, the book invites a long overdue critical reflection on the relationship between scale and social organization. For this effort to be successful and make its mark properly in social theory, more interdisciplinarity and comparison will be needed, including, but not limited to, the Scandinavian societies.

University of Oslo Thomas Hylland Eriksen
Oslo, Norway

REFERENCES

Gullestad, Marianne, and Martine Segalen, eds. 1997. *Family and kinship in Europe*. London: Pinter.

Todd, Emmanuel. 1985. *The explanation of ideology: Family structure and social system* (Trans. David Garrioch). Oxford: Blackwell.

Acknowledgments

The idea for this book emerged while we organized the seminar "Denaturalizing Egalitarianism in the Nordic Countries: Historical and Anthropological Perspectives", at the Department of Social Anthropology, University of Bergen, Norway, November 24–25, 2015. The workshop was a part of the theory-driven project, "Denaturalizing difference: Challenging the Production of Global Social Inequality" (DENAT), funded by the Norwegian Research Foundation, in the Department of Social Anthropology, which brought together scholars to discuss new avenues for research on difference and inequality. The generous funding of DENAT made it possible to bring most of the contributors in this book together for that seminar, and to make this book possible.

We are grateful to the staff at Palgrave Macmillan, in particular Kyra Saniewski and Alexis Nelson, for their support, professionalism and encouragement in this book project. Palgrave's anonymous reviewer gave valuable feedback on the book proposal that pushed this book project forward. Our gratitude extends to Bjørn Bertelsen, Thomas Hylland Eriksen, and Ørnulf Gulbrandsen for their critical engagement with an early draft of the Introduction to this volume. Last but not least, we would like to thank the contributors for their engagement with issues at the core of the Scandinavian societies.

Bergen, Norway
28 February 2017

Synnøve Bendixsen, Mary Bente Bringslid,
and Halvard Vike

Contents

1 Introduction: Egalitarianism in a Scandinavian Context 1
  Synnøve Bendixsen, Mary Bente Bringslid,
  and Halvard Vike

Part I The Tradition of Egalitarianism 45

2 The Cultural Construction of Equality in Norden 47
  Bo Stråth

3 The Cradle of Norwegian Equality and Egalitarianism:
  Norway in the Nineteenth Century 65
  Jan Eivind Myhre

4 *Likhet* Is Not Equality: Discussing Norway in English
  and Norwegian 87
  Simone Abram

Part II   Institutionalizing Egalitarianism — 109

5 The Protestant Ethic and the Spirit of Political Resistance: Notes on the Political Roots of Egalitarianism in Scandinavia — 111
Halvard Vike

6 Social Imaginaries and Egalitarian Practices in the Era of Neoliberalization — 135
Maja Hojer Bruun

7 Normative Hierarchy and Pragmatic Egalitarianism in Municipal Policy Development — 157
Christian Lo

Part III   Egalitarian Welfare? — 179

8 Social Differences in Health as a Challenge to the Danish Welfare State — 181
Camilla Hoffmann Merrild

9 How Deep into Their Lives Can We Really Go? Diverse Populations, Professionals, and Contested Egalitarianisms in an Institutional Setting — 201
Ida Erstad

10 The Limits of Egalitarianism: Irregular Migration and the Norwegian Welfare State — 223
Marry-Anne Karlsen

Part IV   Egalitarianism, Inequality, and Difference — 245

11 Riding Along in the Name of Equality: Everyday Demands on Refugee Children to Conform to Local Bodily Practices of Danish Egalitarianism — 247
Birgitte Romme Larsen

12	Egalitarianism Under Siege? Swedish Refugee Reception and Social Trust Kjell Hansen	269
13	Conditional Belonging: Middle-Class Ethnic Minorities in Norway Monica Five Aarset	291
14	The (In)egalitarian Dynamics of Gender Equality and Homotolerance in Contemporary Norway Christine M. Jacobsen	313
15	Postscript Jonathan Friedman	337
Index		347

List of Contributors

Monica Five Aarset holds a PhD in Social Anthropology and is a researcher at NOVA—Norwegian Social Research, Centre for Welfare and Labour, Oslo, and Akershus University College for Applied Sciences, Norway. Aarset has been working with the theme of minority families and minority youth, and on research projects concerning minority youth, generations, families, migration, asylum seekers, as well as national minorities. Her PhD dissertation concerns family life and belonging among descendants of immigrants in Norway.

Simone Abram first did ethnographic fieldwork in Norway in 2000. Her current research project explores Norwegian kinship through material practices and ownership of property. Her books include *Green Ice. Tourism Ecologies in the European High North* (2016), *Elusive Promises: Planning in the Contemporary World* (2013), and *Culture and Planning* (2011).

Synnøve Bendixsen is a postdoctoral fellow in the Department of Social Anthropology, University of Bergen, Norway. Her research interests include irregular migration, political mobilization, Islam and Muslims in Europe. She has written a number of articles, book chapters, and edited volumes and one monograph: *The Religious Identity of Young Muslim Women in Berlin* (Brill 2013). Since 2013, she has been the co-editor of the *Nordic Journal of Migration Research*.

Mary Bente Bringslid is Associate Professor in the Department of Social Anthropology, University of Bergen, Norway. Her main areas of research are rural Norway, rural development and social integration, heritage, locality, and place.

Maja Hojer Bruun received her PhD in Anthropology on cooperative housing and changes in the Danish welfare society from the University of Copenhagen in 2012. She is now an Associate Professor in Applied Anthropology at Aalborg University. Her research interests include technology, organizations, political and economic anthropology.

Thomas Hylland Eriksen is Professor of Social Anthropology at the University of Oslo, Norway. He has written numerous books, the most recent, *Overheating: An Anthropology of Accelerated Change* (2016). He is currently PI of the ERC project "Overheating" and President of the European Association of Social Anthropologists (EASA).

Ida Erstad holds a PhD in Social Anthropology from the University of Oslo, Norway. Her PhD research was on socialization and migrant motherhood, and the governing of these, in ethnically diverse Alna borough in Oslo, Norway. Erstad has previously conducted research on professionals in local health clinics and hospitals, and SOS Children's Villages in Southern Africa. She currently works in the Department of Research and International Affairs at the Norwegian Directorate of Education and Training.

Jonathan Friedman is Directeur d'études (retired) at the Ecole des Hautes Etudes en Sciences Sociales in Paris, and distinguished Professor of Anthropology emeritus at University of California, San Diego. He has done research on the anthropology of global systems and processes, on Marxist theory in anthropology, the study of crises, and social and cultural movements as products of global systemic crisis. He has done research on South-east Hawaii, Europe, and Central Africa and has written numerous books, including *Modernities, Class, and the Contradictions of Globalization: The Anthropology of Global Systems* (with Kajsa Ekholm Friedman, AltaMira Press, 2011).

Kjell Hansen is Associate Professor of European Ethnology, and works as senior lecturer in the division of rural development at the Swedish University for Agricultural Sciences in Uppsala, Sweden. His main research focus is the relationships between central policies and local, rural practices. Presently he is doing research on the integration processes of refugees, and on the role of civil society organizations in rural areas.

LIST OF CONTRIBUTORS xvii

Christine M. Jacobsen is Professor of Social Anthropology and Director of the Centre for Women's and Gender Studies (SKOK) at the University of Bergen, Norway. She specializes in the areas of migration, religion, and gender. Her latest book is *Eksepsjonell velferd? Irregulære migranter i det norske velferdssamfunnet* [Exceptional Welfare?: Irregular Migrants in the Norwegian Welfare State] (Gyldendal, 2015, co-edited with Synnøve Bendixsen and Karl Harald Søvig).

Marry-Anne Karlsen is a postdoctoral fellow at the Centre for Women's and Gender Research (SKOK), and senior researcher at Uni Research Rokkan Centre. She has a background in both Human Geography and Social Anthropology. Her research interests cover migration, welfare state, and border politics.

Birgitte Romme Larsen has a PhD from the Department of Anthropology, University of Copenhagen, Denmark, and is currently a postdoctoral fellow at The Saxo Institute, Centre for Advanced Migration Studies, University of Copenhagen. Her main research interests concern the dynamics of neighborliness and the processes of inclusion, exclusion, and belonging in the everyday encounter between refugees and asylum seekers and local inhabitants in rural areas of Denmark.

Christian Lo is a senior researcher at the Nordland Research Institute (*Nordlandsforskning*). He holds a MSc in Social Anthropology, and a PhD in Sociology. In his PhD work, he conducted ethnographic studies within municipal organizations in Norway, exploring the relationship between hierarchical government and networked governance in municipal policy development.

Camilla Hoffmann Merrild is an anthropologist working as a postdoctoral fellow at the Center for Research in Cancer Diagnosis in Primary Care, the Research Unit for General Practice, Institute of Public Health, Aarhus University, Denmark. Her research focuses on social differences in experiences of health, illness, and the body as well as care-seeking practices, and she has carried out fieldwork among different social groups in Denmark.

Jan Eivind Myhre is a Professor of Modern History at the University of Oslo. He has had research stays at universities in Berkeley, Oxford, Cambridge, Berlin, Leicester, and Osnabrück. His latest books are *Boundaries of History* (ed., 2015); *Norsk historie 1814–1905* (2nd ed.,

2015); *Historie. En introduksjon til grunnlagsproblemer* (2014); *Kunnskapsbærerne 1811–2011. Akademikere mellom universitet og samfunn* (2011); and *Intellectuals in the Public Sphere* (ed., 2008).

Bo Stråth is a Professor emeritus, fil.dr, and was 2007–2014 Finnish Academy Distinguished Professor in Nordic, European and World History, and Director of Research at the Department of World Cultures/Centre of Nordic Studies (CENS), University of Helsinki, Finland. In 1997–2007, he was Professor of Contemporary History at the European University Institute in Florence. Stråth's research has focused on the philosophy of history and political, social, and economic theory of modernity, from a conceptual history perspective with special attention to questions of what keeps societies together or divides them.

Halvard Vike is Professor of Welfare Studies at the University College of Southeast Norway, and senior researcher at Telemark Research Institute. Formerly Professor of Anthropology at the University of Oslo, Vike has published extensively on local politics, political culture, bureaucracy and organizations, historical anthropology, psychiatry, and cognitive anthropology.

CHAPTER 1

Introduction: Egalitarianism in a Scandinavian Context

Synnøve Bendixsen, Mary Bente Bringslid, and Halvard Vike

John Barnes was the first anthropologist to carry out Malinowskian fieldwork in Norway, in the early 1950s, in the island parish of Bremnes on the west coast. Barnes (1954) identified "committees and [social] class" as salient features of the local world he observed. According to Barnes, Bremnes and other peripheral areas of Norway were characterized by an absence of conventional state apparatus as a result of Norway's separation from Denmark (in 1814) and Sweden (in 1905). Instead, various forms of local politics were gradually filling this political void: committees, for example, represented "a common pattern of organization … in every instance of formal social life" (Barnes 1954, 50). Thus, Barnes noted, there was a committee for each association, elected at an annual meeting, with an executive council, a chairman, treasurer, and a secretary—with all positions

---

S. Bendixsen (✉) • M.B. Bringslid (✉)
Department of Social Anthropology, University of Bergen,
Bergen, Norway

H. Vike
Department of Health, Social, and Welfare Studies, University College of Southeast Norway, Porsgrunn, Norway

© The Author(s) 2018
S. Bendixsen et al. (eds.), *Egalitarianism in Scandinavia*,
Approaches to Social Inequality and Difference,
DOI 10.1007/978-3-319-59791-1_1

filled on the basis of a simple majority vote. Furthermore, Barnes speculated about what type of social class system Bremnes would have in the future. He saw the social process he was observing, with its "gradual emergence of part-time peasants in key positions of government", as necessarily transitional. In the future, he expected increasing class differences to undermine the current role of part-time peasants, as well as that of the committees. In Bremnes, at the time of Barnes's fieldwork, social inequality was clearly present, but a strongly egalitarian code of behavior seemed to make this largely irrelevant. Barnes's assumption was that this situation would change as inequality increased.

Today, as far as class relations are concerned, Barnes was partly right. Norway and the other Scandinavian countries have indeed been profoundly shaped by social class. As Barnes noted, the "part-time peasants" in the coastal areas in Bremnes were involved from the start in the commercial fish trade, in much the same way as peasants in other parts of the country were involved in the timber trade. At the time of his fieldwork, the fishing industry was expanding, establishing what Barnes saw as a more "modern" system of hierarchical relations than the ones he observed in politics and social networks in the community.

As indicated by Barnes's description of "part-time peasants", the "equality" that many observers (as well as many Scandinavians themselves) have regarded as a characteristic feature of Scandinavia has not come about because penetration of Europe's northern periphery by capitalism—in commercial, industrial, and financial forms—has been incomplete in any way.[1] Rather, Barnes's observation of political activity among part-time peasants noted an egalitarian social relationship, operating within a specific institutional and historical context. His anthropological informants were members of formally organized committees that overlapped with informal networks of kin, neighbors, friends, and workmates. In Bremnes, egalitarianism emerged as a combination of a particular worldview, certain universal citizen rights, a style of interaction, and—perhaps above all—an *institutional mechanism* for dealing with political conflict. Barnes emphasized that political conflicts, when channeled through committee discussions and the municipal assembly, mostly ended in unanimous votes.

Around the same time as Barnes was writing his seminal article on class and committees in Bremnes, anthropology was becoming established as an academic discipline in Scandinavia. Interest in the field grew quickly over the following decades, although relatively few anthropologists exhibit ethnographic interest in this region. The majority have concentrated on other parts of the world, aiming to contribute to the discipline's ambition to map disappearing worlds and compare cultures on a global scale. To the extent that anthropologists representing the dominant research environments in Britain and the USA have been interested in Scandinavian ethnography, and in carrying out fieldwork in the region, the focus has mainly been on the Sami people in the North. To date, the ethnographic study of Scandinavia has been fragmented, and hardly constitutes a coherent research tradition or agenda. The exceptions to this are the fields of ethnic relations and minority studies, which have grown considerably since the 1990s, partly inspired by an interest in majority–minority relations emerging from the initial focus on the Sami.

A quarter of a century after Barnes's study of Bremnes, Swedish ethnologists Jonas Frykman and Orvar Löfgren published the influential *Cultured Man* (in Swedish, *Den kultiverade människan* 1979) on Swedish modernization. They argued that the old bourgeois and the new middle classes had been so successful in using the state as a means for influencing the lower strata of the population in the twentieth century that most people seemed to have forgotten how to perceive of categorical differences relating to social class. All types of difference were reduced to versions of individual deviation in relation to a hegemonic notion of "normality". The aspiration to become socially mobile had penetrated the agrarian population and the working classes so thoroughly that they had enthusiastically embraced middle-class culture and made it their own, assisted by the institutions of the state, through which the means of discipline were also disseminated (Sejersted 2005).

Frykman and Löfgren came from an intellectual tradition inspired by German *Volkskunde*, and they remained committed to studying historical folk traditions. They were also strongly influenced by social anthropology, neo-Marxism, and by the work of Michel Foucault (Löfgren 1987). Their own influence on later Scandinavian scholars was considerable. Indeed, the importance they placed on historical aspects and perspectives is no less significant today, and this focus has been an inspirational source for the present research, which is an interdisciplinary venture among anthropologists, historians, and one ethnologist.

A decade after Frykman and Löfgren, Marianne Gullestad, a Norwegian anthropologist educated in (what was then known as) the Bergen School (under the direction of Fredrik Barth), brought anthropology "home" in yet another sense. Gullestad became interested in the everyday life of urban people, particularly the working class, and explored patterns of interaction in detail. Drawing on the scholarship of Dumont, Gullestad (1984) explored the concept of "egalitarian individualism", which became highly influential in studies of Scandinavian culture. She emphasized that the dominant code of behavior she had observed in a variety of social contexts, where equality in status was ritually emphasized, was a pragmatic one. As Gullestad saw it, it was more about partners making each other similar over the course of interactions than about an objective form of equality.

Taken together, these three approaches encapsulate much of what the authors of this Introduction regard as analytically significant when studying egalitarianism in Scandinavia. Barnes investigated political activity through the lens of actors' membership in voluntary associations and municipal decision-making bodies. Frykman and Löfgren explored the historical trajectory of the disciplining state and the capacity of public institutions to generate new worldviews and ideas. The rise of bourgeois ideals that spread and became almost universal instituted particular forms of individual aesthetics, materiality, and bodily manners. Lastly, Gullestad demonstrated how the cultural ethos of equality as sameness is socially embedded in Scandinavia, in specific interactional patterns and styles.

These three analytical perspectives are complementary and together indicate a specific dynamic; they cover different aspects of social reality and represent different analytical levels—all of which are necessary tools for constructing a more thorough, relevant model of Scandinavian egalitarianism. Over the course of the present volume, we present a fuller understanding of the phenomenon of egalitarianism in Scandinavia, in which endeavor we draw on the political institutionalization that Barnes explored, the historical perspectives developed by Frykman and Löfgren, and Gullestad's exploration of egalitarianism as a pragmatic value.

Gullestad's analytical term "equality as sameness" may be applicable to many different social contexts outside Scandinavia. However, in light of Barnes's study of municipal politics, in our present context, it may be hypothesized that Gullestad's forms of social interaction, which she associates with life in informal contexts in Scandinavia, may in fact have penetrated "the state" via associations and municipal governance. Lastly, Frykman and Löfgren describe perceptions of the national community and the grand visions that guide state policies, which largely mirror municipal policies. The municipal political life described by Barnes was neither authoritarian nor very powerful, yet the institutional strength of Scandinavian municipalities has proved to be considerable. From the early nineteenth century onwards, they have been based on broad participation, have had important representative functions, and in tandem with the local clergy and local courts, they have had a significant disciplining capacity. Pragmatically motivated policies developed locally by municipalities—for example, in the fields of poverty relief, education, elder care, banking, transport, and infrastructure, and later in childcare and pension systems—have been quite far-reaching (Baldersheim et al. 1987; Nagel 1991; Seip 1992).

In short, then, we ask the following important questions of our Scandinavian context. How can we understand egalitarianism in the context of Scandinavian welfare states? How does egalitarianism in the Scandinavian context differ from other contemporary versions of egalitarianism? If any form of egalitarianism must be understood in relation to a particular historical and socio-cultural background, what happens to egalitarianism in times of larger socio-historical changes? What can an exploration of egalitarianism in a Scandinavian context tell us more broadly about egalitarianism as an analytical concept and as an empirical possibility?

This volume approaches egalitarianism from a variety of analytical perspectives. As proposed by Solway (2006, 2), for example, it can be understood "as a theoretical possibility, an historical fact, and a political project". In the Scandinavian case, egalitarianism may also be fruitfully understood as a process of institutionalization, as illustrated by Barnes. Here, we consider the institutionalization of egalitarianism as a particular Scandinavian feature, tied to popular (membership-based) movements, municipal politics, and the welfare state (see Chaps. 5 and 8). As established in several of the following chapters (Chaps. 9, 11 and 13), egalitarianism is also in part about cultural and social values and models, and in this introduction we also suggest that egalitarianism may be an unintended effect of historical contingencies. From this perspective, egalitarian practices and imaginaries are emergent properties of conflict and social tension relating to class, gender, and ethnicity, for example. Furthermore, we illustrate how *resistance movements* have played an important role in the history of egalitarianism in Scandinavia, which highlights out new dynamics among the region's fundamental ideas, practices, and social organization. A historically informed perspective suggests, for example, that there is a particular Scandinavian interrelation between the state and the people, where the state has tended to incorporate, or co-opt, resistance movements and organizations rather than fighting or attempting to marginalize them. Can this historically informed tradition have implications for the state's potential capacity to meet new groups of immigrants today?

These different ways of understanding egalitarianism are neither exclusive nor disconnected. Rather, in understanding egalitarianism as a political project, for example, we can view it as an aspect of institutional structures and forms of redistributive policy. It is, thus, closely intertwined with associational life, membership, democratic representation, welfare policies that are universally oriented, entitlements and services, and access to means of economic security. As Scandinavian ideas of self and community are increasingly challenged by growing cultural complexity, social inequality, and migration, we explore how these ideas are being transformed.

Part of the remit of this introductory chapter is to discuss substantive issues of egalitarianism in Scandinavian countries. It does not intend to provide an overview of anthropological engagement with the concept of egalitarianism, which recent scholarship has already addressed (see Barth et al. 2014; Bruun 2015; Bruun et al. 2011; Bryden et al. 2015; Lien et al. 2001). Rather, we set out different ways of engaging with and grasping the concept of egalitarianism in a Scandinavian context.

After briefly discussing egalitarianism in Solway's (2006, 2) terms, as a "theoretical possibility", we explore it in relation to the ideological and social construction of Scandinavian welfare states, investigating in particular the role of civil society and politics. Then, through an empirical discussion of egalitarianism in Scandinavia as an unintended effect, in historical terms, we show how egalitarian popular movements have become *institutionalized* and tied to state policy. Alongside this, we discuss how movements driven by ideas of equalitarianism have become embedded in state structures. We move this discussion forward, elaborating on what egalitarianism as a cultural and social value in Scandinavia may mean, and explore its institutionalization in this context as well. The last section of the Introduction positions the ways in which egalitarianism as a political project has been pursued (or not), and this project's—sometimes unintended—consequences in an era of migration. In this section, we also engage with the political project of gender equality—a trademark of Scandinavian countries—and with how the social conditions for the political ambition of gender equality have changed over time. We end this introductory chapter by asking what the future of the institutionalization of egalitarianism might be.

Egalitarianism as a Theoretical Possibility

The legacy of the French Revolution is an important starting point for understanding egalitarianism, in Scandinavia and elsewhere. Perhaps the most important driving force for the French Revolution was the desire to get rid of the old regime's oppressive structures of inequality, through constructing a contradiction between the individual and social structures, situating the notion of the egalitarian in a so-called natural individual who was bounded by social structures. As Bruce Kapferer argues:

> The egalitarian spirit of the Revolution was founded in the fundamental illegitimacy in nature of any necessary right to authority or to govern, or any such claim based on hierarchy or morality. Only egalitarianism, equality, has legitimacy in nature, not society or, especially, the state. Equality is pre-value, pre-ideological, the condition for what may follow. Egalitarianism is the only thing that is naturally legitimate, and it is thus upon equality that everything else rests. (2015, 108)

Thus, egalitarianism became linked to an idea of "the natural individual", while social structures became associated with inequality and oppression. Consequently, in the legacy of the French Revolution, certain perceptions steer our thoughts about the relations between the individual and the state or social structures. According to Kapferer, the French Revolution and the spirit of egalitarianism that fueled it were directed against both society and the state. That is, egalitarianism emerged as a legitimate form of anti-structure.

Scandinavian societies have particular characteristics when it comes to the appropriation of this mind set, for example, as outlined by Lars Trägårdh in *The Cultural Construction of Norden* (Sørensen and Stråth 1997), to which this volume will return. As explored in some of the following chapters, rather than being characterized by a tension or contradiction between the citizen and the state, Scandinavian societies are characterized by high levels of trust in the state. The state in Scandinavia is to a considerable extent regarded as an extension of a political community, the legitimacy of which rests on the perception of broad participation and popular control

In the European Enlightenment tradition, egalitarianism is one of the most celebrated ideas; as such, it has become a defining attribute of Western democracy and of the infrastructure of human rights. In this tradition, egalitarianism encompasses the idea that each individual has equal moral worth, as well as being linked to the natural rights of each individual; as indicated above, it also means protection from arbitrary state actions. Today, most modern state constitutions are committed to the Enlightenment notion that all humans have equal dignity and worth, which should provide all citizens with the value of equality before the law.

The notion of the free individual, however, as many have observed, does not necessarily sit well with the notion of the egalitarian individual. Sociologist Georg Simmel (1971, 220) writes of eighteenth-century individualism as "the deepest point of individuality", and "the point of universal equality". He explains, "[w]hether it is nature, reason or man, it is always something shared with others in which the individual discovers himself when he has discovered his own freedom, his own selfhood" (Simmel 1971, 221). According to Simmel, as individuals are reliant upon their essential self, and stand on the same footing as everyone else, freedom reveals equality. However, he also observes that this universal feature of individualism is in conflict with another key aspect of it, namely, an understanding of the individual that emphasizes the uniqueness of their qualities and values, which Simmel believes generates inequality rather than equality. His work thus exposes an inherent contradiction between individualism and egalitarianism: "As soon as the ego became sufficiently strengthened by the feeling of equality and universality, it sought once again inequality—but this time an inequality from within" (Simmel 1971, 222).

Simmel suggests that this discord within the individual was latent in the European understanding of individuality until the nineteenth century, when it was finally articulated. Indeed, historical traits confirm this: the liberal individual, cultivating a traditional capitalist society, produced inequality. Politically, it has been commonplace to distinguish between egalitarian in principle and egalitarian as a result (Heywood 2004, 285–291), between equality of opportunity and distributive equality. In the liberal tradition, emphasis is placed on the former—on making individuals alike from the beginning in terms of basic human rights and legal rights as citizens of a state. With the advent of neo-liberalism, however, the framework of what a state should do to contribute to equality has become rather narrower. The individual differences, in Simmel's words, "the equality posited from within" (1950, 78) are understood as natural and to be guarded; here, it is the state's role to facilitate competition based on inequality (Hayek 2007, 90).

Egalitarianism as an Enlightenment ideal and theoretical possibility, however, does not necessarily lead to egalitarianism as an empirical reality. In his discussion of European egalitarianism, Kapferer sees the French revolutionary heritage of European egalitarianism as contradictory and in struggle with itself:

> In-egalitarianism is the enduring potential of egalitarianism's other side, the many-headed Hydra that continually springs up against egalitarianism in the moment of egalitarianism itself. (2015, 106)

Kapferer here shines a light on the paradoxical feature of the powerful and "egalitarian" support for those who were struck by the terrorist action in France: "the expression of egalitarian community in reaction to the Charlie Hebdou event had as a paradox of its effect, the very inegalitarian exclusion of French Muslims" (Kapferer 2015, 109). The French Revolution ignited the politicization of egalitarianism, but the course of events following the initial transformation of the autocratic order very rapidly led to another transformation: terror in the name of egalitarianism. Referring to the last year's immigration, egalitarianism in Scandinavia can be understood as particular forms of understanding, appropriating, and acting upon the dialectic between the two sides of egalitarianism, the egalitarian and its possibility of inegalitarian consequences.

These insights lay the foundation for our discussion in the latter part of this Introduction, which explores how egalitarianism in Scandinavia can be understood as a particular forms of understanding, appropriating and acting upon the dialectic between the two sides of egalitarianism, that is, between the egalitarian and its possibility of inegalitarian consequences. Egalitarianism in Scandinavia might historically be seen as a dialectic between egalitarian resistance movements and as principles of social organization. Central to social organization in Scandinavia is the welfare state.

Egalitarianism and the Welfare State

Seen as a political project, egalitarianism in Scandinavia is firmly tied to the ideological and social construction of a strong welfare state. With its redistributive ideology, the welfare state is generally interpreted as expressing commitment to egalitarian values (Siim 1993), and is expected to attend to inequalities in economic resources, political power, and influence, and regional variation (Ellingsæter and Leira 2006). In economic terms, contemporary Scandinavia may be characterized by an exceptional degree of "wage compression" (relatively small differences between high and low wages), a collective bargaining system, and political emphasis on full employment. Labor market policies conform to a logic of "flexicurity" (Vulkan et al. 2015), involving the facilitation of "creative destruction" in the business/industrial sector, combined with a high degree of public support for the unemployed (including income protection and support to acquire higher/new professional skills). All these factors appear to stimulate market cooperation (between employers and unions), productivity, and a widely shared preference for high welfare spending (Barth et al. 2014). However, the increasing influence of "the culture of neo-liberalism" (Comaroff and Comaroff 2011) in Scandinavia, which has been influencing governance and policy, public institutions, and ideological sensitivity since the 1980s (Bruun et al. 2015; Sejersted 2005), has generated substantive changes, and there is widespread concern that it legitimizes increasing inequality. For example, the combined effects of the politics of austerity and neo-liberal managerialism are clearly visible through the restructuring of the relationship between the state and local democratic institutions (municipalities). They have generated large-scale centralization, and today municipalities are increasingly being transformed into implementation tools for national-level state institutions (Blom-Hansen 2010; Granberg 2008; Tranvik and Selle 2007). Despite this, it should also be emphasized that scholars working in the field of comparative welfare state research seem to agree that the effects of neo-liberal policies have not (yet) fundamentally transformed or undermined the distinctive features of the Scandinavian model (Arter 2008; Glyn 2006).

The institutionalization of egalitarianism through the welfare state must be understood in historical terms: traditionally, Scandinavian populations have not really imagined national solidarity in opposition to the state, at least, not to any significant extent. On the contrary, there seems to be a strong tendency to imagine the state pragmatically as a medium, and as an executive aspect of the democratic, collective will. This, presumably, constitutes a key component of the development of the Scandinavian version of welfare capitalism, and seems to have much to do with how large sections of its populations have embraced the public responsibility assumed by the growing states—and their redistributive measures and public services in particular. Indeed, this has been experienced as a strengthening of personal autonomy. According to Gøsta Esping-Andersen (1990), a leading theorist of egalitarianism in Europe, the Scandinavian version of welfare capitalism was inspired by broad mass movements rising to parliamentary power in the twentieth century, which made the Scandinavian states exceptionally active in terms of influencing market competition and regulating the life trajectories of individual citizens. Furthermore, according to Esping-Andersen, the concept of *de-commodification* encapsulates this phenomenon, in reference to (Scandinavian) state policies that seek to shelter the population (qua individuals) from market dependence—that is, from the negative effects of market competition, broadly understood: thus, the state guarantees the means of livelihood for all. The other significant aspect of de-commodification in this context is the emphasis on social reproduction: social investment policies aim to maintain and strengthen citizens' capacity for self-help across generations.

The universalist orientation guiding the welfare policies of the Scandinavian states may play a significant role in this. Scholars generally agree that universalism promotes popular support for the welfare state—most crucially among the middle classes, who otherwise tend not to view public services as a common good from which they themselves benefit (Kildal and Kuhnle 2005). In this light, associating the universalism of Scandinavian welfare policies with "generosity" misses the point (Headey 1999). Universalism was probably never intended to be "generous", but was, in historical terms, a practical means by which associations (missions, women's associations, sport associations, neighborhood associations, philanthropic associations, and the labor movement, for example) that initiated and developed collective welfare arrangements gained support, recruited members, and ran the business in the most unbureaucratic way possible. When universalism later became a foundational policy principle, it emerged as a class compromise (Kildal and Kuhnle 2005; Knudsen 2000).

According to Esping-Andersen (1985, 154), when the Social Democrats achieved parliamentary power in the early years of the twentieth century, they "had to cultivate, and fabricate, unity among workers, peasants, and the rising white collar strata". Perhaps for these reasons, welfare as a societal ideal was to some extent de-coupled from the negative associations linked to being "on welfare". In the early twentieth century, when civil (and later, municipal) arrangements of this type were taken over by municipalities and thereafter by states, universalism was reinforced as a result of the widespread fear that social insurance would become a class issue, rather than an inclusive measure for "the people" (Sejersted 2005). An important side effect was that welfare policies—and the public services provided by the municipalities in particular—tend to mobilize large coalitions throughout Scandinavia, seeking to protect and expand them.

Policies of de-commodification make for strong states. For many political thinkers, this fact is logically linked to the Enlightenment idea that freedom and equality are difficult to balance out (Sørensen and Stråth 1997). At one extreme, the political ambition to establish equality is potentially authoritarian. Thus, a key question has concerned how the exceptionally active, de-commodifying Scandinavian states have achieved legitimacy without (as yet) transforming into vast and alienating bureaucracies. This question seems logical in relation to liberal reactions to the French Revolution: individual freedom depends on freedom both from arbitrary power exercised by feudal lords and absolute kings, but also from state power. An outline of political and scholarly discourses on civil society may serve as an illustration of what we mean when we seek to identify the sources of state legitimacy in Scandinavia.

The State and Civil Society

What is civil society in the context of a state-centric welfare state? From the theories of Hegel, Habermas, and American communitarianism, to liberal notions of democratic sustainability (Alexander 2006; Bellah et al. 1985; Putnam 2000; Trägårdh 2007), scholars have assumed that any liberal, democratic regime is in need of some sort of civil society that stands apart from the state and is capable of sustaining itself in the form of genuine, autonomous "life-worlds" in the Habermasian sense (Habermas 1987). Accordingly, civil society autonomy is often regarded as essential to cultivate a political culture that reproduces egalitarian social bonds, the motivation among citizens to be involved in caring for the common good, and nourishing a sense of individual responsibility (Etzioni 1995). This requires a relatively clearly bounded state that refrains from absorbing and transforming such essential qualities. However, while the perspective outlined here may be fruitful, it largely fails to account for some Scandinavian characteristics, such as unique levels of growth and the viability of voluntary activity, stimulated by state expansion (Sivesind and Selle 2010).

As Swedish historian Lars Trägårdh (2007) explains, in Scandinavia, voluntary activity has never been seen as separate from the state, but, rather, has always been an integral part of it, and because ideas of freedom are so strongly attached to individual autonomy, public policy and services are regarded as essential means by which to realize both. The classical liberal notion that individual freedom depends on a limited state has proven to be very weak indeed in this context. To Scandinavian populations, the state is more an ally than an external, powerful agent representing a threat to their autonomy, although the conservative and liberal parties (the Conservative Party and the Liberal Party), as well as the populist right (the Progress Party), have capitalized on presenting the state as neither an ally nor "non-harmful".

Trägårdh (2007, 2008) observed that in Scandinavia, extensive public entitlements and services have contributed to the generation of a radically individualist ethos. Although dependence on the state is a characteristic feature of Scandinavian welfare states, this dependency has not generally been viewed as especially problematic. The right to receive state support in the form of economic benefits and public services (which is largely experienced as conducive to freedom and individual autonomy) seems to be more highly valued than freedom from state (or municipal) interference in private life, as well as the right to choose not to pay relatively high taxes. One important aspect of this, which this volume addresses in depth, is the fact that the institutional arrangements of Scandinavian welfare states are both *individualizing* and at the same time encourage the institutionalization of highly collectivist, "one-size-fits-all" policy solutions. Welfare policies have contributed significantly to reducing individual dependency, not only in the markets, but also in the family, the neighborhood, and in other social structures. This effect seems to be mirrored in the relatively widespread preference for organizing social relations on the basis of formal membership (in voluntary associations), as well as in the overlapping forms of responsibility assumed by those associations on the one hand, and by municipalities and the state, on the other. A relevant case in point concerning the apparent amalgamation of the state with civil society is the temperance movement in Sweden and Norway. In the early twentieth century, this movement mobilized large parts of these populations to combat alcohol abuse. It grew out of voluntary associations (Christian, socialist, and philanthropic) and rapidly became an integral part of public policy, intervening in people's lives in the name of the common good (Knudsen and Rothstein 1994; Stenius 2010). The temperance movement thus serves to symbolize both the way in which state and society may be seen as a single entity, and the relative absence of a deep-seated liberal concern that the boundaries of the state may become blurred and thus threatening (Dahl 1986)

The Local Level of the State

To understand institutionalized egalitarianism in the context of the Scandinavian state, and as a historical unintended effect, it is worth noting that although they are strong states Scandinavian countries are characterized by a decentralized political system. This not only refers to the devolution of power from the state to the local level, but also encompasses a kind of institutional tension with deep historical roots. Here, the main responsibilities taken on by the welfare state are managed locally. This combination of an expansive welfare state and relatively small, local service providing institutions governed though democratic representation creates a situation in which many people's idea of "the state" is often very general and diffuse, partly because so many of the big political issues are translated into practical, municipal concerns (Knudsen 2000; Vike 1997).

An interesting case in point is sociologist Apostolis Papakostas's (2001) analysis of bureaucratic traditions in Sweden. During the seventeenth and eighteenth centuries, the Swedish state bureaucracy had grown strong and enjoyed a significant degree of autonomy in relation to both political power and popular demands. Drawing analytical inspiration from historical sociology (and the work of Stein Rokkan and Charles Tilly, in particular), Papakostas argues that the Swedish population was then incorporated into state institutions and policies at the point of democratic mass mobilization in the late eighteenth and early nineteenth centuries. There was little room here for patrons and other powerful mediators.[2] In relation to contemporary Sweden, Papakostas suggests that complex bureaucracies at the local level, responsible for organizing and providing a wide array of services, can now function in small-scale contexts without becoming absorbed by informal power relations and systems of personal dependency. According to Papakostas, the historical (and partly accidental) timing is essential. For example, as street-level bureaucracy (providers of public services) grew strong and became a key feature of the welfare state, the discretion that was required at the interface between "the state" and local populations was appropriated from bureaucratic traditions that stemmed from the monarchical *Rechtstaat*, and in this way they retained relative autonomy. This autonomy seems to have facilitated dealing with clients as instances of general cases, as well as the ability to strike a balance between street-level bureaucrats' many—and potentially contradictory—roles in the context of this interface.

More generally, these "street-level bureaucrats" of the Scandinavian welfare state at local and national levels have yet to be fully explored (although Papakostas's discussion is a significant contribution). As representatives of ambitious welfare institutions, with a strong tradition of professional autonomy and discretion, they have carried out their work in a world of conflicting loyalties and identities. As advocates for the users, local communities, their own professions, and their employers (the municipalities), they have—together with local political representatives in the municipal assemblies—played an important role as representatives with a double agenda. Such local alliances represent a challenge to the autonomy of state elites—and perhaps particularly so when austerity measures and ambitions to strengthen control over unruly municipalities are high on the agenda.

Egalitarianism as an Unintended Effect

One of the most important comparative explorations of the Scandinavian countries (and Finland) to date is Øystein Sørensen and Bo Stråth's *The Cultural Construction of Norden* (1997). The contributors take issue with the core idea discussed in the book's introductory chapter, namely, that Nordic modernization represents a European *Sonderweg*, particularly in the sense that the Enlightenment came to mean something different in this region when compared to Germany and other major European countries. Here, the majority of yeoman farmers rose above their status as heroic symbols of the nation, as construed by intellectual and bourgeois elites, and seized a role as key actors in political and economic modernization. Nordic Enlightenment, according to Sørensen and Stråth, was mainly pragmatic and inclusive, and contributed to striking a balance between freedom and equality.

Scandinavia is unique in Western Europe in that there has been no real class war; the internal history of these countries has been remarkably non-violent, and the labor movements' increasing inclination to use strikes as a political weapon was never criminalized (Stenius 2010). The opportunity to use non-violent paths to initiate and provoke change may partly explain why the labor movement and the parties on the left did not become socialist in the revolutionary sense (only, at times, rhetorically so), but remained committed to parliamentary political means. Moreover, the labor movements' paths to parliamentary power were remarkably swift in all three countries, and when in power the social democratic governments—from the 1930s onwards—had considerable success. They did not initiate the reform agenda that would eventually lead to the post-war welfare state, but what the preceding liberal governments had initiated they were able to appropriate and significantly extend (Sejersted 2005; Slagstad 1998; Stråth 2005). Moreover, they gained considerable majorities in their respective parliaments due to significant compromises agreed between labor and the agrarian parties in the crisis-ridden period between the world wars. During the same period, the conservative parties in all three countries declined to embrace fascism, thereby defining a political middle ground that could incorporate alienated groups that in many other parts of Europe turned more extreme (Sejersted 2005).

The red/green alliances of the 1930s (between the social democrats and agrarian parties), and their affinity with the liberal agenda, constitute an interesting point of departure for identifying some deeper insights in comparative anthropological terms. Scandinavian political culture seems to be extensively influenced by agrarian modernization (Dahl 1986), and the public sphere may be seen as an extension of the municipal assembly (Aronsson 1997). Agrarian modernization enabled farming populations to play a decisive role in challenging and transforming urban culture and state bureaucracy, particularly in terms of undermining the privileges upon which the latter rested, as well as in establishing a template for political mobilization, organization, and identity. Class dynamics under the old regime were initially an important element of this; in Denmark, the autocratic kings required the support of the agrarian population in their struggle to destabilize the power of the aristocracy, to generate tax income, mobilize soldiers, and to balance the power of the rising urban commercial bourgeoisie.

Yet, in Denmark, the relationship between the ruling elites and the population at large remained tense, politically, which created a need to cultivate a space for freedom from the state (in a liberal sense)—which to some extent explains why the temperance movements of Sweden and Norway never saw the light of day in Denmark. It was the highly bureaucratic and meritocratic set-up of the Danish state that later reduced this tension, as state bureaucrats tended to identify with the economically liberal bourgeoisie and the entrepreneurial farmers (Knudsen and Rothstein 1994). The Swedish state was much more corporatist, and quite similar to Britain in its tendency to seek support among the nobility, which, like the British gentry, gradually became deeply involved in capitalist endeavors. Thus, it seems reasonable to regard the more hierarchical structure of Swedish society as the product of a form of corporatism originally arising from elitist interests. This made for a high degree of state-centeredness, but also led to an emerging social democratic order of a more paternalist type than in Denmark and Norway, where grassroots mobilizations seemed to have left deeper imprints of the nature of state power. The Swedish experience of being a key actor in European wars—and a colonial power—may in part account for this phenomenon, as may the fact that the relationship here between the pre-democratic state rulers and the nobility was much less hostile than in the Danish case. What stands out in the case of pre-modern Sweden, in contrast to continental Europe and Britain, is the relative freedom of the agrarian masses.

A common feature of all three countries in the late nineteenth century was that agrarian, grassroots radicalism was allied with both the new middle-class elites and with the growing labor movement. This pattern is most evident in Norway, where almost no feudal traditions existed. However, in Denmark as well, the peasants were freed from feudal dependency as late as the mid-eighteenth century, and then followed a path toward agricultural innovation (that is, toward commercial farming based on cooperative organization) and political mobilization: it may well constitute one of the most extraordinary, and peaceful, revolutions in modern history (Østergård 1992).

In summary, we offer the following generalization: in Norway and Denmark, popular modernization preceded the democratization of the state. The big difference was that in Norway, popular modernization had a more immediate and lasting influence on the state, mainly because the state was formed by an institutional infrastructure left by the colonists, rather than constituting a framework of political authority. Another difference was that the "one-norm society" syndrome was weaker in Denmark, where popular movements and the state represented more distinctly different universes (Stenius 2010). In Sweden, both political incorporation of the farmers and the development of a solid industrial capitalism took place before democratization, leaving a more hierarchical, but strongly integrated societal structure (Knudsen and Rothstein 1994).

Egalitarianism: Cultural and Social Values

In their Introduction to a special issue on egalitarianism in Scandinavia, Bruun et al. (2011, 5–6) criticize anthropologist Marianne Gullestad, who writes on this issue, for being "more interested in the ideology of egalitarianism as a generalized cultural value than in equality as a characteristic of certain forms of social organization". Their main argument is that Scandinavian egalitarianism has a social dimension, a differentialized social practice in which it is important to understand Scandinavian egalitarianism as addressing explicit values and a specific ideology (see Chap. 4 for a discussion of their contribution).

A key analytical question posed in the present volume concerns how the values, identities, models of understanding, and forms of social reciprocity that guide people's lives relate to institutions of power in the state and in the market. Insofar as institutions of power appeal to any given population (in a state) as means of solving conflicts, inducing cooperation, and symbolizing collective identities of whatever kinds, we ask to what extent they are subject to popular influence and appropriation—that is, whether they perform tasks of representation in some meaningful sense. This is a politically informed perspective on culture, and we are particularly interested in how cultural worlds relate to interests, how interests become political, and what happens next—as culturally shaped interests are negotiated in institutional worlds and thus shape identities and social relations. The following Scandinavian history of gender struggle (*likestillingskamp*) helps to exemplify this issue.

In Norway, the fight for suffrage and access to academia at the end of the nineteenth century was based on an insistence that women and men were equal. In 1884, women's access to academic examinations was discussed in Parliament: MPs were reminded in arguments in favor of the reform of the basic tenet of the French Revolution: "All human beings are created equal when it comes to the ability to understand truth in all its forms" (Agerholt 1973, 63). It was added that "the need to provide for yourself is the same for women as for men" (Agerholt 1973, 63). Ten years later, Liberal MP Ole Anton Qvam contended that the word "citizen", as it appeared in the constitutional paragraph that dealt with suffrage rights, meant women as well as men (Blom 2016, 53). However, gaining equal rights for women and men remained a slow process.

In the 1980s, Helga Hernes (1987, 15) introduced the concept of the "woman-friendly" welfare state, where "injustice on the basis of gender would be largely eliminated".[3] Later research suggests that notions of women-friendliness and state feminism were coined in "the golden period of Scandinavian gender equality policies" and may now need to be reconsidered (Borchorst and Siim 2008). New socio-economic and political conditions that are a result of increased immigration and globalization in general may suggest a need to include perspectives on "intersectionality" when evaluating and discussing ideas about woman-friendliness.[4] Nonetheless, since the 1970s, gender equality has increasingly been presented as a summarizing symbol of the welfare state model. Specific perceptions of gender equality became an important part of the welfare state model, politically speaking, and legislation facilitating the reconciliation of work and family was passed to this end. Equality between women and men in labor market participation and in terms of economic independence became tied to work/family arrangements within a dual-earner family model. A key to understanding gender relations in Scandinavia is recognizing the significance of the principle of freedom from personal dependence as a cultural value and political ideal, which is to some extent institutionalized through welfare state rights and policies.

The Institutionalization of Egalitarian Social and Cultural Values

Agrarian modernization in Scandinavia took place in the relative absence of church domination, but was simultaneously strongly shaped by Lutheran ideology and representatives of the church as agents of the state. As Henrik Stenius (2010) notes, the Reformation in Scandinavia laid the foundation for a form of the "one-norm society" (which he has also labelled "islamization") in which the very idea of society as made up of sub-cultures was fundamentally alien. The phenomenon of universalism, which later became a characteristic of the Scandinavian welfare state model, may be seen in this light. According to Stenius's analysis, universalism is conformity (of a type found in local communities, voluntary associations, and municipal politics) translated into national policy.

Two observations are of particular relevance here. First, the idea that cultural (and partly social) differences—religious and regional, for example—were to a considerable extent encompassed by the idea that there is only one way of life (depicted by the image of the Lutheran, independent farmer). Indeed, in Norway in particular, cultural identity became deeply politicized—mainly as but one aspect of a broader, cross-cutting system of conflicts from which a reinforced sense of national unity emerged. "You don't go to Scandinavia to have your ideas challenged by creative minorities", as Hans Fredrik Dahl (1986, 106) observed. Second, as indicated above, the idea of universality seems to have emerged historically from conventional forms of labor sharing, which was common throughout Scandinavia. The basic challenge for most farmers was scarcity of labor, particularly in seasonal peak periods. "Equality" was never an important criterion for inclusion in labor-sharing activities, but the effect of the organization of such activities was that people—presumably as a means by which to enable reciprocity—tended to deal with each other as though they were equal—in the sense of conforming to standard ideas of personal responsibility.

The cultural continuity of these arrangements is significant, even though the municipalities—and, in part, the central state—were later to appropriate almost all of them. Since labor was in short supply, and freedom from dependence was a basic criterion for personal dignity, self-help became the dominant practical principle. Later, an emphasis on work and employment became the basic element in the idea of inclusion in the welfare state. According to Stenius (2010), equality was relative and graded, but was a way to secure the participation of as many people as possible: inherent in the principle of inclusion here was the individual's will to do his best to conform (to work hard). According to Sejersted (2005, 115), it was generally assumed that people of this type were to be "helped and lifted, formed and cultivated"—in a form of a gift that established a reciprocal relationship of a strongly moral kind. This principle of inclusion may be a key to understanding the rationale behind the welfare state's tendency to establish "one-track" solutions (Dahl 1986), or "one-size-fits-all arrangements" (Knudsen and Rothstein 1994).

The importance of what may reasonably be called *performative criteria* for inclusion can also be seen in Scandinavian nationalism, which seems in some ways less ethnically essentialist than performatively orthodox (Frykman and Löfgren 1979; Sørensen and Stråth 1997; Østergård 1992). Frykman and Löfgren (1979) suggest that the politics of social integration was as much about universalizing opportunities for living "normal" lives as about nationalist ideology in the essentialist sense. The countries' geopolitical positioning in relation to the great powers of Europe, and their colonial trajectories, distinctly shape nationalism on the northern periphery of Europe. Norway was a colony (or, in technical terms, a part of Denmark from the fourteenth century to the early nineteenth century, and thereafter in a "union" with Sweden until 1905); Norwegians developed a form of nationalism that linked the idea of the national community to resistance, a struggle for democracy, and freedom from external dominance. This form of "heroic" imagined community may be understood as a blend of the German and the French versions, yet it was also quite different from these cases. Its mooring in performative and political criteria prevented the imagined community from becoming a servant of authoritarian political ideologies and ends. In comparative terms, it is significant that in Norway, nationalism has played an important part in anti-elitist political mobilizations, seeking—twice successfully—to keep the country outside the EU. In the battles waged prior to the referendums in 1972 and 1994, the anti-EU movement won much support for the argument that staying outside was the better way to protect democratic institutions and popular influence.

Furthermore, performative nationalism seems to have been extended along multiple axes: health and outdoor life may serve as an illustrative example—particularly in Norway. In such discourses of national identity, identity becomes a question of appropriate competence, projected at specifically selected categories of others, who tend to lack it. "Foreigners" hiking in Norwegian mountains without the appropriate equipment and experience, and thus needing to seek the aid of rescue services, are said to "stumble in their own incompetence" (Horgen 2016). Nothing similar is expressed when Norwegians on summer vacation along the coast get involved in increasing numbers of accidents caused by "un-Norwegian" behavior (often involving alcohol) when driving luxury boats.

In Denmark, where the relationship with Germany was an important foundation stone of national identity—particularly after Denmark's traumatic defeat in the war over Schleswig Holstein in the 1860s—"performative" nationalism was anchored in language, Protestant/Lutheran values, educational ideals (deeply inspired by the Enlightenment hero, Grundtvig), and later, what Richard Jenkins (2011, 296) terms "everyday social democracy". Jenkins, who conducted ethnographic fieldwork in a small town in Jutland in the early 2000s, observed that his informants cultivated a sense of living in a "special country". They saw themselves as constituting a "homogenous *folk*", struggling to maintain moral boundaries, moored in a sense of responsibility that related to being a member of a highly valued welfare state. Being different involves a categorical threat to the solidarity assumed to constitute the basis for this sense of community.

Contemporary Sweden, on the other hand, emerges from a very different nationalist trajectory. Nationalism here has been more statist, deeply conservative, and elitist, but as it became associated with forces resisting democratization, it became discredited. Consequently, nationalism here became associated with an emerging image in the early twentieth century of Sweden as being the avant-garde of modernity (Sejersted 2005). Notably, the Sami on Swedish territory were subject to fewer assimilationist measures than those on the Norwegian side, well into the twentieth century.

If political populism plays a more important role in Norway and Denmark, this may speak to the question of why the moral demand directed toward immigrants to integrate seems more insistent in these two countries.

Egalitarianism as a Political Project in the Era of Migration

How is egalitarianism as a political project shaped by the increased migration and diversity in Scandinavian societies? Today, migration researchers, politicians, and public figures question the sustainability of the ambition of material safety and social leveling in the face of cultural diversity. An important issue is whether cultural difference can be recognized without also weakening social cohesion and the welfare state community which, accordingly, is predicated upon common values as the glue of society. These doubts must be understood within the context of how welfare states have received and sought to incorporate newcomers.

Non-European immigration began in the late 1960s, after the three countries had established comprehensive welfare states. While some differences in their political approach toward immigration exist, the Scandinavian states resemble each other in terms of their institutional and normative framing. All three countries applied some form of multicultural integration policies from the 1970s onwards. Based on an evaluation of how 21 established democracies are fulfilling eight criteria, which they define as multicultural policy, Will Kymlicka and Keith Banting (2006) classify Norway and Denmark as following a weak multiculturalist integration policy, while Sweden is classified as following a mid-level multiculturalist integration policy. Generally, Scandinavian nation states have sought to prevent social and economic marginalization, and to secure some form of cultural diversity (Brochmann 2016). In Sweden, multicultural ideology as part of nation-state building was reconceptualized in the late 1990s when the state's responsibility was turned toward safeguarding individual rights, instead of group rights. Norway, for a while, took on the Swedish multicultural model. In Denmark, however, it was modified: Danish language and culture were to be prioritized and the idea of "setting requirements for immigrants" was implemented earlier in Denmark than in Norway and Sweden.[5]

The ambition to integrate immigrants has largely involved resorting to traditional welfare state arrangements, and particularly labor market policies. An important characteristic of the Scandinavian welfare state model is the organization of the labor market (Brochmann 2016). *Arbeidslinjen*, a directive prioritizing employment, has become a central feature: it dictates that in order to maintain a high level of welfare spending, people must engage in productive work. There is a presumption that a universal, "generous" welfare state rests on a well-functioning and strongly regulated labor market, and that this is not sustainable if some people or groups are not participating in the labor market. This idea and its historical patterns that are presented above, together with the performance criteria of inclusion, have been constitutive of how various governments have dealt with immigrants over the past 20 years. The equality ideal, which in this context means conforming to the ethos of wage labor as means of securing autonomy and signaling the right kind of commitment to collective goals, is far stronger than the multicultural ideal (Rugkåsa 2012). Integration policies are founded on individually based rights and obligations. Ethnic minorities in the Norwegian welfare state are essentially offered conditions equal to those of the majority population, and there are few statutory prerogatives (Rugkåsa 2012). Nation-building has thus served as a powerful legitimation of a generalized policy of Norwegianization (Haagensen et al. 1990), which has been aggressively pursued toward some minorities, but not all.[5]

Multiculturalism and Equality

Multiculturalism is a highly contested domain. In particular, the question of whether it fosters or undermines equality is subject to debate, among both scholars and politicians, as well as among the wider public (Kivisto and Wahlbeck 2013). Thomas Faist argues:

> No matter which words we use—integration, assimilation, incorporation or insertion—all of these normatively loaded terms hold the promise of equality for immigrants. Nonetheless, the other side of the coin reveals manifold inequalities, such as high unemployment, residential segregation and religious extremism. Multiculturalism, along with assimilation, has been one of the main paradigms of integration and of policy aimed at addressing such inequalities and promoting further equality. (2013, 24)

The promise of multiculturalism is that it may bring a high degree of substantive equality and contribute to a national unity of social cohesion. In taking this approach, "inequality" refers to the "boundaries between categories" (Faist 2013, 26), which "arise from categorizations of heterogeneities". The central principle in multiculturalism is its "normatively oriented intellectual lineage: to overcome social inequalities based on cultural markers (heterogeneities) by shaping cultural, civic, politician and economic relations via public policies" (Faist 2013, 24).

The Norwegian approach to multiculturalism after the 1970s has a tripartite structure: a homogeneous nationhood, the welfare model, and an integration ideology that was imported from Sweden (Brochmann and Djuve 2013). One outcome of this approach, is that immigrants are generally perceived as potentially like "us"—and thus as having a potential for becoming civilized, that is to say, as being capable of embracing the ethos of wage labor and collective commitment (Gressgård 2007). "The Norwegian" is depicted as "an aggregate of equal, autonomous individuals", as opposed to "the other", who are depicted as representatives of their culture. "We" tends to appear as universally inclusive, as opposed to the culturally distinctive and exclusive "Other" (Gressgård 2005, 56–57).

Regarding Denmark, Schmidt (2013) has suggested that even though, at the level of state policy, it seems strongly opposed to multiculturalism, the issue looks very different from the local point of view. In Copenhagen, for example, both ethnic diversity and social diversity are celebrated. The city's integration policies are seen "as a means to access the resources of its citizens and to prevent ethnic tensions" (Schmidt 2013, 197).

When it comes to Sweden, it took a particular turn in 1975 with the introduction of principles of *equality, freedom of choice, and partnership* in their migration and minority policies. In an effort to implement these principles, the political approach involved supporting new members of society in achieving the same socio-economic standards as the majority population, but they should at the same time be able to retain the right to maintain cultural attachments (Olwig 2011). They received state subsidies as means to "preserve" their culture, and cultural rights accorded to immigrants were protected by the Swedish Constitution (Borevi 2010). Thus, rather than pursuing a cultural policy of homogenization, Sweden followed a form of multicultural liberalism. The "everyday culture" of immigrants was to be left in peace (Brochmann 2016). This, it has been argued, was in stark contrast to the social engineering policies directed at the majority population, which, as part of the Swedish welfare state trajectory, involve emphasizing the need to guide people's values and attitudes (Brochmann 2016; Sejersted 2005). One consequence of this focus on group attributes and needs was, according to Brekke and Borchgrenvik (2007, 16), that difference (*annorlundaskap*) was accentuated and migrants were given a status as outsiders (*utanförskap*). In other words, welfare state interventions targeting "problematic difference" or specific groups may reinforce boundaries and generate exclusion mechanisms (Eastmond 2011).

All three Scandinavian countries have developed extensive policies aimed at monitoring and governing the majority population, especially in the domain of family life (and child rearing in particular) and their health (in a very broad sense). Egalitarian ideals serve as important points of reference for such policies, and in this context we are interested in how, in more precise terms, they are carried out and legitimized. Moreover, we ask: How is the political project of egalitarianism being transformed in a society that is becoming more economically and culturally heterogeneous, at the same time as it insists on being a "one-norm society"?

In areas of migration and integration, policies pursued in the name of egalitarianism are becoming increasingly ambiguous: migrants face policies that are supposed to grant equal access to the welfare state, at the same time as they are expected to become "the same" as prototypical Norwegians (that is, in accepting wage labor, certain gender values and specific forms of parenting, and conforming to social values such as work parties—*dugnad*) in order to be recognized as equal. One obvious problem is that willingness to conform is often the criterion for access. Ideas and policies of gender equality have come to play a particular role in generating particular notions of social incorporation and conformity.

Gender Equality as a Political Ambition

In recent years, multiculturalism and integration policies have increasingly been tied to issues of gender equality in Scandinavia, as in other European countries (Siim and Skjeie 2008). International and national debates have questioned whether multiculturalism and gender equality are incompatible policy orientations (Borchgrevink 2002; Gressgård and Jacobsen 2002; Gullikstad 2010; Okin 1999). Together with "gay tolerance", gender equality has become a trademark and part of the self-representation of the nation state, and particularly so for Norway and Sweden (Danielsen et al. 2013).

Minority groups tend to be evaluated according to the way they treat "their" women (as the majority population tends to express it), and this has become a litmus test for whether they are seen as integrated in society. This is not a specific Scandinavian feature. Anthias and Yuval-Davis (1996) have argued that gender and sexuality play a central part in the construction of ethnic identities and in the production of ethnic boundaries. The social construction of women frequently serves as a decisive point of reference for the ways in which markers of difference come to life (Anthias and Yuval-Davis 1996). Yet the role the welfare state takes, and is expected to take, to promote gender equality is specifically Scandinavian. Gender equality in Scandinavia is generally thought of as something more than just equality of opportunity: "equality of outcome is an important part of policy thinking. Ideologically, the promotion of gender equality policies is legitimated as central to the promotion of continuing processes of democratization" (Ellingsæter and Leira 2006, 7). Politically, equality is not only thought of in terms of labor market participation and economic independence, it also concerns the sharing of the workload in the family and in caring for children. However, despite comprehensive gender equality policies, the labor market is highly divided in terms of gender, and a very large number of women work part-time in low-paid jobs.

More than 20 years ago, Norwegian anthropologist Unni Wikan blamed Norwegian authorities for failing to intervene in dysfunctional immigrant families, particularly in relation to raising their children (and this particularly related to the raising of daughters). This, she argued, necessarily led to poor language skills, high unemployment, and social welfare dependency (Wikan 1995). In consequence, she further argued, social integration was being prevented and immigrants were becoming the new underclass, which in turn threatened the egalitarianism of Norwegian society.

In contrast to Wikan, other scholars have focused on how boundaries of "Danishness" (Schmidt 2012) and "Norwegianness" (Gullestad 2002) are enacted, and how ideas of cultural sameness and ancestry have become part of the production of an "invisible fence" vis-à-vis immigrants (Gullestad 2002). According to Gullestad, immigrants are expected to play down their differences or otherwise risk being viewed as compromising the narrative of Norway as "a homogeneous, tolerant, anti-racist, and peace-loving society" (Gullestad 2002, 59). Being "similar to the local population" is considered as a prerequisite to being treated on an equal basis, thus programs targeting refugees and migrants are part of efforts to create such similarities (Olwig 2011). The political welfare project of Scandinavian societies is founded on notions of strong similarities and cultural notions of equality (Olwig 2011), which produce specific policies and ideologies of social incorporation. The image of egalitarianism entertained by majority populations seems increasingly to be viewed as dependent on whether non-Western immigrants are seen to perform according to standards of normality. Thus, one consequence of the present construction of egalitarianism as a social norm and cultural value—namely, as a one-norm society, particularly in Norway—is that it has contributed to exclusionary mechanisms as the society grows more heterogeneous.

The Political Construction of Inegalitarian Egalitarianism?

Despite egalitarian ambitions, the attempt to follow one mainstream gender equality ideal in a plural society has opened up a form of "inegalitarian egalitarianism". Frequently, ethnic minorities or immigrant-citizens are represented as suppressed and not following "our" egalitarian gender conventions (Brochmann et al. 2002; Gullestad 2002; Kristensen 2010). One consequence of this focus on "their" lack of equality is that "Norwegian" or "Danish" equality is confirmed, and appears to be both distinct and unifying. This is also the starting point for descriptions of equality that highlight differences between "us" and "them", which suggests that gender equality is both emerging as a prerequisite for integration and a measure of how integrated and "Norwegian" a person is (Kristensen 2010, 73). At work here is the above-mentioned problem of egalitarianism: the aim to establish equality for everyone may end with the unintended consequence that some will be kept or constructed as an "outsider". It has become politically vital that equality is understood in a "Norwegian" way, both in terms of gender equality's relevance to national self-esteem and in its role as a boundary marker.

Equality and diversity are central tenets of current political debates on how to develop an inclusive society. While *equality* of women and men, according to political authorities, should be a prerequisite for an inclusive society, *diversity* is presented as a way to enrich this society. As a policy strategy, diversity (primarily ethnic) has been strongly linked to the labor market (Berg and Håpnes 2001). Diversity as a concept and labor market principle starts from the assumption that we are all different in some way, and that this is positive. However, the concept of gender equality contains a tension between equality and diversity: Equality should provide equality of rights and opportunities. At the same time, in Swedish bureaucratic culture, equality is frequently understood as conformity, which is both expected and valued (Graham 2003). In her analysis of Swedish political culture, Norman (2004) observes the tendency to present equality (*jämlikhet*) as a core value in order to ensure sameness as a basic norm (*likhet*). When sameness becomes a scale for measuring whether a given person may be identified as equal, certain kinds of difference can be constructed as problematic and even interpreted as an anomaly or a lack. This resonates with Gullestad's (2002) analysis of Norway, that is, of the ways in which the cultural construction of egalitarianism as sameness has become entangled with nationalism and the racialization of difference: "'immigrants' are asked to 'become Norwegian', at the same time as it is tacitly assumed that this is something they can never really achieve" (Gullestad 2002, 59). When "equality", which should be applied to all, is founded on (cultural) sameness, a contradiction arises (in this volume, see Erstad, Chap. 9; Larsen, Chap. 11; Aarset, Chap. 13).

With reference to the relationship among ideas of national identity, gender equality, and constructions of otherness, Mouritsen argues that, in the Danish case,

> The meaning of Danish values has become a contested issue in the public discourse, and the intersection of gender and ethnicity is often used as a strong marker of "Danishness". Danish nationalism represents a particular civic nationalism, where the dominant political discourse equates Danish values with universalist civic values, and thus perceives democracy and egalitarianism as a Danish way of life. (2006, 78–79)

The welfare state model is partly built on the cultural construction of homogeneity (Jöhncke 2007). Historically, the image of a homogeneous population draws upon specific experiences (in Denmark, most people spoke Danish) that left little room for acknowledging heterogeneous categorizations (rural/urban, class differences, and different economic interests) that were at least equally important in people's daily lives. One response to the increased migration from non-European countries was a new form of categorizing that could potentially express and articulate the already existing differences within the majority population (Gullestad 2002), but which instead silenced them even more systematically. In the Scandinavian countries, the ideology of sameness contributes to the construction of the nation state's history as homogeneous and with deep historical roots (Jöhncke 2007).

The social construction and institutionalization of the Danish, Norwegian, or Swedish versions of the welfare state as egalitarian sociocultural orders may also be seen as incorporating performative criteria of inclusion. To some extent the social construction of the welfare state has promoted a perception of society as an integrated whole. Norway/Denmark/Sweden as "the good society" has largely become the national populations' master narrative about their country (Jöhncke 2007).

In "Diversity without boundaries", Tordis Borchgrevink and Grete Brochmann (2008) ask whether the emphasis on diversity among the Norwegian public creates avoidance in talking about other more imperative issues than gender equality, such as economic inequality. The diversity concept conceals existing class differences and makes it harder to understand the nature of the different types of systematic differences, as well as the similarities, that exist among the different population groups (Andenæs 2010). For example, the fact that employment rates among non-Western immigrant women are relatively low may to a considerable extent be attributed to more or less subtle forms of discrimination, resulting in marginalization in the labor market, in politics, and in society in general (Brochmann and Hagelund 2005; Midtbøen and Rogstad 2012).

Overall, the social conditions for Hernes's so-called woman-friendly state and state feminism have changed. The political project of using gender equality as an important symbol of the egalitarian society seems to have lost some of its momentum, and has failed on several counts.

THE FUTURE OF THE INSTITUTIONALIZATION OF EGALITARIANISM

The Scandinavian states are undergoing a process of transformation that is a result of a social, economic, and political situation in which social inequality is increasing, neo-liberal policies are seeping into the conceptualization of the welfare state, and the labor market is changing, including as a result of increased social dumping. This is occurring at the same time as skepticism toward migrants and refugees is rising, and as people are experiencing increased competition for access to welfare state services. While these aspects are publicly interrelated, how they are constructed as connected, and the direction of any suggested future path, are necessarily contingent on an individual's political orientation. The increased diversity among the Scandinavian population, in terms of religion, culture, and language, has raised questions concerning the capacity of the welfare model to facilitate immigrants' entrance to the labor market, and about the normative foundation of gender equality and woman-friendliness in the Nordic model (Borchorst and Siim 2008).

It might be concluded that welfare states with an egalitarian-oriented ideology have created political and economic arrangements with broad popular legitimacy. This has had a marked integrative effect on the notion of Denmark/Norway/Sweden—creating an image of unity and equality in the respective populations, in both a political and an economic sense—a notion the nation states have both built on and contributed to (Jöhncke 2007). On the other hand, it cannot simply be assumed that the welfare state creates a more egalitarian society, empirically speaking. For example, although economic inequalities have been less pronounced than in many comparable countries, Norway is not a classless society (Barth et al. 2015), and economic difference has sometimes increased, and at other times decreased (Aaberge 2016).

In some sectors, institutionalization and institutional practice, as important dimensions of egalitarianism in Scandinavian countries, have been particularly significant—as in education, where democratic reforms have provided broad and popular access to the public school system (Dahl 1986). Such popular movements came from a joint project based on egalitarianism and anti-authoritarian ideals. Here, the role of the Nordic people's movements in the development of their welfare states is clearly visible. While these movements were local and grassroots-oriented, they also had a national orientation, in which the state was the frame of reference (Vike 2004). With time, labor unions took over this type of training, and of "Enlightenment", which was then directed toward the new class of wage laborers. From the late nineteenth century onwards, this kind of Enlightenment thinking has been mainly oriented toward adult migrants (Rugkåsa 2012).

However, despite the foundational egalitarian ambitions, politics, schools, and health care reflect largely middle-class values (Rugkåsa 2012). A middle-class way of life has come to represent the norm against which everything is measured: it has become the civilizing normality (Löfgren 1987; Rugkåsa 2012). Research shows that when it comes to school achievement and subsequent life chances, the impact of class (Stefansen and Aarseth 2011) and ethnic background (Welstad 2014) is well documented. Further, the Norwegian government's *knowledge-promise/ improvement* (*kunnskapsløftet*) program—a reform of schools' content, organization, and structure, introduced in 2006—is characterized by arguments that promote universalism, and emphasize shared values and equality among students; it begs the question of whether equality is an appropriate value in a multicultural society (Welstad 2014). This suggests that the effects of egalitarianism as a motivating idea in educational policy are limited. Its outcomes are profoundly shaped by existing, and changing, socio-economic and cultural structures.

Welfare states are key institutions in terms of the structuring of class and social order. As sociologist Gøsta Esping-Andersen (1990, 23) argues, the welfare state is not just a mechanism that intervenes in, and possibly corrects, inequality structures. It is in itself a system of stratification, and an active force in the ordering of social relationships. The organizational features of the welfare state shape how social solidarity, class, and status differences are expressed. While welfare states are built into the cultural construction of heterogeneity and cultural conditions, which in turn become rather narrow with specific cultural frames, they are also an autonomous device through which individuals are expected to become economic agents and to gain individual independence from social relations and the market. Even if Scandinavia is marked by strong egalitarian ideals and egalitarian-oriented politics, they nonetheless tend to reproduce dominant norms of social class and distinctions of ethnicity and religion (Larsen 2011). Jöhncke (2007) suggests that the integration criteria in this ideology must evolve in the context of an increasingly plural society, namely, by accentuating new similarities and reducing new differences.

Neo-liberal politics have brought increased emphasis across a wide range of policies on notions of individual responsibility and self-sufficiency, which has brought to the forefront questions about citizen formation and potential interventions to teach new immigrant residents how to become resourceful citizens and "free agents" (Eastmond 2011), or "individualized" and "autonomous" agents (Larsen, Chap. 11, in this volume). On the whole, such neo-liberal approaches toward immigrants represent a continuum of the Scandinavian states' attempt at nation building through citizen formation. The strong state presence with its vision of social harmony, as we have seen, has long had popular legitimacy. However, it is a model that is generalist and authoritative, at a time when tolerance for certain kinds of difference is at a low level. It may be reasoned, then, that normative standards were more explicit in earlier times when the poor and the marginalized had to "learn to change their ways" in order to achieve similar life chances to those who were better off (Brekke and Borchgrenvik 2007; Eriksen 2001). Today, social equality still comes with a demand for conformity (Eastmond 2011; see also Erstad, Chap. 9, Larsen, Chap. 11, and Aarset, Chap. 13, in this volume), sometimes in the name of egalitarianism. The prominence of autonomy in social relations in the Scandinavian countries has become particularly visible in social expectations of, and policies targeting, migrants and their children.

Conclusion

This Introduction has aimed neither to be a complete review of egalitarianism in Scandinavia, nor to present a comprehensive comparative analysis. Instead, the aim has been to explain relevant aspects of the history of these three countries and to create a framework of Scandinavian themes and positions regarding egalitarianism, which provides a background to, and a framework for, the following chapters.

In terms of theory, the arguments outlined here are based on the strong influence of egalitarianism in the European heritage, as well as on the history of Scandinavia. We have highlighted the particularities of Scandinavian combinations of egalitarianism with notions of the one-norm society, the welfare state, and individual autonomy. We have also engaged with the elusive and sometimes paradoxical character of egalitarianism and the (in)egalitarian, which are particularly evident in the face of increased immigration to Scandinavia. In approaching egalitarianism as partly an unintended effect of complex historical circumstances, we understand egalitarianism not simply as a relationship between certain Enlightenment ideas, patterns of traditional ("peasant") culture, and patterns of policy, but also as an element of societal tensions that, in Scandinavian countries, seem to have generated institutionally specific ways of dealing with class, gender, and ethnic relations. Moreover, egalitarianism has been explored with reference to the ways in which individuality is conceptualized here (individual autonomy in particular), and the social forms in which such conceptualization is incorporated and reproduced.

One characteristic of this region, historically speaking, appears to be a different kind of relationship between people's movements and the state compared to other states in Europe. Egalitarian movements in Scandinavia have largely been picked up, co-opted by, and made part of the state and its institutions. In comparative terms it may seem surprising that this has not (or not yet) undermined associational life nor individual autonomy as paramount cultural values. Egalitarianism and the egalitarian are not specifically Scandinavian phenomena, but perhaps the institutionalization of egalitarianism particular to this region constitutes a rather unique feature. Even if egalitarianism is rightly frequently linked to resistance, opposition, and class conflict, as it was during the French Revolution, and later to the liberal struggle to protect vital interests and sensibilities relating to civic life lived at arm's length from the state, the Scandinavian case represents a somewhat different trajectory. As this case indicates, egalitarianism may also be part of a continuous negotiation of the ways in which the state, associational life, patterns of interaction, and values relating to individual autonomy and social conformity interact and partly reinforce—and partly undermine—each other. Under conditions of increasing neo-liberal governance and centralization of power, this pattern, which has traditionally depended more on the social embeddedness of the state in society at large than on independent, autonomous agency on the part of the state, may well change.

Structure of the Book

This introductory discussion of some ways of understanding and engaging with egalitarianism in a Scandinavian context, evolving not only from different disciplines, but also different analytical perspectives and theoretical questions, informs the following main chapters of this book. The Scandinavian context represents a particular case in terms of how various elements of egalitarianism intersect. The chapters that follow address a variety of these issues using historically oriented or empirical data. In order to contribute the fullest possible insights into this complex subject, we combine anthropological, historical, and political science approaches.

Part I, *The Tradition of Egalitarianism*, historicizes egalitarianism in Norden, and thus contributes to the exploration of egalitarianism as a social construct, and reflects on how the story of Nordic egalitarianism is produced and translated in research. In Chap. 2, Bo Stråth argues that the Nordic countries managed to keep the tension between freedom and equality under better control than elsewhere in Europe. This control might be seen as a form of Nordic *Sonderweg*, which dealt with the political and cultural implementation and *management* of the vision of equality. This chapter shows that particular to the Nordic enterprise was the idea that the *bønder/bönder* (farmers) were not only the *object* of a Romantic idealization of a heroic past going back to the world of the sagas, but also an actively participating *subject* in political processes. This study shows that Norden became, rather than "originally" was, in some sense more equal than in many other societies, and that people's movements were crucial for this development.

In Chap. 3, Jan Eivind Myhre explores various dimensions of equality and how they are connected. Myhre argues that in the nineteenth century, social equality was more prevalent in Norway than in other European countries, and to some extent more so than among its Scandinavian neighbors. Norway was the only country in Europe where the backbone of society, the peasants (farmers), had a say in national political matters and were represented in the parliament (although not proportionately). Equality, Myhre argues, played an important role in generating economic growth, in the quality of governance, and in the development of democratic institutions.

In Chap. 4, Simone Abram provides a perspective on Norwegian egalitarianism from the outside. She argues that English-language accounts that describe a welfare state marked by national egalitarianism are misleading, and that such idealistic images are doing the work of nationalism rather than contributing to critical analysis. Contrasting such accounts with critiques of the notion of *likhet* (sameness) in the Norwegian language and with writings on the nationalism of Norway by Norwegian anthropologists, the chapter demonstrates how non-Scandinavian-speaking social scientists risk misinterpreting the politics and sociology of Scandinavian countries.

Part II, *Institutionalizing Egalitarianism*, draws on various ethnographic fields to discuss how egalitarianism can be understood as institutionalized in Scandinavia in a number of ways. Part II begins with Halvard Vike, in Chap. 5, exploring the emergence of the contemporary Norwegian—and more generally, the Scandinavian—welfare state model with reference to political contestation, or resistance, which he sees as constitutive of egalitarianism. His underlying hypothesis is that the welfare state model may be seen as the product of a long-standing political tension that relates to class struggles, which took place from the Middle Ages onward. Because of the nature of the relationship that was formed between the state and the sections of the population that challenged it (or acts and practices conducted in its name), a pattern of conflict and cooperation developed that gradually became an institutional aspect of the state (municipal institutions included). A significant element in this, as Vike sees it, is the fact that popular political mobilization in Scandinavia was more successful in influencing the state than is the case in most other Western, democratic societies.

In Chap. 6, Maja Hojer Bruun explores housing cooperatives, and their role in meeting citizens' right to housing in Denmark as an instance of welfare institutions that transgress the conceptual boundaries among the state, the market, and civil society. This, Bruun explains, has recently been challenged by neo-liberal housing policies. In leaving the economic development of the cooperatives to a housing market in flux, and by installing short-term interests in members to adopt the highest possible share prices, the state and central government are heading for a neo-liberalized welfare state.

In Chap. 7, Christian Lo is inspired by F. G. Bailey's outline of *normative* and *pragmatic* rules in political struggle, and draws on ethnographic fieldwork among administrators and local politicians to discuss how both groups conceive of their roles as actors in policy processes. According to

Lo, a general sense of pragmatism draws on a source of political legitimacy that provides an alternative to the hierarchical Weberian principles expressed as axiomatic by his informants. Exploring cases of policy development, Lo finds that their characteristics are balanced between the legitimacy drawn from the hierarchical command chain of the municipal organization and horizontal policy alliances operating with a sense of egalitarian-rooted pragmatism. He calls the latter a *pragmatic policy alliance*, and its characteristic is the possibility of withdrawing from commitments while maintaining social cohesion and relations with the same persons in other arenas.

Part III, *Egalitarian Welfare?*, interrogates the egalitarian aspects of welfare institutions and practices in view of increased social and cultural differentiations in the Scandinavian states. To that end, in Chap. 8, Camilla Hoffmann Merrild discusses how differences in morbidity and mortality across the population cast light on fundamental structures of inequality in the otherwise egalitarian Danish welfare state. In Denmark, as in most other parts of the world, socially deprived people most often lead shorter lives, and often experience more illness, than people who live in more affluent social situations. Paradoxically, because of the egalitarian ideology of imagined sameness in Denmark, differences are frequently overlooked or ignored, which has important social and health consequences for the lives of people from lower social classes.

In Chap. 9, taking interactions between front-line bureaucrats (public health nurses) and migrant mothers in Norway as a case study, Ida Erstad discusses how these interactions have been shaped not only by the governmental techniques of health care workers who aim to empower mothers, but also by the mothers' expectations and desire for tangible advice that they can use. Erstad's chapter illustrates how egalitarianism in a pluralistic Norway has been reshaped to also embrace difference in the form of diversity, although only to some extent: the same-ness dimension of equality and egalitarianism is played down by the nurses. Erstad suggests that this takes place concurrently with a racialization and essentialization process in relation to migrant mothers.

In Chap. 10, Marry-Anne Karlsen explores how the exclusion of irregular migrants in terms of social rights is justified within a welfare state based on egalitarian notions of justice. In Norway, the egalitarian welfare approach implies that migrants should have the same formal rights to welfare as every other citizen, and that regular welfare state institutions should cover this. However, the adherence to egalitarian norms from within have been linked to restrictive admissions policies, following "the hard on the outside, soft on the inside" model of citizenship (Bosniak 2006). According to this government rationale, distributive justice presupposes a territorially bounded world within which distribution takes place. Karlsen shows how irregular migrants who are legally excluded, but still physically present within state borders, pose a particular challenge to this rationale.

Part IV, *Egalitarianism, Inequality, and Difference*, addresses how ideals, ideas, and practices of egalitarianism are, on the one hand, contesting, and, on the other, challenged by, various forms of difference—be it gender, ethnic, or class difference, which frequently intersect. In Chap. 11, Birgitte Romme Larsen draws attention to the irony of a small-scale rural Danish society's work to include refugee children and adolescents as individuals. The society emphasizes individuality, difference, and autonomy, yet the realization of these valued characteristics must be pursued through specific Danish practices in order to be recognized as such. Larsen suggests that migrants are "made Danish" through particular concrete social and bodily practices, such as "everyone should learn to ride a bicycle", through which the will to individualize and be made autonomous subjects should both transpire and be demonstrated. Larsen suggests that paradoxically such social expectations turn the envisioned *emancipation from discipline* into an everyday *discipline in emancipation*.

The focus remains on refugees in Chap. 12, where Kjell Hansen explains how the large influx of refugees to Sweden in 2015 highlighted a number of tensions in relation to the welfare state. The liberal Swedish reception of asylum seekers may reflect a particular form of international solidarity that can be seen as an extension of national egalitarianism. However, the large numbers of refugees arriving in Sweden contributed to changing the preconditions of how to meet the refugees in rural areas. This chapter draws particular attention to the fact that the real crisis emerging from the great influx of migrants was less about the refugees and more about changes in state–local relations, and the mechanisms by which trust is produced in Swedish society.

In Chap. 13, Monica Five Aarset examines how Norwegian egalitarianism may play out in a given context, in her exploration of how aspiring families with a migrant background work on their social habitus to become accepted as middle class. Based on a study of educated descendants of migrants from Pakistan, the chapter demonstrates the precarious work to "fit in" for middle-class ethnic minorities in order to be viewed as equal and achieve belonging. She uses the term *conditional belonging* to explore how feelings of belonging to Norway co-exist with an awareness of the conditionality of this belonging, and the consequences of not being in control of these conditions.

In the final chapter, Chap. 14, Christine M. Jacobsen engages with the ways in which gender equality and sexual equality have come to be articulated as constitutive of Norwegian identity and as societal values. Drawing on Bridget Anderson's (2013) notions of "the good citizen" and the "community of value", Jacobsen scrutinizes how the good citizen is anchored in ideas about the individual, autonomy, and equality, and is defined by what lies "outside" these concepts—the non-citizen and the failed citizen. Drawing on policy documents on gender equality, homosexuality, and citizenship, she argues that gender and sexual equality have become crucial to the understanding of Norwegian society as a particular kind of national imagined community (Anderson 1983). Ultimately, it would seem, borders of the national community and its citizenry are patrolled by entrenching gendered and racialized differences between "us" and "them". Jonathan Friedman, in his postscript, takes his long-term familiarity with Sweden as his starting point to discuss how egalitarianism in Scandinavia is a social project related to forms of sociality. He draws our attention to janteloven or jantelagen as a type of equalizer specific to Scandinavia, and suggests that the transformation of an egalitarian political order in Sweden has taken place among others through changes in the social construction of shame and the infringement of the state in the local. The erosion of the sociality of equality since the 1980s, he argues, must be seen as connected to the decline of Western hegemony.

Notes

1. With the exception of Chap. 2 by Bo Stråth and Chap. 10 by Marry-Anne Karlsen, this volume mainly refers to the Scandinavian countries—Norway, Sweden, and Denmark. The term "Norden" includes additionally Finland, Iceland, and their associated territories Greenland, the Faroe Islands, and the Åland Islands. "Norden" calls to mind images of folk spirituality, human–nature relations, and the landscape with which the ethnography of that region is concerned (Bruun et al. 2011); "Scandinavia" evokes political history and the image of the modern welfare state. Today, Norway, Sweden and Denmark share comparable welfare institutions at the state level in municipalities and small communities. "Scandinavia" is the focus of this volume and, thus, is the term we use throughout. When we make reference to scholarship concerned with the Nordic countries, we use that term.

2. The notable contrast in the European context may be Greece, where the modern state has largely been incorporated into informal structures of authority and loyalty.
3. Hernes's argument was based on welfare policies that provided generous parental leave schemes, extensive public care services for children and the elderly, and the idea that there were relatively high numbers of women in positions of political power, which enabled them to influence political decisions.
4. Notions such as "state feminism" and "woman-friendliness" risk disregarding differences among women and men not only in terms of gender and class, but also according to race/ethnicity, religion, and nationality.
5. See Brochmann and Hagelund (2010) for a comparison of the development of the three countries in this area.
6. Some groups, such as the Kven and Forest Finns, were exposed to relatively mild assimilation policies, while other groups, such as the Sami and the Norwegian and Swedish Travellers, faced more drastic measures.

References

Aaberge, Rolf. 2016. Inntektsulikhet i Norge i lys av Piketty-debatten, SSB. *Samfunnsspeilet* 1: 3–9.

Agerholdt, Casperi A. 1973 [1937]. *Den norske kvinnebevegelsens historie*. Oslo: Gyldendal Norsk Forlag.

Alexander, Jeffrey C. 2006. *The civil sphere*. New York/Oxford: University of Oxford Press.

Andenæs, Ellen. 2010. "Nok norsk" til å være "norsk nok"? Språk, arbeidsliv, likestilling. In *Likestilte norskheter. Om kjønn og etnisitet*, ed. Anne-Jorunn Berg, Anne Britt Flemmen, and Berit Gullikstad. Oslo: Tapir Akademiske Forlag.

Anderson, Benedict. 1983. *Imagined communities*. London: Verso.

Anderson, Bridget. 2013. *Us & them? The dangerous politics of immigration control*. Oxford: Oxford University Press.

Anthias, Floya, and Nira Yuval-Davis. 1996. *Racialized boundaries*. London: Routledge.

Aronsson, Petter. 1997. Local politics – The invisible political culture. In *The cultural construction of Norden*, ed. Øystein Sørensen and Bo Stråth. Oslo: Scandinavian University Press.

Arter, David. 2008. *Scandinavian politics today*. Manchester: Manchester University Press.

Baldersheim, Harald, Hans Eivind Næss, Edgar Hovland, and Rolf Danielsen. 1987. *Folkestyre i by og bygd. Norske kommuner gjennom 150 år*. Oslo: Universitetsforlaget.

Barnes, John. 1954. Class and committees in a Norwegian island parish. *Human Relations* 7 (1): 39–58.
Barth, Erling, Karl O. Moene, and Fredrik Willumsen. 2014. The Scandinavian model – An interpretation. *The Journal of Public Economics* 127: 17–29.
Barth, Erling, Henning Finseraas, and Karl O. Moene. 2015. Political reinforcement: How rising inequality curbs manifested welfare generosity. *American Political Science* 59 (3): 565–577.
Bellah, Robert N., Steven M. Tipton, William M. Sullivan, Richard P. Madsen, and Ann Swidler. 1985. *Habits of the heart. Commitment and individualism in American life*. Berkeley: University of California Press.
Berg, Berit and Tove Håpnes. 2001. *Mellom likhet og forskjellighet – mangfoldsstrategier i arbeidslivet*. Trondheim, rapport, SINTEF IFIM.
Blom, Ida. 2016. Troubled and secure gender identities in a changing society: Norway at the end of the long nineteenth century. In *Gendered citizenship: The politics of representation*, ed. Hilde Danielsen, Kari Tegerstedt, Ragnhild Muriaas, and Brita Ytre-Arne. 37–60. London: Palgrave Macmillan.
Blom-Hansen, Jens. 2010. Municipal amalgamations and common pool problems: The Danish local government reform in 2007. *Scandinavian Political Studies* 33 (1): 51–73.
Borchgrevink, Tordis. 2002. Likestilling. Det flerkulturelle demokratiets hodepine. In *Sand i maskineriet. Makt og demokrati i det flerkulturelle Norge. Makt og demokratiutredningen 1998–2003*, ed. Grete Brochmann, Tordis Brochgrevink, and Jon Rogstad. Oslo: Gyldendal Akademisk.
Borchgrevink, Tordis, and Grete Brochmann. 2008. Mangfold uten grenser. *Samtiden* 3: 22–32.
Borchorst, Anette, and Birte Siim. 2008. Woman-friendly policies and state feminism: Theorizing Scandinavian gender equality. *Feminist Theory* 9 (2): 207–224.
Borevi, Karin. 2010. Sverige – mångkulturalismens flaggskepp i Norden. In *Velferdens grenser. Innvandringspolitikk og velferdsstat i Skandinavia 1945–2010*, ed. Grete Brochmann and Anniken Hagelund. Oslo: Universitetsforlaget.
Bosniak, Linda. 2006. *The citizen and the alien: Dilemmas of contemporary membership*. Princeton: Princeton University Press.
Brekke, Jean-Paul, and Tordis Borchgrenvik. 2007. *Talking about integration: Discourses, alliances and theories on labour market integration in Sweden*. ISF-rapport 2007: 009. Oslo: Institutt for samfunnsforskning.
Brochmann, Grete. 2016. Innvandring til Skandinavia. Velferdsstater i pluralismens tid. In *Det norske samfunn, bind 1*, ed. Ivar Frønes and Lise Kjølsrød, 130–155. Oslo: Gyldendal Akademisk.
Brochmann, Grete, and Anne Britt Djuve. 2013. Multiculturalism or assimilation? The Norwegian welfare state approach. In *Debating multiculturalism in the nordic welfare states*, ed. Peter Kivisto and Östen Wahlbeck, 219–245. Basingstoke: Palgrave Macmillan.

Brochmann, Grete, and Anniken Hagelund. 2005. *Innvandringens velferdspolitiske konsekvenser. Nordisk kunnskapsstatus.* ANP 2005: 701. København: Nordisk Ministrerråd.

———. 2010. From rights to duties? Welfare and citizenship for immigrants and refugees in Scandinavia. In *Conflict, citizenship and civil society*, ed. Patrick Baert, Sokratis Koniordos, Giovanna Procacci, and Carlo Ruzza. London: Routledge.

Brochmann, Grete, Tordis Borchgrevink, and Jon Christian Rogstad. 2002. *Sand i maskineriet. Makt og demokrati i det flerkulturelle Norge.* Oslo: Gyldendal Akademisk.

Bruun, Maja Hojer, Gry Skrædderdal Jakobsen, and Stine Krøijer, eds. 2011. Introduction: The concern for sociality – Practicing equality and hierarchy in Denmark. *Social Analysis* 55 (2): 1–19.

Bruun, Maja Hojer, Stine Krøijer, and Mikkel Rytter. 2015. Innledende perspektiver: Forandringsstaten og selvstændghedssamfundet. *Tidsskriftet Antropologi* 72: 11–37.

Bryden, John, Ottar Brox, and Lesley Riddoch, eds. 2015. *Northern neighbours: Scotland and Norway since 1800.* Edinburgh: Edinburgh University Press.

Comaroff, Jonn, and Jean Comaroff, eds. 2011. *Millenial capitalism and the culture of neoliberalism.* Durham: Duke University Press.

Dahl, Hans Fredrik. 1986. Those equal folk. In *Norden: The passion for equality*, ed. R. Stephen and Graubard. Oslo: Norwegian University Press.

Danielsen, Hilde, Eirinn Larsen, and Ingeborg Winderen Owesen. 2013. *Norsk likestillingshistorie 1814–2013.* Oslo: Fagbokforlaget.

Eastmond, Marita. 2011. Egalitarian ambitions, constructions of difference: The paradoxes of refugee integration in Sweden. *Journal of Ethnic and Migration Studies* 37 (2): 277–295. doi:10.1080/1369183X.2010.521323.

Ellingsæter, Anne-Lise, and Arnlaug Leira, eds. 2006. *Politicising parenthood in Scandinavia. Gender relations in welfare states.* Bristol: Polity Press.

Eriksen, Thomas Hylland, ed. 2001. *Flerkulturell forståelse.* Oslo: Universitetsforlaget.

Esping-Andersen, Gøsta. 1985. *Politics against markets: The social democratic road to power.* Princeton: Princeton University Press.

———. 1990. *The three worlds of welfare capitalism.* Cambridge: Polity Press.

Etzioni, Amitai. 1995. *The spirit of community. Rights, responsibilities and the communitarian agenda.* London: Fontana Press.

Faist, Thomas. 2013. Multiculturalism: From heterogeneities to social (in)equalities. In *Debating multiculturalism in the Nordic welfare states*, ed. Peter Kivisto and Östen Wahlbeck, 22–47. New York: Palgrave Macmillan.

Frykman, Jonas, and Orvar Löfgren. 1979. *Den kultiverade människan.* Stockholm: Liber forlag.

Glyn, Andrew. 2006. *Capitalism unleashed. Finance, globalization, and welfare.* New York/Oxford: Oxford University Press.

Graham, Mark. 2003. Emotional bureaucracies: Emotions, civil servants, and immigrants in the Swedish Welfare State. *Ethos* 30: 199–226.
Granberg, Mukael. 2008. Local governance "in Swedish"? Globalisation, local welfare and beyond. *Local Government Studies* 34 (1): 363–377.
Gressgård, Randi. 2005. *Fra identitet til forskjell*. Oslo: Scandinavian Academic Press.
———. 2007. Det beste fra to kulturer: Frihet og fellesskap (The best of two worlds: Freedom and community). In *Grenser for kultur. Perspektiver på minoritetsforskning* (Cultural limits: Perspectives on minority research), ed. Øivind Fuglerud and Thomas Hylland Eriksen, 80–110. Oslo: Pax.
Gressgård, Randi, and Christine M. Jacobsen. 2002. En kvinne er ikke bare en kvinne. Kjønnsproblematikk i et flerkulturelt samfunn. In *Kjønnsrettferdighet. Utfordringer for feministisk politikk*, ed. Cathrine Holst, 189–230. Oslo: Gyldendal.
Gullestad, Marianne. 1984. *Kitchen-table society. A case study of the family life and friendships of young working-class mothers in urban Norway*. Oslo: Universitetsforlaget.
———. 2002. Invisible fences: Egalitarianism, nationalism and racism. *Journal of the Royal Anthropological Institute* 8 (1): 199–226.
Gullikstad, Berit. 2010. Når likestilling blir ulikhet. Interseksjonalitet i arbeidslivet. In *Likestilte norskheter. Om kjønn og etnisitet*, ed. Anne-Jorunn Berg, Anne Britt Flemmen, and Berit Gullikstad, 101–132. Trondheim: Tapir akademisk forlag.
Haagensen, Eva, Laila Kvisler, and Tor Birkeland. 1990. *Innvandrere – gjester eller bofaste? En innføring i norsk innvandringspolitikk* (Immigrants- Guests or permanent residents? An introduction to Norwegian immigration policy). Oslo: Gyldendal Norsk Forlag.
Habermas, Jürgen. 1987. *The theory of communicative action*. Vol. I–II. Boston: Beacon Press.
Hayek, Friedrich. 2007. *The road to serfdom*. Chicago: Chicago University Press.
Headey, Bruce. 1999. *The real worlds of welfare capitalism*. Cambridge: Cambridge University Press.
Hernes, Helga. 1987. *Welfare state and woman power: Essays in state feminism*. London: Norwegian University Press.
Heywood, Andrew. 2004. *Political theory. An introduction*. New York: Palgrave Macmillan.
Horgen, André. 2016. Sikkerhet trumfer alt? Sikkerhetsdiskurser i og omkring friluftslivet. University College of Southeast Norway (Unpublished manuscript).
Jenkins, Richard. 2011. *Being Danish. Paradoxes of identity in everyday life*. Copenhagen: Museum Tusculanum Press.

Jöhncke, Steffen. 2007. Velfærdsstaten som integrationsprojekt. In *Integration: Antropologiske perspektiver*, ed. Karen Fog Olwig and Karsten Pærregaard, 37–62. København: Museum Tusculanum.

Kapferer, Bruce. 2015. Afterword. When is a joke not a joke? The paradox of egalitarianism. In *The event of Charlie Hebdo: Imaginaries of freedom and control*, Critical interventions 15, ed. Alessandro Zagato. New York: Berghahn.

Kildal, Nanna, and Stein Kuhnle. 2005. The Nordic welfare model and the idea of universalism. In *Normative foundations of the welfare state. The Nordic experience*, ed. Nanna Kildal and Stein Kuhnle. New York: Routledge.

Kivisto, Peter, and Östen Wahlbeck. 2013. Debating multiculturalism in the Nordic welfare states. In *Debating multiculturalism in the Nordic welfare states*, ed. Peter Kivisto and Östen Wahlbeck, 1–21. New York: Palgrave Macmillan.

Knudsen, Tim. 2000. Inledning. In *Den nordiske protestantisme og velfærdsstaten*, ed. Tim Knudsen, 7–20. Aarhus: Aarhus Universitetsforlag.

Knudsen, Tim, and Bo Rothstein. 1994. State building in Scandinavia. *Comparative Politics* 26 (2): 203–220.

Kristensen, Guro Korsnes. 2010. Trad eller trendy med tre? Om barnetall, likestilling og "norskhet". In *Likestilte norskheter: Om kjønn og etnisitet*, ed. Anne-Jorunn Berg, Anne Britt Flemmen, and Berit Gullikstad, 71–99. Trondheim: Tapir akademiske forlag.

Kymlicka, Will, and Keith Banting. 2006. Immigration, multiculturalism, and the welfare state. *Ethnics and International Affairs* 20 (3): 281–304.

Larsen, Birgitte Romme. 2011. Drawing back the curtains: The role of domestic space in the social inclusion and exclusion of refugees in rural Denmark. *Social Analysis* (Special issue title: The concern for sociality in Denmark, eds. Stine Krøijer, Maja Hojer Bruun, and Gry Skrædderdal Jakobsen) 55 (2): 142–158.

Lien, Marianne E., Hilde Lidén, and Halvard Vike, eds. 2001. *Likhetens paradokser. Antropologiske undersøkelser i det moderne Norge*. Oslo: Universitetsforlaget.

Löfgren, Orvar. 1987. Deconstructing swedishness: Culture and class in modern Sweden. In *Anthropology at home*, ASA Monographs, 25, ed. Anthony Jackson, 74–93. London: Tavistock Publications.

Midtbøen, Arnfinn H., and Jon Rogstad. 2012. *Diskrimineringens omfang og årsaker*. ISF-rapport 2012: 1. Oslo.

Mouritsen, Per. 2006. The particular universalism of a Nordic civic nation: Common values, state religion, and Islam in Danish political culture. In *Multiculturalism, muslims and citizenship*, ed. Tariq Modood, Ricard Zapata-Barrero, and Anna Triandafyllidou, 70–93. London: Routledge.

Nagel, Anne Hilde, ed. 1991. *Velferdskommunen. Kommunenes rolle i utviklingen av velferdsstaten*. Bergen: Alma Mater.

Norman, Karin. 2004. Equality and exclusion: "Racism" in a Swedish town. *Ethnos* 69 (2): 204–228.

Okin, Susan Moller. 1999. Is multiculturalism bad for women? In *Is multiculturalism bad for women?* ed. Joshua Cohen, Matthew Howard, and Martha C. Nussbaum, 7–26. Princeton: Princeton University Press.
Olwig, Karen Fog. 2011. "Integration": Migrants and refugees between Scandinavian welfare societies and family relations. *Journal of Ethnic and Migration Studies* 37 (2): 179–196. doi:10.1080/1369183X.2010.521327.
Østergård, Uffe. 1992. *Europas ansigter. Nationale stater og politiske kulturer i en ny, gammel verden.* København: Rosinante.
Papakostas, Apostolis. 2001. Why is there no clientelism in Sweden? In *Clientelism, interests, and democratic representation. The European experience in historical and comparative perspective,* ed. Simona Piattoni. Cambridge: Cambridge University Press.
Putnam, Robert D. 2000. *Bowling alone. The collapse and revival of American community.* New York: Simon & Schuster.
Rugkåsa, Marianne. 2012. *Likhetens dilemma. Om sivilisering og integrasjon i den velferdsambisiøse norske stat.* Oslo: Gyldendal Akademisk.
Schmidt, Garbi. 2012. Nørrebro and "muslimness": A neighborhood caught between national mythscapes and local engagement. In *Islam in Denmark: The challenge of diversity,* ed. Jørgen Nielsen, 95–114. Lanham: Lexington Books.
———. 2013. "Let's get together": Perspectives on multiculturalism and local implications in Denmark. In *Debating multiculturalism in the Nordic welfare states,* ed. Peter Kivisto and Östen Wahlbeck, 197–218. New York: Palgrave Macmillan.
Seip, Anne Lise. 1992. *Velferdsstatens utvikling. Trangen til trygghet og en ny rasjonalitet.* Oslo: Ad Notam.
Sejersted, Francis. 2005. *Sosialdemokratiets tidsalder – Norge og Sverige i det 20. århundre.* Oslo: Pax Forlag.
Siim, Birte. 1993. The gendered Scandinavian welfare states: The interplay between women's roles as mothers, workers and citizens in Denmark. In *Women and social policies in Europe: Work, family and the state,* ed. Jane Lewis, 27–48. Aldershot: Edward Elgar.
Siim, Birte, and Hege Skjeie. 2008. Tracks, intersections and dead ends – Multicultural challenges to state feminism in Denmark and Norway. *Ethnicities* 8 (3): 322–344. doi:10.1177/1468796808092446.
Simmel, Georg. 1950. Individual and society in eighteenth- and nineteenth century views of life. In *The sociology of Georg Simmel,* ed. Kurt H. Wolff, 58–84. New York: Glencoe Free Press.
———. 1971. *On individuality and social forms. Selected writings.* Edited by Donald Levine. Chicago: University of Chicago Press.
Sivesind, Karl Henrik, and Per Selle. 2010. Civil society in the Nordic countries: Between displacement and vitality. In *Nordic associations in a European perspective,* ed. Henrik Stenius and Risto Alapuro. Baden-Baden: Nomos.

Slagstad, Rune. 1998. *De nasjonale strateger*. Oslo: Pax.
Solway, Jacqueline. 2006. *The politics of egalitarianism. Theory and practice*. New York/Oxford: Berghahn.
Sørensen, Øystein, and Bo Stråth, eds. 1997. *The cultural construction of Norden*. Oslo: Scandinavian University Press.
Stefansen, Kari, and Helene Aarseth. 2011. Enriching intimacy: The role of the emotional in the "resourcing" of middle-class children. *British Journal of Sociology of Education* 32 (3): 389–405.
Stenius, Henrik. 2010. Nordic associational life in a European and an inter-Nordic perspective. In *Nordic associations in a European perspective*, ed. Henrik Stenius and Risto Alapuro. Baden-Baden: Nomos.
Stråth, Bo. 2005. *Union og demokrati – dei sameinte rika Norge-Sverige 1814-1905*. Oslo: Pax.
Trägårdh, Lars. 2007. The "civil society" debate in Sweden: The welfare state challenged. In *State and civil society in northern Europe. The Swedish model reconsidered*, ed. Lars Trägårdh. New York/Oxford: Berghahn Books.
———. 2008. Det civila samhällets karriär som vetenskapligt och politiskt begrepp i Sverige. *Tidsskrift for Samfunnsforskning* 49 (4): 575–594.
Tranvik, Tommy, and Per Selle. 2007. More centralization, less democracy: The decline of the democratic infrastructure in Norway. In *State and civil society in northern Europe. The Swedish model reconsidered*, ed. Lars Trägårdh. New York/Oxford: Berghahn Books.
Vike, Halvard. 1997. Reform and resistance. A Norwegian illustration. In *Anthropology of policy: Critical perspectives on governance and power*, ed. Chris Shore and Susan Wright. London: Routledge.
———. 2004. *Velferd uten grenser. Den norske velferdsstaten ved veiskillet*. Oslo: Akribe.
Vulkan, Patrik, Antti Saloniemi, Jørgen Svalund, and Anna Väisänen. 2015. Job insecurity and mental well-being in Finland and Norway and Sweden. Consequences of flexicurity in a Nordic welfare setting. *Nordic Journal of Working Life Studies* 5 (2): 33–53.
Welstad, Trond-Erik. 2014. Elevenes faglige utdanning og menneskelige utvikling i skolen. Rettslige utfordringer og praktiskedilemmaer. In *Kompetanse for mangfold: Om utdanningens rolle og skolens utfordringer i det flerkulturelle Norge*, ed. Kariane Westrheim and Astrid Tolo, 119–149. Oslo: Fagbokforlaget.
Wikan, Unni. 1995. *Mot en ny norsk underklasse. Innvandrere, kultur og integrasjon*. Oslo: Gyldendal.

PART I

The Tradition of Egalitarianism

The Cultural Construction of Equality in Norden

Bo Stråth

Some Points of Departure: A Nordic *Sonderweg*?

Denaturalizing egalitarianism is to deconstruct it, to show that it is a social construct, to historicize it, and emancipate it from any connotation of permanent essence or deep roots. This means to emphasize equality as a social or cultural construct. Equality is a discourse. Equality is not inherent in history or in social structures.

Social constructs are more than the production of symbols or brandings by ruling elites ("invented nations", "invention of tradition"). Neither is it a matter of silent traditions or long chains of ideas as in the imageries of a specific European Enlightenment heritage regarding concepts like freedom and equality. The construction of community is a matter of appealing to, and activating, such traditions and legacies for political use. Strong concepts loaded with contested meaning, like equality and freedom, are the building blocks in the social work on community. The construction of community does not occur in a void, but traditions and legacies do not as such provoke action in the building of community. Construction requires human action in the present.

B. Stråth (✉)
University of Helsinki, Helsinki, Finland

Like everywhere else, the construction of community in the Nordic societies drew on imaginaries of the past when experiences were translated into the future horizons of expectation that promoted action. The discourse on equality in Norden was entangled with the discourse on freedom and outlined visions of a society of free and equal individuals. The discourse picked arguments from the Nordic history and had more appeal in certain social strata than in others. Since the French Revolution, there had been a tension between the ideals of equality and the ideals of freedom. The language of freedom of equality in the North reflected this tension at the same time as it tried to transcend it. The image of a society of free equals was not intrinsic in the Nordic history or social structures, and the Enlightenment thought as such did not mean its political implementation. The idea should not be confused with political and cultural practice. However, the Nordic history and social structures were, like the Enlightenment thought, points of reference in the political work on the implementation of the vision of a society of equals.

The social work on community is seldom a matter of consensus but is a contentious affair. Conflicts between ideals and interests constitute politics. Without such conflicts, there would be no politics. However, politics requires shared concepts such as equality, freedom, reform, modernity, etc., which all agree on as such. Without this agreement there is no shared framework of politics. Politics begins with disagreement on what people really mean in terms of good or bad or in terms of defining the substance. The conflict and the search for compromises mold together societies in the construction of community.

The peasants in the North played a double role in the work on community regarding the concepts of equality and freedom. In contrast to many other countries they were key figures in the production of community. They were no doubt the lowest stratum in the political decision-making at the local and national levels, but they were nevertheless participants with influence in the political process, at least its core of freeholders. *Bonde* (plural *bønder/bönder*) is the Scandinavian term that covers both peasants and farmers. From their early role as peasants in subsistence economies, in the nineteenth century, they became increasingly involved in market relationships as farmers. Instead of peasants in a subsistence economy, commercialization with farmers as producers and consumers in markets emerged. However, long before that, for centuries, they had been active participants in local government politics. In Sweden, since early modern times they had constituted a separate fourth estate of the Diet.

Besides this role as political actors, the peasant was also the key figure in the symbolic representation of equality and freedom. The historical peasant figure was part of the foundation myths in Norden. This was the second role of the peasants/farmers.

Thus, the Nordic specificity was that the *bønder/bönder* were not only the *object* of a Romantic idealization of a heroic past going back to the world of the sagas, but also were an actively participating *subject* in the political processes. The peasants/farmers created their own political future. In particular, they made politics in the local communities (Sørensen and Stråth 1997).

There is a photo from the 1890s of a village meeting in the Swedish province of Västergötland. It shows some ten farmers sitting and standing around a table in the open air of a farmstead. They radiate self-confidence, authority and equality, freedom, and autonomy. They radiate equality but what does equality mean? Yes, equality between equals, but where are the cottagers, the crofters, and the social substrata? Where are the women? How free and equal were the farmers? Where are the squires? Where are the vicar and the representatives of the state? Where is the feudal landlord, who probably felt as free as the farmers? The photo does indeed give an impression of what equality looks like but through questions about the absent people, it also shows how relative concepts like free and equal are.

In the myth of the Nordic peasant as it emerged in the nineteenth century, and in the self-understanding of the farmers, the peasant was the bearer of freedom, equality, and education. Freedom and equality belonged together in the motto of the French Revolution, but in political practice the concepts soon split up. In the 1820s, in post-revolutionary Europe, two ideologies emerged, each of them emphasizing one of the two concepts, liberalism stood for imagery of freedom and socialism for the imagery of equality. The two ideologies tried to cope with what from the 1830s had become the big European problem—the social question, which emerged as a problem for the ruling elites in the wake of the spread of industrial capitalism. This division deepened during the rest of the century, in particular from the 1870s onward, when the top-down perspective for coming to terms with the social question shifted to the bottom-up approach of the class question.

The argument here is that the Nordic countries managed to keep the tension between freedom and equality under better control than elsewhere, which is something different from arguing about concepts like freedom and equality in absolute terms. This control of the tension between freedom and equality might be seen as a Nordic *Sonderweg*, which dealt with the political and cultural implementation and management of the vision of equality rather than something given from history, the Enlightenment heritage, social structures, or nature, although history, heritage, and social structures provided specific preconditions for such implementation and management.

Freedom and Solidarity from a Theoretical Perspective

The Latvian-British-Jewish philosopher Isaiah Berlin distinguished between negative freedom and positive freedom, "liberty". Negative freedom is the freedom to do whatever one wants and becomes in the end a question of power. Positive freedom refers to the right to unify and create rules against abuses of power. Positive freedom has a solidaristic, collective focus whereas negative freedom has the individual as its carrier, the strong individual, one might add (Berlin 1969 [1958]).

The construction of community in Norden mainly followed Berlin's trajectory of positive freedom. There were certainly many examples of practices of negative freedom during the social conflict in the old agrarian society and in the wake of the spread of industrial capitalism, but the point is that they largely were pushed back onto the positive track through politics and legislation. This was the core of Nordic modernity.

Alexis de Tocqueville had, a century before Berlin, tried to find a unifying formula in his idea of social justice as equal *opportunities* to develop one's talents. The French aristocrat based his reasoning on his experience of going to America in the 1830s where he saw the future as both a threat and an opportunity. He saw the future as democracy and was afraid of it at the same time as he considered it to be unavoidable. Aristocracy in Europe was the past, democracy in America was the future, for good and for evil. Therefore, one had to cope with it through emphasizing the opportunities it brought. A key question was how to cope with "equality" and with a society of equals. He found the answer in the vision of equal opportunities. This imagery was the core of the American dream that he envisaged (Tocqueville 1988 [1835–1840]). Everybody had a chance of self-realization and to climb socially, which, of course, implied also the risk of falling. Social positions were not predetermined by birth or social hierarchy. However, in social practice, history after Tocqueville has demonstrated that the American dream of a society of equals often came close to the negative freedom as defined by Berlin.

The argument against the backdrop of this theoretical framework is that the Nordic countries managed to contain the tensions between freedom and equality better than in many other places. Positive freedom in Berlin's ideas matched and corrected the abuses of negative freedom relatively well. A brief outline of the European framework of the hundred years from the 1870s until the 1970s will demonstrate this difference and what was specifically Nordic and also that there were differences between the Nordic countries.

The Political Practices in the Construction of Social Community: The European Framework

In 1871, Otto von Bismarck accomplished German unification with blood and iron. As a consequence of the simultaneous collapse of the French Empire, the Paris Commune was proclaimed. The contours of a workers' republic emerged. The year 1871 was a social earthquake in Europe. The Vienna order broke down. Talk of class spread across Europe. The top-down social question how to avoid new social unrest changed to the bottom-up class question of the emancipation of what increasingly emerged as a working class in the singular as opposed to the earlier more diffuse working classes. The workers began to replace the peasants/farmers as the voice of the lower classes.

Otto von Bismarck came to the conclusion that future politics had to deal with the question of how to appropriate the national question from the liberals and the social question from the socialists. He began to look for a top-down alternative to the bottom-up claims for national unification and social integration. The unification of Germany through war was his answer to the national challenge. The Paris Commune and the growing talk of class convinced him of the urgency of getting control over the social conflict. He was certain that social integration had to follow the national unification of Germany.

In 1872, a group of German professors of political economy, *Nationalökonomie*, met to discuss how to promote state intervention in social issues on the basis of historical-economic investigations. After the solution to the question of national integration, they put the problem of social integration on the agenda. In 1873, they founded the *Verein für Sozialpolitik*, the Association for Social Politics. The call for its foundation expressed the desire to connect politics and social science explicitly:

> ... the strife between capital and labor appears for the time being as endangering. We are therefore of the opinion, that there are urgent tasks of peaceful reform for state and society. At first, the condition of the workers and their relationships to the employers must be clarified [by social sciences] ... In the same way all other social and economic problems of the time, like health care, education, communications, shareholding and taxes must also be taken into consideration. (Wagner 1990, 80)

The Association aimed to become a forum in which academic, economic, and political-administrative elites could discuss what measures should be taken on the basis of the results of social scientific research. There was a pressing need for a public debate. The idea of social politics was based on the conscious insight that state and society necessarily had to be activated in order to establish a balance between the social interests that were drifting apart (Wagner 1990, 81).[1]

The program of the Association fitted like a hand in a glove with Bismarck's policy for social integration of the growing number of industrial workers with ever-louder voices. Occasionally he called himself a state socialist as opposed to the class-struggle socialism of the workers. By this, he did not refer to any idea of state ownership of industry but to a general concern about the allegiance of the workers through the provision of certain social standards. Bismarck's approach focused on insurance programs designed to increase productivity, and included sickness insurance, accident insurance, disability insurance, and a retirement pension, none of which were then in existence to any great degree. The long-term vision of a welfare state, a *Sozialstaat*, emerged around the Bismarckian anti-liberal approach.

Bismarck and the argument for social politics by the moderately conservative German professors were the case in point in a more general development. In England, Disraeli's government's program of social reform in 1874–1875 signaled a new approach to the social question. National integration meant social integration of the working classes. The British Prime Minister had revealed his attention to the social question already in his 1845 novel *Sybil, or the Two Nations* (the rich and the poor), where he referred to "the only duty of power, the social welfare of the people". In 1874, his concern became political programs for social reform in housing, savings and labor relations, against slum buildings, and for public health. The Employers and Workmen Act 1875 established equality before the law regarding labor contracts. Other laws allowed peaceful picketing and regulated labor standards in factory work.

Similar developments based on the work of Émile Durkheim occurred in France, who argued for a new kind of organic solidarity. In Italy, the so-called *statalisti* among the lawyers and economists emphasized the crucial role of the state for social integration in opposition to the market apologists and adherents of a liberal economy. They tried to emulate the German approach to national and social unification.

In Sweden, conservative political science professor Rudolf Kjellén argued for a national socialism in response to the class-struggle socialism. He was just one in an academic chorus there on the need for social nationalism or national socialism for the social integration of the workers in the nation, which was understood as the conservative unification of the people under the king rather than as the emancipation of the subjects to become citizens (Stråth 2016; Wagner 1990). He tried to give the concept of people a conservative shape with the concept of *folkhem*, the nation as the home for the people, but a conservative shape with a social dimension.

The backdrop of Bismarck's social-state approach and the more general European conservative social reform and concession strategy in the wake of the German example was the lengthy economic crisis that began with a speculation bubble and bank crash in 1873. The crisis was soon referred to as the Great Depression which destroyed the credibility of the vision of a liberal, global, free-trade order which had legitimized the British global commercial and geopolitical power since 1815, although was never fully implemented.

Bismarck and Germany provided the model to emulate. In Germany, the *Centralverband deutscher Industrieller* (the Central Federation of German Industrialists, CdI) was established in January 1876. The federation represented the whole spectrum of industry and its central idea was the rejection of liberal free trade. It became a powerful lobbying organization. Somewhat later than industry, the agrarian sector ceased to benefit from free trade. Cheap cereals from Canada, the USA and Russia (Ukraine) closed export markets to German agrarian products. A month after the establishment of the CdI, the *Großagrarier* founded the *Vereinigung der Steuer- und Wirtschaftsreformer*, the Association of the Tax and Economy Reformers, which began to lobby for protection of the German agrarian market.

The emergence of centralized interest organizations promoted the development of state institutions for social integration and reconciliation as well as for arbitration in the class conflict. This was the emergence of organized modernity. Austrian social democratic theoretician Rudolf Hilferding spoke about organized capital which established a state apparatus that the social democrats relatively easy could take over and transform into a social democratic welfare state. In Sweden, the social democrats were interested in Rudolf Kjellén's conservative home-for-the-people concept although they wanted to give it a different shape and substance. A 30-year discursive struggle between the conservatives and the social democrats about giving meaning to the *folkhem* concept began. The opposite of the social conservative reform strategy was the louder class language of the workers and the trend toward social polarization. The social democrats competed with the conservatives over how to create social integration in polarized societies. Bottom-up approaches provoked top-down responses and vice versa, in polarizing or in compromise-oriented directions. In the Nordic countries, the trend mainly followed the latter tendency.

However, the trend toward social compromises and the hopes invested in the social-democratic expectations could not conceal the fact that Europe in 1914 was in firm conservative hands. Through the skillful use of concessions, the authoritarian regimes in Europe warded off the threats of the class-struggle language. The social democrats were far from the reins of political power. From the 1870s onward, the conservatives gave up the hope of crushing the working class. Their main problem became how to integrate the workers into the nation through concessions. Sweden and Finland were well suited to follow this development. They both had conservative political regimes in 1914, Finland as a Russian Grand Duchy. They both struggled to come to terms with the democratic threat through concessions.

Denmark and Norway did not follow this European pattern to the same extent as Sweden and Finland. In Denmark, the liberal Left broke through as a political force around 1900 and in Norway the liberal Left enforced the dissolution of the union with Sweden in 1905. The Left had mobilized the nation in a campaign against the union since 1890, indeed, since the 1870s, a campaign which in the end also the conservatives joined. The destiny of the union was tied to its incapacity to cope institutionally with the fact that Norway was more democratic than Sweden. In Norway, in the 1830s, the peasants/farmers had already become a powerful political force reinforced from the 1870s onward. Norway was different from the other Nordic countries in one crucial respect: there was historically no landed aristocracy or nobility as a social formation. The freeholding farmers dominated rural Norway. There was a strong liberal merchant bourgeoisie and a conservative reform-oriented formation of civil servants and professors, which produced specific preconditions for the approach to the question of social integration.

It was not the French Revolution but the world wars that brought the breakthrough of democracy in Europe. The mass mobilization for the war created mass societies of a new kind. The war sacrifices of the masses required a tribute to them. The politics of slow concessions came to an end. This European framework is important for the question of equality in the North.

Denmark and Norway were similar, on the one side, and Sweden and Finland, on the other, beyond the fact that Sweden and Finland were more aristocratic, and there were similarities between the Nordic countries that distinguished them from the European stage as the next section will show.

THE SOCIAL PROTEST: THE PEOPLE'S MOVEMENTS

What made Norden unique in this European pattern was the people's movements, folkebevegelsene (Norwegian)/folkebevegelserne (Danish)/ *folkrörelserna* (Swedish), the social protest movements, which, with tensions between and within them, from the 1870s formed a social, religious, and cultural protest against the *ancien régime*. In Norway, there was no really old society in the aristocratic sense as was found in Sweden and Finland. The ruling political and economic elites were representatives of enlightened liberalism and conservatism in commerce, industry, and government administration. There the unifying target of attack was rather the union with Sweden with its conservative establishment.

The shared dimension of the social conflict in the North was that it was much less a polarized class conflict between organized labor and organized capital as occurred in other parts of Europe. The religious protest against the exegetic power of the Lutheran state church clergy was particularly strong in Sweden, whereas the churches in Denmark, Norway, and Finland had less of a High Church profile. However, the claim for more laity influence in the interpretation of Lutheranism, for less ostentation and ritual show, and the search for a more immediate divine relationship circumventing the mediation of the clergy was common. There was a strong moralist dimension in the religious protest which was closely linked to the campaign against alcohol of the temperance movement but was also visible in the social protest of the labor movement. There was also a strong social dimension in the religious protest which reinforced the links to the labor movement.

The people's movements cut straight through the middle classes and split them between lower and upper middle classes. The people's movements were coalitions between the lower middle classes in the towns and in the rural districts with the labor movement. The dimension of bottom-up was obvious in the mediation of the tension between freedom and equality in these popular coalitions. They promised to dissolve the tensions. The distinctive Nordic mark was that bottom-up did not mean the working class against the rest but involved a broader protest coalition involving the lower rural and urban middle classes and connecting religious and social protest.

They challenged the conservative use of education in the schools, the army, and at the universities, which propagated national and Lutheran moral values as the tool for social integration from above. The people's movements represented the Nordic *Sonderweg*. The social protest from below in Norden must be understood against the backdrop of conservative concessions from above for national integration, which emerged in a Swedish-Finnish more aristocratic version and a Norwegian-Danish less aristocratic version. The confrontation dealt with the connection between Lutheran religion and social values, a more or less social and economic hierarchy, and the interpretation of the Enlightenment values around the key concepts of equality, freedom and education.

The tension between the ideals of equality and freedom was kept under better control in the Nordic debate on the social question. The debate was less polarized even if, of course, the class language since the 1870s rumbled also there, and a strong liberal cultural-radical tradition, inspired by French and German (Nietzsche) philosophy, introduced by the Danish critic Georg Brandes and propagated loudly by Henrik Ibsen and August Strindberg, since the 1880s frontally confronted religion, economic concentration, and the double morals of the church and royal court establishments. The debate was not necessarily more muted than elsewhere but followed a different line of conflict, not between the rising working class and the rest as in the standard stereotype, but between lower and higher rural and urban middle classes, where through the people's movements the working classes were more involved with the lower middle classes.

There was in addition to their struggle for freedom and equality, whatever that meant, a third key dimension on their road toward the promised land of emancipation: education, self-education. The Nordic peasants/farmers and workers were carriers not only of freedom and equality but also of education which became a key tool in the struggle of the people's movements to define the meaning of the concepts of equality and freedom. Already at the conceptual level, there were particular preconditions in the Scandinavian languages for the struggle about giving meaning to what, in English, is called education. This term is derived from the Latin verb *educare*, "to draw out" or "to bring up". The German term *Erziehung* is based on a direct translation of this Latin word, "drawing up". In Danish and Norwegian the term is *dannelse*, which means "forming, shaping", and in Swedish it is *bildning*, which means "forming and shaping", too, but the word is also connected to building, to build something To bring up somebody means that the teacher is the active agent whereas to shape or build something moves the agency more toward what in "education" is the pupil. The people's movements developed this dimension of self-education looking for alternative knowledge to the teaching found in schools and universities.

The farmers were the core of the ambitious Enlightenment program of the Danish clergyman N. F. S. Grundtvig in the nineteenth century. It is difficult to exaggerate his influence all over the Nordic countries. His program emerged in the framework of a Danish popular mobilization against an experienced threat of a militarily and culturally expansive Germany. The program of *dannelse* was both far-reaching and widespread. From the point of departure in an imagined Christian community based on the Holy Communion and baptism, his scheme embraced the establishment of farmers' producers' cooperatives and a farmers' political party for political reforms. Against what he called the artificial Latin-based scholarship at the universities, he set the "real" *dannelse* as an emancipative instrument in the hands of the farmers. *Folkehøjskolen*, the "folk high school", became a veritable movement, which spread from Denmark then to other Nordic countries. They became formation and education centers, where the popular thirst for knowledge was satisfied. The peasants/farmers (and the workers in Grundtvig's plan) as carriers of education were no doubt an alternative role to most stereotypes (Sørensen and Stråth 1997).

A comparison between Grundtvig and the father of the modern university, Wilhelm von Humboldt, is instructive. Both were influenced by English liberalism and utilitarian ideas. They embraced both Enlightenment and Romantic ideas. They considered education (*Erziehung*, *dannelse*) to be an emancipative instrument. Education and freedom were closely connected in their perspective. However, they did not mean the same thing by freedom. While Humboldt required the state both to guarantee academic freedom and pay for it, Grundtvig's view was that education had to be organized independently of the state and in conscious opposition to the mandarins of the universities. Humboldt's academic freedom paved the way for the emergence of the German *Bildungsbürgertum* under state control, which never really emerged as a social formation in Norden. There the concept of *dannelse/bildning* meant much more the people's (revivalist, temperance, labor) movements which all had study circles and local libraries as organizational cornerstones. The role of the peasants/farmers and the workers in the people's movement as carriers of education gave the modernization of the North its specific shape. This was particularly true of the way in which national Romanticism developed in a much more common-sense and Enlightenment-oriented direction than in, for example, Germany. It is true that the civil servants and the *borgerlig* society were skeptical of the cultural and political maturity of the *bönder* and the workers, but this skepticism never resulted in the emergence of a bourgeois alternative, such as the German *Bildungsbürgertum* (Sørensen and Stråth 1997). Bourgeois is too charged with Marxist meaning to be a good translation for *borgerlig*, which means citizen, and the German *bürgerlich*. The word for citizen is *medborgare*, for instance. These conceptual nuances reflect crucial socio-economic differences.

The comparison of Grundtvig's and von Humboldt's approaches reflects two opposite approaches to education in the processes of social integration, from below and from above respectively. These alternative integrative processes were not *caused* in a simple way by the different approaches to education, of course. The different solutions reflect deeper cultural differences between the Scandinavian/Nordic and the German societies. Not least the role and the social self-esteem of the *bönder*, the peasants/farmers are important in this connection.

The peasant myth based on the peasants as carriers of freedom and equality under the concept of "people" or "nation" was a general characteristic of the nineteenth-century European nation-building. The addition of education gave this process a particular twist in the North. The Scandinavian concept of *folk* and the Finnish *kansa* are less holistic and less ideologically charged than the German *Volk*.

Folk/Volk emerged as a key concept in a Romantic search for holistic unity in an industrializing world where experiences of atomization produced alienation. Romanticism was a critical corrective to modernity and Enlightenment. Romanticism and Enlightenment were two parallel ideological movements which constituted one another, in the sense that they defined themselves through the demarcation from each other, rather than being subsequent phases of history. The precise mix between the two was different in different societies. In the politically unfulfilled German nation, Enlightenment rationalization and the emphasis on individualism not only were experienced in terms of emancipation but also provoked longings for holistic community. The discursive development on the theme Enlightenment-Romanticism had a more experienced-based, pragmatic, less philosophical connotation in Norden and did not merge with a holistic nation concept to the same extent.

There were interesting similarities between Nordic and British modernity, between the Nordic people's movements and the British social-religious protest movement, and in terms of the individualistic orientation in the organization of society in both Norden and Britain. "Individualistic" here was something very different from the kind of dogmatic individualism detached from social ties propagated by the neo-liberal ideologues in the 1980s and the 1990s. It was a matter of individual liberty within a collective identification provided by local self-governing units in the *bonde* and working-class communities. Individualistic meant individual self-realization based on collective performance, which, in turn, was based on deep value patterns within the framework of a puritan and moralistic Protestant ethic. The revivalist movement was strong in both Britain and Norden. Puritanism and moralism were not linked to fanaticism and fundamentalism, however, but to pragmatism in the search for compromises in the social conflict. This was in Norden a kind of Protestant Romanticism as opposed to the German more holistic dialectics of *Sturm und Drang*. In the more polarized Germany, the collectivist organization under the *Volk* concept meant the restoration of holistic visions from above. In the triangular patterns of social organization in Britain, Germany, and Norden, the historically more aristocratic Sweden and Finland with bigger industrial companies and capital concentration in the nineteenth century had links not only to British modernity but came in crucial respects close also to the German organized form of modernity, however (cf. Stråth 1996). In a triangular Britain-Norden-Germany comparison of the patterns of social organization, Norden came between Britain and Germany, but Sweden and Finland were closer to Germany and Denmark, and Norway was closer to Britain. In an internal Nordic comparison, Sweden and Finland were more polarized along the axis property-poverty and aristocracy-democracy than Denmark and Norway.

Norway represents probably a European *Sonderweg* among the development patterns as outlined here. Francis Sejersted described this Norwegian *Sonderweg* in his study, *Demokratisk kapitalisme* (Sejersted 2002 [1993]).[2] Democracy and capitalism are often seen as counter-concepts, although liberal theory tries to keep them together, like the concepts of freedom and equality. Sejersted unified them on the empirical basis of Norwegian historical experiences. It was not the social-democratic state-governed capitalism after 1945 he had in mind, but the imagery of liberal commercial and entrepreneurial middle classes—bourgeoisie, with its Marx-inspired connotation of French concentration of economic power, industrial capitalism and *haute bourgeoisie*, would here be the wrong label—who together with enlightened civil servants, state officials, and professors of law, statistics, economics, and similar disciplines developed a dynamic economy based on commerce and small enterprises. Their normative value scale went far beyond individual-based maximization of utility. This model opened economic growth and social integration. This was a model that the social democrats later could take over and transform into what Sejersted in his last great work called the century of social democracy (Sejersted 2005). Francis Sejersted confirmed on the Norwegian empirical basis Jürgen Habermas's ideal-type of the civic liberal public as the basis of democracy.

Sweden and Finland were more in the mainstream European trend with the emergence of big business and the corporate organization of interests. There the conservative social nationalism with an ethnic blend of social integration had more of a hierarchical top-down profile than the Norwegian enlightened liberalism of the commercial and entrepreneurial middle classes and the enlightened conservatism of the state officials. Denmark was more agrarian and had, as opposed to Norway, a landed aristocracy, but the agrarian economy there was based more on *Gutswirtschaft*, manor economy, than on *Gutsherrschaft*, manorial power. There was a clear liberal commercial profile after the abolition of serfdom in 1788.

To sum up, yes, Norden became, rather than was, in some sense more equal than many other societies, and the people's movements were crucial for this development. The work on shaping the modern world and on coming to terms with new kinds of inequalities in the wake of the spread of industrial capitalism put the social question on the political agenda in Norden as in Europe in general. The people's movements gave the debate a particular twist where ideals of equality connected to ideals of positive freedom in the sense of Isaiah Berlin and to ideals of self-realization through *bildning/dannelse*.

Toward the Social Democratic Welfare Governments

After World War I, the people's movements became more immediately involved in government politics via social democratic and social liberal parties, in the 1930s ever more so. The 1930s was the breakthrough of red-green coalition governments in all the Nordic countries in response to the global economic crisis. This was the North European democratic version of mass politics against the economic crisis. As we know, mass politics could under the conditions of economic crisis lead to politics in very different directions which did not necessarily mean democracy. The Nordic *Sonderweg* had a fourth dimension besides freedom, equality and education: welfare by the state. The Nordic welfare states became the instrument of a new political elite where bottom-up shifted to top-down. This was the social-democratic takeover of the conservative Swedish and Finnish authoritarian states for social integration from above and of the state of the enlightened Norwegian and Danish state functionaries.

The Nordic welfare democracies provided a serious proposal to show how one can solve the tension between freedom and equality, although there was all the time criticism from the opposition that the politics for equality destroyed the basis of freedom. This criticism kept the debate and the contention about the good society alive. The distinction between society and state, *samhälle* and *stat* as in Hegel's distinction disappeared. Olof Palme talked about the strong society, *det starka samhället*, when he meant the welfare state. *Civilsamhället*, the civil society, was a new concept in the political language in the North coined to mark a new kind of society in the neo-liberal vision in the 1980s and 1990s. Before that there was no need for the prefix of civil because "*samhälle*" meant both society and state. The new term *civilsamhälle* in the 1980s signaled a demarcation from the state.

The problem was that the Nordic social democracies became increasingly technocracies which under the label of welfare wanted to order the lives of their citizens. Through a vulgarization of the economic theory of Keynes, they developed a tool kit for the political management of the economies under promises of permanent affluence ahead. The hubris grew. At the same time as this happened in the 1960s, the claims for more equality increased and radical voices began to argue that it was harvest time. A few years later the labor markets, the basis of the welfare states, collapsed. The time of neo-liberalism was approaching. The long-term answer to the economic crisis in the 1970s became ever more obvious in the 1980s. It was the end of organized modernity as it had emerged in response to the economic crisis a century earlier. A new kind of disorganized or individualized modernity emerged with freedom as its core value. Equality was played down as a mobilizing concept and its meaning shifted from equality through state-guaranteed welfare to equal opportunities to develop one's talent. There were certainly few formal obstacles to equal opportunities, like birth rights or expensive school and university fees, but it soon became clear that some enjoyed better preconditions to exploit their opportunities than others.

The division into institutional arrangements and interpretative frameworks from the 1870s onwards until the 1970s set the stage for the development of different kinds of society in the North in a European comparison. From the 1980s, the Nordic countries became more mainstream in their disconnection of state and welfare, in their trend toward privatization and the marketization of welfare.

THE QUESTION OF EQUALITY TODAY AND FOR THE FUTURE

What is the Nordic pattern of reducing the tension between equality and freedom, historically based on an agricultural farmer and industrial manufacturing economy, with all its variety, worth today? The economies and the organization of the labor markets have changed dramatically since the 1970s, with decreasing political control over economies and much greater opportunities for capital evasion from state control. The bonus rewards to managements of dramatically new dimensions and the increased speculative kind of capitalism do not provide the same kind of legitimacy for economic concentration as the ownership of manufacturing enterprises with thousands of employees. Political control of the economy was a precondition for the political guarantee of legitimacy for private economic concentration. This control is no longer as it was. It has become more difficult to attach legitimacy to economic power, and to combine economic legitimacy with democracy. At the same time the economic basis for political redistribution and promotion of the equality ideal has declined. The social gap has increased. Both economic and political legitimacy are eroding and it is not easy to find value criteria on which a new legitimacy might be built. What the implications of the European banking crisis will mean in the long run for the Nordic countries in this respect is an open question (Stråth 2012).[3]

The issue at stake is one of value transformation and the extent to which the political imagination is sufficient to transfer old virtues like equality, freedom, and solidarity into new patterns of economic organization where terms like growth, profit, and reform mean new things. Or, rather than transformation as such, the issue at stake is what direction the transformation will take. This is very much an open question for which historical experiences do not offer much guidance.

It is clear that the neo-liberal value basis that from the 1980s began to replace the previous value basis—culturally constructed during more than a century of social conflicts, contentious debate, and search for compromises—for a decade has been eroding dramatically, too. This does not mean that there is a value vacuum. Ethnic xenophobic nationalism and authoritarian policy ideals with cries for strong leadership are growing everywhere. This seems to be the substitute for, and the response to the signs of social disintegration and to the collapse of the legitimacy of global financial capitalism.

What until the 1970s looked like a Nordic particular path to modernity based on a particular capacity to use long-term economic conjunctures to reduce the tension between the ideals of equality and freedom is difficult to discern any longer. Here it is important to emphasize that Norden was never isolated from its international entanglement, as this chapter has demonstrated. The particularity emerged in comparison and entanglement with the world outside Norden. However, the digital revolution with the acceleration of time and the shrinkage of space has opened up a global dimension in the debate of quite new proportions that transcends the Nordic framework with much more intensity than previously. It is important to bear this fact in mind in any reflection on the future of the Nordic value basis. At the present moment with 60 million refugees on the move globally trying to escape wars and violence, persecution, and destitution, the question of equality has become more crucial and at the same time more difficult to handle than ever, since it emerged in Enlightenment thought. To see it as a Nordic particularity is even more difficult. However, this does not mean that the political question about how to construct a more equal world on the ideal of equality has disappeared or become less relevant, on the contrary. This is the challenge for the future, in Norden and elsewhere.

NOTES

1. See also Eisermann (1956, 231–242) and Winkel (1977).
2. Cf. Sejersted (2001 [1984]).
3. Cf. Stråth (2001, 2004, 2005).

References

Berlin, Isaiah. 1969 [1958]. *Four essays on liberty*. Oxford: Oxford University Press.
Eisermann, Gottfried. 1956. *Die Grundlagen des Historismus in der deutschen Nationalökonomie*. Stuttgart: F. Enke.
Sejersted, Francis. 2001 [1984]. *Demokrati og rettstat*. Oslo: Pax.
———. 2002 [1993]. *Demokratisk kapitalisme*. Oslo: Pax.
———. 2005. *Socialdemokratiets tidsälder. Norge og Sverige i det 20. århundre*. Oslo: Pax.
Sørensen, Øystein, and Bo Stråth, eds. 1997. *The cultural construction of Norden*. Oslo: Universitetsforlaget.
Stråth, Bo. 1996. *The organisation of labour markets. Modernity, culture and governance in Germany, Sweden, Britain and Japan*. London: Routledge.
———. 2001. Nordic capitalism and democratisation. In *The democratic challenge to capitalism. Management and democracy in the Nordic countries*, ed. Haldor Byrkjeflot et al. Oslo: Fagbokforlaget.
———. 2004. Nordic modernity: Origins, trajectory and prospects. *Thesis Eleven* 77 (1): 5–23.
———. 2005. The Normative foundations of the Scandinavian welfare states in historical perspective. In *Normative foundations of the welfare state: The Nordic experience*, ed. Nanna Kildaland and Stein Kuhnle. London: Routledge.
———. 2012. Nordic modernity: Origins, trajectories, perspectives. In *Nordic paths to modernity*, ed. Jóhann Páll Árnason and Björn Wittrock. New York/Oxford: Berghahn.
———. 2016. *Europe's utopias of peace: 1815, 1919, 1951*. London: Bloomsbury.
Tocqueville, Alexis de. 1988 [1835–1840]. *Democracy in America*. New York: Harper and Row.
Wagner, Peter. 1990. *Sozialwissenschaften und Staat. Frankreich, Italien, Deutschland 1870–1980*. Frankfurt/Main: Campus.
Winkel, Harald. 1977. *Die deutsche Nationalokonomie im 19. Jahrhundert*. Darmstadt: Wissenschaftliche Buchgesellschaft.

CHAPTER 3

The Cradle of Norwegian Equality and Egalitarianism: Norway in the Nineteenth Century

Jan Eivind Myhre

POINT OF DEPARTURE[1]

The point of departure for this chapter is one element—social equality—in what has been called the Nordic Model, or its Norwegian counterpart, the Norwegian Model. The model in the twenty-first century is generally characterized by generous social benefits, strong collective movements, extensive cooperation in industrial relations, publicly financed education, stable economy through state governance, high degree of work participation among women—and relative social equality.

Behind these characteristics lurk some general social and political traits often referred to as legitimate and stable institutions, good governance (little corruption and other evils of governance) and widespread social trust. Where do these come from?

J.E. Myhre (✉)
Department of Archaeology, Conservation and History,
University of Oslo, Oslo, Norway

© The Author(s) 2018
S. Bendixsen et al. (eds.), *Egalitarianism in Scandinavia*,
Approaches to Social Inequality and Difference,
DOI 10.1007/978-3-319-59791-1_3

My contentions are:

1. That the source of the model and the social and political traits dates back to the nineteenth century, in some cases even earlier.
2. That social equality was more prevalent in Norway than in other European countries, to some extent more than its Nordic neighbours. However, the Nordic countries, with considerable differences in governance, economy and social make-up early in the century, grew steadily closer to each other in the course of the century up to World War I.
3. That equality, in a wide sense of the word, is closely connected to many of the elements of the Nordic model and to the social and political traits mentioned. In the nineteenth century in particular, equality played an important role in economic growth, the quality of governance and the development of democratic institutions. What the causes and effects are in this relationship, I will return to below.

In what follows, I will first consider what is meant by "social equality" and the related concepts of egalitarianism, social structure and social mobility. I will then go on to show how Norwegians have portrayed themselves as egalitarian in opposition to other peoples, in the nineteenth century and later. Thereafter, I will discuss, on the bases of sources, the reality or myth of Norwegian nineteenth-century social equality, ending by presenting its roots and effects.

SOCIAL EQUALITY AND EGALITARIANISM: THE TERMS AND THEIR CONNOTATIONS

What do we mean by *social equality*? It is, of course, a concept with many connotations, varying in time and place. We commonly distinguish between *absolute* equality on the one hand (sometimes called equality of results, "*resultatlikhet*", and formal equality or equality of *opportunity* on the other, "*sjanselikhet*". The first is usually, but not necessarily, associated with economic equality, as measured, e.g., by income or wealth. The equality of opportunity concerns people's possibilities to obtain benefits; rising in the social structure, to receive education, to enter a desired occupation, in other words, to experience social mobility.

Mobility, in its turn, has two main varieties. There is first mobility within a given structure, meaning that if somebody rises socially, somebody else falls. Second, there is structural mobility. When the structure of society changes, mobility must necessarily take place. The first might be called voluntary mobility, the second necessary mobility. This is not to say that structural mobility counts for nothing. Moving from a working-class to a middle-class occupation, from a lower to a higher income, will normally be experienced as a step upward in society and as an improvement in well-being, notwithstanding that the whole of society moves in that direction. Looking at Norwegian history in the nineteenth century, it is easy to see that both versions of mobility took place.

Egalitarianism, or the ideology of equality, is easy to spot among nineteenth-century Norwegians. Did social equality breed egalitarianism, or was it the other way around? Or perhaps egalitarianism was an ideology without connections to actual equality? That is hardly probable, and my hunch is that equality came before egalitarianism, but that the two mutually reinforced each other.

No fairly advanced society is without economic, social and cultural differences and is in this respect unequal. This applies surely to Norwegian society in the nineteenth, as well as the twentieth and the twenty-first centuries. However, a prerequisite for a fairly just society with possibilities for social mobility is the quality of governance, in particular, equality before the law and a low level of corruption or other instances of malfeasance, creating what we may call social trust (Rothstein 2015; Rothstein and Teorell 2015; Teorell and Rothstein 2015). Behind this, of course, looms the big word: freedom. This is where Norway, and later in the century the other Nordic countries, parted from most other countries during the nineteenth century. Freedom, in rhetoric and reality, was closely connected with equality.

Norwegian Social Equality: As Seen by Norwegians and Others

Let me start by presenting some cases, pictures if you like, portraying nineteenth-century Norway while contrasting it to other countries.

Venezuela experienced its Bolivarian revolution in 1810 and became independent in 1821, contemporaneous with Norway. Its ideals were roughly the same: freedom, equality and brotherhood. However, Venezuelan society possessed a social order firmly based on "religion, the Castillian monarchy and a blind obedience to authority, an order built on duty and obedience" (Uslar Pietri, according to Skutlaberg 2012). Its nineteenth-century trajectory, therefore, became very different from the Norwegian one, with less equality, less freedom and bad governance.

The Norwegian historian Ingrid Semmingsen in 1954 received an assignment akin to that of her Nordic colleagues, "the dissolution of estate society in Norway in the nineteenth century" (Semmingsen 1954). She was a little surprised: Unlike its Nordic neighbours and most other European countries, Norway had no estate society, no *ancien régime*, to dissolve, since there was no nobility with privileges. She solved the task by taking "estate society" to mean something different, namely, an informal paternalistic structure whose structure of social relations melted into air in the course of the century.

Historians and social scientists, as well as politicians, journalists and the public at large, have for a long time cherished the notion of Norway since 1814 as a peculiar case, with no nobility and a fair amount of social equality in general, in the twentieth century accompanied by the other Nordic countries. Economically and socially, Norway's way has been depicted as a "*Sonderweg*", a unique path, where the lack of a strong capitalist class was remedied by a relatively active state, which, on behalf of the nation, and with the aid of stable infrastructural institutions, helped foster economic growth (Sejersted 1993).

Behind it all, it is thought, was an all-pervasive ideology, perhaps a mentality, of social egalitarianism. Norwegians, in general, supported social harmony. There was a willingness to compromise in the inevitable situations of conflicts of interest. There is, and was, in the title of a famous book from almost three decades ago, "A passion for equality" in the Nordic countries, particularly in Norway and Denmark (Graubard 1986; Nielsen 2009). The Norwegian contribution in Graubard's book is entitled "Those equal folk" (Dahl 1986).

In a book synopsis, the University of Bergen historians Jan Heiret and Hans-Jacob Ågotnes (2010) have discerned three tales of equality in the Norwegian tradition. The first is called "the primordial myth" (*urmyten*), the contention that Norwegian egalitarianism hails from the long-term existence of a dominant class of peasant freeholders (yeomen), fairly equal in social standing. It thus combines equality with freedom.

The second tale revolves around the so-called "integration thesis", first developed by Halvdan Koht, later to be elaborated upon by Stein Rokkan and Francis Sejersted. The thesis refers to the gradual development—through conflicts to be sure—of national unity by the piecemeal integration of new social groups, first, the burghers, then the peasants, and lastly the workers (some of them were also immigrants, and one wonders what will happen to the immigrants of the last wave since the 1970s).

The third tale is called "From pluralism to unity" ("*Fra mangfold til enhet*") and concerns mainly the twentieth century, although visible from the late nineteenth onwards. It is about what in abstract English language is called "industrial relations", namely, the thrust of the labor movement resulting in the situation variously described as "class compromise", a "social democratic order" (Furre 1999), "the age of social democracy" (Sejersted 2011) or the three-partite cooperation between employers, employees and the state, the latter frequently mentioned as an important element of the Nordic model.

Heiret and Ågotnes are sceptical of the frequent use of these tales as frameworks for understand modern Norwegian history. They want to "challenge the claims that there is a unified egalitarian tradition in Norway which can be traced back to the nineteenth century", without refuting that there are, and were, social and economic egalitarian traits in Norwegian society (Heiret and Ågotnes 2010, 2). There are variations in the uses of the concept, they say, and there has historically taken place a struggle over the contents of the word equality, *likhet*.

It is certainly easy to agree with this, but on the other hand difficult to see how it might have been otherwise. Although a relatively homogeneous society, Norway in the nineteenth or twentieth centuries was never monolithic, neither economically, socially, politically, nor culturally (in particular).

In what follows, I will try to assess the degree of equality one might find in Norwegian nineteenth-century society, starting with how various actors looked at society, and continuing with equality within various societal spheres, such as law, politics, economy, social structure, and culture.

Nineteenth-Century Norwegians Look at Themselves

The statistician, historian, and professor of law Torkel Halvorsen Aschehoug (1822–1909) was a conservative politician. Like his fellow members of the Norwegian elite of higher civil servants (*embetsmenn*) and wealthy businessmen, he despised nobility and all forms of aristocracy, and would use words like extortion or fleecing (*udsuge*) to describe their activities (Seip 1975; Winther 2007). These viewpoints would also be shared by peasant politicians and Norwegians in general.

Norwegians were fond of pointing out how favourably their country stood out compared to others when it came to democracy and equality. The union partner was often singled out. Sweden's parliament (*Riksdagen*) consisted of independently elected estates (clergy, nobility, burghers and peasants) until 1867, and even then with a very restricted vote. The peasants in the parliament largely followed the politics of their social superiors, in contrast to their Norwegian counterparts. Sweden got its first non-noble prime minister as late as 1883. Denmark was an absolute monarchy until 1848/1849, when a constitution was drawn up, and even then for many decades the country was effectively ruled by landowners, *godsejer-regeringer* (Nielsen 2009, 190). Most other countries were regarded as worse, and were loosely lumped together as "despotic states", e.g., when the parliament (*Stortinget*) debated and unanimously voted to abolish the use of passports, seen as an anachronistic institution in a free and liberal country (Myhre 2003). Even the leader of the parliamentary opposition, Johan Sverdrup, declared in the 1870s that "there do not exist any deep lines of conflict (*konfliktlinjer*) in Norwegian society, as exist in other European countries" (Winther 2007, 77). In Norway, as well as in the other Nordic countries, social *harmony* was an explicit and implicit ideal, even within much of the lower classes, and even to some extent in the first years of the labour movement.

The basis of the somewhat self-congratulatory tone among Norwegian politicians was, of course, the liberal Constitution of 1814 and the liberal politics that followed, particularly concerning the economy, religion and the freedom of the press, and particularly after 1850. In Norway especially, but also in the other Nordic countries, their societies were described with nouns such as light, freedom, nature, progress, truth, as opposed to other countries' barbaric customs, serfdom, chains, moral corruption and depravation (Nielsen 2009, 166). These views of supremacy were probably strengthened by the fact that the Norwegian Constitution and its political system were admired by liberals and other opposition parties around Europe, particularly in the wake of 1814 and in the years around the revolutions in 1848. This happened in Austria, Bohemia, various German states, the Duchies of Slesvig and Holstein and even in England (Myhre 2015a, 143). The Norwegian Constitution was translated into a number of languages, 31 in all until 1850 (Hemstad 2016). Swedish liberals would look to Norway throughout the century, with an "exoteric (*eksotiserende*) worship of the Norwegian constitution" (Nielsen 2009, 196).

This, however, was the upside of the medal. The reverse side is well known. Norway was to a large extent a country of the propertied classes, including the peasant freeholders. The propertyless—cottars and workers being the most numerous—saw the situation differently. The Thrane movement (Ringvej 2014), organizing a sizeable amount of cottars, workers, artisans and smallholder peasants—would argue that they were facing an "aristocracy" of civil servants, businessmen and even larger peasants, a term one would think was well considered. They felt disadvantaged politically (no vote, except the smallholders), economically (poor, unpropertied), and socially (disregarded). The elites, from Aschehoug and his follow civil servants to the peasants in the parliament, notwithstanding their scorn of aristocratic societies, had no thought of enfranchising these lower strata of society, not until late in the century, at any rate. Such a measure, they thought, would seriously upset the balance of power in society. But even Aschehoug conceded that, although he was against it, the right to vote for all (men) probably would take place.

Equality Before the Law?

With the abolition of the nobility in 1821 (the principles laid down in the Constitution, the Act passed in the parliament in 1815 and 1818, and was finally sanctioned by the king in 1821), no citizen was exempt from the law. According to § 96 in the Constitution, no one could be judged or sentenced except by law. In line with the principle of separation of powers, the judiciary was independent.

One should note that there was no law formally stating citizenship in Norway until 1888. Any person with a few years' stay in the country was a subject or a Norwegian. Common people (*allmue*) played a certain part in local courts (*tingene*), and were also represented in the high courts (*lagretten*) in cases involving life, honour and allodial matters (*odel*). Trusted locals would commonly sit in the local arbitration courts (*forlikskommisjoner*), established in 1797.

This is not to say that everyone had equal rights. The right to vote was denied to all women and propertyless men (around 60 percent of all men above the voting age of 25). The civil servants were particularly protected in the sense that they could only be dismissed by rule of law. The unpropertied also had the obligation to take service (the so-called *tjenestetvang*, introduced in 1754), a provision modified in 1818 and abolished in 1854. This entailed, however, no bondage, villeinage or adscription (*livegenskap, hoveri, stavnsbånd*), and from 1854 onwards, in practice earlier, Norwegian cottars and workers were in this respect free individuals.

The personal freedom of Norwegian citizens (or subjects) in religious matters was secured by the abolishment of *konventikkelplakaten* in 1842, a remnant from pietistic absolutism which forbade people congregating without an ordained priest, the law regulating religious dissenters in 1845, and the opening of the country to Jews in 1851. Before this, Jews were occasionally admitted temporarily. You could also be a Catholic or a Quaker, but had to keep it private. There is no doubt, however, that a Norwegian was envisioned as a Lutheran Protestant. The obligation of civil servants to be members of the Lutheran state church was abolished in 1890.

Henrik Wergeland tells a story called "Hans Jacobsen's cheese" (*Hans Jacobsens ost*). He encounters a man eating his sandwich consisting of bread only. "That's a meagre lunch you've got there, Hans", Wergeland comments. "I have plenty spread on my sandwich", the man replies, "I have freedom" (Wergeland 1934 [1844]). This freedom, of course, was rather formal and abstract, but still a prerequisite for equality. Contemporaries would sometimes claim that freedom also meant equality. In most cases, however, we must keep the two apart. The makers and defenders of the Norwegian Constitution were more preoccupied with freedom than with equality (Nielsen 2009, 177ff), which will become evident when speaking about politics. They were, however, also preoccupied with property. True freedom came with property, meaning that the majority of the population possessed limited freedom in this sense.

Politics

The Constitution gave voting rights to around 40 percent of all men, making it the most democratic nation in Europe until mid-century in terms of suffrage. The vote was extended in 1884 and manhood suffrage came in 1898. Even with its new Constitution in 1849, only 15 percent of all Danish males could vote. The Swedish and Finnish franchise was even more restricted, also after the abolition of the Swedish estate Diet in 1866. After this date, only Austria and Finland had estate Diets. The Norwegian parliamentary system was more democratic and egalitarian than that of other countries not only because of the wide franchise, but also because Norway had, for all practical purposes, a one-chamber system, while most other states had two-chamber systems, with one chamber acting as a conservative guarantor.

The Norwegian franchise, however, became somewhat more restricted with time, since the proportion of propertyless men increased, relatively speaking. The voting rights divided the Norwegian population roughly in two, gave the vote to higher civil servants, burghers in the cities and towns (merchants and artisans, *næringsdrivende borgere*), other propertied people in cities and towns, and notably independent farmers and even leaseholders (*leilendinger*) in the countryside (§ 50 in the Constitution).

What does this add up to, in terms of democracy and equality? It means that Norway was the only country in Europe where the numerical backbone of society, the peasants (farmers), even the tiniest smallholder, in principle, had a say in national political matters. The peasants were well represented in the parliament (although not in proportion to their share of the voters), particularly from the 1830s onwards, but even before (Hommerstad 2012). Their interests were heard, and their wishes and demands sometimes met, in a political atmosphere dominated by the higher civil servants. From the 1870s, however, in a coalition with radical academics, the peasants gained the upper hand, culminating in the introduction of parliamentarianism in 1884. In achieving this, they were first in Europe to do so.

Already from 1814 on, the peasants in the parliament demanded local self-determination, which was granted in 1837. Soon the peasants occupied the majority of the mayor positions. Among the Nordic countries, Norway was the first to achieve local self-rule, although in Sweden the old institution of *Sockenstämmar* (a local gathering of the whole population) had some of the characteristics, but with less power. Swedish and Finnish peasants were represented in the Diet (estate assembly), where they had little influence. They seem for a long time to have been content with this, and—contrary to Denmark and especially Norway—were conservative in political matters (Nielsen 2009, 213).

What about the remaining more than half of the male population? They were, and felt, definitely pushed aside in political matters, as, e.g., the socialist Thrane movement around 1850 clearly showed. But the absence of serious violence during the whole of nineteenth century is noteworthy. There were protests, rallies and strikes to be sure. One person was killed by the police during a strike in 1881. Were the common people somehow included in society? We shall in a moment look at the associations, but first note that the ideology of the civil servant state, stressing harmony, certainly had a vision of the common weal, reaching out to all. Was the Norwegian state a legitimate one, even for oppositional groups, like the peasants and the unpropertied?

To a certain degree it was, notwithstanding the justified complaints from the Thrane movement and other oppositional groups about social injustice and other social evils, demonstrable also to all contemporaries.

The Norwegian political system was to a large degree considered legitimate in the sense that there was a common platform of understanding, also beyond the 40 percent (20 percent when we include women) who had the vote. What were the reasons for this?

In the first place, Norwegians (as well as the other Nordic peoples) were not in general afraid of a strong state, which was something they were used to, at least since the introduction of absolutism in Denmark-Norway in 1660. The state as such was considered just (Lien et al. 2001; Vike 2004), at least before the radical labour movement early in the twentieth century. The parliament as such was a legitimate institution although somewhat restricted by the fact that it represented less than half of the male population. Even the Thrane movement turned to the king and the parliament with their hopes of improving their lot. That the Constitution of 1814 and its semi-democratic system in principle were designed to curb the strong state and to protect the population, only made the system more legitimate.

The basis of the legitimacy of the state was of course the Constitution. The ruling class, the higher civil servants, were elected representatives. The government (the cabinet), however, did not emanate from the parliament, which was an increasing problem, solved by the introduction of parliamentarism in 1884.

The higher civil servants (*embetsmennene*) enjoyed also for other reasons than being elected a higher degree of legitimacy than other European elites. Their elite status was founded on their superior education (they were the only education-based elite in Europe) and their claim to being impartial. They regarded themselves as a kind of "headmaster" in society, a paternalistic attitude, to be true, and therefore for a long time were approached with deference. However, they did not constitute an elevated mandarin class, aloof from the rest of society, but were an actively politicizing and governing elite.

A major strength was a certain lack of material interests, although some of their income was based on charges for their services (*sportler*). This was a thorn in the side of the public at large, who demanded they be put on fixed salaries. In general, however, the bureaucracy was considered fairly non-corrupt, and definitely less corrupt with time, although it would frequently have a tint of nepotism. The trend towards a Weberian kind of bureaucracy was undoubtedly an advantage in creating and retaining the social trust upon which democracy and equality had to rest (on corruption, see Myhre 2015b, 43; Teige 2015; and, for Sweden, Rothstein 2015; Rothstein and Teorell 2015; Teorell and Rothstein 2015).

Their education and claim to disinterestedness and impartiality made the civil servants formidable adversaries in the election process (which was a complicated one, with many steps). There was also an open ballot, which often made opponents like the peasants lose their nerve when voting.

The interest of the elite certainly consisted in staying in power, and keeping the peasants on the sidelines as much as possible and the unpropertied classes out of politics was one way of doing this. In the numerous parliamentary debates on a possible extension of the franchise, the fear of the unpropertied was sometimes voiced, especially in the wake of the Paris Commune in 1871.

In spite of their dominating position in politics and bureaucracy, the civil servants were not *ersatz* nobility. They were never able to govern all by themselves, for several reasons. The civil servants seldom had the majority in the Parliament, and locally they were usually in a tiny minority. They governed by the Constitution, whose paragraphs encompassed all of society, and potentially opened society for a wide electorate to gain power and influence. The Constitution, as one historian has remarked, gave "a taste of freedom" to a large part of the population (Storsveen et al. 2015).

The politics of the elite was also guided by what they considered as the common weal. That meant paving the way for economic growth and general welfare by liberalizing the economy while building out the infrastructure. The latter meant not only the construction and establishment of roads and railroads, harbours and coastal steamers, telegraph lines and postal service, a map service and statistical bureau, a financial infrastructure, but not least an educational system for the whole population (more about this below). In a certain sense, all this served as an equalizer That it also in the long run caused the downfall of the regime, was an unintended consequence.

The second factor accounting for a common platform of understanding was the existence of a fairly common rationalistic and pragmatic view of society, with a basis in the Enlightenment. Norwegian Enlightenment, it is held, was a horse-trading rationalism (Nielsen 2009, 253; Skirbekk 2010; Sørensen and Stråth 1997), encompassing the literate peasants as well as the higher echelons of society. Liberal Enlightenment ideas were quite common among the peasants, several of which presented outlines of a constitution before the first national assembly at Eidsvoll in 1814. No later than the 1840s, the civil servants built their politics on professionalism and science. Norway was a country of Christians to be sure, and with a state church, but hardly founded on religion. The king was not so by the grace of God, but the sovereignty of the people. The Constitution did not use religious arguments. Some have spoken of a "Christian Enlightenment" (Witoszek 1997). Nineteenth-century Norwegian society was already on its way to something described as secular Lutheranism (Bendixsen, Bringslid, and Vike, Chap. 1, this volume; Sørensen and Stråth 1997).

Social Structure

The third unifying factor is what I will call relative social equality. The emphasis here must be on the word "relative". In spite of the absence of nobility and the contemporary rhetoric about equality, the social differences in living standards were, needless to say, considerable, and much greater than they became in the twentieth century. The differences between Norway in 1850 and, say, in 1980 are vast. However, there are reasons to believe (although the sources are not very good, and this is an under-researched area) that social equality in the meaning of living standards was less marked in Norway than in other countries, certainly Sweden and the Continent. The social differences decreased in the course of the century. What are the arguments for this?

In the nineteenth century, Norway was a country of freeholding peasants (sometimes described as yeomen farmers). Reaching a peak around 1860, the number of crofters and other people with no land property exceeded the number of freeholders. In some areas, parts of Østlandet and Trøndelag in particular, the crofters were in a very subordinate position, and the gap between freeholders and crofters was great. In other parts, like Vestlandet, Sørlandet and Northern Norway, the gaps were less marked, partly as a consequence of the fact that most freeholders had farms of a modest size, and that they had considerable additional income, like fishing.

In the southwestern area of Jæren, the differences between freeholders and crofters were consciously under-communicated in the service of an ideology saying that all were part of the same community (Langhelle 2011). Towards the end of the century certain distinguishing symbols disappeared, like the tradition stating that the biggest peasants should have the best seating in church. This tradition was outlawed in 1897. In many places, notably along the coast, the existence of additional occupations could place crofters and other workers almost on par with freeholders, as in fishing or crafts. The mortality among crofters in Trøndelag was no higher than among the peasants, which was lower than the Norwegian average (Lindbekk 2016), which in turn was the lowest in the world throughout the nineteenth century.

Poverty was surely widespread, according to later standards, but also to contemporary ones. Reports on poverty were common. But how does one measure "poverty"? Between 1851 and 1866 the share of the population who were partly or fully supported by poor relief was between 4.5 and 5 percent. This appears to be a small number, and the criteria were strict. Tveite (1987) claims that the criteria for calling someone "poor", and therefore give poor relief, were stricter in Norway than elsewhere. For him, that is an indication that poverty was modest in an international perspective. One could add that, although many people experienced hunger, at least from time to time, there was no famine after 1813. The large-scale Norwegian overseas emigration, second only to that of Ireland in relative numbers, is sometimes taken to mean that living conditions in Norway were particularly harsh. This was not the case. The causes of the relatively large emigration was probably due to literacy (see below) and the pull exerted via close connections across the Atlantic (Myhre 2015a; Østrem 2014).

Did Norwegians in the nineteenth century have a chance to rise socially? This is not easy to measure or evaluate. It does follow from what is said above, though, that Norway was a fairly open society, especially in the last half of the century. During the first half, however, the strong growth of the rural population in combination with the allodium caused many sons and daughters of peasants to settle down as crofters, a structural downward mobility. In the second half it was the other way around. The crofting system gradually disappeared as a result of the introduction of new technology and alternative livelihoods, both in rural areas, in the growing towns and cities and across the Atlantic. Norwegians were free to move. Moving from rural work to the growing manufacturing industry was generally seen as a step upwards in society (Bull 1985). The first phases of industrialization in Norway were not, as some English historians claim in the English case, accompanied by a reduction in living standards.

The educational system promoted social advancement. The Norwegian population as a whole was increasingly literate after compulsory schooling for both boys and girls was introduced in 1739. After the School Act of 1860 all Norwegians born after c. 1850 could write and calculate; they already knew how to read. This certainly facilitated upward mobility, and many peasants as well as others could improve their lot by taking up new or additional occupations (see below).

New middle-class occupations also came available for peasant sons in particular. Teachers' seminars and schools for non-commissioned officers (*underoffiserer*) were filled with rural boys. A number of secondary schools, like technical schools, engineering schools, nursing schools, schools for agriculture, seamen's schools, home crafts' schools, schools for commerce and the like, provided opportunities for young men from the lower echelons of society and for young women from (mainly) better-off families. We are seeing a combination of structural and "pure" mobility.

The high schools (*gymnasium*), preparing for the university, were for most of the century an institution peopled by sons of higher civil servants (about half) and, to some degree, better-off businessmen (about a quarter). From the 1860s and 1870s, however, other social groups gradually entered the high schools, in particular, sons of peasants, artisans and the new middle-class groups, like clerks, teachers and other public servants. This also meant that the university itself opened to new social groups (Myhre 2011), especially in the case of theology. Whereas the share of sons of higher civil servants and businessmen graduating from theology was 85 percent in 1810–1829, it had dropped to 54 percent in 1890–1909. Medicine and law had been slightly more open to students from below, since a provision said that students could enter these studies without having gone through the Latin schools, instead taking another preparatory exam (*preliminæreksamen*), often encouraged by local civil servants or others with ability to help. These students could go far in public service, but not to the highest posts. Women were admitted to secondary schools (*middelskole, realskole*) in the 1870s, to the gymnasium and thereby to university in 1882/1884. It was not until the twentieth century that their numbers in higher education became substantial.

There were certainly economic, social and cultural (but less legal) hindrances for people to rise socially in nineteenth-century Norway, but there were possibilities, and they became more frequent towards the end of the century. The most important incitement for people, the Opposition Leader Johan Sverdrup said in 1868, was the possibility to rise and reach the highest post that society could offer (Solheim 1976, 52). It was definitely easier to rise in the economic sphere than in the bureaucracy.

Equality and Economic Growth

Despite what one can hear from politician and journalists nowadays, Norway was one of the rich countries in Europe and the world already around 1870, probably somewhere between number five or ten in Europe early in the twentieth century, measured in GDP per inhabitant (Hodne and Grytten 2000). It was also fairly advanced technologically speaking. This meant that measured by the standard of living, Norway ranked even higher, since the distribution of wealth was more equal (Kiær 1908; O'Rourke and Williamson 1997; Pounds 1985).

It is possible to argue that Norwegian relative social equality promoted general economic well-being not only through the distribution of wealth, but also promoted economic growth as such. It is sometimes held, particularly among economists, that democracy with wide participation, a non-corrupt legal system, general trust of the laws, freedom of expression and free education, is a result of economic growth. This chapter, following, e.g., Jerome Kagan, will turn the argument on its head (Kagan 2009, 197). The amazing economic development of Norway in the nineteenth century followed from the other societal traits. These do not mention social equality explicitly, but it is indeed an integral part of them.

The elements of the economic growth contained productivity growth in agriculture, growth (with increased exports) in the fisheries, industrialization (with exports in particular of the forest products) and not least shipping, creating considerable income for the country. Behind it all there was the colossal building of state-led infrastructure, from lighthouses to geological surveys and education.

The independent Norwegian freeholder had stronger incitements for investments than his unfree colleagues abroad, a fact that helped to compensate for the tendency to adopt large-scale farming elsewhere. The Norwegian peasant also had the advantage of not paying income tax to the state between 1836 and 1882, and had ample opportunities to borrow money from the state or local banks, especially after 1850. The rise of numerous local savings banks from 1822 onwards testifies to the thrift and ability to organize among peasants and middle classes alike (Thue 2014). The peasant would specialize, and some peasants could with time rather be called farmers than peasants (the Norwegian term is in any case *bonde* or *gårdbruker*, the debate about the English terms and the character of Norwegian agriculture need not be debated here).

The freedom of the peasants also had other benefits conducive to economic development. They often had occupations on the side, at sea, in the forest, as craftsmen, with the municipality. As forest owners they would deliver timber to the shipyards, and could thereby become shareholders in one or more of the shipping companies, which based their success on having many small joint owners (*partsrederi*). They might, together with other "businessmen", buy stocks in the railroad companies.

The religious revival around 1800, built around the charismatic leader Hans Nielsen Hauge, was in part a reaction against the rationalist religion preached by many contemporary representatives of the state church.

He was outlawed for breaking the *konventikkelplakat* regulation which forbade others than priests to lead services. What concerns us here, are two things. The Hauge movement was pragmatic, and it was egalitarian. It was anything but millenarian or otherworldly. Hauge and his followers put an emphasis on a variety of practical economic pursuits, improvements in agriculture, developments in the crafts, the extraction of salt and even undertakings in manufacture (a textile mill), the first ones in the country, as a matter of fact. Many well-known entrepreneurs in Norwegian industry in the nineteenth century were *haugianere*, followers of Hauge. The followers were encouraged to read and write, for both religious and mundane purposes. Not least, the revivalists were considered equal, not only in the eyes of God, but also among themselves.

In the crafts, manufacturing and the trades, the policy of liberalization meant that the threshold for starting businesses was low in most cases. This was visible, e.g., in the case of the many mechanical workshops and other small industrial firms that were created. The numerous small businesses is the basis of what Francis Sejersted has named the Norwegian "*Sonderweg*", an economy built on small units, and where the state had to provide the infrastructure (Sejersted 1993).

The role of women in the economy was considerable. The director of the Central Bureau of Statistics, argued in a commentary to the census of 1875 that housework was productive in an economic sense, without the argument entering into economic statistics. Women were indispensable in agriculture, in the fisheries (as "coastal peasants" while the men were out fishing), in parts of the manufacturing industry (producing textiles, tobacco, matches), in commerce and in service occupations, with time also in middle-class occupations, as teachers, telegraphers and shop assistants.

Schooling and Civil Society

This section will deal with two societal traits which acted as equalizers, namely, education and civil society (associations).

Norwegian society in the nineteenth century has sometimes been described as a society with two cultures, roughly corresponding to the urban, Danish and European-oriented, commercialized culture versus the culture of the rural, genuinely Norwegian with a largely self-sufficient economy (Steen 1957; Try 1979). Although rather approximate, it portrays a country of two different cultural systems. Late in the century this division became less visible. However, the two societal traits mentioned at an early stage cut across the division.

The educational system, already mentioned, has a long history. Already in 1739 compulsory schooling for boys and girls was introduced in Denmark-Norway, a measure that brought all of society up to certain reading level. The regulation of 1739 had a religious pietistic background, but no later than in the middle of the nineteenth century was taken over, so to speak, by secular interests. The laws about schools in towns of 1848 and the countryside in 1860 made all children fully literate, as one of the first countries to do so.

In the towns and cities the social differences in the schooling system were considerable, with children of the elite going to Latin schools (grammar schools) and the children of the middle ranks going to the private so-called *borgerskoler* (burghers' schools or citizens' schools). The latter were in the second half of the century taken over by the municipalities and named secondary schools (*middelskoler, realskoler*). The girls of the middle and upper classes went to private girls' schools or were taught in private. With the new school laws of 1889 (one for urban areas and one for rural ones) a uniform public elementary school system was created, with children of different social backgrounds going to the same school, sometimes in the literal sense. The urban-rural divide was to a large degree overcome. This no doubt, at least for some time, was a powerful social equalizer. At about the same time (1896), a uniform system for secondary schools was legislated, although such schools in the rural districts had to await the creation of rural gymnasia (*landsgymnas*) until early in the twentieth century.

Contemporaries from the 1840s onwards spoke of a "spirit of association", *Assosiationsaanden*, the massive upsurge of voluntary associations, established with political, social, philanthropic, economic, social, and cultural aims in mind. This is not the place to present details about this powerful rise of a civil society, but to present its egalitarian effects on Norwegian society.

First, the associations, based on the freedom of expression, were open to everyone who had an interest in the purpose of the organization in question. Second, they would cover the void created by a liberalistic government when it came to remediating social ills, like poverty, alcoholism, and bad moral conduct (*usedelighet*). It also exerted a pressure on the authorities for social legislation, a pressure which proved quite successful towards the end of the century. Third, the associations became an important spokesman for disadvantaged groups in society, the trade unions and the women's organizations being the most obvious examples. The national trade union, comprising all other unions, was founded in 1899, the employers association the year after. In 1900, thus, two-thirds of the tripartite cooperation in industrial relations (the third being the state) was already in place. Fourth, the associations turned out to be schools in micro-democracy, with all members having the same rights to speak and vote. They would also improve the members' abilities to read, write and manage a budget.

Conclusion

The relative equality of nineteenth-century Norway thus rested on several factors:

It was based on the combination of a strong state and liberal Enlightenment ideas. The liberal 1814 Constitution had its shortcomings, but potentially opened the way for more freedom and equality, a potential that was to a large degree realized in the second half of the century.

Based on economic freedom, another gift from the Constitution, Norway had a small-scale economy, with free peasants, fishermen, craftsmen, tradesmen and manufacturers.

Stable political, economic and social institutions were created, acting as a trustworthy infrastructure. It was, particularly after c. 1840, manned by a professionalized, meritocratic, bureaucracy that was largely non-corrupt.

A strong class of enfranchised peasant freeholders remained the numerical backbone of the population guaranteed by the Constitution. The lack of nobility and, for a long time, a strong capitalist class, paved the way for the higher civil servants as a ruling class, an elite enjoying, for a long time, considerable legitimacy.

Freedom of expression, guaranteed by the Constitution, allowed the rise of a large civil society sector, acting as interest groups for large segments of the population, as an impetus to reform, and as schools in local democracy.

A high degree of literacy based on compulsory schooling from 1739 on, acted as a formidable leveller.

Note

1. This chapter is a revised and enlarged version of Myhre (2015b).

REFERENCES

Bull, Edvard. 1985. *Arbeiderklassen blir til (1850–1900)*. Oslo: Tiden Norsk Forlag.
Dahl, Hans Fredrik. 1986. Those equal folk. In *Norden—The passion for equality*, ed. Stephen Graubard. Oslo: Norwegian University Press.
Furre, Berge. 1999. *Norsk historie 1914–2000. Industrisamfunnet—frå vokstervisse til framtidstvil*. Oslo: Det Norske Samlaget.
Graubard, Stephen R., ed. 1986. *Norden—The passion for equality*. Oslo: Norwegian University Press.
Heiret, Jan, and Hans-Jacob Ågotnes. 2010. *Det norske likhetssamfunnet*. Manuscript, University of Bergen.
Hemstad, Ruth. 2015. Translations of the Constitution of the Kingdom of Norway, 1814–1920. A bibliography. In *Editions and translations of the Norwegian Constitution*, ed. Ola Mestad. Oslo: Pax forlag.
Hodne, Fritz, and Ola H. Grytten. 2000. *Norsk økonomi i det 19. århundre*. Bergen: Fagbokforlaget.
Hommerstad, Marthe. 2012. *Politiske bønder—Bondepolitikk og Stortinget 1815–1837*. PhD thesis, University of Oslo.
Kagan, Jerome. 2009. *The three cultures. Natural sciences, social sciences, and the humanities in the 21st century*. Cambridge: Cambridge University Press.
Kiær, Anders Nicolai. 1908. Indtægtsforholdene i Norge og andre lande. *Statsøkonomisk Tidsskrift*: 53–76.
Langhelle, Svein Ivar. 2011. Idealisert og inkludert, men ikkje likeverdig: ei drøfting av egalitet og mentalitet på Jæren omkring 1850. *Heimen* 1: 3–18.
Lien, Marianne, Hilde Lidén, and Halvard Vike, eds. 2001. *Likhetens paradokser. Antropologiske undersøkelser i det moderne Norge*. Oslo: Universitetsforlaget.
Lindbekk, Kari. 2016. *"Et fast og tilstrekkelig levebrød". En livsløpsanalyse av trønderkohorten 1855 og foreldrene deres ca. 1825–1920*. PhD thesis, University of Oslo.
Myhre, Jan Eivind. 2003. Det liberale innvandringsregimet. In *Norsk innvandringshistorie. Vol 2. I nasjonalstatens tid 1814–1940*, ed. Knut Kjeldstadli, Jan Eivind Myhre, and Einar Niemi. Oslo: Pax forlag.
———. 2011. *Kunnskapsbærerne 1811–2011. Akademikere mellom universitet og samfunn*. Oslo: Unipub.
———. 2015a. *Norsk historie 1814–1905. Å byggje ein stat og skape ein nasjon*. Oslo: Det Norske Samlaget.
———. 2015b. Sosial likhet på 1800-tallet: Et forstadium til den norske modellen? In *Myndighet og medborgerskap. Festskrift til Gro Hagemann på 70-årsdagen 3. september 2015*, ed. Kari H. Nordberg et al., 113–127. Oslo: Novus forlag.
Nielsen, Niels Kayser. 2009. *Bonde, stat og hjem. Nordisk demokrati og rasjonalisme—fra pietismen til 2. verdenskrig*. Aarhus: Aarhus University Press.

O'Rourke, Kevin H., and Jeffrey G. Williamson. 1997. Around the European periphery 1870–1913: Globalization, schooling and growth. *European Review of Economic History* I: 153–190.

Østrem, Nils Olav. 2014. *Norsk utvandringshistorie*. Oslo: Det Norske Samlaget.

Pounds, Norman. 1985. *An historical geography of Europe 1800–1914*. Cambridge: Cambridge University Press.

Ringvej, Mona R. 2014. *Marcus Thrane. Forbrytelse og straff*. Oslo: Pax forlag.

Rothstein, Bo. 2015. *De samhälleliga institutionernas kvalitet. Slutrapport från et forskningsprogram*. Stockholm: Riksbankens Jubileumsfond/Makadam forlag.

Rothstein, Bo, and Jan Teorell. 2015. Getting to Sweden, part II: Breaking with corruption in the nineteenth century. *Scandinavian Political Studies* 38 (3): 238–254.

Seip, Anne-Lise. 1975. *Vitenskap og virkelighet. Sosiale, økonomiske og politiske teorier hos T. H. Aschehoug 1845 til 1882*. Oslo: Gyldendal.

Sejersted, Francis. 1993. Den norske "Sonderweg". In *Demokratisk kapitalisme*. Oslo: Universitetsforlaget.

———. 2011. *The age of social democracy: Norway and Sweden in the twentieth century*. Princeton: Princeton University Press.

Semmingsen, Ingrid. 1954. The dissolution of estate society in Norway. *Scandinavian Economic History Review* 2: 166–203.

Skirbekk, Gunnar. 2010. *Norsk og moderne*. Oslo: Res Publica.

Skutlaberg, Erlend. 2012. *Las Lanzas Coloradas—historie eller fiksjon? Relasjonene mellom historie og litteratur i Venezuela*. Master's thesis, University of Oslo.

Solheim, Klaus Frode. 1976. *Oppfatningen av forholdet mellom samfunnsklassene slik det kom til uttrykk i stemmerettsdebattene på 1800-tallet*. Hovedfag thesis, University of Oslo.

Sørensen, Øystein, and Bo Stråth, eds. 1997. *The cultural construction of Norden*. Oslo: Scandinavian University Press.

Steen, Sverre. 1957. *Det gamle samfunn*. Oslo: J. W. Cappelens Forlag.

Storsveen, Odd Arvid, Amund Pedersen, and Bård Frydenlund, eds. 2015. *Smak av frihet. 1814-grunnloven. Historisk virkning og sosial forankring*. Oslo: Scandinavian Academic Press.

Teige, Ola. 2015. Korrupsjon i det danske og norske embetsverket etter 1814. In *Den rianske vending*, ed. Finn-Einar Eliassen, Bård Frydenlund, Erik Opsahl, and Kai Østberg, 193–208. Oslo: Novus Forlag.

Teorell, Jan, and Bo Rothstein. 2015. Getting to Sweden, Part I: War and malfeasance, 1720–1850. *Scandinavian Political Studies* 38 (3): 217–237.

Thue, Lars. 2014. *Forandring og forankring. Sparebankene i Norge 1822–2014*. Oslo: Universitetsforlaget.

Try, Hans. 1979. *To kulturer. En stat. Norges historie, vol. 11*. Oslo: J. W. Cappelens Forlag.

Tveite, Stein. 1987. The Bumble-Bee of economic history: Norway 1800–1850. In *Historiographie-Protoindustrialiserung-Arbeiterbewegung-Faschismus. Bericht über das 1. Deutsch-Norwegische Historikertreffen in Bergen 1986*. Bergen.
Vike, Halvard. 2004. *Velferd uten grenser. Den norske velferdsstaten ved veiskillet.* Oslo: Akribe.
Wergeland, Henrik. 1934 [1844]. Hans Jacobsens ost. In *Samlede skrifter III, bind 3*, 567–571. Oslo.
Winther, Vegard. 2007. *Egaliret i liberalismens århundre. En undersøkelse av egalitære holdninger slik de kom til uttrykk i stemmerettsdebattene fra 1851 til 1898*. Master's thesis, University of Oslo.
Witoszek, Nina. 1997. Fugitives from utopia: The Scandinavian enlightenment reconsidered. In *The cultural construction of Norden*, ed. Øystein Sørensen and Bo Stråth, 72–90. Oslo: Scandinavian University Press.

CHAPTER 4

Likhet Is Not Equality: Discussing Norway in English and Norwegian

Simone Abram

INTRODUCTION

Around 2009–2010, prior to the election of the Conservative-LibDem Coalition Government in the UK, a lively debate was held in the media about the values of equality in response to the publication of Wilkinson and Pickett's polemic, *The Spirit Level* (Wilkinson and Pickett 2009). In the face of increasing inequality in the United Kingdom, Wilkinson and Pickett leaned heavily on evidence from Scandinavia to argue for the value of socio-economic equality in improving the quality of life. Critics argued over the statistical analysis (Snowdon 2010), but not over the idea of Scandinavia as equal.

In Anglophone debates, Scandinavia has long stood rather uncritically as a general icon of egalitarianism and democracy. A vision of the Norwegian welfare state, supported by abundant oil income, is often invoked either to dismiss the reality of the welfare state as a viable political structure without excessive income, or to idealize the Norwegians as environmentalist egalitarians with, perhaps, naïve expectations of human nature. Such an

S. Abram (✉)
Department of Anthropology, Durham University, Durham, UK

image of the egalitarian North does not spring from innocent observation but is, like most national myths, carefully and continually reproduced by key actors in both academic and political contexts. In this chapter, my aim is to show how internal debate—particularly among Norwegian anthropologists and historians—is poorly represented in the comparative literature that is published in the English language for an international audience, which, instead, over-represents the notion of an egalitarian nation. This mismatch in the quality and depth of debate poses particular problems for comparative research, particularly at the macro-level. A researcher wishing to paint with a broad brush and to take in varied examples from a wide range of contexts, or a policy researcher on the look-out for policy lessons from abroad, for example, is unlikely to speak the language of the country compared with, and will thus turn to general summaries of national conditions, or, at best, to a range of English-language literature available about a country. Unsurprisingly, this leaves them at risk of meeting and reproducing poorly examined stereotypes, rather than a thorough and nuanced understanding.

McDonald (1993) has pointed out how national stereotypes serve as shorthand way-markers, relying on a kernel of truth in order to be convincing. National stereotypes also serve a particular purpose in the maintenance of nation-states, in reinforcing images of one's own nation in comparison to others. Such stereotypes can easily find their way into policy analysis, especially when the literature is limited. The reference to policy analysis is perhaps particularly important, since its consequences can be profound in terms of new policy introductions in other countries and the material impact this may have on the lives of very many people. In other words, what we think we know about other countries can have significant impacts on how we think about our own political situation.

My aim in this chapter is to demonstrate that what Anglophone readers know about Norwegian equality is not the same as what Norwegian readers know. What I present here fills out an overview of a critical Norwegian literature on equality and sameness, that both demonstrates how partial the representations of Norway abroad are and adds a degree of nuance to Anglophone discussions of Norwegian equality.

The Ideal Egalitarians

The widely held belief that Norwegians are egalitarian, and that Norwegian politics is generally democratic and participative, is often used to suggest that Norwegian political processes might hold out a model of participatory government and planning that should have lessons for other countries. It is not surprising that Norway has this reputation, since it has been carefully nurtured, both locally and internationally, by a relatively small group of influential intellectuals writing in both domestic and international contexts. As a prime example, Øyvind Østerud's striking narrative of the political history of Norway exemplifies the promotion of Norwegian egalitarianism in English language publications, in contrast to the much more nuanced picture found in his Norwegian publications. Østerud served as the chair of a three-year-long research programme funded by the Norwegian Research Council into domestic notions and practices of power, and was responsible for the authoritative summary of the project's findings (Østerud 2005). The summary's forceful narrative of the Norwegian state provides an easy reference point for international comparison, one which has already been taken up by international scholars. Although the article is quite clearly a summary that lacks the nuance of an internal debate, most of the more nuanced literature is not available outside Scandinavia, nor in the English language. The article is thus an important gatekeeper to international academic representations of the Norwegian state.

In "The Peculiarities of Norway", Østerud sets out a basic political science definition of what makes Norway different from other countries (Østerud 2005). In doing so, he draws on a long tradition of characterizing both the Norwegian state and nation in terms that are deeply lodged in popular and political consciousness within Norway. Østerud sets out three key features that make Norway an interesting political case for international comparative studies:

1. Norway is a stable democracy ... a society with striking egalitarianism, a strong public sector, and a culture of cooperative institutions which merges private with public interests.
2. Norway's peculiar international position as a rich country on the north-western Atlantic fringe of Europe, struggling to retain a faltering security guarantee from the United States, and having twice turned down in national referendums government proposals to join the European Union.
3. Norway's posture in international affairs, strong in its defence of national resource protection and its assertion of sovereignty, but equally strong in its moral policy of engagement as a champion of foreign aid and the global environment, and as an eager peace negotiator in the Middle East, Sri Lanka, Columbia and elsewhere (Østerud 2005, 705).

Within these three factors, it is the idea of a rich yet egalitarian nation which has positioned Norway as a most exotic land on the European periphery, often invoked (not by Østerud) as a kind of welfare paradise, courtesy of oil income, high taxation and its egalitarian culture, and, as such, as a kind of exception to the normal rules of European economics and politics. On the basis of this egalitarian culture, Norway can be seen as both a source of inspiration for other countries and as an impossible ideal, or as an anomaly requiring explanation (Graubard 1986).

The theme of egalitarianism can be seen as a leitmotif of Norwegian political history and social science, reflecting as it does a political trope which has been dominant for much of the twentieth century, and continues to hold a central position in public debate. However, the notion of egalitarianism can easily drift from being used to describe a political project to suggest a homogeneous state of affairs. This move reached some kind of apotheosis in the 1986 volume, "Norden, the passion for equality", first published as articles in the *Journal of American Academy of Arts and Sciences, Dædalus* (Graubard 1986). Here, Graubard argues that the Nordic states fulfil the dream of Alexis de Tocqueville of a "true passion for equality" where comprehensive welfare produced nations free of poverty or racial tension. Indeed, he goes as far as to argue that, in the Nordic countries, "the dreams of nineteenth-century utopians have been fully realized" (Graubard 1986, 11). And yet, even in these utopian lands, where criticism of the state is not only tolerated but welcomed, the populations appear unsatisfied and the model of the egalitarian welfare state has somehow not broken through as a global model of ideal statehood. Hans Fredrik Dahl accuses "those equal folk" not only of being so much more "leftish" than other Europeans in their egalitarian demands for the dismantling of privileges, but of simultaneously being "slightly conceited, perhaps even a little provincially moralistic, in their pride of the equity in their national systems of distribution" (Dahl 1986, 99). What Nordic nations share, he argues, is a profound commitment to the notion of *rettferd* (or justice), and an unrelenting social-democratic propaganda of equality. "There is little pathos in the style of Nordic man, less mythos in his conceptions of the world. Pragmatism is what filters out when Nordic value preferences, be they laborite in orientation or bourgeois, are probed", he states (Dahl 1986, 100). Such claims and statements serve as all stereotypes serve, to gather around them an aura of unity and solidity. They lend credence to the idea of national and pluri-national characters and beliefs, and must be read as nationalism in action rather than analytical arguments. They highlight the way that it is the Norwegian (member of the nation), not the inhabitant of Norway (resident or citizen), who participates in this inclusive unity.

This interpretation of Norwegian history is called into service to support what I will call the "Egalitarian view" of Norway in Anglophone literature. Østerud's (2005) more scholarly description calls on the same image. This narrative consistently under-emphasizes a critical literature on the idea of "*likhet*", Nordic nationalism, and discourses of the egalitarian state that can be found within the Norwegian language literature, largely out of sight of the interested non-Norwegian-speaking observer (e.g., Bruun et al. 2011; Eriksen 1993; Gullestad 2002; Lidén et al. 2001).

Østerud begins his reassuring description of "the Norwegian System" by describing "a stable democratic tradition going back to the early nineteenth century", characterized by a smooth transition from a weak nobility, to a strong Constitution asserted in 1814 as Norwegian sovereignty emerged from the Danish empire into a union with Sweden (see Myhre, Chap. 3, in this volume). The assertion of Norway shortly after independence as "one of the most democratic systems in Europe" (which Østerud takes directly from Rokkan 1966, 75) is based on the establishment of broad, then universal, suffrage early in relation to other European nation-states. Norway was one of the first European states to offer all adults the vote, both in relation to land-ownership and to gender. Secession from the union with Sweden (in 1905) is thus allied to a fundamental democratization through universal suffrage. According to Østerud (again in line with Rokkan 1966), a form of "democratic nationalism" thus emerged, which was to be recognizable through much of the twentieth century. The emergence of the Labor Party as a hegemonic force after 1945 consolidated the autonomy of the local state, in a nation-state "tied to centre-left forces for more than 100 years" (Østerud 2005, 707). Popular mobilization was expressed through the activities of a number of social movements (including language, religious and philanthropic movements), in contrast to the weak elitist centre in a capital perceived as the " 'least national' place in Norway" (Østerud 2005, 707).

In comparison, Rokkan's account of "Numerical democracy and corporate pluralism" (Rokkan 1966), does not present Norway as an egalitarian culture of ethnic homogeneity. Instead, he emphasizes the conflicting political mobilizations that swept the country through independence, and he outlines both the weaknesses and the fragile coalitions wrought even within the dominant Labor Party. His point, rather, is that cleavages in early twentieth-century Norwegian politics did not coalesce on any one axis, and therefore allowed a multi-party system to flourish. Even with a dominant Labor Party post-war, conflicting pressures led to electoral strategies that ploughed a centrist course, with bargaining between alliances of associations and corporations (Rokkan 1966, 106). In other words, Rokkan emphasizes diversity and agonistic striving towards consensus. In contrast, Østerud's summary account of Rokkan seems to formulate an argument relating some kind of national force or tradition for equality that supported the development of a particular kind of welfare state. He slips from stating that "egalitarianism has been a strong force in the normative fabric of Norwegian society" (Østerud 2005, 707), to reinforcing this position with reference to the strength of the farmer and peasant freeholder movements and the weakness of elites, leading to a unique form of cooperation between capital and labour, taking in what has become a normative history of Norwegian nationalism. Yet he also asserts that "the character of Norwegian capitalism partly explains Norway's egalitarian and popular state policies and its universalistic welfare system" (Østerud 2005, 707), hence arguing that both a tradition for egalitarianism accounts for the particularly shared capitalism in Norway, and that Norwegian democratic capitalism accounts for the popularity of egalitarian politics. This neat symmetrical argument is now well established in accounts of the Norwegian welfare state and forms a canon of political literature internationally. It is odd, even so, to find it resonating in the English language work of an author who has written in Norwegian of the construction of an idealized farming culture as authentically Norwegian by nineteenth-century elites.[1] Their vision, of an independent yeomanry as the foundation of the polity, is a seductive symbol for national identification and serves well to legitimize the notion of an inclusive egalitarian state, but while it works as a rhetorical strategy, it is more problematic as a "fact" for comparative political analysis.

A partial critique of these approaches from within the Norwegian political economy literature is found in Barth et al.'s (2003) account of the Scandinavian model of fiscal redistribution, carried out under the auspices of a national programme of research on democracy ("*Maktutredningen*", led by Østerud, see above). They start with a view of Scandinavia, according to the UN's Human Development Report, which suggests that "the Scandinavian lands are among the most egalitarian in the world" (Barth et al. 2003, 8, my translation), in particular in having the lowest pay gap before tax. The UN report's elision of economic details into nationalist generalizations occurs again and again throughout the English literature on the Scandinavian welfare states, even where it is the focus of critique. Barth, Moene, and Wallerstein begin by identifying classic explanations of the limited transferability of the Scandinavian model of economic redistribution, which they set up as "straw-men" for their preferred explanation. These straw-men include reference to the strength of the labour movement that has pressed capital interests into political and economic concessions, and the notion that Scandinavian states rely on small homogeneous societies with strongly egalitarian preferences. Some of these different aspects are helpfully weighed up by Myhre in Chap. 3 in this volume who specifies three separate discourses around equality. These more nuanced arguments have much to contribute to broader debates about whether welfare-egalitarianism is a political strategy that can be applied anywhere, or is so purely a product of national beliefs and history that it must remain unique. Barth, Moene, and Wallerstein question why the Scandinavian lands have such an egalitarian distribution of incomes (i.e., why Scandinavian *salaries* are the most egalitarian in the world), and challenge the notion of egalitarianism being based on some kind of social *Zeitgeist*, with a clear focus on the economic mechanics of the state.

Two further comments on accounts of national political histories are relevant here. First, national histories rely on a narrative structure that remains causal, drawing links between conditions and actions, and between social organization and political organization. These may remain implicit—indeed, implicit links are those that have become successful enough not to require comment—yet they are essential for political historical narrative to function as a legitimizing rhetoric. In the widely read, landmark volume, *The Cultural Construction of Norden* (Sørensen and Stråth 1997), Trädgårdh remarks on the force of the idea of "peasant Scandinavia" in political rhetoric, despite it being recognized as a mythical national narrative invented in the nineteenth century and recently largely debunked (Trädgårdh 1997, 258). For the narrative to have its convincing effect, it relies on the belief in a logical continuity between the relative autonomy of land-owning farmers and fishermen, individualism, the anti-authoritarian tradition and stable social democracy, which continues to carry weight in the Scandinavian context. From outside, though, the narrative's credibility is less obvious. For example, the idea that anti-authoritarianism sits comfortably alongside low levels of tax evasion will strike most English (and probably many US) readers as anti-intuitive (since tax evasion is often understood there as the concretization of anti-authoritarianism, the individual good often considered to be irreconcilable with fiscal redistribution). Associations between citizenship and taxation do not carry the same force of common sense outside the Nordic context.

Trädgårdh shows that such ideas are based on contrary understandings of both the state and the individual. It is not always clear whose understandings these are, but the unit of analysis is clearly the nation, despite Sørensen and Stråth's clear account of the invention of these nations as an "identity-producing projection from within", and the desire from the outside for a model of social organization that could be labelled as "Nordic" (Trädgårdh 1997, 21). Narratives that appear to give an explanation for a national character often break free from historical evidence, yet continue to exert rhetorical force. For example, historical narratives about the significance of feudalism as an absence in Scandinavian history ignore the awkward fact that feudal relations were already in decline in England in the thirteenth century and were legally outlawed in 1660 (Brown 2016). Can its absence from medieval Scandinavia really be a powerful explanatory force in the story of post-war Nordic welfare states?

Second, the taken-for-granted use of national terms serves consistently to reinforce the idea of nation-hood in itself, in the kind of everyday reinforcement that Billig calls "banal" (Billig 1995). This is visible in Lafferty's 1981 challenge to Martinussen's 1973/77 claim (Martinussen 1977) that the majority of Norwegians were apolitical and apathetic, not participating in democracy or political life. For Martinussen, this suggested that the health of Norwegian political engagement was not so rude as many politicians and political scientists preferred to believe, thus proffering a critique of the idealized egalitarian Norwegian polity. In response, Lafferty examines a different set of criteria to ascertain what level of participation existed, and by widening the criteria for political participation beyond voting behaviours, shows that in his definition, political participation was in fact higher in Norway than in most other countries (Lafferty 1981). What such arguments take for granted is that a country is a relevant unit of comparison for political activities, and this itself is central to the performance of nationhood. By assuming a correlation between nation-state and political tradition, practice or pattern, the nation-state itself is implicitly supported as a unit of cultural analysis. In the search for discernible regularities, differentiation is negated and an unreflective nationalism reinforced (Wimmer and Glick Schiller 2002).

The vision of Norway as egalitarian is paradoxically strengthened by accounts of current changes in governing structures. Even while arguing that the vision of Norway put forward in the Norwegian tradition of comparative political research—that of a "corporatist mode of government, the strength of the rural districts and the periphery, the egalitarianism and the deep structure of social democratic norms across the political spectrum"—is now an outdated stereotype, Østerud normalizes the sense of an earlier period in which the representation was fair (Østerud 2005, 705). There is a very intriguing rhetorical effect here from the use of the term stereotype that at once undermines the image yet also reiterates it as a vision. So while we read that this description is not true, we also read that it is less true now than it once was. A similar effect emerges from Østerud and Selle's argument that "[r]ule by popular consent is weaker than it was just a few decades ago, even if citizens do have a stronger position in terms of formalised rights, consumer options, welfare and education" (Østerud and Selle 2006, 25). The implication of statements that Norway had "a stable democratic tradition going back to the early nineteenth century" (Østerud and Selle 2006, 27) is to homogenize a long historical period, reinforcing this idea of stability by seeing recent changes as radical and contrary. It sidesteps the findings of another of the *Maktutredning* publications that the vision of the monolithic state as solitary provider of welfare was never entirely accurate. Given the history of cooperation between government and voluntary organizations from at least the nineteenth century, and the existence of market-actors who have always delivered services in Norway (Eikås and Selle 2000), the description of the egalitarian comprehensive welfare state serves more to reinforce the idea of egalitarianism, rather than account for the ups and downs that would be found in an empirical description.

Østerud details the kinds of changes in political stability which have occurred in recent years, with the move towards a more neo-liberal politico-economic system which has led to increased decentralization and privatization of public services, and to what he terms the emergence of a "new working class" of "immigrants … working in low-paid jobs or unemployed and receiving welfare benefits" (Østerud 2005, 716). This "immigrant population", described as split "along ethnic lines", and being "in constant demographic flux", is, according to Østerud, structurally unable to form popular movements along the lines of Norwegian class history. Østerud briefly mentions "a kind of minority hierarchy in Norway", with Sami at the top with their own representative institution, the Sami parliament. Rhetorically, this set of statements reduces ethnicity to a set of segregated unities, none of which can rise to the political organization of the social movements, which formed the unified Norway he refers to. Who is it, we might ask, that hierarchizes these minorities? How many of the working class are "immigrant", and why is it suggested that they enjoy no forms of solidarity with other working-class persons? Such statements do little to account for the political realities in different localities across the Norwegian territory or across generations or other social spectra. Nor do they pass without criticism within Norway, where a lively controversy surrounded the publication of a critique of implicit Norwegian racism by the anthropologist Marianne Gullestad (Gullestad 2002, published in English in 2006). Gullestad's work is not difficult to access, and she had a high media profile. Norway was not ethnically homogeneous before the establishment of the Sami parliament, suggesting that the mythical Norwegian unity might always have been cast into doubt. It should be noted that the first Sami National Congress was held in Trondheim in 1917. It was during the supposed heyday of Norwegian equality that the presence of a nation within the nation was so problematic for Norwegian nationalism that repressive Norwegianization policies were elaborated. We might call this the dark side of equality-as-sameness. Sami were, of course, by no means the only ethnic minority in Norway; we need only acknowledge the Tater, Kven and Jews—before and after exclusion—before drawing attention to the presence of nationals of other European countries, particularly the other Nordic countries. Østerud's mentions, almost in passing, of immigrant workers as a feature of the new neo-liberalized Norway, ethnicizes immigration, and makes it into a sign of the fall of the Norwegian egalitarian state.

It can be argued that the national consensus which Østerud describes (as being in the process of disappearing) is one that confuses a fictive kinship for political unity. If the imagined Norway is one of ethnic unity (the "nation" of the essentialized nation-state), it is one in which only certain foreigners are considered ethnically different. The immigrant working classes identified are not Finns or Danes, for example, but are those considered ethnically separate. Scandinavians who for generations have crossed borders and intermarried are not considered significantly ethnically different, and these other white Scandinavians are easily incorporated into the Norwegian national family. On the other hand, it appears to be more difficult to include those who maintain an element of ethnic difference, be they Sami or Pakistani. While Myhre (Chap. 3, this volume; see also Neumann 2001) notes the introduction of this more "ethnicized" form of citizenship in the nineteenth century, the kinship-basis of Norwegian citizenship has become much more apparent with the emphatic rise in international adoption into Norway. A generation of adult Norwegians who "look different" are accepted, as Signe Howell puts it, by being tied into familial relations and transformed into "typical Norwegian" children through processes of "kinning" which create the "Norwegian family" (Howell 2001, 84). This is not a pseudo-biological discussion about race, but an argument about nationality. If Norwegian-ness is achievable through incorporation into a family, yet not through civic participation or language acquisition, then it is clear that nation is an effect of kinship, either biological or social. Just as Bowie demonstrates for Welsh nationalism (Bowie 1993), belonging is tied to kinship, even if the core of that kinship can be remarkably slippery (Strathern 1981). We ought not to be surprised at this, as some definition of kinship has been central to all European national movements. I identify kinship rather than biological relatedness in order to highlight that kinship is a selective relation with strongly normative social rules.

English Nordic

Sadly, the distinction between different meanings and spheres of "equality" and "egalitarianism" are hard to find in comparative political research outside the Nordic debate. Barth et al.'s critique appears only in the Norwegian language, reinforcing my suggestion that nuanced critique of Nordic politics is rare in English. Beyond academia, the stereotypes that circulate globally have invited equally platitudinous responses from the political Right and the Left, such as the British Conservative suggestion that Scandinavian capitalism lacks entrepreneurs since excessive social security reduces the risk-taking qualities of capitalists, and the critique from the Left that union leaders fail their members' interests by agreeing to consistent pay moderation in the public sector. Trädgårdh reports complaints from Swedish Liberals, identifying slippage between the workings of a particular form of welfare state and the notion of egalitarianism that in no way explains how some states have achieved accommodation between conflicting interests.

In contrast, Barth and his colleagues present a more pragmatic and circumstantial argument, that centralized national wage bargaining could not survive without the support of both workers and capitalist interests. The state's representative, as arbitrator, completes a triad of negotiators, with wage moderation helping to stabilize economic conditions to the benefit of the government of the day. In brief, their argument suggests that the more centralized and coordinated wage settlements are, the smaller the pay gap; the smaller the pay gap, the greater the political support for welfare state social security and the greater the generosity of social security and the smaller the section of population living under the poverty line. In their view, this virtuous political-economic circle of stabilizing pressure between centralized organizations has been the basis for financial stability. In contrast, they point to Sweden and Norway's disastrous histories of employment conflict and strikes with the world's highest number of work days lost in the 1920s and 1930s (which Trädgårdh waves aside), and to their poverty and inequality prior to the establishment of the particular constellation of powerful interests in the post-war period. Thus, they emphasize that the Scandinavian countries were not magically endowed with personal or collective qualities of egalitarianism. The harsh capitalist conditions described by authors such as Hamsun (2001 [1890]) and Kielland (2006 [1882]) are otherwise absent from the historical characterizations of the "egalitarian Norwegian". Although Myhre shows that in the historical context, Nordic societies were remarkably progressive (cf. Østerud's remarks on universal suffrage), the lack of equality in this period suggests that it is not possible to explain the strong welfare state through actually-existing inherent equality, and leaves us with the same conundrum of how the equality-loving people so invoked reached this sensibility and then put it into action. Even Weber noted that the Protestant ethic led as much to concentrated economic wealth as it did to privation from luxury (on this issue, see Sørensen and Stråth 1997). On the contrary, Barth et al. (2003) seem to suggest that a happy coincidence (and the weakness of entrenched elite opposition) enabled the Scandinavians to discover that centralized wage bargaining and generous welfare reinforced each other in the interests of generalized economic stability.

It is when commentators attempt to identify explanations for such effects that they so often resort to heuristic concepts of national culture, social contracts or political culture. As anthropologists have found, culture is a relational product that largely arises through comparison at different scales—one must invent a "field" to identify "culture", at what is effectively a quite arbitrary scale (Amit-Talai 2000; Olwig and Hastrup 1997). Hence, tricky questions can always be raised. How consistently does the egalitarian principle hold in different parts of Norway? Over what period could we align wage-equality with puritanism? For how long was the welfare state universal and/or comprehensive? These questions indicate that the discussion about equality is less an empirical quest than a narrative construction. As Trädgårdh notes, it is rather the power of the narrative of egalitarianism that seems to facilitate negotiations between capital, labour and state, rather than the factual existence of a nation of egalitarian people. Unfortunately, opportunistic politicians or social scientists looking for international comparison have often been immune to this kind of distinction. On the contrary, it appears that many discussions of national determination are primarily for internal consumption and offer little that would satisfy a detailed comparative project.

One is left with an external vision of the Norwegian state having been a benign consensus between capital and social movements, peopled by strongly egalitarian individuals supported by a generous welfare state. This vision seems to have withstood the emergence of contradictory evidence, such as the forced sterilization of disabled or mentally ill people in Sweden, the mistreatment of the children of German officers and Norwegian women (the so-called "tyskerunger"), the persistence—if in small numbers—of violent neo-Nazi organizations, and the presence of a significant streak of authoritarianism. The days of unchallenged Labour government are over, and a series of much more conservative political parties have held power since the 1990s, including quite extreme libertarians. While these examples might be explained away as exceptions to prove a general rule, it is also possible that they are systematically underemphasized in the general narrative of Norwegian politics and history. One might, for example, wonder where Norway's experience of World War II fits into the strikingly egalitarian stable, cooperative and democratic nation described by Østerud as going back though the nineteenth century.

CHALLENGING ORTHODOXIES

There are other arguments which cast doubt on the impeccable image of egalitarianism. Among the texts that interrogate Norwegian egalitarianism, Marianne Gullestad's detailed ethnographic research into everyday life in various Norwegian contexts is the most detailed, and several of her books have been translated into English, alongside various English-language articles (Gullestad 1992, 1996). She herself summarizes her work in a Norwegian-language collection of essays devoted to empirical interrogation of the notion of "*likhet*", a term that encompasses sameness, egalitarianism and equality (Liden et al. 2001). Gullestad argues, first of all, that egalitarian individualism is often said to be a characteristic of the whole of the Modern Western world (Gullestad 2001). Various authors have asserted a particular Norwegian variety with a specially strong link between similarity and equality which, she suggests, forms a culturally-specific means to resolve the ideological conflict in Modernity between the individual and society.

Gullestad's empirical research on family life, neighbourliness, friendship and personal narrative leads her to a particular argument that, in informal contexts Norwegian people need to feel alike in order to feel equal, leading to a tendency to reinforce similarity (or sameness, as Gullestad refers to it) and avoid situations where difference is emphasized. Once likeness has been established, differences can then be explored and individuality again becomes a positive quality. The positive emphasis on similarity contributes to established narratives about the Norwegian welfare state, which Gullestad describes in the context of Østerud's third face of Norway, the role of international peace broker and aid-giver, where Norwegians are presented as a "particularly homogeneous, with equal opportunities, tolerant, antiracist and peace-making people" (Gullestad 2001, 63). Gullestad explains how the presence of immigrants who do not seek to make their difference invisible threatens the imagined community of Norwegianness, such that immigrants are systematically trained to play down their difference through obligatory "integration" training. Hence, "*likhet*" is central to domestic notions of nationhood, which explains why this is put forward on the international stage as a characteristic of Norwegianism.

Yet there is a tension, even here, between abstract theorizing about the notion of egalitarianism and the recognition that narratives of nationhood are, indeed, narratives, which seldom have secure or consistent content, as Eriksen stresses (1993). Lien, for example, points out that Gullestad's empirical work on *likhet* is very much based in southern Norway, and has less applicability in the far northern coastal town where she conducted extensive ethnographic field research in the 1980s and more recently. There, she explains, difference is much more taken for granted, and newcomers are incorporated in quite different ways, through stages of partial incorporation into local social exchanges. The closest form of social relation is established through exchange of goods, particularly foods (Gullestad 2001). These different ways of managing difference reflect the problem with national discourse, which tends to assemble sets of discourses rather than constituting accurate reflections of practice.

Paradoxically, equality in Norway has been practised differently in the regions. Brox's *What's Happening in Northern Norway* is an ethnographic investigation into the impact of centrally developed post-war economic development plans for the northern region of the country (Brox 1972). Brox set out to examine the effects of centralized ambitions based on rational-choice economic theory developed from the central state perspective of national cohesiveness. The plan could be conceptualized by its authors as progressive because of the categories and measures used to define the regions. In a classic policy process of defining a problem into existence, a research consultancy set up in 1948 to study the economics of northern Norway observed that despite having around 12 percent of the population, the region produced only 6 percent of the national product, in other words, production in the north was only half the national average per head of population. This was put down to the fact that economic activity was mostly in areas with low profits, and that production levels were too low. With this starting point, Brox details how it was impossible for central state policy actors to appreciate the value of subsistence activities that lay outside the economic realm, and which, in turn, contributed significantly to the livelihoods of people living in the North. A traditional pattern of combining seasonal salaried labour with non-monetary exchange practices and mixed subsistence farming and fishing was then undermined by a set of economic and infrastructure plans, which aimed to resettle the population in more concentrated settlements. Although this was more convenient for factory-style labour, it made subsistence activities almost impossible, and hence reduced much of the population to a form of economic dependency, while depopulating the villages of the coast in a scale hitherto unseen.

Brox shows that throughout the post-war period (most of the second half of the twentieth century), quite apart from any "cultural" differences within the country, there were quite different economic systems operating in the different regions. Furthermore, these systems were held in a colonial relationship with the urban governing centre (Oslo)—often described, as noted above, as the least Norwegian part of the country—which not only failed to realize the significance of its actions, but believed that its form of economic rationalizing was superior to those in the rest of the country. As Brox comments, there is no doubt that the Plan for Northern Norway emerged from a real desire to help fellow Norwegians, but that the unintended unfortunate consequences can be blamed on a lack of understanding of the situation of subsistence farmers/fishermen, and a fundamental lack of respect for others' ability to recognize their own best interests (Brox 1972, 125). Ironically, Brox notes that at the time of the implementation of the Plan, which was to all intents and purposes a plan for the industrialization of an agrarian economy, Northern Norwegian society was experiencing a period of heightened local egalitarianism, and was therefore able to resist the most unwelcome parts of the Plan (Brox 1972), but not without a decrease in what we now call quality of life for many fishing and farming communities. The grand vision of an egalitarian country where all citizens should be equal thus reveals itself, even in its early days, as being perilously close to an ambition to impose a centrally-steered economy on all regions, in spite of local differences, and as such constitute the kind of colonialist state-centric development planning that Scott criticizes for creating economic dependency in peripheral regions even within nation-states (Scott 1998).

Following Brox, the greatest chorus of critique of national generalizations is based on detailed ethnographic studies of concepts included in the Norwegian term "*likhet*". Thomas Hylland Eriksen's coruscating demolition of Norwegian nationalism begins with a head-on dissection of the "myth of the homogeneous Norway", and proceeds to elaborate on the differentiation over both time and space in the country (Eriksen 1993). He analyzes a wave of introspected examinations of Norwegian identity, and finds that many of the classic national symbols of popular culture are far from shared across generations or regions, but also that many of the traits considered to be specific to the Norwegian nation are actually widely shared beyond Norway. For example, the "*Jante*" laws endlessly quoted from Sandemose's nihilistic novel to characterize puritanical egalitarian Norwegians were actually written about a village in Denmark and, as Eriksen remarks "*Jante*-like moral rules are characteristic of peasant societies across the world" (Eriksen 1993, 26, my translation). In his criticism of nationalism, Eriksen shows the myriad ways in which national sentiment is espoused and practised and the range of symbols, which are called into its service. This critique, like Brox's, is published in the Norwegian language.

A more recent critique of discourses of Scandinavian equality can be found in Bruun, Jakobsen, and Krøijer's equally critical look at Gullestad's analysis of equality-as-sameness (Bruun et al. 2011). This English-language collection offers a welcome nuanced glimpse of the internal Scandinavian debates about equality for a global audience, placing equality and sameness into a context among broader forms of sociality. Bruun, for example, places greater emphasis on the Danish notion of "*fælleskab*" (which she translates as "community", although "fellowship" offers another metaphor for the sense of egalitarian togetherness) (Bruun 2011). According to Bruun, the social pressure to manage and live without hierarchy in Danish cooperative housing is mirrored in the ideal of the nation as a broader cooperative fellowship of equals, through metaphorical scaling effects, such as that outlined in Anderson's thesis on nationalism (Anderson 1983). Bruun's account of the transition from a community-focused, kinship and friendship-based structure, to a market in cooperative housing also reveals how far the cooperative movement in Denmark was a political movement as much as a social movement, and how far that national political movement has been weakened, although social principles among cooperative housing participants persist. Linnet argues that the notion of *hygge* has offered a route for the idealization of equality in Denmark, combining thrift and luxury in a familial sociality that offers a retreat from social disharmony outside intimate domestic settings (Linnet 2011). *Hygge* is a means to emphasize ordinariness in a conflicted and divided society, while marking a stringently normative middle-class sociality as the hallmark of Danishness (Larsen 2011). It is perhaps no coincidence that "*hygge*" has emerged increasingly strongly as an international marketing concept, as the question of Danishness has become more politically heightened in recent years.

A sense that fragile and weakened fellowship and increasing diversity are undermining Scandinavian equality today reflects both the brevity of the success of the social movements that emphasized equality in the twentieth century, and the ephemerality of some versions of the notion of equality itself. Scandinavian equality stands in opposition to the extreme capitalist economies of European Austerity and also in opposition to the former communist dictatorships with their evident injustices and systems of privileges. Why, then, should we want to critique the political discourse on Norwegian equality and its benefits today? Is it to suggest that egalitarianism does not "really" exist in Norway, and thus by extension cannot be achieved elsewhere? Given the detailed ethnographic accounts on the different nuances and materializations of "*likhet*" found in the Norwegian language literature, it would be foolish to suggest that similarity and equality are not of continued significance as a social category within Norway and across wider Scandinavia. On the contrary, it is the widening gap between English-language portrayals of Scandinavian egalitarianism and the nuanced and detailed debates in the Scandinavian languages that gives rise to misapprehensions and mistakes in evaluating what actually-existing equality really is, and how egalitarianism is effected in practice. This divergence must be addressed if Scandinavian forms of equality are to be relevant to, and appropriately interpreted for, international political debates.

Conclusion

Is the intention of this chapter to suggest that the Norwegian welfare state failed to bring its citizens to a universally good standard of living? Folk memory and economic surveys suggest that this would be to do a great disfavour to the welfare state, which, to a great degree allowed a generation to take universal welfare for granted, so much so that the majority were unable to conceive, for example, that the Norwegian national health service could go the way of the British NHS and collapse into a dysfunctional economic quagmire only months after its devolution. And yet, in contrast to the UK, health services were never wholly free on demand, nursery care had to be paid for until children reached school age, and student maintenance for higher education was financed through loans: hardly the socialist paradise that outsiders might imagine. Norway has had much stronger policies in favour of regional maintenance than its neighbours, yet internal regional difference cannot be denied. Cross-border trade in the Arctic North made the region economically different to other areas, for example, and certainly more socially diverse (Lien 2001). The treatment of Sami people reveals the "dark side" of equality-as-sameness. It may be argued that Norway has been no worse than other nations, and in many cases has remained much more egalitarian than other countries, but this is a long way from the suggestions in some of the English-language literature that it straightforwardly *is* egalitarian.

My intent, first, is to alert comparative researchers and policy-makers to treat with caution the representation of a whole nation with characteristics otherwise used to describe individuals, i.e., to resist the attribution of personhood to the nation. A number of factors crucial to comparative research, including scale, category and context, flag up large questions. While the nation-state seems to presents itself as a primary unit for comparison, we must always ask "why compare nation-states?" If it is the national legal system, electoral process, or some other structure that operates at the national scale, then comparison of state-level activities might indeed be feasible. But to slip over into indulging in nation-talk is not appropriate for scholarly analysis.

Second, it makes sense to align empirical material with analytical discourse. Barth et al.'s (2003) use of economic data to inform economic history is convincing, whereas the heavily-cited, ill-tempered debates between Lafferty and Martinussen (Lafferty 1981; Martinussen 1977) about whether Norwegians were on the whole more or less a/political (which first inspired this critique), now appear to be based on an erroneous desire to characterize all Norwegians as this or that: to stereotype by majority, and to interpret voting habits and local social or other activities in the interest of some broader holistic judgement. What does it tell us that citizens of Norway vote more or less than the citizens of some other country, except that they vote more or less? Exploring local or regional differentiations or reasons for such would require a wholly different form of empirical enquiry than an examination of voting records and association membership. If arguments about political institutions and social coercion are to be valuable, close attention must be paid to the narratives that are silenced in the promotion of Nordic egalitarianism: the systematic under-emphasis of difference described by Gullestad, the recognition of the geographical and social limits to such analysis, and serious attention to the darker forms of nationalisms that bubble just under the surface of Nordic public life.

Third, the great challenge that all of the historians and anthropologists grapple with is in evaluating which of the very many and diverse contextual factors might carry explanatory weight. One can certainly speculate on the significance of puritan Protestantism on relations to authority and wealth, but without engaging in teleological or counterfactual history, these remain unproven, interesting, and challenging speculations. And since any discussion of context depends on the questions of scale and category mentioned above, the limitations of international comparative research and analysis can be seen to be significant. The great values of comparison lie in questioning assumptions (such as the relevance of the nation-state as an axis of comparison), the challenge to justify conclusions when faced with counter-examples, and the rigour of separating speculation, explanation, and reflection. Such subtleties, as evident in the historical and anthropological literature, particularly in the Scandinavian-language literature, are missing from much of the English-language debate about Scandinavia, most particularly from those in the well-defended discipline of Political Science. The intention of this chapter is to underline why that matters, and why this volume is an important step forward.

Norwegian politicians have traded for many years on the notion of egalitarianism to promote their particular political projects, both at home and abroad. Attributing egalitarianism as a personal quality of members of Norwegian society generates a kind of reified national character, a stereotype that may mislead with potentially disastrous consequences. That much of the discussion about equality is published by only a few prominent individuals in the English language, when much of the critique of their work is published largely in Norwegian allows those few representations to dominate the idea of Norway in the wider world. When Norwegian policies are adopted as ideal models by other governments (such as the Oslo model for cabinet-format local government adopted in the UK, or the Norwegian model of comprehensive planning transformed into "community planning"), these adoptions both underestimate the local difference of the Norwegian context (its political, economic and social history, the development and powers of local government and the allegiances of the actors in whom those powers are vested, see Abram and Cowell 2004), and overestimate the apparent "egalitarianism" of the imagined nation. International debates on social inequality (such as the Wilkinson and Pickett debate) will remain narrow and misleading unless a properly contextualized debate on Scandinavian egalitarianism prevails.

Note

1. Østerud 1984, cited in Eriksen (1993), 49.

References

Abram, Simone, and Richard Cowell. 2004. Learning policy—The contextual curtain and conceptual barriers. *European Planning Studies* 12: 209–228.

Amit-Talai, Vered, ed. 2000. *Constructing the field: Ethnographic fieldwork in the contemporary world*. London/New York: Routledge.

Anderson, Benedict. 1983. *Imagined communities: Reflections on the origin and spread of nationalism*. London: Verso.

Barth, Erling, Karl Ove Moene, Michael Wallerstein, and Makt- og demokratiutredningen 1998–2003. 2003. *Likhet under press: Utfordringer for den skandinaviske fordelingsmodellen*. Oslo: Gyldendal akademisk.

Billig, Michael. 1995. *Banal nationalism*. London: Sage.

Bowie, Fiona. 1993. Wales from within: Conflicting interpretations of Welsh identity. In *Inside European identities*, ed. Sharon Macdonald, 167–193. Oxford: Berg.

Brown, Elizabeth A.R. 2016. Feudalism. *Encyclopaedia Brittanica*. https://www.britannica.com/topic/feudalism. Accessed 26 Sept 2016.

Brox, Ottar. 1972. *Hva skjer i Nord-Norge? En studie i norsk utkantpolitikk*. Oslo: Pax forlag.

Bruun, Maja Hojer. 2011. Egalitarianism and community in Danish housing cooperatives. *Social Analysis* 55 (2): 62–83.

Bruun, Maja Hojer, Gry Skrædderdal Jakobsen, and Stine Krøijer. 2011. The concern for sociality—Practicing equality and hierarchy in Denmark. *Social Analysis* 5 (2): 1–19.
Dahl, Hans Fredrik. 1986. Those equal folk. In *Norden—The passion for equality*, ed. Stephen R. Graubard. Oslo: Norwegian University Press.
Eikås, Magne, and Per Selle. 2000. *A contract culture even in Scandinavia*. Oslo: Makt- og demokratiutredningen.
Eriksen, Thomas Hylland. 1993. *Typisk norsk: Essays om kulturen i Norge*. Oslo: C. Huitfeldt Forlag.
Graubard, Stephen R., ed. 1986. *Norden—The passion for equality*. Oslo: Norwegian University Press.
Gullestad, Marianne. 1992. *The art of social relations: Essays on culture, social action and everyday life in modern Norway*. Oslo: Universitetsforlaget.
———. 1996. *Everyday life philosophers: Modernity, morality and autobiography in Norway*. Oslo: Scandinavian University Press.
———. 2001. Likhetens Grenser. In *Likhetens paradokser*, ed. Marianne Lien, Hilde Lidén, and Halvard Vike, 32–67. Oslo: Universitetsforlaget.
———. 2002. *Det norske sett med nye øyne kritisk analyse av norsk innvandringsdebatt*. Oslo: Universitetsforlaget.
Hamsun, Knut. 2001 [1890]. *Sult*. Oslo: Gyldendal.
Howell, Signe. 2001. "En Vanlig Familie": Utenlandsadopsjon i Norge, et stadig voksende fenomen. In *Blod—Tykkere enn vann? Betydninger av slektskap i Norge*, ed. Signe Howell and Marit Melhuus. Bergen: Fagbokforlaget.
Kielland, Alexander. 2006 [1882]. *Skipper worse*. Oslo: Fono forlag.
Lafferty, William M. 1981. *Participation and democracy in Norway: The "distant democracy" revisted*. Oslo: Universitetsforlaget.
Larsen, Birgitte Romme. 2011. Drawing back the curtains: The role of domestic space in the social inclusion and exclusion of refugees in rural Denmark. *Social Analysis* 55 (2): 142–158.
Lidén, Hilde, Halvard Vike, and Marianne Lien. 2001. *Likhetens paradokser: Antropologiske undersøkelser i det moderne Norge*. Oslo: Universitetsforlaget.
Lien, Marianne. 2001. Likhet og verdighet: Gavebytter og integrasjon i Båtsfjord. In *Likhetens paradokser*, ed. Hilde Lidén, Halvard Vike, and Marianne Lien. Oslo: Universitetsforlaget.
Linnet, Jeppe Trolle. 2011. Money can't buy me hygge. Danish middle-class consumption, egalitarianism, and the sanctity of inner space. *Social Analysis* 55 (2): 21–44.
Martinussen, Willy. 1977. *The distant democracy: Social inequality, political resources and political influence in Norway*. London: John Wiley and Sons.
McDonald, Maryon. 1993. The construction of difference: An anthropological approach to stereotypes. In *Inside European identities*, ed. Sharon MacDonald, 219–236. Oxford: Berg.

Neumann, Iver B. 2001. *Norge—En kritikk*. Oslo: Pax Forlag.
Olwig, Karen Fog, and Kirsten Hastrup, eds. 1997. *Siting culture: The shifting anthropological object*. London: Routledge.
Østerud, Øyvind. 2005. Introduction: The peculiarities of Norway. *West European Politics* 28 (4): 705–720.
Østerud, Øyvind, and Per Selle. 2006. Power and democracy in Norway: The transformation of Norwegian politics. *Scandinavian Political Studies* 29 (1): 25–46.
Rokkan, Stein. 1966. Norway: Numerical democracy and corporate pluralism. In *Political oppositions in Western democracies*, ed. Robert A. Dahl, 70–115. New Haven/London: Yale University Press.
Scott, James. 1998. *Seeing like a state: How certain schemes to improve the human condition have failed*. New Haven/London: Yale University Press.
Snowdon, Christopher. 2010. *The spirit level delusion*. Ripton: The Democracy Institute.
Sørensen, Øystein, and Bo Stråth, eds. 1997. *The cultural construction of Norden*. Oslo: Scandinavian University Press.
Strathern, Marilyn. 1981. *Kinship at the core*. Cambridge, MA: Cambridge University Press.
Trägårdh, Lars. 1997. Statist individualism: On the culturality of the Nordic state. In *The cultural construction of Norden*, ed. Øystein Sørensen and Bo Stråth, 253–285. Oslo: Scandinavian University Press.
Wilkinson, Richard, and Kate Pickett. 2009. *The spirit level: Why more equal societies almost always do better*. London: Allen Lane.
Wimmer, Andreas, and Nina Glick-Schiller. 2002. Methodological nationalism and beyond: Nation-state building, migration and the social sciences. *Global Networks* 2 (4): 301–334.

PART II

Institutionalizing Egalitarianism

CHAPTER 5

The Protestant Ethic and the Spirit of Political Resistance: Notes on the Political Roots of Egalitarianism in Scandinavia

Halvard Vike

INTRODUCTION

Francis Fukuyama, in a little section of his influential work *Origins of Political Order*, pays a visit to Denmark (Fukuyama 2011, 431–434). In this section, which is entitled "Getting to Denmark", Fukuyama reflects on what he regards as modern Scandinavia's extraordinary historical trajectory. He identifies the particular dynamic that generated relatively peaceful transitions from a feudal-like social order to democratic welfare

---

The following colleagues have contributed with valuable comments to earlier drafts for this chapter: Mary-Bente Bringslid, Synnøve Bendixsen, Jan Eivind Myhre, Christian Lo, and Maja Hojer Bruun. They all helped substantially in improving my argument, and I am very grateful. Also the critical input provided by the participants in the workshop hosted by the Department of Anthropology, University of Bergen, 24–25 November, 2015, "De-Naturalizing Egalitarianism" has been very useful in the process of developing the chapter.

H. Vike (✉)
Department of Health, Social, and Welfare Studies, University College of Southeast Norway, Porsgrunn, Norway

capitalism. According to Fukuyama, Denmark's transformations are above all characterized by the combination of a strong state (which from a very early stage secured some *Rechtstaat* structures that, among other things, facilitated the development of a vibrant capitalist agricultural economy) and popular mobilization leading to a type of gradual democratic development. In Denmark, popular political mobilization did not trigger major, violent reactions from the old elites—even much less so, in fact, than what was the case in Britain, which is the prototypical European case of a non-revolutionary path to constitutional democracy. Concerning "how to get to Denmark", Fukuyama writes:

> Political liberty—that is, the ability of societies to rule themselves—does not depend only on the degree to which a society can mobilize opposition to centralized power and impose constitutional constraints on the state. It must also have a state that is strong enough to act when action is required. (Fukuyama 2011, 431)

Denmark did indeed have a strong state. However, by the year 1500, Fukuyama points out, it was not at all obvious that the nature of change in Denmark or the rest of Scandinavia would differ from that in any other early modern state-organized society in early modern Europe. But the effects of the Protestant Reformation were tremendous, particularly in terms of the path it paved for the spread of literacy among the peasantry. Peasant enlightenment generated a new sense of individuality, as well as political mobilization and economic modernization. In contrast to Britain, representative democracy in Denmark emerged not from a feudal institution—Parliament—but from a more or less continuous struggle from below to increase citizens' rights. Danish peasants (who during the mid-1800s transformed themselves into commercially oriented farmers) were not alone in this struggle: constitutional democracy emerged from a broad alliance across the major class divisions, as both national liberals and the rising labor movement joined in. The old elites were deeply divided: the king had managed to marginalize the class of large landowners and establish a form of absolute rule, but became increasingly dependent on the urban bourgeoisie as well as the peasant farmers (as taxpayers, soldiers, and economic modernizers) (Knudsen and Rothstein 1994; Østergård 1992).

A number of other factors were involved in this historical trajectory. Fukuyama concludes that the Danish case is "full of historical accidents and contingent circumstances", and adds that these "cannot be duplicated elsewhere" (Fukuyama 2011, 434). Nevertheless, he points out that there appear to be many different ways to "get to Denmark" as long as there is some combination of a strong state, rule of law, accountable government, and organized opposition from "below". Charles Tilly (2005), in a comparatively oriented study, has emphasized that the varied forms in which state regimes react to the mobilization of "trust networks" may heavily influence processes of democratization. The trust networks he discusses are of many different types, but he seem mainly to concentrate on those networks that tend to emerge as markets expand. A main problem, he argues, is that "regimes and trust networks often depend on the same resources—labor power, money, information, loyalty, and more" (Tilly 2005, 23) For this reason, such networks are vulnerable to destruction owing to rulers' temptation to seize these resources. But a few processes may promote accommodations and connect trust networks with public politics, thereby establishing some form of mutual—although sometimes highly conflictual—dependency.

What does this have to do with egalitarianism, the main theme of this volume? "Getting to Denmark" is partly about how trust networks become integrated into public politics, and in this chapter, I want to look at processes that have promoted such accommodations. In Scandinavia, this seems to have happened to a rather large extent, and here I wish to explore some aspects of how this occurred, and why, and examine some of the implications. In comparative terms, popular political mobilization in Scandinavia was quite successful in influencing the state, not only by forcing it to make concessions, but also by integrating forms of trust, horizontal loyalty, and certain values and interests that became important for developing policy—such as individual autonomy and universalism (Vike 2012, 2015). A key issue here, as I understand it, is that under some circumstances trust networks may be able to retain and protect vital resources independently of state power.

The chapter has two main sections, both dealing with the case of Norway: (1) a historical review of some important instances of political challenges to state power from below; and (2) a set of ethnographic illustrations from contemporary local politics in Norway. The link between these two is speculative and exploratory. Through the latter part of the chapter, I hope to show that municipal politics in Norway is generally heavily influenced by organized interests (trust networks) that to some extent challenge the logics of state governance. In Norway in particular, local institutions—municipalities, above all—have been key arenas for the social organization of political interests, and have only partially served as extensions of state power. Local political institutions are highly "porous" and allow political interests to operate both within and beyond the formal boundaries of "the state" (represented by the municipality) and the interests of the elites who guard those boundaries and the political-bureaucratic organization these elites are supposed to protect. This phenomenon, it seems to me, has some interesting historical roots, which I explore in some detail in the first section of this chapter. In Norway, and in Scandinavia at large, "grassroots" political mobilization appears historically to have been strong enough to represent a real challenge to state power, but yet at the same time it was not seen as deeply threatening (Skirbekk 2010). Such mobilizations were rarely crushed, and were able to evolve into the form of trust networks that were extended from the local level over time. They did not simply become absorbed by the hierarchical—and partly clientelistic—logic of the state apparatus (Piattoni 2003).

As Bo Stråth has pointed out, the seemingly common view that the Scandinavian welfare state model arose from some general, traditional, and widespread will to agree, a culture of consensus, "is not very relevant when considering Scandinavian political culture" (Stråth 2005, 41). In historical terms there seems to be little evidence to support the assumption that a "passion for equality" (Graubard 1986) has permeated "Scandinavian culture". Until quite recently, particularly so in Norway and Denmark (somewhat less so in Sweden), processes of change were characterized principally by intense conflict. In my perspective, "equality" is more an outcome of such conflicts than an overarching value related to "a culture of consensus". Thus, what interests me in this context is the form and dynamic of such conflicts, as well as the institutional features emerging from them. It seems to me that the Scandinavian states went a long way toward incorporating (some of) the tensions that contributed to forming them, and institutionalized these conflicts by attempting to domesticate interests that opposed state policies. In this sense, egalitarianism can be seen as, among other things, a structural *and* cultural aspect of a specific institutional dynamic—institutionalized resistance, if you will. I use the expression "institutionalized resistance" heuristically in order to pinpoint ways in which conflicting interests are played out, not only outside, but also within the state as more or less normal routine. In the first section, I investigate the forms of political opposition that began to occur in the first phase of political modernization in the late eighteenth century and continued into the twentieth, and discuss some aspects of their form and their effects. First, however, I discuss the nature of political interests that developed among the Norwegian "peasantry" prior to and during this period.

Of Peasants and State Capitalism

In the Introduction to this volume (Chap. 1), it was noted that John Barnes's anthropological construction of the island parish of Bremnes involved the observation that "part-time peasants" took part in an egalitarian political order of a transitional kind (Barnes 1954). Barnes emphasized its transitional state because he assumed that what he regarded as a power vacuum was probably in the process of being filled by a more active, modern state formation, and because the class system was expanding. To some extent, Barnes may have been right, but his observations seem to lend themselves to a different interpretation. What he observed (or failed to observe) may not have been so much a vacuum as an expression of the way in which the Danish, and later the Swedish and Norwegian, state actually worked in places like Bremnes. When Fukuyama speaks of "strong states" as one important condition in the formation of democratic societies, he is somewhat imprecise. In Scandinavia, it was perhaps not the strength of the state that was the salient feature historically, but rather its peculiar unitary nature and its ability to adapt to (and gradually transform) local realities and networks. As Henrik Stenius (2010), Tim Knudsen (2000), and many others have pointed out (see the Introduction to this volume, Chap. 1), the Reformation put an end to subcultural pluralism in a seemingly radical way. This was achieved, it should be noted, not through the elimination of subcultures as such, but rather by subsuming them all under one, singular and conformist authority in religious, administrative, and political terms. In this way, the church, the educational system, the local courts, and municipal institutions could do much of the work of the state, that is to say, perform some kind of "indirect rule" (Tilly 1990).

In this case, the mediating factor was not primarily powerful intermediaries but rather institutions that had emerged partly independently of state power, and partly under local control. This made it relatively easy for the state to exercise its authority through a variety of channels and reach the individual citizen, even his/her inner life, at minimum cost and without to any great extent having to rely on repressive measures (Knudsen 2000). The mutual social control involved in such alliances provided ample possibilities for enforcing discipline, but not without a price. Social control made state authority relatively sensitive to influence from below, since the institutions upon which state authority rested were party external to it and were dominated by trust networks partly beyond its direct control. For example, local priests, schoolteachers, and administrators were often recruited and/or hired locally, and their loyalty tended to be mixed. Simultaneously, the decentralized management of state authority that took place in local courts and municipal institutions was not only characterized by a mixed loyalty of the same kind; it also formed the institutional basis for opposition of a more organized, political type, potentially to be played out within the institutional framework of the state itself. It seems highly productive, along the lines spelled out by Stenius (2010), Knudsen (2000), and Sørensen and Stråth (1997), to view this dynamic in the context of a dominant worldview and language of Protestant Lutheranism, privileging individual discipline, modesty, and organization. In the Norwegian context at least, in hindsight, it seems logical that the first serious controversy between the state/church and the popular movements that challenged its authority was about the right to congregate and to speak freely in such contexts—as well as the freedom to establish businesses, to which I will return.

Barnes's second point, noted above, about the emerging class system, provides another means of approaching the same general process. In my own view, Barnes is but one among many scholars who have failed to acknowledge the penetrating nature of proto-industrial capitalism in premodern Scandinavia, and its effects on identities, class relations, and political mobilization. The "peasants" Barnes observed were not late arrivals to the capitalist world market; they were, as was the case with the majority of farmers in Norway since the sixteenth century (particularly in areas not too far from the coast and major waterways), commercial agents and only involved in subsistence part-time (Østerud 1978). From 1500 to 1850, the population of Norway increased tenfold, but economic growth was even faster and stronger (Dyrvik 1979). Such a growth rate is exceptional in pre-modern economies. In the case of Norway, the most significant aspect of this may not be the growth rate as such, which clearly is related to the relative abundance of available resources such as fish, timber, metals, and available land to be cultivated, but rather its distribution. As resources were relatively easily available to common folk, the need for capital investments was rarely overwhelming. Moreover, some of the most promising commercial activities that grew in importance later in the period, especially shipping and ship brokering, were not to any great extent monopolized by the elites, even though they actively sought protection through royal privileges (which became outdated when economic liberalism gained hegemony in the early 1800s).

A large proportion of the freeholding farmers (who, since the Black Death, always constituted the majority, but were reduced somewhat during parts of the eighteenth century) in Norway found themselves in a favorable situation to exploit the opportunities provided by increasing demand, both in the international and in the internal market. According to economic historians Ståle Dyrvik (1979) and Håvard Teigen (2006), one important factor here was the flexibility of their adaption. Subsistence activities were labor-intensive, but could be carried out by women ("deputy husbands", in the words of Solheim 2016), children, and the elderly when the men were away fishing, cutting and transporting timber, etc. In periods of market failure, they could invest in more animals and intensify the use of available uncultivated land, often forest areas and grassland at higher altitudes. Because of this flexibility, taking part in commercial activities did not constitute a major risk. Micro-level specialization proved highly adaptable and profitable, and this may even help explain why the exceptional pre-industrial growth was both strong and steady (Brox 1966; Dyrvik 1979, 237; Myhre in Chap. 3, this volume).

The political interests of Norwegian peasant farmers were profoundly shaped by their activities and identities as agents in commercial markets. Clearly such activities and identities also influenced their interest in other resources that became available in the pre-democratic state, such as technology to be used for innovating agriculture, cutting and transporting wood/building materials, catching and preserving cod, herring, or trout—and, perhaps above all, the ability to read and write. Not surprisingly, much of the negotiations involving the state and farmers involved access to markets, protection of property, and taxes. There is little doubt that in the same way as the state (the royal sovereign) acknowledged its dependence on farmers as soldiers, it realized that the potential for tax revenue did not depend primarily on subsistence production but also on their role as producers and entrepreneurs in expanding markets. Probably for that reason there seems to have been a conscious policy from around 1670 to be careful not to tax the farmers too harshly (Dyrvik 1979, 251). "The King's weakness was his strength", Norwegian historian Magne Njåstad has pointed out, referring to the attempts to establish a foundation for legitimacy on the part of the king and the state in the late Middle Ages. As result of establishing this foundation on premises already established in local institutions, the state became mainly a guarantee of the status quo (Njåstad 2003, 250; Dørum 2010). It should be noted here that these institutions, local courts in particular, represented a deep-seated tradition of formal judicial-political negotiation reaching back to Viking times (Titlestad 2016).

The Dynamics of Political Change in Scandinavia

The political organization of Scandinavia in the eighteenth century was quite diverse. Denmark was an "absolute" monarchy with a deeply feudal countryside, Norway its colony, and Sweden a former military great power with a strong, centralist state and a rather "un-Western European" mooring in the peasantry (Knudsen and Rothstein 1994; Østergård 1992; Stenius 2010). In cultural terms, their commonalities were above all related to Protestantism and the profound effects of the Reformation. As pointed out above, state and church became one, and in contrast to most other European countries, no alternative sources of authority competed with the political sovereign. This "theocratization" of society (the unity of state and church/religion), and the construction of a "one-norm society" (Stenius 2010, 33), contributed significantly to marginalize the idea that society consists of incommensurable subcultures, and to pave the way for uniform institutions based on Protestant values. Moreover, it provided what Finnish historian Henrik Stenius calls "rigid, but effective practices of inclusion (on work, education, local government, and the production and dissemination of practical knowledge)" (Stenius 2010, 31). However, although this institutional uniformity constituted a powerful mechanism for control and the imposition of discipline, and proved an extremely efficient means for governing the population according to the logic of what we may call "direct rule" (Tilly 1990) of an "indirect" kind, it was less successful in preventing the lower classes from using state institutions for their own purposes. Five aspects should be highlighted.

First, the class dynamics in Scandinavia were tense, and had strong effects on political conflicts long before democratization. The royal sovereign effectively outmaneuvered the aristocracy quite early on, and the peasantry became important as the supplier of soldiers and tax revenue. The urban bourgeoisie played an important role, but it was internally fragmented and its relationship with the state and the peasants remained complex, thus preventing it from becoming an all-dominant actor. In Norway, which is the main case study in this chapter, urban merchants and proto-industrialists depended heavily on the king to protect their privileges (from the fourteenth century to the nineteenth century), but also on peasant farmers, who were in control of much of the timber (and supplied the fish). Political conflicts in the autocratic state reveal complex patterns of alliances between these three sets of actors.

Second, political conflicts—at least from the mid-eighteenth century onward—were nearly always about conflicting economic interests related to the key role of "part-time peasants" in expanding markets. A significant number of urban merchants, shippers, and proto-industrialists were formerly successful peasant farmers, who had moved to town and specialized their business, and most of those who did not make this move were active in the timber trade.

The third factor that helped enable the lower classes to use state institutions for their own purposes was the nature of their political action. Although often seen as deeply provocative and dangerous, political action on the part of the peasant farmers was generally of a highly disciplined and well-organized kind, based on experience from decision-making in local communities. Faced with such a degree of organization, the authorities actively reflected upon their own possibility whether to respond with "the policy of the iron fist" (Sejersted 2003) and attempts at domestication.

Fourth, throughout Scandinavia, municipalities were relatively autonomous but at the same time heavily involved in dealing with the interests of the state locally. Municipalities were not task-specific, but generalist (especially after the municipal laws issued in 1837), and partly due to the broad scope of their activity, the boundaries between them as elected bodies, on the one hand, and voluntary associations, on the other, were not always very clear (Stenius 2010, 39). Social control in the local community was not simply limited to controlling the governed or those governing, mutual and multiplex. It also worked through a sense of equal membership that became strongly reinforced as voluntary organizations became politicized and in part coopted by the state.

The fifth factor concerns patterns of social differentiation. From the early nineteenth century onward, it became common for individuals to be members in several associations. The organizational landscape thus became extraordinarily complex and overlapping, although uniform in its institutional structure and scope. Most movements and organizations had their basis in local communities, organized members formally, operated according to strict procedures, and were joined together in umbrella organizations nationally. They not only took responsibility for one section of society, but also sought comprehensive policy solutions and did not see themselves as outside the state (Stenius 2010, 51; Knudsen and Rothstein 1994).

Challenges to State Power: Some Examples of Political Mobilizations and Their Aftermath

The Lofthus Rebellion

In the 1780s and 1790s, a major uprising took place in Southern Norway—the so-called "Lofthus rebellion", popularly understood as a "peasant rebellion". Its initiator was Jørgen Lofthus, who was frustrated by what he saw as unlawful behavior on the part of local state officials as well as by merchants in the town of Arendal, one of many coastal towns with an extremely vibrant economy (Dyrvik and Feldbæk 1996; Fiskaa 2012). He was able to collect considerable amounts of documentation before anyone tried to stop him, and mobilized large numbers of allies among peasant farmers in the south. He and his followers claimed that officials and merchants alike broke the rules of the game as established by the king, and one of the first things he did was in fact to go to Copenhagen to attempt to deliver his complaint to the sovereign in person. At one point, thousands of followers were ready to march to Christiania, the capital, to confront the officials seen as responsible. The uprising became too much for the authorities, however, and was put down—eventually landing Lofthus and some of his followers in jail (where he died). During the uprising, which was a wholly non-violent affair, a range of conflicting interests were involved. First, Lofthus was a successful entrepreneur and involved in shipping with timber, in addition to owning a small farm. His frustration with the local merchants mainly concerned one merchant pointing out that other merchants in the same town enjoyed and abused privileges. In his attacks on local authorities, Lofthus surely had many of these same merchants behind him. The "peasants" who joined his movement were not marginalized people ready to take desperate action, but mostly farmers who were fully able to document their complaints and appeal to the law in order to protect their economic interests (related to the timber trade in particular). The reaction the uprising eventually triggered was severe in several ways, but it resulted in the establishment of a commission that ended up debating the need for reforms, most notably in the area of economic liberalization. Economic liberalization was one of the most important elements in Lofthus' program, but now it was formulated in even broader terms than he himself had done. Especially in the higher strata of the state bureaucracy, the uprising inspired a concern with corruption at the local level and a more positive attitude to the lower classes as political actors (Dyrvik and

Feldbæk 1996, 65). The process, most probably illustrating a deeper set of common interests between the peasant farmers as entrepreneurs and agents of economic change (and growth) and the state (the king), recurred in Denmark half a century later. As Danish agriculture lost out in the competition in the increasingly internalized grain market, and Danish farmers initiated changing production strategies from plants to livestock, the associational infrastructure which made this possible was supported by the state (mainly for military and economic reasons), even in periods of deeply conservative rule (Østergård 1992; Kaspersen and Ottesen 2001, 114).

The Haugians

Only a few years after "the Lofthus rebellion", another grassroots movement grew to great proportions in Norway, encompassing large parts of the country (Dyrvik and Feldbæk 1996; Dørum 2010; Grytten 2013). Hans Nielsen Hauge, a religiously devoted puritan farmer from the southeast corner bordering Sweden, began a "grand tour" as a preacher and modernizer. He gathered people to preach a form of anti-clerical Lutheranism promoting the (well-known) idea that each man is directly responsible to God, that official mediators do not have a legitimate place in this dyad, and that the path to salvation consists of disciplined conduct. By bringing common people together, preaching the Gospel, and educating them in agricultural innovation, business development, and the ability to read and write, Hauge provoked the representatives of the state, who feared that this could lead to freedom of assembly and political opposition. Hauge himself was moderate in his provocations, but consistent in pursuing his entrepreneurial religiosity among people, and he was extremely successful in both regards. After having been active for about ten years, he was arrested in 1804. Those most provoked by him and the movement were the church, which was an important part of the local state bureaucracy, but also many urban merchants, who saw his business orientation, and the increasing numbers of competitors resulting from his teaching, as a threat to their interests (as holders of commercial privileges). Businesses established by Hauge and his followers included paper mills, paper factories, salt processing plants, shipyards, provision of fishing vessel equipment, fish preservation (smoking, drying, salting), copper mining, shipping, and printing houses (Grytten 2013, 36). In much the same way as the authorities reacted to Lofthus' activities, they ended up treating him with greater leniency than might have been expected. Again, the alliance whose voice became decisive consisted of higher officials and a large portion of all those who could profit from increasing liberalization of the economy. Indeed, Hauge's entrepreneurship had clearly demonstrated that there could be an alternative to the traditional way of collecting revenue (through urban privileges), and a means to stimulate economic growth without losing control. Presumably as a result of this, Hauge's movement began to fascinate leading officials, who chose to express publicly that he was in many ways a respectful man whose morality and discipline were undisputed. Shortly after his death in 1824, it became common among successful entrepreneurs in Norway to call themselves "Haugians".

The Menstad Battle

The largest and most important industrial confrontation between labor and capital in large-scale industry occurred in 1931, at Menstad in the town of Skien (also located in the south-east of Norway) (Kjeldstadli 1994; Berntsen 2014). As a result of the economic crisis, the employer in the town (Hydro, which at the time specialized in producing salpeter), decided that they needed to cut wages, and when the workers rejected to accept this, the company initiated a total lockout. They recruited strikebreakers with impunity, arguing that since there was not a strike but a lockout there could be no strikebreaking. The workers kept guard and for almost a month prevented workers from entering the plant. The Cabinet Minister of Defense, the infamous Vidkun Quisling (who later became the Führer of Norway during the German Occupation in World War II, and a major international symbol of national betrayal), sent a group of military police and a warship to confront them. However, although the police fired one shot, the conflict ended peacefully. The heated national debate that followed nevertheless inspired some fear that a revolution was imminent. Knut Kjeldstadli, one of many historians who has written about the subject, states: "the conflict ended with a draw" (Kjeldstadli 1994, 184). The employers did not succeed in their attempts to cut wages; in fact, the workers ended up keeping a higher wage than the average in most other comparable countries. Shortly after the confrontation, workers' rights were also strengthened in several areas, institutionalized through the "Main Agreement" between the employers' union and the labor movement's foremost organization, the LO (*Landsorganisasjonen*, The National Union), and four years later the first Labor government was established—based on a political agreement with the party Quisling had represented as cabinet minister during "the Menstad battle" in 1931. In hindsight, it seems clear that the Norwegian labor movement was never radically anti-capitalist. It recruited almost all of its members more or less directly from the farming population, which is to say from people intensely interested in, among other things, protecting private property.

Also of relevance here is the conservative-liberal approach to fascism in this period in Norway, which reflects a general Scandinavian pattern. All the major parties on the right ended up rejecting the fascist movement, thereby channeling authoritarian sensibilities and interests toward moderate political programs. One general insight that can be drawn from this is that the political interests of conservative-liberal elites in Norway, who had struggled hard to contain political opposition from the left and democratization more generally, were seen by the same elites as best served by the strategy of non-confrontation (Sejersted 2005). At this time, there was little doubt that political power had to rest on electoral support, and these parties had no significant independent electoral base beyond that which was increasingly mobilized by the social democrats.

POLITICAL MOBILIZATION: SOME PRELIMINARY CONCLUSIONS

From these historical illustrations of political conflict leading to, and resulting from, political mobilization, some patterns emerge. There is no doubt that the experience of social class was a foundational reason why the conflicts took place. However, from a European perspective, the kinds of interests involved, the institutional context in which they were negotiated, and the alliances (and political "consensus") established during the process constituted peculiar features of political contestation and compromise. In fact, state authorities ended up *not* responding to potentially authority-threatening political mobilization by extending the definition of criminal behavior. All examples involve some form of initial concessions followed by reform. Furthermore, in all three cases the initiators and their followers were able to gain from unstable class alliances. This involved, among other things, some elite interests that could somehow benefit from possible change. In addition to this, and perhaps most importantly, the authorities' tendency to choose the path of domesticating opposition meant—at least in the longer run—that the state apparatus (partly through the political parties) extended its scope and incorporated the associations organizing the opposition through corporatist arrangements. One significant aspect of this was that in doing so, it also made itself vulnerable to the mobilizing capacity of the associations that were invited to play a role in decision-making. The major associations became in part an integral part of the state, and tended to maintain and reproduce their organizational form, founded in the idea of membership across social class divisions and regional boundaries (and, we may add, in both town and country). Finally, as Stenius (2010) has pointed out, one of the key "ideological" visions shared by many of these associations—the idea of universalism—gradually became an important premise for policy.

Local Politics: A Contemporary Perspective

In my own ethnographic work on local politics in Norway, I have become fascinated with the institutional tensions resulting from the tight integration between the state and civil society, particularly the way in which this integration seems to have become institutionalized locally. At an early stage of my first fieldwork, carried out in a small industrial community in 1990, I met local politicians who repeatedly problematized their own conscience in relation to what they experienced as major political dilemmas (Vike 1991, 1996, 1997). What appeared particularly difficult for them was aligning the ambitions that had motivated them to participate and get elected to the municipal assembly, on the one hand, with the responsibility to perform their duty as a part of a governing collective, on the other. As representatives, they saw themselves as advocates for people with legitimate claims vis-à-vis the municipality, while as responsible governors, they were often forced to make budget cutbacks because "the economy" and bureaucratic managers (as well as local political elites) demanded it. After a while, I realized that this dilemma was intimately related to the integration of the municipal institutions in the central state. The municipalities constitute highly complex bureaucratic structures in communities where networks of kin, neighborhood, friendship, and membership in voluntary organizations overlap each other and tend to be very dense (Barnes 1954; Vike 2015).

As I became a more experienced ethnographer of local politics, I grew interested in how the local politicians' dilemma could be utilized by political interests in the local environment. Owing to the small scale and density of local networks, they tend to be much more vulnerable to local pressure than are their fellow politicians in the national arena, and they have a harder time escaping the tension between their double mandate as representatives of the local community and the state. This holds true both ways. As a part of a neo-liberal agenda seeking to secure users' rights, the central state aggressively pursues an auditing strategy seeking to detect failures in service delivery, thus reinforcing not only the principle of universalism, but also local alliances that may legitimately utilize this to pursue welfare state expansion though more and better services. Local populations are able to exercise a considerable degree of moral control through the political parties, their programs, and through organizations associated with the parties. The state's double agenda thus establishes an institutional tension that can be used to undermine local politicians' role as responsible guardians of scarce resources, and inspire them to challenge administrative chains of command upon which policies of strict economic responsibility rest. When under pressure, even local political elites may have a hard time maneuvering independently of the majority vote of the local party they represent, and of the moral pressure exercised through overlapping networks of organizational membership and informal contexts. In the following, I will present some illustrations and deal with these as instances of political resistance. It seems to me that an important aspect of the form of egalitarianism found in Norwegian society is political in nature, that it is moored in organizational membership, and that the performance of membership has the capacity to challenge ordinary, conventional bureaucratic governance and the chains of command cultivated by it. The municipal institution maintains an institutional space in which horizontal solidarity may be mobilized. By resistance, I do not mean revolutionary action, nor even political rebellion, but, rather, systematic and often successful attempts to change the course of "necessary" action already chosen by political and administrative elites in ways that partly undermine their autonomy.

During my first fieldwork in Nome municipality, in south-east Norway, an intense political controversy developed around a new plan for the reorganization of elderly care (Vike 1991, 1997). The mayor and other leading politicians had led a planning process that concluded that there was a need for a reform that would channel resources from elderly care institutions to more "open solutions"—providing greater care in the home. The basic idea was that this would improve the quality of care and enable the frail elderly to live longer in their own home, thereby lessening the financial burden involved in maintaining costly institutions. In the beginning there seemed a broad consensus that this was a good strategy, and the leading politicians understood this as a "go" signal. However, after a while, the opposition gained ground and become serious. The mayor, who took the lead in the fronting the plan, argued that his own party, the Labor Party, as well as the municipal health and welfare committee, had already committed to the plan and could not reverse the process. The opposition, which consisted of several backbenchers in his own party and a considerable number of party members—as well as parts of their networks in local voluntary associations—was provoked by the major's conclusion that no further discussion was necessary and stirred to angry protest. In my understanding, the hostility generated in party meetings was unprecedented, and the public meetings that were held to enlighten the public ended up as failures. The one meeting I attended got completely out of hand, and both the leading politicians and the attending bureaucrats were almost literally thrown out of the building and accused of being arrogant. The conflict kept escalating further for a while, but after a couple of months, a compromise was achieved. Most elements in the plan were kept, but the transition from institutional to home-based care was to be slower and less radical.

Three years later, I carried out a similar ethnographic study of the nearby town of Skien, with a population numbering 50,000. I attended the meetings of the municipal health and welfare committee on a regular basis, and experienced a sudden change in strategy and atmosphere when, during the annual budget negotiation phase in the early fall, the municipal council ruled that a serious cutback in health care was needed. The health and welfare committee, which included representatives from all political parties, decided—after a short spontaneous, preparatory meeting—that they would completely reject the council's ruling. In the committee leader's words, they prepared themselves to "oppose elite politicians in all parties". In the meeting they passionately argued that their loyalty was with "the weak groups in our society", and that the formal obligation to follow the council's decision (and to label such blind loyalty "responsibility") would be morally wrong. The "rebellion" among the representatives in the health and welfare committee was, however, not very successful. Later that fall, the municipal assembly confirmed the council's decision and the committee members lost their case. Yet the case they raised did have some more lasting effects: it was not only an isolated instance of emotional ecstasy, but an index of something more profound. As I experienced during this process and later, the rebellion mobilized not only the committee members, but also certain bureaucrats, backbenchers in the assembly, local branches of several political parties, as well as user groups. For a number of reasons, this type of alliance proved more efficient in other instances, and in some cases efficient enough to situationally undermine the local elites.

Over the last three decades, Norwegian municipalities have been subject to a very strong pressure to increase efficiency, and the emphasis has been on budget control, leadership, loyalty, and, more generally, the neoliberal urge to distinguish as clearly as possible between ordering and delivering functions (in part to clear the way for privatization) (Christensen and Lægreid 2011; Mydske 2011). Clearly, from a managerial perspective, this has made the municipalities less messy and at the same time much more unambiguously hierarchical. In hindsight, I realize more clearly that the horizontal alliances I observed when conducting my ethnographic work in the 1990s and early 2000s could be understood as a foundational aspect of this type of institution—one that is perhaps best characterized by its *porous boundaries*. Politicians, employees, and civil society organizations (users' organizations especially) have been able to mobilize networks beyond these boundaries. Thus, to the extent that egalitarianism is an aspect of this, it seems to have to do with how the institutional infrastructure of the local "state" makes it possible to craft alliances that cut across and influence not only policy as such, but also the way hierarchically derived power is allowed to work. The phenomenon seems very much like what Christian Lo in Chap. 7 in this volume calls "pragmatic policy alliances". As Maja Hojer Bruun's Chap. 6 in this volume indicates, recent changes in state policies in Scandinavia (non-ironically often labeled "liberalization") may be interpreted as involving a gradual seizure of collective resources from trust networks (in Tilly's sense), thus eroding their control. My case may illustrate that Norwegian elites have been less successful in this pursuit than has been the case in Denmark.

One useful analytical strategy for understanding the kind of embeddedness I have in mind here is Fredrik Barth's classic discussion of political leadership in Swat (Barth 1959). Barth looked at the phenomenon of cross-cutting ties and its implications for political power and conflict—the same problem that concerned Max Gluckman in "The peace in the feud" (Gluckman 1955). In the Swat Pathan case, patrilineal descent may ideologically serve as the paramount principle of loyalty, but in reality, other interests—and the alliances such interests may generate—challenge and in turn modify it. There is, however, an important limitation involved: the hierarchical social order of Swat society is not transformed by this dynamic, even though political relations among the elite may be shifting and "anarchic". In the Norwegian case, by contrast, it seems that the social and political control made possible by cross-cutting ties at the grassroots level may be extended upwards, at least to some extent.

In my research on local politics, I have observed that overlapping membership and cross-cutting cleavages not only tend to make conflicts unpredictable; they also make it difficult to "manage" oppositional policy alliances and keep them firmly within the institutional boundaries ultimately controlled by bureaucratic and political elites, the authority of which rests on loyalty. Subordinates may both have good professional arguments (anchored in the universalist rhetoric of the central state) and find allies in various camps, which, together, in turn may influence political decisions through majority votes and undermine the authority of leaders. Also, this mechanism seems to have given rise to what we may call a culture of negotiation; one that often effectively penetrates and challenges the boundaries between bureaucracy, politics, and civil society. The cultural pattern emerging from this dynamic has three key elements. First, the application of bureaucratic rules easily becomes politicized and requires negotiations, depending on the degree and nature of political mobilization. Second, political leaders have to be very careful about stretching their mandate, and administrative leaders often need to check out what their employees think, as the latter sometimes ally themselves with politicians and voluntary organizations that have a stake in a given policy. Third, bureaucratic formalities may mediate interests, facilitate negotiation, and be influenced by political mobilization, rather than simply be followed. In sum: rules, mandates, and roles must be interpreted, and the question is what type of political context—formal and informal—facilitates or undermines (or serves to deny) this process.

Conclusion

In Chap. 4 in this volume, Simone Abram argues that narratives of Norwegian modernization tend to highlight social harmony, thus—intentionally or not—presenting a picture that makes it seem as though a certain deep-seated cultural ethos has worked its way through history, as it were, and laid the foundation of a stable system glued together by trust and cooperation. In this chapter, I have argued that in the Norwegian political experiment and perhaps the Scandinavian one more generally, egalitarian practices seem to have emerged from conflict and tension.

When seen in this light, "trust" seems less like a strong and widely shared value than an outcome of a certain way of fighting political battles (Grimen 2009; Trägårdh 2007; Tilly 2005; Stenius 2010). Political mobilization often proved successful, in part because in most cases it recruited broadly across class divisions and represented cross-cutting cleavages and shifting alliances, and in part because most often neither the agenda nor the form of action taken was militant. The cases described in this chapter serve to illustrate that the largely peaceful transitions characterizing the political history of modern Scandinavia may not be that hard to explain in institutional terms. Traditional elites were generally rarely strong or unified enough to reject compromise wholesale. In particular, I have emphasized some of the ways in which such conflicts give rise to institutional tension within the state, or public sector in the broad sense, allowing alternative loyalties and resistance to become a real factor within public institutions and policy-making processes. In Scandinavia, state-governing elites have relied quite heavily on strategies of domestication by incorporating opposition into decision-making arenas, rather than keeping them at arm's length (Trägårdh 2007). Over time, this seems to have contributed significantly to institutionalizing cooperation, but also tension and conflict.

The principle of welfare state universalism may be understood in such terms. In Norway, and in Scandinavia in general, the struggle for democratic rights united people across class divisions, and the policies they fought to realize followed from it: for the most part they were oriented toward solutions that would unite them and help the recruitment of new members. Universalism as a principle was hardly motivated by a desire to establish "generous" welfare arrangements; it seemed rather to follow from what appeared logical from the point of view of local decision-making, where the Protestant outlook, property relations, way of life, and institutional structure made the self-help principle a practical option (Stenius 2010; Knudsen 2000). Providing assistance on a universal basis went hand in hand with the ambition and ability on the part of membership-based associations to educate and discipline their members. Moreover, universalism was sensitive to people's sense of dignity, easy to manage, compatible with the principle of low spending, and a useful mechanism for spreading risk, securing conformity, and mobilizing shared interest in protecting the common good. In political terms, universalism represents a system of social security that sewed the historical alliances between the labor movement and the parties representing the agrarian population. In fact, it also attracted the interest of the conservative parties, which sought to prevent the labor movement from appropriating welfare arrangements as an exclusive (and particularistic) property of the social democratic electorate, thus contributing to a broadening of the scope of universalism as a policy principle (Sejersted 2005).

Once universalized and needs-driven, the welfare state's great responsibilities in the field of service provision, which in Scandinavia largely rests on the municipalities, prove very hard to contain. Those who fight to protect and expand them have, for natural reasons, grown in numbers, and at the local level, they have access to key arenas in the municipal organization (political and administrative) and at its margins (voluntary associations, political parties). Welfare needs, which increasingly are moored in formal rights to services, tend to follow a self-propelling dynamic of expansion. The significance of a decentralized institutional system of decision-making and service provision is hard to overestimate when the state's responsibility is not clearly bounded; when the public tends to understand political parties' welfare-friendly rhetoric literally, and the bureaucratic chain of command may be overwhelmed by political mobilization. Indeed, in local politics, public services have become a common good of major importance, and the struggle to protect (and extend) them mobilizes party members from all camps.

In institutional terms, it may be interesting to note that although "civil society" in Scandinavia never existed as something separate from "the state" (the central state and the municipalities combined) (Trägårdh 2008), it had a profound effect on how welfare state arrangements were perceived. Both local politicians and the welfare professions have tended to see themselves as representatives not simply of the state, but also of voluntary associations and the forms of reciprocity that characterize them—as I have tried to illuminate in my discussion of membership as a social metaphor. This constitutes one important source of the institutional tension described above; a tension that may explain why, in Scandinavia, "the state" is rarely viewed as an authoritarian or paternalist big brother. For most people, the "double identity" that has characterized local politicians and service providers has helped enable those receiving services to negotiate their form and content.

The Scandinavian welfare state has been extraordinarily service-intensive, and "grassroots bureaucrats" and local politicians enjoyed relative autonomy during the great expansion that took place between the 1960s and the 1990s. Most importantly, perhaps, the key (municipal) decision-making arenas have been unusually close to the receiving end of welfare provision. In this chapter, I have tried to indicate that institutional arrangements of this kind may be, at least in part, an unintended consequence of the force, form, and influence that large-scale political mobilizations from below have had in modern Norwegian political history. It may represent a slightly different route to "get to Denmark", and an illustration of how trust networks (Tilly 2005) can prevent conventional chains of command within the state apparatus from seizing hegemonic status.

REFERENCES

Barnes, John. 1954. Class and committees in a Norwegian island parish. *Human Relations* 7 (1): 39–58.
Barth, Fredrik. 1959. *Political leadership among Swat Pathans*. London: Athlone Press.
Berntsen, Harald. 2014. Det røde fylket. In *Telemarks historie*, ed. Olav Rovde et al., vol. 3, 197–217. Bergen: Fagbokforlaget.
Brox, Ottar. 1966. *Hva skjer i Nord-Norge? En studie i norsk utkantpolitikk*. Oslo: Pax.
Christensen, Tom, and Per Lægreid. 2011. *New public management: The transformation of ideas and practice*. Hampshire: Ashgate Publishing Limited.
Dørum, Knut. 2010. Opprør eller legitim politisk praksis? Kommunalisme og folkelige aksjoner i Norge ca. 1700–1850. In *Demokratisk teori og historisk praksis. Forutsetninger for folkestyre 1750–1850*, ed. Hilde Sandvik, 71–105. Oslo: Spartacus.
Dyrvik, Ståle. 1979. *Norsk økonomisk historie 1500–1970*. Vol. 1, 1500–1850. Bergen: Universitetsforlaget.
Dyrvik, Ståle, and Ole Feldbæk. 1996. Mellom brødre 1780–1830. In *Norges historie*, ed. Knut Helle, vol. 7. Oslo: Aschehoug.
Fiskaa, Ingrid. 2012. Lofthusreisinga i Agder og Telemark 1786–87. In *Opptøyer i Norge 1750–1850*, ed. Knut Dørum and Hilde Sandvik. Oslo: Spartacus.
Fukuyama, Francis. 2011. *The origin of political order. From prehuman times to the French revolution*. New York: Farrar, Strauss, and Giroux.
Gluckman, Max. 1955. The peace in the feud. *Past and Present* 8 (1): 1–14.
Graubard, Stephen R. 1986. *Norden: The passion for equality*. Oslo: Norwegian University Press.
Grimen, Harald. 2009. *Hva er tillit?* Oslo: Universitetsforlaget.
Grytten, Ola. 2013. The protestant ethic and the spirit of capitalism: Entrepreneurship of the Norwegian puritan leader Hans Nielsen Hauge. *Review of European Studies* 5 (1): 31–44.

Kaspersen, Lars Bo, and Laila Ottesen. 2001. Associationalism for 150 years and still alive and kicking: Some reflections on Danish civil society. *Critical Review of International and Political Philosophy* 4 (1): 105–130.

Kjeldstadli, Knut. 1994. Et splittet samfunn. In *Norges historie*, ed. Knut Helle, vol. 10. Oslo: Aschehoug.

Knudsen, Tim. 2000. Indledning. In *Den nordiske protestantisme og velfærdsstaten*, 7–20. Aarhus: Aarhus Universitetsforlag.

Knudsen, Tim, and Bo Rothstein. 1994. State building in Scandinavia. *Comparative Politics* 26 (2): 203–220.

Mydske, Per Kristen. 2011. Book review of *New public management: The transformation of ideas and practice*, ed. Tom Christensen and Per Lægreid (2011). *Norsk Statsvitenskapelig Tidsskrift* 27 (4): 253–256.

Njåstad, Magne. 2003. *Grenser for makt. Konflikter og konfliktløsning mellom lokalsamfunn øvrighet ca. 1300–1540*. Trondheim: Institutt for historie og klassiske fag, NTNU.

Østergård, Uffe. 1992. *Europas ansigter. Nationale stater og politiske kulturer i en ny, gammel verden*. København: Rosinante.

Østerud, Øyvind. 1978. *Peasant politics in Scandinavia. A comparative study of rural response to economic change*. Oslo: Universitetsforlaget.

Piattoni, Simona, ed. 2003. *Clientelism, interests, and democratic representation. The European experience in historical and comparative perspective*. Cambridge: Cambridge University Press.

Sejersted, Francis. 2003. *Opposisjon og posisjon. Høyres historie 1945–1981*. Oslo: Cappelen.

———. 2005. *Sosialdemokratiets tidsalder: Norge og Sverige i det 20. århundre*. Oslo: Pax.

Skirbekk, Gunnar. 2010. *Norsk og moderne*. Oslo: Res Publica.

Solheim, Jorun. 2016. Bringing it all back home—familien som generativ kulturell formasjon i det moderne. *Norsk Antropologisk Tidsskrift* 27 (1): 7–21.

Sørensen, Øystein, and Bo Stråth, eds. 1997. *The cultural construction of Norden*. Oslo: Scandinavian University Press.

Stenius, Henrik. 2010. Nordic associational life in a European and an inter-Nordic perspective. In *Nordic associations in a European perspective*, ed. Henrik Stenius and Risto Alapuro. Baden-Baden: Nomos.

Stråth, Bo. 2005. *Union og demokrati—dei sameinte rika Norge-Sverige 1814–1905*. Oslo: Pax.

Teigen, Håvard. 2006. Bønder flest er ikkje forretningsmenn? *Historisk Tidsskrift* 83 (1): 107–120.

Tilly, Charles. 1990. *Coercion, capital and European states, A. D. 990–1990*. Cambridge/New York: Cambridge University Press.

———. 2005. *Trust and rule*. Cambridge/New York: Cambridge University Press.

Titlestad, Torgrim. 2016. *Vikingtid: Motstandsrett og folkestyre.* Stavanger: Saga Bok.
Trägårdh, Lars, ed. 2007. The "civil society" debate in Sweden: The welfare state challenged. In *State and civil society in northern Europe. The Swedish model reconsidered.* New York/Oxford: Berghahn Books.
———. 2008. Det civila samhällets karriär som vetenskapligt och politiskt begrepp i Sverige. *Tidsskrift for Samfunnsforskning* 49 (4): 575–594.
Vike, Halvard. 1991. *Contested signs: Political discourse in a Norwegian industrial community.* Universitetet i Oslo, Sosialantropologisk institutt.
———. 1996. *Conquering the unreal: Politics and bureaucracy in a Norwegian town.* Universitetet i Oslo, Sosialantropologisk institutt.
———. 1997. Reform and resistance. A Norwegian illustration. In *Anthropology of policy: Critical perspectives on governance and power*, ed. Cris Shore and Susan Wright. London: Routledge.
———. 2012. Varianter av vest-europeiske statsformasjoner—Utkast til en historisk antropologi. *Norsk Antropologisk Tidsskrift* 23 (2): 126–142.
———. 2015. Likhetens natur. *Norsk Antropologisk Tidsskrift* 25 (1): 7–21.

CHAPTER 6

Social Imaginaries and Egalitarian Practices in the Era of Neoliberalization

Maja Hojer Bruun

INTRODUCTION

There are several different meanings of equality in the ethnography of Scandinavia. Vike et al. (2001) state that one important distinction in the different understandings of equality is between equality as a regulating principle for political institutions and equality as a premise for social interaction. In the former, equality refers to social and political equality as a political principle for equal rights and equal access to social and economic goods and services in society, and in this sense equality is the opposite of inequality (*ulighed* in Danish, *ulikhet* in Norwegian and *ojämlikhet* in Swedish). This meaning of equality is generally linked to the Scandinavian universalist welfare states that have developed since World War II. The other understanding of equality, which anthropologists have emphasized, refers to similarity or sameness as the opposite of difference (*forskel, forskellighed*). This is the crux of Gullestad's (1992) theory of "equality as sameness", according to which people emphasize similarities in their social interaction, suppress differences, and seek conformity, or, alternatively, create distance or "symbolic fences".

M.H. Bruun (✉)
Department of Learning and Philosophy, Aalborg University, Aalborg, Denmark

© The Author(s) 2018
S. Bendixsen et al. (eds.), *Egalitarianism in Scandinavia*, Approaches to Social Inequality and Difference, DOI 10.1007/978-3-319-59791-1_6

Several anthropological and ethnological studies have linked these two main understandings of equality and exposed how the political ideal and regulating principles of equality in Scandinavian welfare states are connected to norms of sameness and cultural conformity: Löfgren (1987) has pointed out how the middle-class way of life and consumption patterns came to represent normality during the formation of the modern Swedish welfare state. Gullestad (1984) and Ekman (1991) have emphasized that even though there may be actual social differences and inequalities among social classes, people identify themselves and their fellow citizens as the "same kind of people", and feeling superior or of a higher class than others is socially prohibited. Gullestad (2006) and Jöhncke (2011) show how welfare state institutions that are built on equality as similarity and cultural homogeneity lead to other kinds of exclusions, e.g., of immigrants. Bruun et al. (2011) argue that equality in social interaction and other forms of sociality are models of and models for Danish society at a larger scale. They show that people's concern for certain forms of sociality—not only equality but also spaciousness (*rummelighed*), cosiness (*hygge*), community (*fællesskab*) and other valued forms of sociality—reflect a relationship of imitation and identification between sociality enacted in smaller groups (e.g., families and communities) and emic conceptions of society.

According to Taylor (2002), "society" as a social imaginary and powerful understanding of the social order is one of the key figures of modernity. Taylor and other political philosophers tend to speak about Western modernity as a unified concept, but some admit the existence of alternative or multiple modernities (Eisenstadt 2000), indicating that non-Western cultures have modernized in different ways, with their own divergent social imaginaries. In line with this anthology's exploration of the Nordic or Scandinavian version of modernity, this chapter investigates the relationship between social imaginaries of the modern Scandinavian welfare society, governing practices and everyday sociality in local welfare institutions, in particular, in Danish cooperative housing associations.[1] In housing cooperatives, equality is both a regulating principle and sought in social interaction among members in the housing communities, and the local community is imagined as an instance of modern Danish society (Bruun 2011). The chapter discusses what happens with such egalitarian governance principles, social practices, and social imaginaries in a time of neoliberal reforms when the cooperatives' community economies are opening up for commodification and financialization. Thus, it is an ethnography of a new era. Many ethnographic studies of Scandinavian societies have shown how equality and egalitarianism are configured and the effects of these configurations. The present study leaves the impression that equality and egalitarianism are potentially fragile and reliant on particular social, political and institutional arrangements that may be rearranged. In that sense, egalitarianism as found in Danish cooperatives and associations, whether in housing cooperatives or other similar civic associations, may also be seen as an emergent property of particular institutional arrangements that are about to change (see Introduction, Chap. 1, in this volume).

The egalitarianism and universalism of modern Scandinavian welfare institutions are not restricted to *state* institutions. Before the incorporation of the welfare state, many social needs were met by the labor movement, the cooperative movement, and other social movements that were built on egalitarian principles, and these organizations either continued parallel to welfare state institutions, intertwined with them, or became part of the welfare state's administration (cf. Papakostas 2001). Today still, there is a long tradition of different kinds of independent welfare institutions, e.g., free schools (*friskoler*), child daycare institutions, and housing associations that have explicit egalitarian ideals and provide services in the education, health, social, and housing sectors. The particular social movements that they have grown out of bind them together in larger interest groups that work together with and defend their interests against government and market actors, but they are also organized in a decentralized manner. In this chapter I show how the tendency toward decentralization and the so-called arm's length principle that also characterizes housing cooperatives make these organizations prone to neoliberal "change without reform". The universalistic and egalitarian cooperative principles as a non-codified political culture form the backdrop against everyday interaction and regulation in the housing cooperatives, but each cooperative's economy also has to be settled on an annual basis in the cooperatives' general assemblies. Here structural changes and the state's retraction from regulations of the housing and mortgage markets affect members' economic decisions and their long-term consequences. As Charles Tilly points out, "*when* things happen within a sequence affects *how* they happen" (Tilly 1984, in Papakostas 2001, 49, emphasis added). In a neoliberalizing economic order since the mid-2000s, apparently small changes in the Cooperative Housing Act spurred local cooperatives to follow the market, which may lead to unforeseen and yet quite fundamental changes in notions of equality over time.

Welfare services are provided by many different public and private, non-profit and for-profit organizations, e.g., third sector organizations that work for the profit of their members (cf. Alexander 2010). The practical and conceived boundaries between "the public sphere", "the market", "civil society", and other social forms that, according to Taylor (2002), characterize Western modernity and enable modern imaginaries of society are rather blurred in Scandinavia. Scandinavian citizens generally do not contrast "welfare society" and "the welfare state". They are integrated (Jöhncke 2011), and it is difficult to determine where one begins and the other ends. Richard Jenkins (2011, 199) even suggests that Danes see the state as their ever-watchful and interested but not necessarily interfering neighbor. Vike (2015a) argues that civil society as such barely exists in the Nordic countries. Most civil society associations never had the explicit goal of standing outside the state, and public goods are often managed collaboratively by civil society associations and municipalities, which have popular legitimacy independent of the central state agencies, even though they are an integrated part of the state's regulation and distribution politics.

Anthropological debates about egalitarianism and the welfare state in Scandinavia mainly focus on the nearly invisible boundary between civil society and the state. In an age of economic globalization and international neoliberalization, however, the boundary between civil society and the market is no less interesting. In this respect too we find a particular form of integration in Scandinavia, one where the welfare state and civil society institutions have built strong coalitions to regulate, and indeed create, markets, notably the labor market, but also, as discussed in this chapter, by way of the example of cooperative housing, the housing market. The modern Scandinavian welfare state builds on a powerful social imaginary of socio-economic integration where the state balances the market through de-commodification and where households, markets, the state, and civil society institutions work together as an organic whole. These forms of integration both exist at the national level and, as I will show, at the smaller social scale of communities such as cooperative housing associations.

In the following sections, I show how the Danish welfare state has adopted an association-based model for social housing that was originally developed by the cooperative housing movement. The welfare state's universalism in its housing provision was based, at least in the first post-war decades

before the mass construction of privately-owned, single-family houses set in, on the de-commodification of social housing that was owned by housing associations and not by the state or municipalities. Later, private housing cooperatives consolidated as third sector housing with a particular mix of collective ownership, do-it-yourself management and the cooperative ideology. The fact that members own shares of the collective property has, however, been lying low the whole time as a potential for the recommodification of cooperative flats. This process started in the 2000s with the introduction of market-orientation and mortgage-liberalization at a time of general economic boom and boom in the housing market. The chapter also offers a discussion of neoliberalization in its Danish variant, based on political scientist Ove K. Pedersen's influential book, *The Competition State* (2011). In the chapter's next sections I analyze recent developments in two particular cooperatives in the era of necliberalization, and in the conclusion I gather up the threads of this story.

HOUSING FOR ALL

Housing is one of the main welfare services that European welfare states provide for their citizens, along with education, health care, and pensions. In Denmark, the Social Reform Act of 1933 that laid the groundwork for different welfare institutions not only included retirement pensions and unemployment and sickness benefits but also public subsidies for social housing construction and the development of social housing associations (Vestergaard 2004). As distinct from the other main welfare services of education, health care, and pensions, nobody expects that housing should be provided for free or financed through the general tax system; citizens buy or rent their dwellings in a housing market, and tenants, even in social housing, pay rents. The welfare state's housing policy guarantees citizens a right to housing, but the capitalist welfare state relies heavily on the market and a range of private and public organizations that have developed over a long time to make good quality and affordable housing available for all (Bengtsson 2001).

In the period leading up to the Social Reform Act in 1933, a range of non-state actors were involved in the social housing movement. The first attempts to improve the housing conditions in the industrializing cities and towns in the period between 1850 and World War I came from a mix of philanthropic projects, mutual building societies, and cooperative associations (Bro 2009). The first social housing initiative in Denmark was the medical association's semi-detached houses with small gardens built with the capital that was left over from the relief funds that the medical association had disposed of during the cholera epidemic in Copenhagen in the 1850s. In the following decades more affluent workers joined the wave of new building societies that received state and municipality loans on the principle of self-help. These building societies were dissolved and the members became individual private owners when they had paid off their loans. By the way, these former building societies' row houses are among the most attractive, and expensive, dwellings in Copenhagen today. In 1912, the first non-profit cooperative housing associations were established as a speculation-free alternative to the building societies. Here the ownership of the property remained collective. Members only held a share of the building and got use-rights to their dwellings.

The Social Reform Act of 1933 was a compromise between the Social Democratic Party and the liberal parties, and unlike Sweden, where the local council owns social housing, an association-based and market-based model was adopted (Larsen and Hansen 2015). The labor movement demanded that housing construction be a municipal responsibility and had for a long time been skeptical of housing associations, but with the new political settlement, housing associations on the edge of the market and the state became a compromise. After the Social Reform Act, housing associations developed in two different directions: (1) non-profit housing associations (*almene boligorganisationer*) received direct economic support from the state and were regulated by social housing politics. Capital savings are placed in a trust and reserved for new housing construction. In the non-profit housing associations, residents are tenants of their association, yet with a strong tradition of participatory democracy; (2) autonomous private housing cooperatives (*andelsboliger*) continued to be governed in a decentralized manner by the local cooperatives' members through general assemblies and local bylaws (since 1972 also by the Cooperative Housing Act).[2] In the cooperatives that are the subject of this chapter, residents are members of cooperative association and own a share of the association's common property. The housing cooperatives became decentralized self-governing communities that work for the benefit of their members, but they also, through the cooperative ideology and the Cooperative Housing Act, are connected to egalitarian principles of governance, and many members saw themselves as guardians of a common good in Danish society (Bruun 2015). Thus, social housing in the Danish welfare state has never been state-owned but owned and regulated by local associations, and the rationality of these institutions (cf. Eriksen and Loftager 1996) draws strongly on organizations that developed outside the state.

Universality in the Scandinavian welfare model means that welfare benefits are for *all*, not just for those in need, as in the liberal welfare model, or for those who have saved up for them, as in the corporate welfare model (Esping-Andersen 1990). The principle of universality and the Scandinavian notion of egalitarian individualism (Gullestad 1992) are interlinked, in that everybody is treated equally/the same. In principle, there is no difference or hierarchy between those who give and those who receive, and it is not stigmatizing to receive benefits because everybody pays taxes, even people with very low incomes, and everybody receives free education, health care, and basic public pensions, even those with very high incomes. In the case of housing, universality means that the welfare state's housing policies are not only directed towards the poor but the whole population. There is no separate housing market for social housing, and, thanks to rent regulation, only a limited difference between the rent level in private rental housing and social rental housing. The social housing associations bear the telling name *almene boliger* (common housing), and, in principle, all types of households should be able to live in all types of housing, including all three types of tenure: owner-occupied housing, rental housing and cooperative housing (N. Nielsen 2010b). In spite of the universal access to social housing, there is, in fact, a significant income difference between those who live in owner-occupied housing and those who live in social housing, and the standard and sizes of dwellings are also different (Kristensen 2007).

Inspired by the work of Karl Polanyi, Esping-Andersen (1990) regarded the extension of social rights in different types of welfare states as a question of the state's capacity for "de-commodification", that is the degree to which people are permitted to maintain their living standards independent of market forces. Through de-commodification, the welfare state released people from relations of dependency in markets and contributed to their personal autonomy (Vike 2015b). Vike reminds us that universalistic welfare policies are linked to notions of egalitarianism, personal autonomy, and people's personal freedom to participate in government and gain access to resources for their livelihood, and that freedom and autonomy are achieved through state and collective solutions, contrary to what is assumed in liberal theories of state-citizen relations (see also the Introduction, Chap. 1, in this volume). Welfare institutions do, however, also create and institutionalize new forms of personal dependency and stratification (Esping-Andersen 1990; Vike 2015a). In the context of housing cooperatives, it is interesting that cooperative communities as collectives struggle for self-governance and autonomy both in relation to the market (they offer alternatives to private, profit-seeking landlords) and the state (they dissociate from municipalities and the public administration, often spoken about as "the system"). At the same time, members seek independence and a room to maneuver free from the interpersonal relations within the cooperative associations.

Esping-Andersen largely based his welfare regime typology on the analysis of social security and pension systems, which allow workers to opt out of the labor market to some degree. He did not take the de-commodification of other welfare services such as health, education, and housing into account, but many of these welfare services were de-commodified in the Scandinavian welfare states too. The welfare state not only de-commodified different welfare services. It also created its own markets, not in the free market sense but in the Polanyian sense where markets constitute the means for the allocation of different needs for livelihood and must be seen as subordinate to larger social goals. The most prominent example is the labor market where employers' organizations and unions enter into voluntary agreements. The housing market does not have the same partners and unions as the labor market, but as we shall see in the example of two housing cooperatives, the housing market is also created through different agreements. Yet, the past 15 years have witnessed a recommodification of housing.

Two Cooperatives

In the following I want to draw on two particular housing cooperatives in Copenhagen that I have chosen to call AB Svanebo and AB Freja.[3] Both are located in the neighborhood of Nørrebro,[4] but, as we will see, their size, history, and composition of residents differ. Each in their own way is an example of how housing cooperatives are governed locally, the kinds of control produced, and the moral dilemmas that exist in cooperatives.

In 1975, the cooperative housing scheme was revived. Tenants received the right of first refusal when landlords in private rental housing estates put their properties up for sale, and the majority of tenants could form a housing cooperative and buy their estate at the market price.[5] In the following years, many cooperatives were established in existing buildings as an alternative to privately owned rental housing. In 1981, a group of tenants established the small cooperative AB Svanebo with 18 flats in Nørrebro. The municipal authorities had scheduled the six-storied apartment building for a comprehensive renovation as part of the Urban Renewal Act, but the owner of the building, like so many other private landlords at that time, did not have the capital to enter into a large construction project. So the building could either be bought by one of the municipality's provisional urban renewal companies, or the tenants could take over the building as a housing cooperative. Though most of the tenants were against the Urban Renewal Act in general, they feared that their rents would rise and decided to buy their building, so that they could "steer the urban renewal themselves" and become "the masters in their own house". In 2009, I interviewed one of the original members, Niels, who was a squatter before he rented an apartment in the building in the 1970s, became one of the founding members of the cooperative and still lived there, and he told me:

> We were really eager to take over the house, you know. This thought that this is *our* house and that we decide on our own! And of course we knew that it was a lot of responsibility too, because we have to make sure that the house is maintained properly. Moreover, we chose to manage the house on our own and have done so since then [i.e., no professional firm to collect rents or do the annual accounts]. Not without problems I would say, but out of the idea of "why not?" We were very community-minded at that time, so why not take care of the house together, have work weekends, collect rents, and so on? And save something like, at that time, maybe twenty or thirty thousand crowns a year, which must be good for our economy? That was the main idea. To have a house together, and make sure it is good and cheap and that you are not dependent on some speculator who owns the estate, rents the flats and just makes those improvements that allow him to take more money from the tenants. Basically, it is about controlling our own house and not being controlled. It is about living in a communal way and supporting each other.

Other founding members confirmed the original idea of self-control and self-organization from the grassroots as an alternative to private ownership and central planning authorities. The new cooperative took care of the urban renewal project in their building and arranged many work parties, work weekends, and communal dinners for all members. The members insulated the roof and installed new bathrooms, windows, and central heating. In these work parties, all members participated according to their abilities and built an egalitarian sense of community (Bruun 2011).

Not far from AB Svanebo lies AB Freja with around 500 flats. The estate was originally built by the municipality in the 1920s, but in 1998 the municipality decided to sell off all its social housing estates as part of a large restructuring of the city, including further urban regeneration and gentrification (Larsen and Hansen 2008). An initiative group formed in the large rental estate, and after intense campaigning and canvassing, a majority of tenants decided to buy the estate and form a cooperative. Here too tenants feared that a "speculator" or "property shark" would buy their estate. The tenants' relations with public institutions were, however, more mixed here than in AB Svanebo: Many tenants received sick pensions or other welfare benefits, and most tenants got to rent their flats through the municipality's housing administration that allocated dwellings to homeless people, the mentally ill and others who had difficulties finding housing, including students who moved to the city from other parts of the country. Municipal housing was "at the bottom of the housing hierarchy", as a social worker explained to me, because the standard was very poor, typically no bathrooms and bad insulation (single glazing when double glazing was already standard) and sometimes no central heating. Those who received welfare benefits had no interest in joining the cooperative, because the value of their shares in the cooperative would be set off against their pensions. In this estate there were, however, so many students, activists and people with jobs that a majority signed up to become cooperative members, paid the relatively low deposit of 5–10,000 USD and the cooperative was established. The others stayed in the buildings as tenants of the cooperative, but when these tenants moved out, their flats would be sold as shares in the cooperative. In this way the many new cooperatives that were formed in the 1980s and 1990s in the old working-class neighborhoods of Copenhagen were introducing gentrification processes (cf. Larsen and Hansen 2015).

In both AB Svanebo and AB Freja, just as in all other housing cooperatives, the cooperative's highest authority is the general assembly of all members that convenes once a year. Each member has a vote, or rather: there is one vote per flat independent of the size of the flat or household. At these annual meetings the members pass the annual report, last year's accounts and the next year's budget. They discuss various issues of social life in the cooperative and elect the cooperative's executive board that manages the cooperative day-to-day. Importantly, the general assembly also settles on the prices of flats in the cooperative, that is shares (*andele*), and passes amendments to the statutes, such as rules about how flats are sold and new members recruited.

The share values, the so-called *andelskrone*,[6] became a hot topic in all housing cooperatives in Nørrebro in the end of the 1990s and the beginning of the 2000s, because urban regeneration had caused property values to go up in the whole city. In housing cooperatives, the general assembly each year has three different options on the basis of which they can calculate the value of their property: (1) the original purchase price when the cooperative was first established; (2) the latest valuation by the tax authorities, the so-called public property valuation; or (3) the market value of the property as assessed by a real estate appraiser. In principle, each autonomous housing cooperative can change its method for settling their property value each year. The value of individual shares value is arrived by dividing the associations' collective funds by the buildings square meters, not counting collective loans and savings for repairs.

In the 1980s and the 1990s, most housing cooperatives used the original purchase price or the public valuations to fix the value of their property and thus shares, in line with the original non-profit ideology of cooperative housing. By the end of 1990s and onward more and more often different members proposed to let a real estate appraiser assess the property. Such proposals usually came from members who had plans to move out and sell their shares and cash in a larger profit than the customary few percentage that the public valuation of the property usually increased. The proposals were routinely rejected by the majority of members who defended the existence of cheap cooperative flats in the city on moral grounds and also had friends or siblings on the cooperatives' waiting lists who wanted to get a cheap apartment. While the first camp provided evidence of the increasing property values and complained that they could not afford to buy other flats or a house for their family elsewhere due to the high prices in the general housing market, the other camp claimed the moral principles that "cooperatives should offer affordable dwelling for all" and "everybody should have the right to a cooperative flat".

These internal discussions in the cooperatives might have continued for ever if it had not been for a small amendment to the Cooperative Housing Act in 2005 that allowed members in all cooperatives to mortgage their individual shares. Previously, local cooperatives could forbid their members to use their individual shares as security for loans. This opportunity to raise cash based on the equity in individual shares further encouraged members to vote for a higher valuation, including all the members who wanted to stay in the cooperative. The discourse on home equity (Sjørslev 2012) was pervasive at that time, and many members of cooperatives asked why cashing in the equity should be reserved for private home-owners.

The amendment to the Cooperative Housing Act was a small part of the Liberal-Conservative government's neoliberal housing policy program entitled "More housing: growth and renewal on the housing market". One of the program's ten objectives was the "market-orientation of cooperative housing", which included the introduction of mortgaging of members' shares in housing cooperatives with the aim of opening and softening the market for cooperative housing flats. Another of the government's objectives was to introduce new mortgage products such as interest-only loans. When the amendments were introduced in 2005, housing prices rose further, adding to cooperative members' incentives to raise their share prices, which members spoke about as "following the market". Moreover, in 2004 and 2006, the tax authorities decided to regulate the public property valuations of cooperative housing estates and let them reflect the general housing market. The public valuation of housing cooperatives in the Copenhagen metropolitan area rose by an average of 55 percent in 2004 and 155 percent in 2006.[7]

The government presented the new housing policy in 2002 as a "retreat of the state". This way of introducing political reforms points to an important contradiction inherent in neoliberalism: "Neoliberal reform 'arrives' through state institutions yet as a commitment to dismantling the state in some respects (by delegation, deregulation, and privatization in particular)" (Greenhouse 2010, 5). The new housing policy course has been called "change without reform" (B. Nielsen 2010a) which is quintessential of neoliberalization, here in a distinct Danish or perhaps Scandinavian form.

THE DANISH VERSION OF NEOLIBERALISM

While the concept of neoliberalism as such is rarely used in the Danish public or political debate, in 2011, the Danish political scientist and Professor of Comparative Political Economy at Copenhagen Business School, Ove K. Pedersen published his book *Konkurrencestaten* [The Competition State], in which he describes *Konkurrencestaten* as the Danish version of a (neo)liberalizing welfare state. Pedersen argues that the central features of the welfare state are being dismantled and that Danish society is entering into a new episteme of discourses, norms and values, institutions, organizations, and forms of regulation that he calls the competition state and that supersedes the welfare state. The book and the concept of the competition state have had an enormous influence on Danish politics—to a degree where the concept was embraced by the Social Democratic Finance Minister—and has set the agenda for many political and social science debates about the ontology and the future of the welfare state (see also Bruun et al. 2015).

Critical social science research in Denmark has engaged with the cultural and sociological consequences of neoliberal policies in different parts of social life, often with reference to Pedersen's book, e.g., in the public school system (Bjerg and Vaaben 2015; Illeris 2014), in public administration (Kaspersen and Nørgaard 2015), and in processes of individualization as manifest in the increasing extension of psychiatric diagnoses (Brinkman and Pedersen 2015). I discuss another aspect of neoliberal change, namely, free market-orientation and financialization. The financialization of the economy is usually debated as a question of national and international economy (e.g., Pedersen 2011), but, especially since the global financial crisis in 2008, it has also been discussed as a matter of daily life and private economies (Martin 2002; Palomera 2014). I focus on the level of communities and how the public goods they hold are financialized and their cultural notions and practices of equality and egalitarianism change. Similar to the way Lana Gershon (2011) described how "liberal selves" own themselves as if persons were property and "neoliberal selves" invest in their own marketable capacities, so communities and their self-conception are changing in the direction of ownership, marketization, and economic investments.

Before discussing how the neoliberal reforms affected the two cooperatives, I want to draw attention to Pedersen's (2011) description of social imaginaries, because it resonates with ethnographic descriptions of Scandinavian societies. Pedersen outlines a particular social imaginary of society—he calls it the socio-economic imaginary (*Den samfundsøkonomiske forestilling*)—that developed and matured together with the welfare state and that is today developing into a new kind of economism, an economistic understanding of society in increasingly neoliberal terms. The socio-economic imaginary of the welfare state includes a "certain notion of society as an economic or organic whole where the decisions of households are believed to have consequences for the state's decisions and where the state, in turn, is obliged to create balance where the market forces cannot create balance" (Pedersen 2011, 18).[8] In many ways Pedersen's socio-economic imaginary of Danish society with its integrated whole and reciprocity between citizens, market forces, and state institutions resembles the images of society and the welfare state in ethnographies of

Denmark, for example, Steffen Jöhncke's (2011) notion of the "integrated Denmark", the popular image of the nation as an integrated whole tied together by solidaristic welfare services, except that Pedersen (2011) more explicitly emphasizes the economistic thinking in the way society is integrated.

According to Pedersen, the economistic socio-economic imaginary is a precondition for the particular ways in which neoliberal policies are adopted in the Danish competition state today. Political discourse emphasizes that households, the state, and the market, particularly the labor market, are integrated as a social whole of reciprocal relations and that neoliberal reforms are necessary to sustain a welfare society. For instance, the way in which the Liberal-Conservative government's cutbacks in unemployment benefits were justified in 2010 reflected that there is a social contract between citizens and the state, according to which individuals who are fit to participate in the labor market and provide for themselves are obliged to do so while the state is obliged to provide for those who are not fit (Pedersen 2014).

Following the Market

In AB Freja the general assembly decided to "follow the market" in Spring 2007 after the public property valuation had more than doubled from October 2005 to October 2006. The members debated heavily whether they should "follow the market" or not, and some members noted that this would change the composition of members and "break with the original founding statement that the cooperative should offer comparatively cheap dwellings" (quote from the minutes of the general assembly in 2007). Some raised the question how it would affect the private economy of members whose pensions would be deducted, because their share value increased so much, but this concern was overruled by others who argued that those affected could live off their equity. In the end, the majority voted for a price rise of the shares that was equivalent to 50 times the original deposits per square meter in 1998.

The commodification of cooperative flats means that the members of AB Freja today live under very differentiated economic conditions. Some of the old members have large equities and some of them, whose income depends on pensions, have to live off their equity. After the financial crisis in 2008 the housing market dropped in Copenhagen, and the cooperative had to reduce the share values, so that many of the new members who bought their shares during the boom became insolvent. This new economic inequality among the members in cooperatives is a new reality in many of the housing cooperatives in Copenhagen. It means that it is difficult for the cooperatives as collectives to vote for further costly improvements to their property. It has also puts a damper on the members' participation in work parties. Many young members told me they do not enjoy work parties that celebrate an egalitarian sense of community in the cooperative when in effect the members live under so different economic conditions.

The economy of cooperatives such as AB Freja has been financialized in the sense that their collective property has become the object for speculation and risk management (cf. Martin 2002). The boards of cooperatives increasingly require financial literacy to manage the cooperatives' economy and rely more and more on lawyers, banks, and property administration companies. Many cooperatives have re-structured their finances so that payments are deferred and they only pay the interest of their collective loans. When AB Freja had to change their roof, the cooperative took a large interest-only loan. This means that payments are deferred to future members of the cooperative. Many cooperatives now try to attract creditworthy members and try to "sell themselves" as communities. Thus, the "community spirit" has changed in character and does not only serve those who live in the cooperative but has also become an asset for the future that needs asset management. It also means that the cooperative community now no longer guards a valuable (public) good potentially for all Danish citizens, but rather manages shared risk and debt.

In AB Svanebo, the discussions of share prices and whether to follow the market or not took a slightly different turn during the era of the economic boom. They have much fewer members, and many of the original members had over the years recruited their close friends and relatives. Apart from a few outsiders, the cooperative was a close group who helped each other out and ran the cooperative almost like a household, including hierarchical relations among the members. The ideological universalist orientation of this cooperative had thus been weakened over the years. In public discourse, cooperatives like AB Svanebo were often accused of nepotism or favoritism and of exploiting the cooperative ideology for people's own benefits and not the good of society. Although the housing cooperatives that worked "like a family" in many ways were more hierarchically organized, they had other traits of egalitarianism that both members and observers valued, e.g., generalized reciprocity and demand-sharing (Bruun 2013). As Laville (2010) notes in a chapter entitled

"Solidarity Economy", civil society that works through interpersonal ties is often marked by inequality. He suggests that it is the role of the state to counter this tendency. The state "results from a universalist orientation, it guarantees social rights while establishing general rules and standardized procedures that correct inequalities, but also neglect the contribution of local relations" (Laville 2010, 234). In the case of housing cooperatives, the egalitarian principles of the cooperative ideology are not codified, and there is no tradition for relying on the state or legal system to secure democracy or equal access, so the state has never taken on this role.

In AB Svanebo, following the market has led to a loss of control of who gets to live in the cooperative, as friends and family members cannot necessarily afford the new high share prices. It has, however, led to new forms of *financial* social control within the cooperative community, because ordinary members can only obtain loans secured by their individual share values if the cooperative's board gives permission. In this way relations among the members in the housing communities have become financialized too. It has become increasingly difficult for the members to vote against the short-term economic interests of the majority of members, and the financial engagements of the whole cooperative with interest-only loans set out a path for the future and limit the decisions they can make. New notions of equality have appeared; now everybody who can afford it can buy a share in a cooperative and get an equal opportunity to "buy into a cooperative" (Bruun 2011). This reflects a liberal notion of equality, which is not foreign to the cooperative movement either, especially in rural cooperatives,[9] but runs counter to the way it has been practiced for some decades in urban housing cooperatives. It also goes against the notions of equality where all, rich or poor, should have equal access or where social equality is created through social interaction (Gullestad 1992, 197–198).

Conclusion

With the Social Reform Act in 1933 and the incorporation of the Danish welfare state, welfare institutions such as housing provision adopted principles and rationalities that had first developed outside the state in social movements and civil society associations. These movements and local associations had built welfare services as alternatives to the market in the *laissez-faire* state, many of them based on egalitarian and universalist principles, such as the cooperative principles. The private housing cooperatives that are central to this chapter were never fully integrated into the welfare state, but have existed parallel to and in symbiosis with welfare state institutions since the 1930s. Cooperative flats were in effect de-commodified and traded in special cooperative housing markets where prices were kept low and members could swap flats internally. The cooperatives regulated themselves in a decentralized manner, not primarily based on public laws but local statutes and traditions, and their economies were more or less closed, yet always affected by financial, housing, and urban policies. The cooperative ideology constituted an egalitarian social ethos, although the egalitarian and universalist cooperative ideology was undermined by interpersonal relations in some cooperatives. Democratic management structures together with work parties and other social events created a strong sense of community in the cooperatives.

Due to their decentralized economy and governance structure, and without detailed codification of the cooperative ideology, but with various possible notions of equality and egalitarianism that may weave together in new ways (see also Abram, Chap. 4, in this volume), the housing cooperatives were prone to recommodify, "follow the market" and practice other forms of equality when new neoliberal housing policies opened up to do that. When the cooperative principles were taken up at a time of neoliberalization and financialization in the mid-2000s, in the midst of a housing boom, this started a process of recommodification and social change in the cooperatives. The notion of egalitarianism is slowly changing in the cooperatives, as, for instance, equal access to cooperative housing now often means equal opportunity to buy an (expensive) share in a cooperative. Some cooperatives offer new models of society, because these are practiced as self-interested corporations that make collective investments and care for their collective asset, with occasional festive events and experiences of communitas, but no longer with the ideal of open, solidaristic, and redistributive communities.

The nearly invisible boundary and symbiosis between the state and civil society with parallel and intertwined welfare institutions that, since the establishment of the welfare state have been working with a similar rationality and political culture, has formally and legally not been violated with the introduction of neoliberal reforms in the cooperative housing sector. It may seem as if the state is still not colonizing or interfering directly in the housing cooperatives—but this image dissolves when the cooperatives' economies are taken into account and we look into the political economy of the social and cooperative housing sector. By leaving the economic development of the cooperatives to a housing market in flux and installing short-term interests for members, e.g., incentives to adopt the highest possible share prices, the state and central government are heading for a neoliberalized welfare state. This may be the beginning of social change in third sector housing and also put the particular forms of egalitarianism and universalism of these institutions at risk. If these institutions were once the model for (parts of) the modern welfare state, it seems that the welfare state has adopted new models and is slowly changing the foundation on which it rests. Just as the association-based and universalist housing policies were the result of a particular historical settlement between citizens, state, and capital, we may now see the beginnings of a new settlement with new forms of integration and new social imaginaries. If the wealth that local housing associations hold and guard is undermined by loans and interest payments in a financialized and neoliberalized housing economy, certain members or whole housing communities may be dispossessed, and individualized citizens may come to depend on the market, once again, or the state. Individualized citizens, no longer the collective owners of self-managed housing, may be portrayed as "receivers" of social welfare and enter into new relations of exchange with increasingly paternalistic state institutions.

Notes

1. The chapter is based on ethnographic and historical material from my fieldwork in Danish housing cooperatives in 2008–2011 as part of my PhD project (Bruun 2012) and several revisits with key informants in the years since then.
2. 20 percent of all dwellings in Denmark are owned by non-profit housing associations, 7 percent by cooperatives, 15 percent by private landlords and the rest are owner-occupied, either single-family houses or freehold flats (Kristensen 2007).
3. AB stands for cooperative association (*AndelsBoligforening*).
4. Nørrebro is one of the oldest working-class neighborhoods in Copenhagen, dating from the time of the industrialization when housing tenements were built outside the old medieval city's ramparts. Today, it is one of the districts with the highest percentage of cooperative housing in Copenhagen, 42 percent in 2016, according to the municipality's key figures: http://www.kk.dk/artikel/statistikbanken-0
5. Housing markets are subject to all kinds of regulation and are dependent on access to loan finance, infrastructure, zoning, and many more political

domains, so what constitutes the market price is highly complex and can be discussed from the perspective of the sociology of markets (Callon 1998).
6. The *andelskrone* is a development index of the members' pro rata shares of the whole cooperative and relates to the members' original deposits at the time of incorporation of the cooperative.
7. "Andelsboliger bliver mere værd", *Politiken*, 19 February 2007 and "Andelshavere er tilfredse med megaprisstigning", *Politiken*, 15 June 2007.
8. All translations in this chapter from Danish to English are by the author.
9. Space does not allow for an elaboration on this point, but one of the reasons why the cooperative association-based model was acceptable as a compromise in the 1933 Social Reform Act was the Danish cooperative movement's rural origins among free farmers and smallholders who were the backbone of the liberal parties in 1933. Today, farmers have lost power in the liberal parties to other businesses and industries, and the cooperative ideology has lost its broad political appeal in the Danish parliament. Interestingly, however, the cooperative ideology is reappearing in new social movements such as the sharing economy (Skytte 2016).

References

Alexander, Catherine. 2010. The third sector. In *The human economy*, ed. Keith Hart, Jean-Louis Laville, and Antonio David Cattani, 213–224. Cambridge: Polity Press.

Bengtsson, Bo. 2001. Housing as a social right: Implications for welfare state theory. *Scandinavian Political Studies* 24 (4): 255–275.

Bjerg, Helle, and Nana Vaaben, eds. 2015. *At lede efter læring: ledelse og organiseringer i den reformerede skole*. Frederiksberg: Samfundslitteratur.

Brinkmann, Svend, and Anders Pedersen, eds. 2015. *Diagnoser. Perspektiver, kritik og diskussion*. Aarhus: Klim.

Bro, Henning. 2009. Housing From night watchman state to welfare state. Danish housing policy, 1914–1930. *Scandinavian Journal of History* 34 (1): 2–28.

Bruun, Maja Hojer. 2011. Egalitarianism and community in Danish housing cooperatives. Proper forms of sharing and being together. *Social Analysis* 55 (2): 62–83.

———. 2012. *Social life and moral economies in Danish cooperative housing: Community, property and value*. PhD thesis, Department of Anthropology, University of Copenhagen, Copenhagen.

———. 2013. Som én stor familie: husfællesskab og slægtskab i danske andelsboligforeninger. In *Familie og slægtskab: Antropologiske perspektiver*, ed. Hanne O. Mogensen and Karen F. Olwig, 171–187. Frederiksberg: Samfundslitteratur.

———. 2015. Communities and the commons: Open access and community ownership of the urban commons. In *Urban commons: Rethinking the city*, ed. Christian Borch and Martin Kornberger, 153–170. London/New York: Routledge.

Bruun, Maja Hojer, Gry Skrædderdal Jakobsen, and Stine Krøijer. 2011. Introduction. The concern for cociality—Practicing equality and hierarchy in Denmark. *Social Analysis* 55 (2): 1–19.

Bruun, Maja Hojer, Stine Krøijer, and Mikkel Rytter. 2015. Indledende perspektiver: Forandringsstaten og selvstændighedssamfundet. *Tidsskriftet Antropologi* 72: 11–37.

Callon, Michel, ed. 1998. Introduction: The embeddedness of economic markets in economy. In *The laws of the markets*, 1–57. Oxford: Blackwell.

Eisenstadt, Shmuel N. 2000. Multiple modernities. *Dædalus* 129 (1): 1–29.

Ekman, Ann-Kristin. 1991. *Community, carnival and campaign. Expressions of belonging in a Swedish region*. Stockholm: Department of Social Anthropology.

Eriksen, Erik Oddvar, and Jørn Loftager. 1996. *The rationality of the welfare state*. Oslo: Scandinavian University Press.

Esping-Andersen, Gøsta. 1990. *The three worlds of welfare capitalism*. Cambridge: Polity Press.

Gershon, Ilana. 2011. Neoliberal agency. *Current Anthropology* 52 (4): 537–555.

Greenhouse, Carol J., ed. 2010. *Ethnographies of neoliberalism*. Philadelphia: University of Pennsylvania Press.

Gullestad, Marianne. 1984. *Kitchen-table society. A case-study of the family life and friendships of young working-class mothers in urban Norway*. Oslo: Universitetsforlaget.

———. 1992. The art of social relations. In *Essays on culture, social action and everyday life in modern Norway*. Oslo: Scandinavian University Press.

———. 2006. *Plausible prejudice. Everyday experiences and social images of nation, culture and race*. Oslo: Universitetsforlaget.

Illeris, Knud, ed. 2014. *Læring i konkurrencestaten*. Copenhagen: Samfundslitteratur.

Jenkins, Richard. 2011. *Being Danish – Paradoxes of identity in everyday life*. Copenhagen: Museum Tusculanum Press.

Jöhncke, Steffen. 2011. Integrating Denmark: The welfare state as a national(ist) accomplishment. In *The question of integration: Immigration, exclusion and the Danish welfare state*, ed. Karen F. Olwig and Karsten Pærregaard, 30–53. Newcastle upon Tyne: Cambridge Scholars Publishing.

Kaspersen, Lars Bo, and Jan Nørgaard. 2015. *Ledelseskrise i konkurrencestaten*. Copenhagen: Hans Reitzels Forlag.

Kristensen, Hans. 2007. *Housing in Denmark*. Copenhagen: Centre for Housing and Welfare.

Larsen, Henrik Gutzon, and Anders Lund Hansen. 2008. Gentrification—Gentle or traumatic? Urban renewal policies and socioeconomic transformations in Copenhagen. *Urban Studies* 45 (12): 2429–2448.

———. 2015. Commodifying Danish housing commons. *Geografiska Annaler B* 97 (3): 263–274.
Laville, Jean-Louis. 2010. Solidarity economy. In *The human economy*, ed. Keith Hart, Jean-Louis Laville, and Antonio David Cattani, 225–235. Cambridge: Polity Press.
Löfgren, Orvar. 1987. Deconstructing swedishness: Culture and class in modern Sweden. In *Anthropology at home*, ed. Anthony Jackson, 74–93. New York: Tavistock Publications.
Martin, Randy. 2002. *Financialization of daily life*. Philadelphia: Temple University Press.
Nielsen, Birgitta Gomez. 2010a. *The hidden politics of a haunted sector—Retrenchment in Danish housing policy 2001–2009*. PhD thesis, Department of Political Science, Faculty of Social Sciences, University of Copenhagen.
Nielsen, Nikolaj. 2010b. *Retten til et hjem—Ejendomsret, privatliv og forsørgelse*. PhD thesis, Faculty of Law, University of Copenhagen.
Palomera, Jamie. 2014. Reciprocity, commodification, and poverty in the era of financialization. *Current Anthropology* 55 (S9): S105–S115.
Papakostas, Apostolis. 2001. Why is there no clientelism in Scandinavia? A comparison of the Swedish and Greek sequences of development. In *Clientelism, interests, and democratic representation. The European experience in historical and comparative perspective*. ed. Simona Piattoni. Cambridge: Cambridge University Press.
Pedersen, Ove Kaj. 2011. *Konkurrencestaten*. Copenhagen: Hans Reitzels Forlag.
———. 2014. *Markedsstaten*. Copenhagen: Hans Reitzels Forlag.
Sjørslev, Inger. 2012. Cash the equity and realize yourself. An anthropological approach to house values. *Housing, Theory and Society* 29 (4): 382–400.
Skytte, Claus. 2016. *Den nye andelsbevægelse*. Copenhagen: Skytsengel.
Taylor, Charles. 2002. Modern social imaginaries. *Public Culture* 14 (1): 91–124.
Vestergaard, Hedvig. 2004. Boligpolitik i velfærdsstaten. In *Den danske velfærdsstats historie*, ed. Niels Ploug, Ingrid Henriksen, and Niels Kærgård, 260–287. Copenhagen: Socialforskningsinstituttet.
Vike, Halvard. 2015a. Likhetens natur. *Norsk Antropologisk Tidsskrift* 26 (1): 6–21.
———. 2015b. Forord: Antropologien og den skandinaviske velferdsstaten. *Tidsskriftet Antropologi* 2015 (72): 5–10.
Vike, Halvard, Hilde Lidén, and Marianne Lien. 2001. Likhetens virkeligheter. In *Likhetens paradokser. Antropologiske undersøkelser i det moderne Norge*, ed. Marianne Lien, Hilde Lidén, and Halvard Vike, 11–31. Oslo: Universitetsforlaget.

CHAPTER 7

Normative Hierarchy and Pragmatic Egalitarianism in Municipal Policy Development

Christian Lo

INTRODUCTION

Anthropological investigations in Norway have been particularly vigorous in demonstrating how Norwegian culture is highly influenced by the rural life-modes of its recent past (Gullestad 1989). This is particularly visible in descriptions of the political culture, where the construction of the Nordic democratic welfare states has assertively been understood as a generalization of the political culture of the "traditional" local peasant communities (Park 1998; Trägårdh 1997). A key topic of investigations into the political culture has been the seemingly egalitarian tradition in Norway (and other Nordic countries), and how its attached ideas of equality, sameness, and trust underpin the relative success of the modern welfare state (Sørensen and Stråth 1997; Vike 2013). While "egalitarian individualism" has been claimed to be a general characteristic of many "Western" societies, Marianne Gullestad's (1991) attempt to formulate the particularities of

C. Lo (✉)
Nordland Research Institute, Bodø, Norway

Faculty of Social Sciences, Nord University, Bodø, Norway

© The Author(s) 2018
S. Bendixsen et al. (eds.), *Egalitarianism in Scandinavia*,
Approaches to Social Inequality and Difference,
DOI 10.1007/978-3-319-59791-1_7

the Scandinavian configuration of this trait as "equality as sameness" has proven influential in the understanding of Norwegian culture.

Gullestad's perspective has, however, been subjected to critical reading and modifications in more recent literature (e.g., Bruun et al. 2011). One such recent modification originates from Halvard Vike (2013), whose criticism of Gullestad's notion of egalitarianism relates to her application of the private/public dichotomy in the understanding of "equality as sameness". Gullestad argues that egalitarianism is associated with the realm of home, the local community, and nature, while Norwegians associate public spheres such as the state and the market with hierarchy, formality, and impersonality (Gullestad 1991, 1992). Vike's point is that by making the "home" a shelter from the impersonal relations of the "modern" society, Gullestad fails to comprehend the interlinks between egalitarianism and the formalized relational forms associated with the state and public life. Thus, Vike (2013) argues that Gullestad's perspective is in need of modification, if it is to encompass the historical significance of formalized relations in the Nordic countries and their profound role in shaping the modern welfare state's institutions.

Vike's understanding of egalitarianism as a by-product of formalized relational forms is important, I argue, not only in understanding the particular configuration of *egalitarian individualism* found in the Nordic countries, but also in understanding the coexistence of seemingly contradictory notions of political legitimacy I found to characterize the practices of local government explored in this chapter. Drawing on F. G. Bailey's division between *normative* and *pragmatic* rules of political struggle, my notions of such coexistence originates from an exploration of how political and administrative personnel conceive their roles as actors in policy processes, and then juxtaposing their normative notions to empirical accounts of actions during political struggle. More than Bailey's (1969) depictions of normative rules bending as pragmatic rules proved successful in changing the playing field, I argue that the sense of pragmatism, displayed in the cases of policy development bellow, rests on a source of political legitimacy alternative to the hierarchical Weberian principles expressed as axiomatic by my informants in normative descriptions of their roles. The explored cases of policy development are therefore characterized by a balancing act between the legitimacy drawn from the hierarchical command chain of the municipal organization and more pragmatic policy alliances which, I argue, operate within and reproduce a sense of egalitarian-rooted pragmatism.

The findings presented in this chapter are based on ethnographic fieldworks conducted among administrators and local politicians in two neighboring municipal organizations, each being among the 50% of Norwegian municipalities inhabiting less than 5000 people.

The *Village* and the *State* as Sources of Political Legitimacy

As noted in the Introduction, Chap. 1, in this volume, the observation of a seemingly egalitarian tradition informing the enactment of local government is salient in one of the earliest ethnographic accounts from Norway, namely, John Barnes's seminal paper "Class and committees in a Norwegian island parish" (Barnes 1954). Since then, the political practices deemed transitional by Barnes have, however, proved less endangered and far more resilient than what was originally anticipated. While the rule of part-time peasants may have been gradually replaced by a professional administrative machinery (Park 1998), the notions of equality and conformism expressed in Barnes's account remain salient in descriptions of political culture (see, particularly, Archetti 1984). As Trägårdh (1997) has argued, rather than generalizing noble or bourgeoisie privileges as in the building of many western democracies, the construction of modern democracy in Scandinavia can be seen as a process of generalizing the egalitarian political culture of the local peasant assembly.

Trägårdh's assertion provides a fitting explanation for Sørhaug's (1984) observation of two competing notions of political legitimacy coexisting in Norwegian public life. Sørhaug argues that political culture and the Norwegian self-image are highly influenced by the egalitarian and rural modes that he metaphorically characterizes as the social formations of the *village*.[1] This village, Sørhaug argues, is characterized by social proximity, stability, interwoven social relations, and, importantly, a fundamental idea of equality. The latter point does not imply that everybody actually regards each other as equal but, rather, a strict behavior code that emphasizes equality in the sense that no one is better than any other. Furthermore, leaning on Gluckman (1955) to understand the interactional forms associated with the *village*, Sørhaug argues that:

> The village is full of conflicts of which everyone are aware, and because of this it becomes unnatural and improper to speak of these directly, at least in public settings. Gossip therefore becomes an important element in the

social life of the village. The conflicts do not in any way threaten the existence of the village, because everybody "knows" that at the end of the day, everything is actually personal relations and affairs. (Sørhaug 1984, 64, my translation)

In this sense, social cohesion becomes a product of a range of activities and actions that the villagers are not necessarily aware actually contribute to maintaining the village, and leadership and social control become integral parts of actions and institutions that are simultaneously committed to other purposes.

Sørhaug contrasts this *logic of the village* to the *logic of the state*, with the latter operating in accordance to the legal-rational principles associated with the modern state. In contrast to the aggregated form of steering characterizing the *village*, the *state* is considered (and considers itself) a result of systematic and deliberate processes of governing. Furthermore, the state largely organizes power by separating it from the rest of the society. As the legitimacy of the state is derived from the totality of the society within its borders, legitimate administration of state power is dependent on barriers separating economic and political power. Both bureaucrats and politicians must, therefore, appear as independent from specific economic interests. Rather than the multiplex relations characterizing the village, the relations of the state must therefore remain factual, uniplex, and impersonal. While the contradicting logic of the *village* can undermine the logic producing the legitimacy of the *state*, Sørhaug demonstrates how the legitimacy of the village can also support the state; for example, by portraying structural problems as solvable by personal involvement (1984, 66).

In the following, I will discuss how this coexistence between the logic of the *village* is expressed in municipal policy development. First, however, I begin with a description of how the rational and universalistic logic of the *state* is expressed in normative descriptions of roles during political struggles in the municipal organization.

Normative Hierarchy

According to his proper vocation, the genuine official ... will not engage in politics. Rather, he should engage in impartial "administration". This also holds for the so-called "political" administrator, at least officially, in so far as the *raison d'état*, that is, the vital interests of the ruling order are not in question. *Sina ira et studio*, "without scorn and bias". He shall administer his office. Hence, he shall not do precisely what the politician, the leader as well as his following, must always and necessarily do, namely, *fight*. (Weber 1946 [1919], 95)

Weber's ideal-type description of the administrator is remarkably fitted to the occupational ethos among the municipal administrators who are the subjects of this study, conducted almost a century later. In a few cases my informants (many of whom held degrees in political science) would even refer to Weber themselves when describing their rules of conduct. But even those with no outspoken knowledge of Weber's work would describe the relation between politics and administration through principles matching Weber's emphasis on a hierarchical relationship, in which the rules of conduct within the two spheres are defined in hierarchical opposition to each other.

Particular normative emphasis was also given to the so-called "hourglass model", asserting that all contact between the administrative sphere and the political sphere should pass through the Chief Municipal Executive (CME), whose relation to the mayor represents the formal link between politics and administration within the municipal organization. All my informants within the municipal administration would affirm strict adherence to this principle of a chain of command rising through the municipal administration and passing through the CME before crossing the boundary into the political sphere, that is, to the mayor and municipal council. As explained by Frode, an administrator at the executive level, when I asked him why he chose to approach the CME, rather than the mayor, when promoting a suggestion for the municipality that required political treatment:

> No, it was natural for me to speak to the CME, it was not natural for me to speak with the mayor directly. Not in the line that I was within … particularly after [name of the mayor] became mayor. Me and him [the mayor], we have a pretty close; you can call it a friend and family relation. We both have [children], and have in a way had a relation for over 20 years. You know, celebrations, baptisms – in total a pretty close [relation]. Because of that, we have become extra observant and careful about what you can label as the differences between administration and politics. So everything that somehow relates to work, and the dialog with the political side, that's handled by [the CME].

Frode's account conforms not only to the normative ideal of a separation between the political sphere and the administrative sphere, but also to the hierarchical "hourglass" model linking the two spheres to the roles of the

CME and Mayor. However, the account also displays the impossibility of separating the political from the administrative sphere by abstaining from contact. In reality, politicians and administrators do, of course, interact in both the local community and within the municipal hall where politicians and administrators will often work closely together during policy processes. In this case, Frode was also known to retain a close personal relationship with the current mayor. The separation between politics and administration could, therefore, not rest on an absence of interaction but, rather, on rules of interaction in which the administrative actors refrained from obtaining political roles (and the politician refrained from obtaining administrative roles). Consequently, the administrator has to refrain from *doing politics*—"namely, *fight*".

While the general normative rule of administrators abstaining from political struggle was widely established, the exact implications of this rule—in essence, the specific content of doing politics—was a more debatable and less ossified matter. One offer of explanation originates from an interview with the CME in one of the studied municipalities:

> *CME*: You can relate it to a case, the process of a case. From it is conceived, to it is processed, proposed and carried out. Then there is a clear separation in time.
> *Researcher*: Process?
> *CME*: Yes, or time. As soon as the CME has provided its proposal, then the case has become politics. And then the CME and the administration will have to act in accordance to the decision that has been made, even if it is contrary to the recommendation of the administration – in an extreme case.

In the dialog above, the CME suggests a timely sequencing distinguishing the political decision-making and the administrative processing. A decision becomes the essential political act, and the administrator can orderly abstain from politics by not participating in the decision-making part of the process. In real life, this timely sequencing between decision-making and preparatory proceedings would, however, seldom be as clear-cut as in the CME's description. Indeed, political fights seemed an integral part of all stages of policy processes. A few days earlier, I had also accompanied the same CME and the municipality's mayor to a meeting in a collaborative forum where they met with their respective counterparts from their neighboring municipalities. During this meeting, one of the mayors present had raised a discussion on initiating a study to examine the possibility of merging municipalities in the area. The CME had then engaged in the discussion, but before presenting a view on the matter, had asked the meeting in a rhetorical manner, "I believe this to be politics, but do we [administrators] still have a right to speak?" I later asked the same CME why the particular topic was deemed as "political":

> *CME*: That's because, regardless, it would be the municipal council that defines what should be, and what should not be, subject. So, I can say yes to merging municipalities as much as I would like, but if the municipal council does not say that "now we are to merge one thing or the other" [nothing will happen]. The politics are at power there. And it's a very sensitive topic.
> *Researcher*: Is that a consideration?
> *CME*: It might be.
> *Researcher*: So the administration should not involve itself in matters that are [sensitive]?
> *CME*: It might be so. But, in our municipality there is a pretty high ceiling on that subject. I think I can say whatever I would like ... at this time in the municipal council. But it is not certain that it would be listened to. If you go too far, then ... But currently there is some rattling around that topic; municipal structure

In the above excerpt, the CME suggests that the matter of initiating a study of municipal mergers remains political as long as the municipal council has not made it an administrative "subject" and granted the administration any mandate in pursuing the matter. Furthermore, the CME also suggests that there is a circumstantial element in the assessment of a particular topic as belonging to the political sphere: it depends on the political sensitivity of the subject and to the "attitude" of the municipal council toward discussing the topic.

In other words, although administrators are responsible for facilitating political decisions, there are normative constraints to the extent to which administrators can propose new and possibly controversial initiatives, thereby introducing a *fight*.

The Paradoxes of Municipal Entrepreneurship

One common observation from my fieldwork, within municipal organizations, was the general difficulty of identifying the very beginning, and initiation, of any given policy process. While the spoken stories about past and present policy processes during lunch, coffee-breaks, and other public arenas in the municipal hall would often identify key actors, the exact origins of policy processes and accounts of how new ideas emerged in the municipal organization would usually be more diffuse. Access to clear statements about origins and personal motives behind municipal policy processes was, therefore, confined to more informal conversations and gossip. This observation, I argue, can partly be explained as a consequence of the paradoxical normative status of administrative entrepreneurship discussed above.

Another illustration of this point originates from another CME, that I have called "Jim". During an interview, Jim provided a rare and detailed narrative on the building of a, then controversial, centralization of his municipality's health care services into a single building, here labeled as the "Health and Service Center" (HSC). According to Jim, the process had started at a conference he attended with fellow CMEs in one of the larger regional cities. During an informal dinner, one of them had told the rest about how they were moving away from institutionally-based health and elderly care to a centralized model combining sheltered housing and nursing homes.

At the time, Jim argued, his municipality was maintaining a costly decentralized structure of such services. Jim therefore saw a need to pursue a more centralized structure, which he thought could be achieved through the model suggested to him by his fellow CME. However, Jim knew that he lacked political support from the current mayor to pursue such a project:

> In total, it was a decentralized structure, an expensive structure, and a very vulnerable structure. And we can clearly see today that we would not have been able to survive with that structure, and we would not have been able to uphold the necessary professional environment. That was the case. And we had a mayor that was not really interested in these matters.
>
> So I thought, to hell with it; should we not do something about this? ... We were running with huge deficits at the time, particularly in the fields of health and nursing. And then the state also launched some of those carrots. They were giving grants directed at building nursing homes.

Seeing the possibility of improving running costs through investments that could partially be sponsored by the state, Jim decided to pursue the matter further even without support from his mayor. However, expecting that the process would be controversial, partly because of a strong general opposition against centralizing services in the municipality, Jim knew that he could not simply propose the matter to the municipal council:

> I understood that starting a process like this … this was a revolutionary thing … So I had to move carefully. I couldn't simply present a proposal suggesting to close everything, the whole damn thing, and build something new … That would never have worked.

This paradox has also been expressed in more general terms by Britan and Cohen, who argue that, "essential to a full understanding of organizational process is the degree of conflict among the rules, regulations, and sanctions governing an office (damned if you do, damned if you don't) and the degree of ambiguity in rules and goals" (Britan and Cohen 1980, 15). Such conflict and ambiguity create a bit of leeway that gives individual bureaucratic actors a variable degree of discretional power and, thus, freedom about how to carry out their duties. Britan and Cohen elaborate this tension between flexibility and discipline as follows:

> The more disciplined or predictable a bureaucracy is, the more it follows a strictly rational Weberian set of operations. However, rationality in this sense may also mean the organization is less flexible and less adaptive. Conversely, the greater the degree of unmonitored autonomy and freedom, the greater the possibility of corruption, incompetence and systematic dysfunction. (Britan and Cohen 1980, 15–16)

The example of the administrative entrepreneur strung between the choice of adherence to the Weberian ideals of loyalty and objectivity—in this case abstaining from political fight—and introducing new and innovative policy suggestions fits well into the dilemma pinpointed by Britan and Cohen. By fronting a controversial policy suggestion, the administrative entrepreneur endangers the legitimacy of the municipal organization by demonstrating the administrative capacity for political agency, which suggests a less than objective administration and, ultimately, a democratic deficit. As the normative (ideal) portrayal of the administrator does not entail a political will or agency, the administrative entrepreneur will be understood as mixing personal political views with the administrative role, thereby carrying the corruptible personal being, burdened by personal loyalties and conflicts, into the office. By having its main protagonist suffer the loss of political legitimacy (for the administrator depending on abstaining from political fight), the policy process will, itself, ultimately be prone to failure.

According to this logic, mirroring the hierarchical logic of the state, the administrative entrepreneur must, rather than single-handedly introducing a controversial political fight, ensure that someone else introduces the fight, or at least somehow obscure its origins. In other words, the administrative entrepreneur will have to create a legitimate reason for pursuing a certain policy goal, particularly if such a goal risks becoming a politically controversial matter. Creating such a legitimate reason for pursuing a policy goal essentially entails creating a legitimate order to act upon for the loyal and objective administrator.

The latter, I believe, often entailed what some of my administrative informants would metaphorically refer to as *planting a seed*. One common way of achieving such planting, was through arranging *open meetings* discussing possible controversial subjects. Returning again to Jim's recollection of the HSC, Jim himself described his first step in initiating the process as the *planting of a seed*.

> *Researcher:* What do you mean by planting a seed?
> *Jim:* Like we did at that brainstorming meeting, or whatever we should call it. I remember one of the head nurses came over to us and said: "This, this sounds very clever."

In his attempt to gain support for the project, Jim's first step had been arranging a large meeting, gathering over 90 participants, through an open invitation aimed at the professional groups working within the concerned services. Although calling it a "brainstorming meeting", suggesting an open-ended approach, he made sure he provided some guidance to the meeting. The CME who had given him the idea at the dinner was invited, and so was another CME from a third municipality that had previously undergone such centralizing reorganizations of their health care and nursing services. While the invited CMEs shared their experiences at the meeting, Jim had also invited potential contractors who could be providers in constructing a building for such a centralized service.

Framing such meetings as "open", both in the sense of having an open-ended approach and for being "open" to anyone wishing to attend,

I argue, served important functions as the political legitimacy of such meetings was heavily dependent on framing them as a stage where different societal interests could interact and achieve general consensus.

The latter point was illustrated by another such open meeting in one of the municipalities of the study, also arranged as a first step in a controversial policy processes. In this case, the meeting concerned the building of a sporting arena, that was, similar to the HSC, considered both a massive centralization and too costly by its political opponents. In the case of the sporting arena, however, the initiating actor was a politician, Raymond, at the time the current mayor, who had invited key actors from the municipalities' sport associations in an effort to gain momentum for the arena. While the meeting had been successful in putting together a task group, that proved itself important in the following political struggle, the meeting had, according to Raymond, also received strong criticism for not being a legitimate starting point:

> We invited them to an open meeting at the café. For those who were interested in working for this project. And we put together a task group, a preliminary task group, at that meeting. But there was ... there has been voiced some critique for that starting point. Because, well, who was invited to this first meeting? Was it really open? Was it only a "hallelujah" crowd, with people praising the project, was it? Well, maybe it was. It might have been. There was no point in inviting people that were strongly opposed to come, people that we knew to be strongly opposed, when we were trying to carry such a cause through. You don't want those people in a group that's supposed to work toward such a project. So there has been voiced some critique over that starting point.

The critique raised against Raymond's "open meeting" illustrates how the political legitimacy of such meetings was highly invested in such meetings being objective in their framing. As such, my observations here are in tune with Archetti's (1984) observations, arguing that political culture in Norway is highly invested in the ideological belief in power as a result of objective processes. The latter, Archetti argues, leads to a strong emphasis on proper and open proceedings, as shared agreement on the framing of a political debate is understood as vital to secure all parties access to participate on a factual basis.

More importantly, the latter example also illustrates how, despite the normative and Weberian portrayal of politicians as proper instruments of political struggle, there were also normative constraints put on the politicians' ability to introduce political *fights*. More than originating from the political end (in accordance to the logic of the state), policy initiatives also had to find legitimacy through conceived objective processes allowing the appearance of consensuses (in accordance to logic of the *village*).

Pragmatic Egalitarianism

Returning once again to Jim, and the case of the HSC, the open meeting had been successful in both recruiting allies, among the concerned professional group, and reframing the issue from being an individual (administrative) initiative to a more collective idea. However, if he was to commit resources more formally toward realizing the HSC, Jim had reached the point where he needed a concrete order from the municipal council. Still faced with a reluctant mayor, he therefore knew that he would have to solicit political support elsewhere. The solution was to contact an oppositional politician, whom he thought might be more positive toward the issue:

> Jim: Well, to be completely honest on how I did it. I saw that it would not be easy to carry forward such a process when I had a mayor that was fighting against it ... So I contacted her [oppositional politician], and asked her how we could do it. How could we get the politicians in on this? ... Then she said: "I can arrange a political meeting, here in the house, gathering all the political parties", because she was intrigued by the same idea as me. So we did it, and one of those small seeds was planted.

With the idea of the HSC firmly planted, the policy process could soon evolve independently, without Jim single-handedly introducing the matter for the municipal council. Publicly, the fight had now been introduced through more normatively legitimate (or at least more diffuse) sources. With the health care and nursing services restructuring now on the political agenda, a formal order for a "factual assessment" was provided by the municipal council. Although not having a final decision from the municipal council, Jim could now actively engage in the policy process (and become the administrative participant of the political fight), on a legitimate order from the municipal council of gaining a factual-based administrative processing of matter.

Such trespassing into the political sphere, bypassing the "hourglass model", was a common element in many of the stories of policy processes I collected during fieldwork. While Jim took a direct approach by contacting a politician, such planting of seeds in the political sphere could also be done through more indirect approaches (e.g., by administrators soliciting third parties to promote issues to the political end of the organization).

Despite the strong normative emphasis on the hierarchical command chain of the municipal organization, alternative alignments were common. Particularly in controversial issues, such *pragmatic policy alliances*, cross-cutting the hierarchical command chain of the municipal organization, often seemed an essential part of political struggle.

Alliances cross-cutting the spheres of politics and administration seemed to provide particularly potent alliances in policy struggles. Partly, I argue, the latter can be accounted for by politicians and administrators controlling different resources in policy struggles. For example, while political actors may publicly solicit support and engage in open political struggles, the administrative actors can engage in political fights through other more subtle, but also possible equally effective means. Jim's recollection of how he worked with other key actors in the municipal administration, in framing the political debate on the HSC, can serve as an example:

> I had a health and social chief that was very bright, and that thought the same way I did. There were many good supporters – the technical chief, and so on. There was no resistance [in the administration]. The municipal organization understood this, and had seen the problems for a long time. But just imagining it, that we would close and lock up [naming the former institutions], and build something new at the municipal center? I don't think anybody could have conceived it possible. "We will never gain political support for it." I remember sitting many long nights creating and shaping the case. Making it as edible as possible.
>
> *Researcher*: Edible?
> *Jim*: Yes, edible. Yes, clarifying everything. As I told you, I could not simply invite them to say, "Yes, we decide to close down now, and build the HSC." I had to phase it. From phase to phase to phase. First phase, throw up some alternatives. Have the municipal council consider this and that alternative. And when they have done so, one will appear as the best. And they will have to go for the best. And then they need some closer reports on one alternative, and we give it to them. And then, they were soon there. It was too late to look back. But, understand, this is not some kind of scam [*bondefangeri*]. It's a process running a process.

More than loyal followers of political decision-making, the sort of *tactical path dependency* described by Jim demonstrates that administrative actors also controlled valuable resources in political struggle. This notion was further supported by many of the politicians interviewed in the study, who emphasized the importance of soliciting the support of administrative actors, and particularly the CME, in controversial political struggles.

Moreover, resources valuable in political struggles were also distributed unequally within the municipal administration itself. While the hierarchical command chain of the municipal organization would be the preferred choice of an administrative entrepreneur attempting to promote a controversial policy development, alternative alignments within the administration could become a necessity, for example, if the CME was expected to oppose the issue at hand.

I asked Thomas, an experienced mid-level administrator, to imagine I was a young, newly appointed administrative employee, then I asked him what advice he would give me if I were to approach him with an idea for a new but possibly controversial policy development. His response illustrates the latter point:

> Well, you would have to, first, you would have to analyze what kind of barriers existed. Why would [for example] the CME be negative? ... It would probably depend on the situation, but I am honestly convinced that in most cases being thorough pays off. It is not going to work with a few pieces of paper and such. Therefore, what I would probably say to you is: "Listen, we are going to sit down together and look at this, and then we might go over to Vegard, and ask him. Talk to him, and maybe we will get some funding to elaborate on this a bit further."

Vegard was another mid-level administrator situated a few offices down from Thomas. Although working in different professional fields, Thomas and Vegard retained a close relationship with each other and had worked on numerous projects together in the past—occasionally also succeeding against the will of their CME. The "funding" referred to was discretional funding administrated by Vegard, aimed at developments in the local community, which they had on previous occasions utilized in preliminary studies when working on controversial policy initiatives.

However, resources such as the funds administered by Vegard are seldom subject to the complete discretion of its administrator alone. Particularly in matters, such as funding, applying such resources often required the approval of someone further up the command chain. Rather than a simple exchange of resources, alliances between such confidantes could more often be understood, therefore, as a strategic coordination of activities. In this light, Thomas's suggestion to approach Vegard and ask his advice about funding should be understood not as actually asking Vegard to simply hand over funds but rather as engaging him to promote the policy development at his end of the organization, to work toward committing such funds to the cause, in this example.

While this latter point may seem obvious, understanding this basic feature of policy alliances becomes increasingly important in order to understand the relations between the municipal organization and external surroundings. While, for example, my informants would frequently express a notion that the general structures of the central state (and particularly the use of earmarked grants and increasingly detailed legislation) represented a threat to municipal autonomy, the concrete relations to state actors were described in very different terms. Rather, the concrete involvement of state actors in providing funding or advice to municipal policy initiatives would usually be described in more personalized terms, and as enablers, rather than threats, to municipal entrepreneurships. This observation is telling to how pragmatic policy alliances vested in egalitarian trust and the personalized relations of the *village* can also extend into the relations between the state and the municipality. More than modifying the hierarchical logic within the municipal organization, such alignments also carry the potential to modify the hierarchical logic of relations between the state and the municipalities.

Embedding the *State* and the *Village*

Despite the normative emphasis on hierarchical Weberian principles, the cases of policy developments discussed demonstrate how municipal policy development was enacted in a tension between a sense of pragmatism and the command-chain principles characterizing the normative perception of the bureaucratic organization. That is a tension between *personalized* relations and the impersonal principles of formal organization, between *forming alliances* across formal organization procedures and representing the totality of the municipality, and, possibly, between the particular interests of society and universalistic bureaucratic procedures. Essentially, I argue that this tension was understood by my informants as a relationship between the pragmatic needs of (the local) society and the need to also anchor policy processes in the democratic legitimacy of the municipal organization—mirroring Sørhaug's notion of legitimacy drawn from the logic of the *village* and from the *state*.

In conceptual terms, these tensions can be understood as the relationship between the pragmatic and normative rules of political struggle (Bailey 1969). In practical terms, these tensions also echo Britan and Cohen's (1980) descriptions of a tension between flexibility and the discipline of Weberian bureaucracy. Following the Weberian set of operations was conceived as lacking the necessary flexibility and ability to adapt required during municipal entrepreneurship. However, I would not draw the conclusion that the pragmatic alternative to Weberian procedures is unmonitored autonomy and freedom. Rather, my findings suggest that informal procedures and alignments were carefully monitored, gossiped about, and could even create sanctions on both the informal and public stages. As such, the informal control of the *village* was highly embedded in the formalized procedures of the *state*, in ways that could often cloud both the meaning and intentions of political actions.

One illustrative example of the latter occurred during a municipal council meeting, during the lengthy processing of the municipal budget. After the CME's briefing on the subject, a council member, whom I have named Astri, stood up and argued against a proposed sale of municipal-owned housing units. Toward the end of her speech, she also proposed an alternative to selling the housing units on the open market as proposed by the administration. Rather than profiting from the possibility of a bidding round that would maximize the price of the units on an open market, she argued that the housing units could be sold for an affordable price to people in need of social housing. Astri revealed that she had been in contact with the county governor's office in an effort to check the rules and guidelines regulating such sales of municipal property; according to the county governor, Astri argued, there was no requirement that the housing units needed to be sold in open bidding rounds. Astri's speech was immediately met with an agitated response from the CME, and a prolonged exchange where the CME questioned Astri about her contact with the county governor on the matter. Finally, the mayor broke in and asked to end the case. Before ending it, however, another council member (and long-time veteran of local politics within the municipality) stood up, delivering a final response to Astri's statements:

Yes, mayor. I have to tell the representative [Astri] that it is good that she does research. But do not present such things to an assembled municipal council! Raise the issue internally to the municipal executive board. It is completely ... it's pretty near undignified to discuss these assumptions, that [you] have asked the county governor this and that ... We can't have it this way in the municipal council! You raise it through the administration—or through the executive board. Let that be said, it is positive if what you are saying is correct.

The incident at the municipal council hardly went unnoticed, and frequently recurred as a topic of discussion in informal conversations, also among many not present at the meeting. When I later discussed the incident with the concerned CME and the mayor, I was told that Astri's actions during the municipal council meeting were understood as provocative due to her contact with personnel at the county governor's office. By doing so, Astri had overstepped the line into administrative affairs—not by arguing politically against the sale but by undermining the CME's factual assessment of the issue.

However, upon discussing the matter further with the CME, an alternative interpretation of Astri's actions also emerged:

Researcher: So you would rather prefer that a correction [to the understanding of regulations] had been brought forward to you in another setting than the municipal council meeting?

CME: But, this was no correction to me. This concerned how the municipality should sell a particular house, to a particular person, by omitting a bidding round. If the municipality wanted to sell to a person living in a municipal housing, there is a way to do it – just as we have previously done it. It is simply a matter of asking if it's possible, asking the administrations if it's possible ... But I found it a bit undignified, because what Astri was doing during the particular meeting was talking on behalf of a particular person. It's so transparent in our tiny local community that everybody sitting there probably knew who it was.

This interpretation of Astri's statements was never uttered publicly during the meeting. According to the CME, the notion that Astri was speaking on behalf of a personalized matter, involving one of the municipality's citizens, was an underlying reason for the strong reactions during the meeting. While crossing into the administrative sphere by contacting the county governor did, in itself, constitute a normative breach, it might, therefore, not have on its own caused the degree of outrage displayed at the meeting.

The incident at the council meeting, therefore, becomes an example of how reactions in the public arena can also be the result of processes not uttered publicly, and how normative breaches in informal arenas can cause reactions in formal arenas without any outspoken linkages. Consequently, informal and formal processes—operating through both the logic of the *village* and the logic of the *state*—become highly intertwined and embedded in the social control regulating policy processes. To the observer, and possibly most of the participants, the formal critique publicly stated (about contacting the county governor) and the informal non-spoken critique (about speaking on behalf of a particular person) become almost impossible to distinguish when trying to interpret the situation.

Organized Egalitarianism and the Morals of Membership

While a society managed on bureaucratic legal-rational principles is certainly different from a "traditional" society, F. G. Bailey reminds us, "such terms stand for concepts, for 'ideal types'" (1969, x). Rather than such pure types, Bailey asserts, the real world is characterized by mixtures.

Within the Norwegian context, Sørhaug's (1984) notions of a tension and interplay between what he conceptualizes as the social formation of the *village* and that of the *state* in Norwegian political culture, represents an expression of the sort of mixtures between ideal-types as depicted by Bailey. However, understanding the mixture of practices characterizing political institutions as a simplified mixture (or transition) between the "traditional" and the "modern", I stress, risks the danger of overlooking the layered reality of social practices, and how practices straying from the ideal description of the legal-rational principles of bureaucracy are not surviving artifacts of a (possibly distorted) "traditional" past, but rather are inextricably embedded and reproduced in modern political institutions. More than existing side-by-side, pragmatic policy alliances regulated by an egalitarian sense of trust are capable of both animating and modifying the hierarchical command chain of the municipal organization, thereby reproducing (in Sørhaug's sense) the egalitarian logic of the *village* within the hierarchical logic of the *state*.

The specific conditions enabling the embedding of such seemingly contradictory logics can be related to the cultural and historical conditions that Vike traces in his concept of *bureaucratic individualism*. Central to his historically oriented analysis is the long-lasting tradition of formalizing social relations within the Nordic societies, which he argues constitute the preconditions for (rather than threats to) Nordic egalitarianism (Vike 2013).

Vike, thus, draws attention to how the important role of associations in the path to political modernization in the Nordic countries continues to shape the practices of the modern political institutions. Moreover, Vike's analysis poses important questions to the understanding of the "traditional" properties of the Nordic "village" at the advent of the Nordic modernization processes.

Within the Norwegian context, the common perception of the peasant communities being embedded into the state and *then* becoming diversified, formalized, and modernized is fundamentally flawed (Vike 2013). In Norway, since the late Middle Ages, peasants could mostly be regarded as freeholders, and the administration of property and autonomy had largely been administered by formal legal procedures (Vike 2013; Park 1998). In this regard, the early juridical protection of autonomy can be understood as a liberal expression of autonomy as *freedom from,* but while the protection *from* hierarchical power, such as indiscriminate state power or privileged city citizens, might have been the primary concern, protection from horizontal threats (i.e., neighbors) may also have provided an important motivation. Expanding the argument, Vike (2013) argues that this notion of freedom also came to inform the view on both central and local government that could occupy the role of the early juridical frameworks, thus becoming protectors of, rather than threats to, personal autonomy. Later, formalized relational forms, through locally based organizations and mass movements, well intertwined with both local and central government long before the advent of the modern welfare state, came to play vital roles in the Nordic state-building processes (Sørensen and Stråth 1997; Vike 2012).

The early success of these associations in gaining control over the governing structures of the state necessitated a form of "formally organized egalitarianism" as a means of ensuring that the delegated power of these organizations remained loyal to their grass-roots (Vike 2012, 128–129). The political morals springing out of this need to control leaders is characterized by a high degree of social control related to specific common moral standards. Important components include conformity, an intense exchange of information about the conduct of members and particularly leaders and, importantly, a normative emphasis on disinterested acts benefitting the common good of the association (Vike 2012, 138). While a high degree of trust is also an important product, Vike argues that such trust is not necessarily related to an enduring faith in the integrity of the leader but rather to the knowledge that the leaders who stray from the group's moral rules of conduct will face consequences.

Simultaneously, this formalized egalitarianism, or "morals of membership", also has the effect of protecting individuals horizontally from each other by limiting the extent of personalized dependencies (Vike 2012). More than facilitating wide participation and commitment to local government (Park 1998) and a system of "governing by committee" (Barnes 1954), the division of political interests into various associations created a complex pattern of cross-cutting conflicts and political alignments. While providing stability, dividing political participation into various cross-cutting alignments has the effect of limiting personal dependencies by providing an easy exit from former commitments and allowing the strategic choice of alternative alignments (Barnes 1954; Vike 2013).

The latter point is important in understanding why personalized relations in municipal policy development seldom develop into personalized dependencies and clientelism. While personalized relations of the *village* and formal relations of the *state* are embedded in social practices, the tension between the two secures the possibility of withdrawing from commitments based on either of the two. The possibility of "switching hats" between formal roles serves an important function, as it allows attachments from ties, commitments and power discrepancies from other social contexts involving the same people. More than confining personnel within roles, the normative emphasis on differentiating roles must also be understood as a way to organize personal autonomy. However, while normative rules prescribe certain roles and alignments in certain situations, the cases of policy development in this chapter display how pragmatic policy alliances can also choose alternative alignments based on strategic and pragmatic needs. Still, the relative transparency of the cross-cutting alignments allows a social control that embeds both formal and informal ties and actions in an attempt to ensure that municipal policy development remains disinterested and focused on the community's common good. Rather than lasting reciprocal relations under the constant threat of becoming asymmetrical, relations in pragmatic policy alliances are characterized by the possibility of withdrawing from commitments while still maintaining social cohesion and relations with the same people in other arenas.

Notes

1. The term *village*, as applied in this chapter, is my own translation of the Norwegian term "*Bygda*" applied by Sørhaug (1984), connoting, in this historical context, a household pattern emphasizing the conjugal bond and nuclear family rather than the emphasis on extended family ties often associated with the social formations of the pre-modern "village" elsewhere (see Solheim 2016). The distinction made here is important as it provides a plausible explanation why local government came to be dominated by relatively autonomous individuals organized in committees (in Barnes's sense), rather than larger kinship-based corporate groups (see Park 1998).

References

Archetti, Eduardo. 1984. Om maktens ideologi – en krysskulturell analyse. In *Den norske væremåten*, ed. Arne Martin Klausen, 45–60. Trondheim: J. W Cappelens Forlag.

Bailey, Fredrick G. 1969. *Stratagems and spoils: A social anthropology of politics.* New York: Schocken Books.

Barnes, John A. 1954. Class and committees in a Norwegian island parish. *Human Relations* 7 (1): 39–58.

Britan, Gerald M., and Ronald Cohen, eds. 1980. Toward an anthropology of formal organizations. In *Hierarchy & society: Anthropological perspectives on bureaucracy*, 9–30. Philadelphia: Institute for the Study of Human Issues.

Bruun, Maja Hojer, Gry Skrædderdal Jakobsen, and Sine Krøijer. 2011. Introduction: The concern for sociality – Practicing equality and hierarchy in Denmark. *Social Analysis* 55 (2): 1–19.

Gluckman, Max. 1955. The peace in the feud. *Past & Present* 8: 1–14.

Gullestad, Marianne. 1989. Small facts and large issues: The anthropology of contemporary Scandinavian society. *Annual Review of Anthropology* 18: 71–93.

———. 1991. The Scandinavian version of egalitarian individualism. *Ethnologica Scandinavica* 21: 3–18.

———. 1992. *The art of social relations: Essays on culture, social action and everyday life in modern Norway.* Oslo: Scandinavian University Press.

Park, George. 1998. *The marke of power. Helgeland and the politics of omnipotence.* Newfoundland: Institute of Social and Economic Research.

Solheim, Jorunn. 2016. Bringing it all back home – Familien som generative kulturell formasjon i det modern. *Norsk Antropologisk Tidsskrift* 27 (1): 7–21.

Sørensen, Øystein, and Bo Stråth. 1997. Introduction: The cultural construction of Norden. In *The cultural construction of Norden*, ed. Øystein Sørensen and Bo Stråth, 1–24. Oslo: Scandinavian University Press.

Sørhaug, Hans Christian. 1984. Totemisme på norsk – Betraktninger om den norske sosialdemokratismes vesen. In *Den norske væremåten*, ed. Arne Martin Klausen, 61–87. Trondheim: J. W Cappelens Forlag.

Trägårdh, Lars. 1997. Statist individualism: On the culturality of the Nordic welfare state. In *The cultural construction of Norden*, ed. Øystein Sørensen and Bo Stråth, 253–285. Oslo: Scandinavian University Press.

Vike, Halvard. 2012. Varianter av vest-europeiske statsformasjoner, Utkast til en historisk antropologi. *Norsk Antropologisk Tidsskrift* 23 (2): 126–142.

———. 2013. Egalitarianisme og byråkratisk individualisme. *Norsk Antropologisk Tidsskrift* 24 (3–4): 181–193.

Weber, Max. 1946. *From Max Weber: Essays in sociology*. Trans. and Eds. H. H. Gerth and C. Wright Mills. New York: Oxford University Press.

PART III

Egalitarian Welfare?

CHAPTER 8

Social Differences in Health as a Challenge to the Danish Welfare State

Camilla Hoffmann Merrild

INTRODUCTION

In the Scandinavian countries, the image of national cohesion and egalitarianism is widely shared by the national populations themselves and by the world at large. The egalitarian ideology, with its values of community and universalism, has provided the grounds for the development and preservation of the modern welfare state and led to the development of the so-called "Nordic model" of welfare (Christiansen and Markkola 2006). This model is perhaps most clearly expressed in an extensive and well-developed welfare system that is based on principles of equality, solidarity, and equal access to welfare benefits. As suggested by Christiansen and Markkola, this form of social and political organization has played a vital role in advancing national cohesion and homogeneity in all the Nordic countries (Christiansen and Markkola 2006). At the national level, it is intrinsically linked to cultural ideals of what Norwegian anthropologist Marianne Gullestad (2001) characterizes as "imagined sameness", and what Danish anthropologist Steffen Jöhncke

C.H. Merrild (✉)
The Research Unit for General Practice, Department of Public Health,
Aarhus University, Århus, Denmark

© The Author(s) 2018
S. Bendixsen et al. (eds.), *Egalitarianism in Scandinavia*,
Approaches to Social Inequality and Difference,
DOI 10.1007/978-3-319-59791-1_8

(2011) coins as "alikeness", by which he refers to shared cultural assumptions that shape Danish national identity. Inspired by the work of Gullestad and Jöhncke, this chapter illustrates how social differences in health may be seen as an example that depict underplayed social hierarchies of class differences in a Danish egalitarian welfare context; findings which may also be relevant for other Scandinavian countries. While the Danish population is often characterized as socially homogeneous, I follow Jöhncke's argument that the construction and operation of the welfare state gloss over the continued existence of class differences and that "the combined cultural ideals of equality and alikeness veil rather than remove class as a structural principle" (2011, 46). This may be accentuated to varying extents across Scandinavia. A recent study of Scandinavian egalitarianism (Kjærsgård 2015), for example, indicates a higher degree of class cooperation and consensus-seeking in Denmark than in Sweden where a more pronounced ideological class struggle is evident.[1]

Gullestad is one of the most important scholars of Nordic egalitarianism and social organization, and she was among the first to describe Norwegian (and Scandinavian) ideologies of what she termed "egalitarian individualism". She introduced the concept of "equality as sameness" as a particularly Scandinavian way of practicing egalitarianism (Gullestad 1984, 1992), which she later developed into the notion of "imagined sameness" (2001). By imagined sameness, Gullestad refers to a shared feeling of equality, similarity, and familiarity, which is not necessarily observable, but which is emphasized in social interaction, thereby reinforcing what is common and shared (Gullestad 2001, 35). Recently, however, Bruun et al. (2011) have argued that rather than uncritically accepting the notion of equality as sameness in a Scandinavian context, it is necessary to look more closely at everyday practices of sociality, as this could offer more in-depth and nuanced insights into life as it is lived in the Scandinavian countries. The point raised by Bruun, Jakobsen, and Krøijer is important as it draws attention to practices of sociality that reproduce practices of hierarchies and stratifications in everyday contexts dominated by ideologies of egalitarianism (Bruun 2011). Such detailed ethnographies of everyday life are often glossed over in broad-brush descriptions of how the hegemonic ideology frames the way in which society's structure is conceptualized and verbalized (Bourdieu 1987; Gullestad 1984, 1992, 2001; Ortner 2003). However, in an attempt to straddle both approaches, Jeppe Linnet (2011) draws attention to how the dominance of the ideology of egalitarianism plays out in everyday practices in his analysis of the concept of "*hygge*" (togetherness, cosiness, informality, homeliness, etc.). Linnet shows how the "in-between middle-class" worldview, which is imagined somewhere in between the higher and lower social classes, dominates, despite a general awareness of stratified lifestyles and social diversities in society at large. He refers to this as the imaginary of Danes as class deniers (Linnet 2011, 25) and suggests that practices of "*hygge*" manifest what he calls the hierarchical egalitarianism of middle-class consciousness (Linnet 2011, 41). The dominance of middle-class in-between-ness resonates with Stine Faber's (2008) research into social class in Denmark. In an interview study with Danish women from different social backgrounds, Faber shows how, although social stratification may be acknowledged, the concept of social class is firmly avoided by the women in her study. When asked about how they perceive their own social position, the women in her study almost unilaterally positioned themselves as middle class, notwithstanding how they might be defined by classic socio-economic measures. Faber found that when addressing the topic of social class, the conversation became somewhat stifled and the discussion shifted toward "the equal worth of people". Social position was downplayed, disregarded, or explicitly denied by all of her informants, and she had difficulties empirically engaging with the concept. Interestingly, Faber also notes how social differences were associated with moral distinctions particularly directed at the higher social classes, which Faber ascribes to the Danish egalitarian ideology, where sticking out and thinking more about oneself is often ill-considered (Faber 2008, 122).[2] These findings of Danish "in-between middle-classness" seem to reflect the fact that the Danes have historically had fewer intra-group differences than, for instance, their Swedish counterparts (Kjærsgård 2015), and that alikeness can be seen as a cultural assumption evident in indigenous ideas about society as well as material constructions of society (Jöhncke 2011, 40).

Although the research referred to above does not constitute an extensive review, it does point to the significance of Scandinavian ideals of individualized egalitarianism, imagined sameness, and cultural alikeness without ignoring or precluding the existence of social hierarchies (Bruun et al. 2015; Faber 2008; Gullestad 1992, 2001; Jöhncke 2011; Linnet 2011). It emphasizes the equal worth of people (*ligeværd*) but at the same time downplays fundamental structural differences that may have very real consequences in people's everyday lives. The central argument of this chapter contributes to these discussions by pointing out how social differences in health and illness highlight fundamental structures of inequality in the Danish egalitarian welfare state, which are most often overlooked or ignored. However, our blindness to such structures of inequality has very real consequences for the lives of people from the lower social classes who suffer in terms of excess morbidity and mortality. In line with the arguments of Jöhncke (2011) and Gullestad (2001), I suggest that the Danish cultural ideal of alikeness or imagined sameness contributes toward maintaining social boundaries and differences. However, certain public debates illuminate just those differences and in effect render them problematic as they bring out social differences that are usually overwritten by the egalitarian ethos of the welfare state. The contemporary discussion of inequality in health in the Danish welfare society, recently described as "the invisible class society" (Olsen et al. 2012), is a case in point. Hence, I suggest that social differences in health direct attention to the mounting challenges of social inequality in society at large. The very concrete social differences in morbidity and mortality raise questions about whether everyone has the same opportunity to reach their full potential and is equally supported in their efforts to do so (see the Introduction, Chap. 1 in this book, for further discussion of how notions of egalitarianism have been conceptualized).

The argument presented below has grown out of ethnographic fieldwork carried out among two different social classes at opposite ends of the social spectrum in Denmark. It is also grounded in my own position as a Dane, born and raised in Denmark. However, following the lives of the two groups of informants, whom I in a descriptive sense have termed the lower working class (LWC) and the higher middle class (HMC), respectively, allowed me to gain insights into life as it is lived in very different social worlds at opposite ends of what I will refer to as the Danish class society. Taking my point of departure in the lives I came to know led me to question the appropriateness of the concept of Danish egalitarianism, which has evolved from notions of universalism, community, and social responsibility to refer increasingly to the values of individualism, personal responsibility, and autonomy; a shift that is also described as the transformation of the welfare state to a competition state (Pedersen 2011). Still, the principles of resource redistribution continue to constitute core principles of the welfare state, and although neoliberal ideas of self-management and cuts in public spending are beginning to influence the character of the welfare state (Bruun et al. 2015), fundamental values of universal access to health, education, and social security still prevail.

Deconstructing Danish Egalitarianism?

The Danish welfare system is based on principles of universalism, equality, and solidarity, and it aims to ensure social justice for all its citizens. It is based on three imaginings about equality: (1) the equal worth of all people (*ligeværd*); (2) equal opportunities for all; and (3) economic equality (Pedersen 2011). To ensure this, the 1933 Social Reform Act, which outlined various forms of tax-financed welfare schemes for the entire population, was implemented (Jöhncke 2011). These schemes included a number of areas such as free education, sickness benefits, pensions, childcare facilities, and healthcare as some of the most celebrated examples. However, inherent notions of solidarity and shared responsibility associated with the welfare state seem gradually to be replaced by an emphasis on individualism and personal responsibility for faring well throughout life (Bruun et al. 2015; Langer and Højlund 2011). Despite the dominance of the egalitarian ideology and the fact that relative poverty and economic disparities are low compared with the rest of the world, different social groupings and hierarchies are, nevertheless, part of Denmark's social structure. In media debates, political discussions, and most research, national differentiation is mostly articulated in terms of ethnic affiliation, sexual orientation, gender, geographical origin or association (e.g., rural/urban). Yet, in recent years, political discussions and more politically engaged research (e.g., Olsen et al. 2012, 2014) have raised the question of social inequality, albeit often from the perspective that it is something new and growing, most probably brought about by the global economic crisis. Statistics, however, reveal a clear picture. One study, for instance, showed that whereas 25 percent of the adult Danish population between 18 and 59 years of age belonged to the middle class, the higher social classes account for 10 percent of the population and the lower social classes for 65 percent (Olsen et al. 2012, 37).[3] Such social differences are usually articulated with reference to individualizing traits such as health, employment or education, using the somewhat neutral language of statistics and socio-economic variables, and intimating that the individual is responsible for how he or she fares in life. Addressing social differences with reference to individual characteristics plays into the move toward neo-liberal ideals of individualism and personal responsibility, which have begun to influence and shape the organization and ideological make-up of the welfare state (Bruun et al. 2015; see also Pedersen 2011). Social differences in broader and structural terms, such as those implied by the concept of class are rarely discussed explicitly in public or academic debates.[4] This may be underlined by the way that the concept of social class as a category of difference brings out internal differentiation, which illuminates how the egalitarian ethos and the Scandinavian notion of imagined sameness downplay social boundaries and under-communicates differences, thereby paradoxically upholding the social class structure (Gullestad 2001, 63–64).

The ideal of egalitarianism was challenged in very concrete ways from the beginning of my fieldwork among the two social classes in suburban Denmark. From my initial experiences of stepping into the everyday lives of my informants, it became evident that cultural and social diversities prevailed in all areas of life. I was somewhat unprepared for this. Being a Dane I shared the egalitarian ideology and had not expected to find the level of hardship and despair that I encountered in my own "backyard". My informants were not living on the street, not substance abusers, not "deviant" or severely deprived people, nor were they part of the elite or super-rich. They were Danish citizens who either had a financial position that was above average or held a university degree or, conversely, had left school after primary and lower secondary level (*Folkeskolen*) and were living on social welfare benefits. My experience of the contrasts between these lives was probably reinforced by the comparative nature of the fieldwork, where the constant shift from one context to the other underlined the challenging lives I encountered among one group of informants, whereas the opposite often seemed to be the case for the other group. This was about much more than financial or social position. The hardship of lives in lower social classes seems to be shaped by the lived realities of physical and mental disease, difficult and damaged family relations, negative social heritage, welfare dependency, and a sense of haphazardness. It was about social concerns, related to, for instance, forced removals of children from home (*tvangsfjernelser*), unemployed and pregnant teenage mothers, difficulties in dealing with the social services, and lack of money. Of course, this is not to say that people in higher social classes have no physical, mental, and social concerns; on the contrary, these are a natural part of most people's lives. But in some lives, these challenges and concerns acquire urgency, circularity, and dominance, which are hard to describe in other ways than by recognizing how such challenges are embedded in difficult social situations.

These difficult social situations were evident when, for instance, LWC informants were subjected to job training requirements that did not take their failing physical conditions into account; when they were instructed to change dietary practices which might not be possible due to lack of teeth (and thereby being "unable to eat vegetables"); and when potentially lifesaving medical appointments could not be attended due to the problem of getting to the hospital when all the money had been spent, and so on. These examples suggest that social inequality exists in something more than individual measures of educational and income level. Social inequality is rooted in social heritage, practices of sociality, and lifestyle; and is produced and reproduced by the very contrast between the daily lives of distinct social classes (Bourdieu 1987; Gullestad 1992, 5–6). It was evident that class was an integral part of my informants' subjectivities and the micro-politics of their lives, as Diane Reay (1998) describes it, lived in and through the body. In terms of everyday life, this meant that the two social classes were essentially living parallel lives in social and cultural worlds that differed from the dominant "in-between middle-classes" (Linnet 2011, 25). Ways of dressing, moving, and talking differed between the two groups of informants, as did forms of social interaction. Social and class-based positions were expressed as forms of social, cultural, and economic capital, through sociality and communication (verbal language as well as body language), body maintenance, and appearance—the very practices, tastes, and preferences that are eloquently described by Bourdieu (1987, 8) as the symbolic construction of class-making.[5] The contrasts were striking both on an emotional, sensational, and visual level: I could almost taste it, definitely feel it, and, of course, I could see it everywhere I turned.

As in Faber's study (2008), the existence of social differences in Danish society was mostly acknowledged among my informants, whereas nobody seemed to have any personal experiences of these differences. Knowledge of and interaction with people living in dissimilar social contexts were limited, and mostly came across in the form of stereotypical descriptions such as "those from the blocks" or "those from cereal hill, who work so much that they only have time to eat oatmeal".[6] Among the LWC informants, the differences were usually verbalized in economic terms, and many times the point was made that the transition from living on a regular income to becoming dependent on social welfare benefits had radically changed their lives. Despite my initial categorization, the HMC informants were somewhat reluctant to describe themselves as well-to-do; and like the women interviewed by Faber, they often downplayed their own social status. The Danish ideology and perception of egalitarianism and equality as sameness may be grounded partly in the fact that people often live together with those who are similar. Social status is reflected in geographical status (and real estate prices), and members of higher social classes mostly live in well-to-do urban neighborhoods, whereas members of lower social classes cluster in social housing associations or rural areas. As such, Danish society can be seen as socially and spatially structured in parallel worlds, which means that it is possible to go through life mainly surrounded by people who are similar to oneself.[7] In the words of Gullestad, equality as sameness "is sustained by avoiding contact with people about whom one has insufficient information, by an interactional style emphasizing sameness and under-communicating difference, and by avoiding people who are considered 'too different'" (1992, 174). Getting to know the everyday lives of people from different social classes in the affluent welfare state of Denmark emphasized the illusory character of the egalitarian ethos of equal opportunities and welfare for all citizens, which is produced and reproduced by the cultural construction of alikeness and imagined sameness. It attested to the paradox of egalitarianism, which Bruce Kapferer (2015) has termed *in-egalitarianism*, referring to the potential exclusiveness of equality as an ideology.[8] I will elaborate on this in the remainder of this chapter, where I will argue that *in-egalitarianism* promotes the "embodiment of inequality" (Fassin 2003), where biological facts become social and structural facts and vice versa.

SOCIAL DIFFERENCES IN HEALTH

Before proceeding to discuss social differences in health, I will briefly describe the health care system, one of the pillars of the Danish welfare state. The tax-funded health care system is based on principles of equity in terms of access, utilization, and outcomes, with the overarching goal being that all citizens should be supported so that they can reach their full health potential (Krasnik 1996). Hence, equality in the Danish health care system is related to outcome rather than services, meaning that although everybody has the right to receive healthcare, some may need more support than others. Most forms of health care are offered free of charge, with the exception of very few services such as dental care or physiotherapy. All citizens access the health care system through primary care, which serves as a gatekeeper system to the secondary sector (in-patient and outpatient hospital services). Although the tax-funded health care system is by far the most widespread, private specialized clinics have become increasingly popular in recent years. In private specialized clinics, services are paid by the patients themselves or are available through private insurance schemes, making it possible to bypass the gatekeeper system and access specialized services directly. This development has led to virulent political and public debates as to how privatization of parts of the health care system may be contributing to health inequalities, splitting the population into two groups—those who can afford to pay for better health and those who cannot, challenging the core ideal of equity in healthcare.

Although the principles of open access and equity are fundamental to Danish health care, social differences are persistent in relation to almost all forms of health and illness (Baadsgaard and Brønnum-Hansen 2012; Diderichsen et al. 2011). For the past 30 years, social research and public health research have illustrated how social differences translate into differences in health and illness outcomes (Marmot et al. 1991, 2008; Popay et al. 2003). The first studies to demonstrate that social disparities in health were not confined to economically disadvantaged and less developed countries were the so-called Whitehall studies (Marmot et al. 1978, 1991) and the Black Report published in the UK in 1980 (Townsend et al. 1992). Focusing on British civil servants, these studies illustrated disparities in health as a gradient rather than as polar expressions of diversity in the population, placing social differences in health and illness firmly on the political agenda in Northern Europe. Similarly, Danish studies have also shown that the prevalence of lifestyle, chronic, and psychiatric diseases is much higher among people with lower socio-economic positions (SEP) than among those with higher SEP, and that people with lower SEP are more likely to suffer from multiple diseases, just as self-evaluated health is also found to be significantly worse among those with lower SEP than among those with higher SEP (Baadsgaard and Brønnum-Hansen 2012; Diderichsen et al. 2011; Larsen et al. 2014). Not only do we see substantial class differences in the risk of getting a disease, but considerable differences are also found in the prognosis. For instance, in 2009, the absolute difference in life expectancy between the two quartiles of Danish males aged 30 years with the highest and lowest income was almost ten years, while the corresponding number for women was six years (Baadsgaard and Brønnum-Hansen 2012). These statistics may indicate what Didier Fassin (2003) has termed the embodiment of inequality as it plays out in a Scandinavian context. Applying Fassin's argument in a Danish context, the embodiment of class may be seen in the way in which power, history, and political truths operate through embodied subjectivities and concrete bodily activity.

Departing from such disparities, social differences in health and illness outcomes play an important role for how health promotion and illness prevention have gained ground in Denmark since the 1980s. With the advancement of new public health, lifestyle practices such as smoking, alcohol and dietary intake, and actively preserving good health and preventing illness are increasingly considered an individual responsibility (Briggs 2003, 288; Lupton 1995, 49–51); and various behavioral demands are articulated through health promotion and illness prevention interventions and campaigns. For instance, the Danish Health and Medicines Authority yearly administers information campaigns that focus on "lifestyle changes" (e.g., in areas of alcohol consumption, diet, physical activity, and smoking), but also that more explicitly address the interface between the general population and the health care system (e.g., in campaigns regarding the importance of seeking care at the "appropriate" time). In the literature, health promotion and illness prevention is often linked with the changing political climate in western Europe, and Ayo (2012, 100), for instance, argues that "existing health promotion policies both reflect and reinforce the prevailing political ideology of neoliberalism and furthermore operate in such a way as to facilitate the making of the 'good' and 'healthy' citizen" (see also Rose 2007). What was previously considered the responsibility of the state, namely ensuring citizens' health and well-being, has increasingly become an issue of personal success/failure and accountability, where unemployment, poverty, and lack of education are considered the result of poor personal choices made by individuals with free choice (Ayo 2012, 102). Another perspective on this move could be that within the context of Nordic welfare states, where, with the extensive welfare society, the state has assumed almost unlimited responsibility for the welfare of the population (Pausewang 2001, 183; Vike 2001, 146), the case of health promotion and illness prevention may be seen as examples of how the state extends its authority by placing behavioral demands on its citizens.[9] This supports a governmentality-inspired perspective on the moral imperative of maintaining good health imposed by the state on its citizens with implicit value-laden hierarchies of lifestyles (e.g., Rose 2007). However, it also seems useful to consider how the principles of the health care system (and, in fact, the entire welfare system) resemble the morality of reciprocity in the sense that in order to get the benefits of health care, people should live "proper" health-enhancing lives, doing their best to maintain or improve their health and prevent potential illness. The increasing financial burden of an aging population, a greater number of people getting chronic and lifestyle diseases, and the increasing biotechnical capacity to identify and diagnose diseases at ever earlier stages mean that the health care (and welfare) systems are stretched to their limits. Many Danes are acutely aware of the fact that the resources of the welfare system are restricted; and that in order to maintain a free health care system, it is necessary to limit its use—that is, to do one's best to stay as healthy as possible for as long as possible. In this way, people are able to repay the welfare system, and thereby establish their "deserving right" to benefits in the sense that they adopt health-enhancing lifestyles and thus compensate for the health care that they may eventually receive. What is more, one of the central obligations of being a Danish citizen is that of contributing toward the welfare system by paying taxes; but if people get sick, this contribution is lost, and the reciprocity is broken.

The duty to live a healthy life and limit the use of health care services was expressed by informants of both social classes. They were all very conscious of how healthy lives were supposedly led and what they might do to prevent illness, albeit they did not always fulfill this obligation. Some smoked, some did not attend screening, and some adjusted their prescribed medicine according to their own understanding and ideas. From the perspective of the policy-makers and health professionals, these localized health and illness practices are often considered to demonstrate lack of knowledge and understanding, rather than being acknowledged as subjective attempts made by individuals to improve their health and deal with illness (Merrild et al. 2016). In the remainder of the chapter, I will use the example of cancer to illustrate how cultural assumptions of imagined sameness and alikeness in many ways blind us to the structural differences in society that may be causing the social differences in health in the first place.

Social Differences in Health as an Amplifier

When considering social differences in health and illness outcomes in relation to socio-economic variables, the prevailing objective seems to be to identify and define those who lack the ability and competency to lead healthy lives. Explanations vary and range from epidemiological explanations of primary associations with education (Townsend et al. 1992); income (Pickett and Wilkinson 2014); wealth (Nowatzki 2012); and abilities to understand, act on, and assess medical information, recently referred to as health literacy (Madsen et al. 2009; Nutbeam 2000). On the other hand, there are also sociologically inspired studies examining the influence of space and place on disease distribution (Cummins et al. 2007; Macintyre et al. 2002).[10] Such studies, which have been referred to as behavioral studies of medicine (Good 1994), suggest the importance of increasing knowledge and awareness of "proper" and "healthy" lifestyles, and rely on the assumption that social differences in health and illness can be eliminated through behavioral changes—the reciprocal repayment to the welfare state.[11] Thus, when, for instance, the eating and smoking practices of my LWC informants rarely followed the official health promotion and illness prevention guidelines, even if most of the informants suffered from multiple physical and mental illnesses, the most obvious explanation might seem to be lack of knowledge and awareness of the potential harmfulness of such practices. Implicit in these assumptions are dominant values of what is meant by the good life and how it is practiced; these values are associated with moralities of the individual, free choice, hierarchies of lifestyles, and obligations of reciprocity. However, focusing on stratified patterns of lifestyle ascribed to moral differences (Linnet 2011, 25) and individualized behavior, such as not knowing how to take care of one's body, may result in the circularity of social deprivation and disease being overlooked. As Halvard Vike (2001, 165–66) argues in his analysis of social class in Norway, lower social positions are attributed to personal competences[12]—which, in effect, obscures and individualizes structural class differences in society at large. Current health promotion and illness prevention initiatives feed into this rhetoric by tying bad health to individual knowledge and morality, supporting the point made by Swedish historian Lars Trägårdh (2010, 235) that the institutional arrangements of the Scandinavian welfare state are essentially individualizing.[13]

If we take cancer as an example, as it is the number one cause of death among Danes and a disease which attracts enormous attention in the media, social differences in prevalence and survival rates are also pervasive (Dalton et al. 2008). Globally, cancer is represented in the media and public debates through metaphors of war as Susan Sontag (1978) amply described decades ago, and its histology is considered complex in both diagnostics and treatment. In Denmark, almost 40 years later, the rhetoric of warfare still holds; now, however, it is accompanied by a strong sense of urgency which depicts cancer as an acute condition and as an epidemic (Tørring 2014). Although most people know someone who has lost what is commonly referred to as "the fight against cancer", or has experienced the often virulent side effects of treatment, the concept of survivorship is gaining ground. Images of devastating personal experiences of individuals suffering or dying from cancer, along with fatalistic predictions representing cancer as one of the greatest threats to the Danish population of modern times, against which all Danes must unite, amplify and reproduce egalitarian ideals of community, solidarity, equality, alikeness, or sameness. For instance, "Unite against cancer" is the slogan of the fight cancer campaign (*knæk cancer kampagnen*), which takes place once every year. For a whole week, the topic of cancer is omnipresent. On all media platforms, in the streetscape, and in many public institutions (particularly educational ones), narratives of personal cancer-related tragedies and victories are told, the progress toward curing cancer is discussed, there are street collections raising money to help "beat" cancer, and awareness campaigns are staged at events in all conceivable forms. The week culminates with a television show broadcast during prime time on Saturday evening, where Danes unite in front of the television with the common goal of fighting cancer. In the spirit of achievement (and with some element of competition—such as, who gives the most, and how much we can all collect), donations are made by individuals and companies, and emotions are shared. In such instances, perhaps the sentiments of imagined sameness are most forcefully at play, in the sense that all Danes are portrayed and probably imagined as being the same (or similar) in relation to their potential risk of getting cancer, winning or losing the battle, or losing a loved one.

However, persistent social differences in cancer prevalence and survival challenge this imagination, by explicitly drawing up boundaries within the population. Why does someone who leaves the educational system after finishing primary and lower secondary school have a higher likelihood of getting cancer than a person who goes to university? What is it that makes people with a high income live longer and have fewer complications if they do get cancer than those on a low income? These very real social differences in quality and length of life highlight fundamental structures of inequality in what may be referred to as a Danish class-based society, differences to which our egalitarian ethos may make us blind. The social differences in incidence and survival across most cancers in Denmark (Dalton et al. 2008), which in public discourse are conveyed in expressions like "cancer has become a social and undemocratic disease" (Lavrsen 2011, my translation) or "your educational level determines if you survive cancer" (Nørgaard et al. 2015, my translation), implies unfairness and a divided community within Denmark's welfare society, challenging the core values of egalitarianism. What is more, they suggest a form of circularity between social and biological dimensions, where social position is inherently linked with physiology and vice versa (Merrild et al. 2017), again pointing to embodiments of inequality (Fassin 2003) where structures of inequality become apparent in unequal bodies.

Conclusion

I have argued that the notion of imagined sameness, which describes a national sense of alikeness and community common to most of the Scandinavian countries, is highly relevant in a Danish context. From an international perspective, Denmark may be a somewhat homogeneous country—in fact, Denmark is often rated as among the most egalitarian countries in the world. However, this is not to say that social differences in Danish society are not discussed and acknowledged internally. In fact, discussions of welfare benefits, poverty, increasing geographical and residential segregation, the coexistence of public and private schools, and the privatization of health are all areas where differences within the population are addressed. Yet, as Gullestad points out, the egalitarian ideology does not preclude the existence of social stratification and hierarchies (1992, 174). Despite the segregation of Danish society in terms of residence, education, or employment, middle-class egalitarianism dominates (Faber 2008; Linnet 2011), which emphasizes sameness and underplays differences. I argue that the social differences that are evident across all areas of health and illness reveal fundamental class differences in the Danish welfare society. Statistical differences in life expectancy and survival rates dramatically challenge the ideals of egalitarianism, solidarity, and welfare for all. Although social differences in health and illness implicitly signify differences in social class, discussions regarding and responses to these differences most often reflect individual socio-economic variables like education and income, which define those who do not understand, are morally inferior, and do not commit to the reciprocal obligations of being a Danish citizen, where one earns the privileges of the welfare state by taking good care of oneself.[14] However, if public health approaches to improving the health of the population remain at the individual level, addressing the underlying structural causes of inequality in Denmark's welfare society is comfortably avoided, and the question of what actually supports equality or egalitarianism is never addressed. Social differences are about much more than economy, education, and where and with whom people live. They are also about what egalitarianism means; they raise questions about what the welfare state has become. Consequently, social differences in health and illness illustrate social hierarchies in terms of lifestyle, morality, and social obligations; and they challenge the egalitarian ethos and our sense of solidarity by raising questions as to who belongs to our imagined sameness and what it means to be alike. Contemporary public health approaches to reducing these social differences in disease outcomes can be considered symptomatic of the increasing institutionalized individualism of welfare states in Scandinavia, which may contribute to increasing exclusion, marginalization, othering, and widening class differences.

Acknowledgements I would like to extend my profound thanks to Rikke Sand Andersen for taking the time to read through this chapter and for offering insightful and critical constructive comments. I would also like to thank the members of CAP anthropology at The Research Unit for General Practice for their valuable comments and input.

Notes

1. Kjærsgård ascribes these differences to the divergent attitudes, media content, and the legacy of the political economies of Denmark and Sweden (Kjærsgård 2015, 40).
2. This aversion to sticking out may also be understood by reference to *Janteloven* (the Law of Jante), which was described and conceptualized by the Norwegian novelist Aksel Sandemose (1992 [1972]). In his novel *En flygtning krydser sit spor* [A Fugitive Crosses His Tracks], he describes the Danish imperative of the need to fit in, not think of oneself as better than anyone else. Although the point of departure for describing *Janteloven* was rural Denmark in the early nineteenth century, the concept remains central to Danish self-understanding and outlook and is still referred to when describing "typical" Danish character traits or tendencies.
3. The lower classes include what is termed the "underclass" and the "working class", and the higher social classes are described as the "upper class" and the "higher middle class". Olsen and colleagues define the middle class as independent business men, senior executives or people with short-range or middle-range education who earn less than twice the average income in Denmark. The lower social classes are defined as skilled and unskilled workers and people who are out of the workforce for 4/5ths of the year. The higher social classes are defined as independent business men, senior executives and people with a higher education who earn more than twice the average Danish income, as well as all university graduates, independent of income (Olsen et al. 2012, 37). The average income in Denmark was 403,500 Danish Kroner in 2012 (Sabiers and Larsen 2014).
4. An exception is the work of ethnologist Thomas Højrup, who carried out pioneering work on different lifeforms (*livsformer*) in Denmark in the early 1980s. He analyzed how different social groups of people practiced their

everyday lives, and highlighted significant social differences within Danish society (Højrup 1983).
5. See Chap. 13 by Monica Aarset in this volume, where Aarset discusses the challenges of transgressing social and cultural boundaries between social classes.
6. See Linnet (2011) for a similar point regarding stereotypical descriptions of social classes.
7. The geographical division of Danish society, especially in rural vs. urban areas, adds to social segregation, and expressions such as the "rotten banana" (*den rådne banan*) and "outskirts Denmark" (*udkants-Danmark*) are commonly used to underline the social and economic hierarchy of the urban-rural division of the country.
8. See the Introduction, Chap. 1 of this volume for further discussion of the egalitarian paradox.
9. See Chap. 9 by Ida Erstad in this volume for a similar point raised in a Norwegian context.
10. Elin Pausewang (2001, 171) makes an interesting point regarding how in the very process of measuring and categorizing, differences in disease prevalence and survival through socio-economic variables (such as economy, education, or employment status differences) are drawn up and explicated, paradoxically, in the attempt to eradicate them.
11. Some scholars have analyzed the ways in which the moral landscape and organizational or social structures influence health practices, looking at, for example, the availability and accessibility of healthy food (Cummins et al. 2014), social and material circumstances (Farmer 1999), and the organization of the health care system (Andersen et al. 2014).
12. Halvard Vike's point is that people with low social positions are often described as lacking personal competences if they fail to live up to the standards of the universal welfare system (Vike 2001).
13. Such neo-liberal transformations of the very idea and the character of the welfare state have also been traced in recent writings on the Danish welfare state (Bruun et al. 2015). The chapters in the volume edited by Bruun, Krøijer, and Rytter analyze the various ways in which the Danish welfare state has changed its expectations of its citizens, indicating a move away from a welfare ideal of imagined sameness.
14. See Offersen, Vedsted, and Andersen for an analysis of the ways in which notions of morality are embedded in perceptions of bodily sensations by their Danish middle-class informants, and thereby create possibilities for interpretations and actions regarding the body, health, and illness. Offersen argues that these possibilities include concerns about the common good of the Danish welfare state, which may legitimize decisions regarding whether or not to seek health care; this is particularly salient among Danish middle-class citizens (Offersen et al. 2017).

REFERENCES

Andersen, Rikke S., Marie L. Tørring, and Peter Vedsted. 2014. Global health care-seeking discourses facing local clinical realities: Exploring the case of cancer. *Medical Anthropology Quarterly* 29 (2): 37–55. doi:10.1111/maq.12148.

Ayo, Nike. 2012. Understanding health promotion in a neoliberal climate and the making of health conscious citizens. *Critical Public Health* 22 (1): 99–105. doi: 10.1080/09581596.2010.520692.

Baadsgaard, Mikkel, and Henrik Brønnum-Hansen. 2012. *Social ulighed i levetiden*. København: Arbejdernes Erhvervsråd. http://www.ae.dk/files/dokumenter/analyse/ae_social-ulighed-i-levetid_0.pdf. Accessed 10 Jan 2016.

Bourdieu, Pierre. 1987. What makes a social class? On the theoretical and practical existence of groups. *Berkeley Journal of Sociology* 32: 1–17.

Briggs, Charles L. 2003. Why nation-states and journalists can't teach people to be healthy: Power and pragmatic miscalculation in public discourses on health. *Medical Anthropology Quarterly* 17 (3): 287–321. doi:10.1525/maq.2003.17.3.287.

Bruun, Maja H. 2011. Egalitarianism and community in Danish housing cooperatives: Proper forms of sharing and being together. *Social Analysis* 55 (2): 62–83. doi:10.3167/sa.2011.550204.

Bruun, Maja H., G. Skrædderdal Jakobsen, and S. Krøijer. 2011. Introduction: The concern for sociality – Practicing equality and hierarchy in Denmark. *Social Analysis* 55 (2): 1–19. doi:10.3167/sa.2011.550201.

Bruun, Maja H., S. Krøijer, and M. Rytter. 2015. Indledende perspektiver: Forandringsstaten og selvstændighedssamfundet. *Tidsskriftet Antropologi* 72: 11–37.

Christiansen, Niels F., and Pirjo Markkola. 2006. Introduction. In *The Nordic model of welfare: A historical reappraisal*, ed. Niels F. Christiansen, Klaus Petersen, and Nils Edling, 9–30. Copenhagen: Museum Tusculanum Press.

Cummins, Steven, Sarah Curtis, Ana V. Diez-Roux, and Sally Macintyre. 2007. Understanding and representing "place" in health research: A relational approach. *Social Science & Medicine* 65 (9): 1825–1838. doi:10.1016/j.socscimed.2007.05.036.

Cummins, Steven, Ellen Flint, and Stephen A. Matthews. 2014. New neighborhood grocery store increased awareness of food access but did not alter dietary habits or obesity. *Health Affairs* 33 (2): 283–291. doi:10.1377/hlthaff.2013.0512.

Dalton, Susanne O., Joachim Schüz, Gerda Engholm, Christoffer Johansen, Susanne K. Kjær, Marianne Steding-Jessen, Hans H. Storm, and Jørgen H. Olsen. 2008. Social inequality in incidence of and survival from cancer in a population-based study in Denmark, 1994–2003: Summary of findings. *European Journal of Cancer* 44 (14): 2074–2085. doi:10.1016/j.ejca.2008.06.018.

Diderichsen, Finn, Ingelise Andersen, and Celie Manuel. 2011. *Ulighed i sundhed. Årsager og indsatser*. København: Sundhedsstyrelsen.
Faber, Stine T. 2008. *På jagt efter klasse*. Phd thesis, Institute of Sociology, Social Work and Organization, Aalborg University.
Farmer, Paul. 1999. *Infections and inequalities. The modern plagues*. Berkeley: University of California Press.
Fassin, Didier. 2003. The embodiment of inequality. AIDS as a social condition and the historical experience in South Africa. EMBO Reports 4 Spec No (June), S4–S9.
Good, Byron J. 1994. *Medicine, rationality and experience: An anthropological perspective*. Cambridge: Cambridge University Press.
Gullestad, Marianne. 1984. *Kitchen-table society: A case study of the family life and friendships of young working-class mothers in urban Norway*. Oslo: Universitetsforlaget.
———. 1992. *The art of social relations: Essays on culture, social action and everyday life in modern Norway*. Oxford: Oxford University Press.
———. 2001. Likhetens grenser. In *Likhetens paradokser. Antropologiske undersøkelser i det moderne Norge*, ed. Marianne Lien, Hilde Lidén, and Halvard Vike, 32–67. Oslo: Univeritetsforlaget.
Højrup, Thomas. 1983. *Det glemte folk – livsformer og centraldirigering*. København: Museum Tusculanum.
Jöhncke, Steffen. 2011. Integrating Denmark: The wellfare state as a national(ist) accomplishment. In *The question of integration. Immigration, exclusion and the Danish wellfare state*, ed. Karen F. Olwig and Karsten Pæregaard. Cambridge: Cambridge Scholars.
Kapferer, Bruce. 2015. When is a joke not a joke? The paradox of egalitarianism. In *The event of Charlie Hebdo: Imaginaries of freedom and control*, ed. Alessandro Zagato, 93–114. New York: Berghahn Books.
Kjærsgård, Andreas P. 2015. *Scandinavian egalitarianism. Understanding attitudes towards the level of wage inequality in Scandinavia*. PhD dissertation, Aalborg University.
Krasnik, Allan. 1996. The concept of equity in health services research. *Scandinavian Journal of Social Medicine* 24 (1): 2–7.
Langer, Susanne, and Susanne Højlund. 2011. An anthropology of welfare. Journeying towards the good life. *Anthropology in Action* 18 (3): 1–9.
Larsen, Finn B., Karina Friis, Mathias Lasgaard, Marie H. Pedersen, Jes B. Sørensen, Louise M.A. Jakobsen, and Julie Christiansen. 2014. *Hvordan har du det? 2013—Sundhedsprofil for region og kommuner—Bind I. Hvordan har du det? 2013—Sundhedsprofil for Region Og Kommuner—Bind 1*. Aarhus: Folkesundhed og Kvalitetsudvikling.
Lavrsen, Lasse. 2011. En sygdom der kender sin klasse. *Information*, 29 Oktober.
Linnet, Jeppe T. 2011. Money can't buy me "hygge". Danish middle-class consumption, egalitarianism, and the sanctity of inner space. *Social Analysis* 55 (2): 21–44. doi:10.3167/sa.2011.550202.

Lupton, Deborah. 1995. *The imperative of health: Public health and the regulated body*. London: Sage.
Macintyre, Sally, Anne Ellaway, and Steven Cummins. 2002. Place effects on health: How can we conseptualise, operationalise and measure them? *Social Science and Medicine* 55 (1): 125–139. doi:10.1016/S0277-9536(01)00214-3.
Madsen, Marie H., Betina Højgaard, and Jens Albæk. 2009. *Health literacy— Begrebet, konsekvenser og mulige interventioner*. København: Sundhedsstyrelsen.
Marmot, Michael G., Geoffrey Rose, Martin Shipley, and Patricia J. Hamilton. 1978. Employment grade and coronary heart disease in British civil servants. *Journal of Epidemiology and Community Health* 32 (4): 244–249.
Marmot, Michael G., George Davey Smith, Stephen A. Stansfeld, Chandra Patel, Fiona North, Jenny Head, Ian R. White, Eric Brunner, and Amanda Feeney. 1991. Health inequalities among British civil servants: The whitehall II study. *Lancet* 337 (8754): 1387–1393.
Marmot, Michael G., Sharon Friel, Ruth Bell, Tanja A.J. Houweling, and Sebastian Taylor. 2008. Closing the gap in a generation: Health equity through action on the social determinants of health. *Lancet* 372 (9650): 1661–1669. doi:10.1016/S0140-6736(08)61690-6.
Merrild, Camilla H., Rikke S. Andersen, Mette B. Risør, and Peter Vedsted. 2016. Resisting "reason". A comparative anthropological study of social differences and resistance towards health promotion and illness prevention in Denmark. *Medical Anthropology Quarterly*, E-pub ahead of print. doi:10.1111/maq.12295.
Merrild, Camilla H., Peter Vedsted, and Rikke S. Andersen. 2017. Noisy lives, noisy bodies: Exploring the sensorial embodiment of class. *Anthropology in Action* 24 (1): 13–19.
Nørgaard, Marie, Peter Korsgaard, and Caroline Clante. 2015. Din uddannelse afgør, om du overlever en kræftsygdom Ekstrabladet, 12 July.
Nowatzki, Nadine R. 2012. Wealth inequality and health: A political economy perspective. *International Journal of Health Services: Planning, Administration, Evaluation* 42 (3): 403–424. doi:10.2190/HS.42.3.c.
Nutbeam, Don. 2000. Health literacy as a public health goal: A challenge for contemporary health education and communication strategies into the 21st century. *Health Promotion International* 15 (3): 259–267. doi:10.1093/heapro/15.3.259.
Offersen, Sarah M.H., Peter Vedsted, and Rikke S. Andersen. 2017. "The good citizen": Balancing moral possibilities in everyday life between sensation, symptom and healthcare seeking. *Anthropology in Action* 24 (1): 6–12.
Olsen, Lars, Niels Ploug, Lars Andersen, and Jonas S. Juul. 2012. *Det danske klassesamfund*. København: Gyldendal.
Olsen, Lars, Niels Ploug, Lars Andersen, Sune E. Sabiers, and Jørgen G. Andersen. 2014. *Klassekamp fra oven*. København: Gyldendal.
Ortner, Sherry B. 2003. *New Jersey dreaming: Capital, culture, and the class of '58*. Durham: Duke University.

Pausewang, Elin A. 2001. Syk og frisk, yter og nyter—Likhetsdilemmaer i et helsefremmende fellesskab. In *Likhetens paradokser. Antropologiske undersøkelser i det moderne Norge*, ed. Marianne Lien, Hilde Lidén, and Halvard Vike, 170–194. Oslo: Univeritetsforlaget.

Pedersen, Ove K. 2011. *Konkurrencestaten*. København: Hans Reitzels Forlag.

Pickett, Kate E., and Richard G. Wilkinson. 2014. Income inequality and health: A causal review. *Social Science & Medicine* 128 (December): 316–326. doi:10.1016/j.socscimed.2014.12.031.

Popay, Jenny, Sharon Bennett, Carol Thomas, Gareth Williams, Anthony Gatrell, and Lisa Bostock. 2003. Beyond "beer, fags, egg and chips"? Exploring lay understandings of social inequalities in health. *Sociology of Health & Illness* 25 (1): 1–23. doi:10.1111/1467-9566.t01-1-00322.

Reay, Diane. 1998. Rethinking social class: Qualitative perspectives on class and gender. *Sociology* 32 (2): 259–275. doi:10.1177/0038038598032002003.

Rose, Nikolas. 2007. *The politics of Life itself. Biomedicine, power, and subjectivity in the twenty-first century*. Princeton: Princeton University Press.

Sabiers, Sune E., and Helene B. Larsen. 2014. *De sociale klasser i Danmark*. København: Arbejdernes Erhvervsråd. http://www.ae.dk/sites/www.ae.dk/files/dokumenter/analyse/ae_indkomster-i-de-sociale-klasser-i-2012_0.pdf. Accessed 10 Jan 2016.

Sandemose, Aksel. 1992 [1972]. *En flygtning krydser sit spor*. Aalborg: Schønberg.

Sontag, Susan. 1978. *Ilness as metaphor*. New York: Farrar, Straus and Giroux.

Tørring, Marie L. 2014. Hvorfor akut kræft? Et bud på en epidemisk forståelse af tid og kræft-tendenser i Danmark. *Tidsskrift for foskning i sygdom og samfund* 20: 13–45.

Townsend, Peter, Margaret Whitehead, and Nicholas Davidson. 1992. *Inequalities in health: The black report & the Health divide*, new 3rd ed. London: Penguin Books.

Trägårdh, Lars. 2010. Rethinking the Nordic welfare state through a neo-Hegelian theory of state and civil society. *Journal of Political Ideologies* 15 (3): 227–239. doi:10.1080/13569317.2010.513853.

Vike, Halvard. 2001. Likhetens Kjønn. In *Likhetens paradokser. Antropologiske undersøkelser i det moderne Norge*, ed. Marianne Lien, Hilde Lidén, and Halvard Vike, 145–169. Oslo: Univeritetsforlaget.

CHAPTER 9

How Deep into Their Lives Can We Really Go? Diverse Populations, Professionals, and Contested Egalitarianisms in an Institutional Setting

Ida Erstad

In her group consultation of 6-month-old babies and parents, public health nurse (PHN, *helsesøster*) Cecilie takes a round and asks parents individually if they have begun to introduce solid foods to their babies. All babies, except one, have started eating solids, commonly as an evening meal. Cecilie listens to the parents, without giving any indications as to whether she thinks that their answers are right or wrong. Elvira, a Norwegian-Bosnian mother says that they have recently introduced porridge to little Adila—"She likes the one from the shop ... I can't remember what it is called, but it has banana in it." Cecilie raises her eyebrows in a sudden alert move and says that one should be "careful" with banana as it can cause allergies. Elvira senses that there is something behind the discreet reaction, and looks at Cecilie, eager for more specific information, which Cecilie does not give her.

I. Erstad (✉)
University of Oslo, Department of Social Anthropology, Oslo, Norway

© The Author(s) 2018
S. Bendixsen et al. (eds.), *Egalitarianism in Scandinavia*,
Approaches to Social Inequality and Difference,
DOI 10.1007/978-3-319-59791-1_9

Many of the consultations at the Parent and Child Health Services (PCHS, *helsestasjon*) in Oslo's Alna borough are organized as group consultations rather than the individual consultations that are more common in Norway. Public health nurses in the borough explain that group consultations, through parents' dialogue with each other and with professionals, facilitate "a sense of community" and installs reflexivity among parents. Yet, during my fieldwork I found that, even with the same group organization, PHNs' governing techniques may vary. In a group consultation for 9-month-old babies, Marit takes an approach that differs from Cecilie's:

> "They can now have regular meals, the same as we have. NAN [baby formula] and milk should be given only in connection with meals; otherwise they should drink water. They should not drink more than 0.5 liters of milk in the course of 24 hours. If they drink more milk than that, they may eat fewer solids." She scans the group with her eyes and asks: "Have many of you have started with normal milk?"

The examples above illustrate two of the different governing approaches public health nurses apply in meeting migrant mothers of babies and toddlers in the Parent and Child Health Services. Marit's tangible information and direct question trigger discussion, and mothers in the group share their experiences of introducing solids to their babies. Some parents ask questions, others offer advice—or share their methods of trial and error. The guiding principle about being "careful" in giving banana porridge to 6-month-olds is vaguer. Through my fieldwork I came to learn that when parents are encouraged to be "careful" in giving their babies porridge with banana, they do not always see how this can guide their actual practice (should they give a child banana porridge or not? How much or how little should one give in order to be *careful*?).

Scandinavian welfare states can be understood as ambiguous in the sense that they are ambitious (Rugkåsa 2011) with an extensive mandate to mold the lives of citizens, while they simultaneously are built upon individual rights to services and support. *Becoming* the state through their direct interactions with citizens, street-level bureaucrats (Lipsky 2010 [1980]) are situated at the continuum between care and control, where Cecilie is positioned more toward care, and Marit toward control—both working at molding the lives of citizens, young and old. As Helena, a welfare state worker working with children in the borough told me:—"We raise parents too ... oh yes, definitely ... the child's family background has always been part of our job ... but the question is, how deep into their lives can we really go?"

In this chapter, I explore the interactions between migrant mothers and public health nurses in the Parent and Child Health Services in Alna borough. I analyze these interactions from two angles. First, I draw attention to the professionals' *dual mandate* (Neumann 2009) and elements of care and control in their governing practices. The mandate is dual in that PHNs are to guide parents to ensure that their children lead safe and healthy lives, while at the same time they are to uncover any deviations, such as reduced hearing, delayed motor-skill development, or child abuse (Neumann 2009, 15). A central concern is the ways in which professionals' practices are influenced by their perceptions of the population they are set to govern and the place in which they do so. Second, I examine migrant mothers' expectations of PHNs, and their strategies in balancing these with expectations of professionals and family members. While egalitarianism, understood primarily through Marianne Gullestad's sameness-oriented definition of equality (1992, 1997, 2002), is often taken for granted as a gatekeeping-concept in Scandinavian anthropology, findings from my fieldwork at the PCHS indicate that it needs to be re-investigated.

Governance in a Diverse Neighborhood

This chapter is based on ethnographic fieldwork conducted in Alna's Parent and Child Health Services (2010–2013) as part of a PhD project about motherhood and socialization, and the governing of these (Erstad 2015). Methods include participant observation in the clinical spaces and in consultations (25 consultations in three different clinics), and semi-structured interviews with PHNs (6) and mothers of babies 0–2 years old (25) in addition to participant observation in families' homes in Norway and Pakistan.

Alna is one of four boroughs in the Grorud Valley in the north-east of Oslo, and has approximately 50,000 residents. In a sense, "all" Alna residents have immigrated to the borough, as the area was agricultural land on the outskirts of Oslo until the 1950s, but the ethnic diversity of inhabitants has increased quite rapidly since the 1980s. The number of residents with a migration background more than doubled between 2000 and 2013, from 11,210 to 23,370.[1] Currently, half of Alna's residents have a migration background (Høydahl 2014, 714–715), and Alna is the most ethnically diverse of Oslo's 15 boroughs, with residents from 148 different nation-state backgrounds (Høydahl 2014, 12).[2]

Through studies of urban neighborhoods in the UK, Steven Vertovec developed the notion of *super-diversity*, underlining "a level and kind of complexity surpassing anything the country has previously experienced", and a condition "distinguished by a dynamic interplay of variables among an increased number of new, small and scattered, multiple-origin, transnationally connected, socio-economically differentiated and legally stratified immigrants who have arrived over the last decade" (2007, 1024).[3] I find that studies of diverse—or super-diverse—neighborhoods tend to focus on *convivial* lives, referring to ways of *living with* each other, through everyday encounters (see Gidley 2013; Rhys-Taylor 2013) and largely ignore the role of the state in governing the people living in these neighborhoods.

Studies of public health nurses in Norway (see Andrews and Wærness 2011; Dahl and Clancy 2015; Neumann 2009) have mainly focused on their governing mandates and practices, and paid less attention to interactions between parents and PHNs. By not paying sufficient attention to the dialogical nature of governing, these studies have missed out on an understanding of how limitations and opportunities in parents' lives shape institutional interactions. Indeed, as Halvard Vike has recently pointed out, there is a lack of empirical studies that map processes in and out of institutions and focus on boundaries between formal institutions and their surroundings (2015, 8).

Unlike many studies of diverse communities, I draw attention to the role of the state through local governance, and analyze interactions in local institutional arenas in a diverse context. Additionally, I explore how both PHNs and migrant mothers actively draw on mothers' social surroundings in clinic interactions. Exploring governing practices in ethnically diverse neighborhoods allows us to comprehend the scope of the state in times of changing population dynamics, such as increasing population diversity, and changing ideological-political circumstances, such as a partial shift from an explicit normativity toward liberalization and individualization.

EQUALITY AND DIFFERENCE, RACIALIZATION, AND EGALITARIANISM

In Scandinavia, egalitarianism and equality are considered a particular kind of ethos or cultural trait (Kjærsgård 2015, 1). For Gullestad (2002), a central feature of egalitarianism as it emerges in Norway is *likhet*, meaning likeness, similarity, identity or sameness. *Likhet,* Gullestad writes "is the most common translation of equality, implying that social actors must consider themselves as more or less the same in order to feel of equal value" (2002, 46). Norwegian everyday life, she argues, is marked by a *passion for boundaries* "expressed in tensions between boundary-setting and boundary-breaking" (Gullestad 1997, 21), which "can be analyzed as a culturally specific way of resolving tensions between the individual and the community" because "this logic leads to an interaction style in which commonalities are emphasized, while differences are played down" (Gullestad 2002, 46–7).

Joel Robbins has argued that anthropologists abandoned the term egalitarianism in the 1980s, due to anthropologists' lack of "any satisfactory theory of what an egalitarian society consists in" (1994, 23). Yet, in Scandinavia, egalitarianism remains somewhat central in anthropological writings. With reference to Denmark, Jeppe Trolle Linnet argues that Gullestad's notion of present-day egalitarianism is built upon norms about not "sticking out" (2011, 21). In her study of refugee integration in Sweden, Marita Eastmond relates ideals of equality and egalitarianism to politics, and argues that the ideal of equality, central to the Swedish welfare state model, becomes a legacy for the belief in, and ideologies of, state regulation and intervention (Eastmond 2011, 280; see also Larsen 2013). Exploring the establishment of a refugee asylum center in a small Swedish town, Karin Norman finds that refugees who look like us, i.e., white or European, are considered by local residents to have more of a reason to stay in the community than those who look different (Norman 2004, 211). Even though Gullestad is referred to in the literature on egalitarianism in Scandinavia, her theories are often used fragmentarily and rarely critically discussed.

In the late 1990s and 2000s, Gullestad (2002) continued to work with "equality as sameness", but now shifted her gaze from the study of everyday life to an analysis of public and media discourse. She found the constructions of difference to contribute to a natural racialization of difference, understanding racialization as "the categorization of people on the basis of characteristics that are assumed to be innate" (Gullestad 2006, 25). However, in her concern with discourse Gullestad may have missed out on some of the complexities in social interactions that could have contributed to an altered understanding of communication, interaction and racialization processes. Certainly, as I show, racialization may become an unintended consequence of a sameness-oriented egalitarianism. Simultaneously, the Parent and Child Health Services is a place where a *uenighetsfellesskap* (community of disagreement), meaning "a group of people with different opinions enter[ing] a common process leading toward a decision" (Iversen 2014, 12, 27, my translation), is negotiated. Shifting our gaze from the study of discourse to practice, and from culturally homogeneous communities, such as those Gullestad studied in Bergen, to culturally diverse neighborhoods, such as Alna borough in Oslo, we need to challenge the assumption that the logic behind social interaction in Norway is an under-communication of differences. As kindergarten teacher Anna says: "The only thing we have in common here is that we are all different." It is this "difference" that PHNs seek to understand and include in what they often talk about as their "mandate" to create a "sense of community" that not only allows for, but is founded upon difference. PHNs have explained to me that this "mandate" is motivated by a sense of responsibility to adjust the impression the media gives of the Grorud Valley as a ghetto[4] and by their personal relationship to the valley; many live or have lived there, others have known families living in the area for generations, caring for children and later their children's children. Background knowledge about migrant mothers, their families, and their private lives becomes integral to their governing.

EGALITARIANISMS OF PUBLIC AND PRIVATE SPHERES

Through my fieldwork I came to realize that for public health nurses, a "different culture", such as extended household living and a more stratified and hierarchical family context where members of the extended family have a right to be involved in parenting, set migrant mothers apart from the majority Norwegian population. These assumptions shape the role the PHN takes toward migrant mothers, such as balancing giving advice and offering guidance. PHNs, in other words, come with presumed perspectives, but also have new experiences through their interactions with mothers. From spending time with migrant families in their homes in Norway, and meeting with some family members in Pakistan, I find that egalitarian relationships are uncommon in the homes of migrant mothers, who often live in more hierarchical and stratified family contexts. Here, they are often met with counter-information from mothers-in-law or other senior family members, which they are expected to follow. This means, many migrant mothers explained to me, that they need professionals to give them tangible *advice* more so than *guidance* both because this meets their own expectations of professionals as experts holding scientific *truths*, and because concrete knowledge stands stronger against the knowledge of authority figures at home.

Gullestad (1992) believed that for Norwegians, equality, independence, and a sense of belonging could be encountered in the positively-marked private home, while people view the state as formal, impersonal, and hierarchical. In his explorations of Gullestad's egalitarianism, Vike (2013) questions the assumption that equality-as-sameness is constituted in private homes and that the public/private boundary is as absolute as Gullestad outlined. Further, Vike argues that despite neo-liberal ideals, in the Nordic countries, the state remains strong and that the population remains inclined to leave great responsibility in the hands of the state (Vike 2013, 2015, 10–1). I find that migrant mothers and their families in Alna borough tend to have great trust in various street-level bureaucrats. This trust aids PHNs in assessing how deep into people's lives they are able to go, but it also means that migrant mothers turn to local professionals as authorities for support when it can strengthen their argument against authorities in the private sphere, such as mothers-in-law.

Empowerment Through Giving Advice or Offering Guidance

Public health nurses are at the core of the implementation of Norwegian state policies due to their close contact with the population (Andrews 2002, 30) and their universalistic dual mandate. Nationally, three services are included in the Parent and Child Health Services: (1) antenatal and maternity care for the mother; (2) regular check-ups for children from birth throughout early childhood; and (3) again through adolescence. Here, I focus on the services provided to families with children of 0–3 years old. National guidelines direct what kind of topics the service is to cover, but local authorities decide how to organize the service in order to meet the guidelines (SHdir 2004). Attendance is not compulsory, but in 2015 a total of 97% of infants in Norway had been for a check-up at the local PCHS within the first eight weeks of life.[5]

According to the national guidelines, the Parent and Child Health Service is to "focus on *methods and processes* that enable parents, children and youth to positively influence their own health, well-being and coping mechanisms (*mestring*)" (SHdir 2004, 38; my translation and italics). Further, "messages must stimulate reflection and action, and not be moralizing" through using methods of "information, guidance and advisory activities" (SHdir 2004, 36, my translation). The guidelines define giving advice as providing "suggestions to solutions based on scientific information (*helsefaglige opplysninger*)", whereas offering guidance is a "planned process" through which "the person who is given guidance him/herself discovers and learns" (SHdir 2004, 28, my translation).

The term empowerment (*myndiggjøring*) does not feature in the 2004 guidelines, but the similar term mastery (*mestring*) does. Professionals in Alna, however, frequently talk about empowerment, a term that features in the draft to the forthcoming revised guidelines.[6] At a seminar for professionals in the borough who worked directly with the parents of toddlers, that I attended as part of my fieldwork, the concept of empowerment came up frequently in discussions. One PHN termed this a "process" of encouraging the ability to "solve own problems", to acquire the necessary resources to exert control over "one's own life", and to activate the ability to "meet own needs". Another PHN defined empowerment as a method to "enable them [parents] to feel confident as parents", requiring "reflection [together] with others". While concerned with empowerment, some PHNs were also worried about becoming "toothless" and "extinct as professionals", arguing that empowerment goes against "our helping gene", ignoring parents' want for "tangible advice". When they raise concerns about becoming toothless or extinct as professionals, PHNs are articulating larger concerns about the implications for their profession if the privileged position that their knowledge has traditionally held becomes challenged, and made equivalent to, rather than superior to, lay knowledge.

Defining a Dialogical Field: Quick Fixes and Not Dictating

Public health nurses' own interpretation of their mandate influences their governing techniques, including communication about knowledge, where they position themselves along a scale of giving guidance and offering advice—of governing more through dialogical care, reflection, and process, or through more direct control and tangible advice. In an interview, Cecilie explains the "empowerment strategy" behind her comment about being "careful" about banana porridge:

> I try not to dictate ... I do not want to give them [parents] the solution, because then they miss out on the educational component. I prefer asking them: "Yes, so how did you do that?" or "OK, what do you [the group] think about that? Do you have similar experiences?" and then try to steer the conversation from there ...

With the deprofessionalization following the Norwegian municipal health care reform in 1984, public health nurses lost their monopoly on duties and leadership positions (Andrews and Wærness 2011). I understand empowerment as a locally adapted ideology facilitated by particular methods and processes related to deprofessionalization, such as giving group consultations rather than the nationally more common individual consultations, and giving guidance more so than advice. One aim of group consultations is that parents may work to correct each other through dialogues or in a relationship of egalitarian reciprocity, institutional practices (Vike 2015, 18). As the first chapter in this book outlines, while institutional arrangements are individualizing, they are simultaneously based on a logic of "one size fits all". Together, this contributes to social relations between parents, and between parents and professionals that potentially open up for diversities in social relations and practices. PHN Elin outlines her contemplations in choosing a method to meet migrant mothers:

> They [non-European migrant-mothers] see public health nurses and the Parent and Child Health Services as authorities. They are concerned with what we tell them. This group often wants a quick fix. Sometimes I give them that, but first I try to get a sense of what they want from me and why.

Norwegian sociologist and social psychologist Stein Bråten has developed the term "pretend dialogue" (*skinndialog*) to describe the processes occurring when a dialogue is conducted on the premises set by those who hold a monopoly on knowledge, limiting the conversational universe so that only one of the participants appears conceptually rich (2000, 143–144). Similarly, anthropologist Brigitte Jordan (1997) has developed the concept of *authoritative knowledge* to analyze domains where several parallel and equally legitimate knowledge systems exist, but where one system is frequently considered more legitimate than the others. Authoritative knowledge is not necessarily correct—but it *counts*. Yet, ranking and communication of knowledge cannot be understood purely in terms of dichotomous models of PHNs' "scientific" knowledge as opposed to migrant mothers' and more so their families' "traditional" knowledge because PHNs' knowledge is not purely scientific, but is combined with personal experience, practical knowledge, and personal discretion (Dahl and Clancy 2015). Neumann argues that PHNs' knowledge is open to negotiation, both internally in that she evaluates different knowledge forms and at an institutional level because she is "expected to tone down her authority as an expert and provide guidance according to a dialogical model for interaction" (2009, 59–60, my translation). Further, the expectations that migrant mothers have of professionals as experts influence interactions between mothers and public health nurses.

While PHNs interpret mothers as wanting a *quick fix* as opposed to empowerment, migrant mothers may seek such forms of knowledge because they need a different organizational and methodological approach from the Parent and Child Health Services to become empowered. I have come across many mothers who visit the PCHS regularly and without an appointment to measure and weigh their children, writing down the numbers in a little notebook. They use this tangible information, they explain to me, as *evidence* to prove to family members that they are good mothers with growing babies. I understand this as another indication of the strength of tangible and scientific knowledge among mothers and their families.

From Elin, we sense that there certainly is a correct answer, or a quick fix, but that she chooses to keep this hidden—at least for some time. As Bendixsen and colleagues argue (Chap. 1, in this volume), the universalist orientation in Scandinavian welfare state was probably not intended to be generous. By underplaying their power by *not dictating* or by more or less informally attempting to solve challenges that formally are sorted under other services, such as the child welfare authorities, as I have found them to do, PHNs can potentially extend their professional power deeper into the private sphere.

Cecilie, more so than Elin, seeks to broaden the dialogical field where mothers can share, discuss, and reflect upon their own and others' experiences and practices, and tries to understand parents' attitudes and levels of knowledge. The aim of this is to provide parents with the information that is required by mothers, but without communicating it clearly as answers to questions. Through their choices of organizational and communication methods, professionals work toward making active and self-reflecting citizens in the nation state. Yet, Elin notes that often "this group", as she terms non-European migrant-mothers, does not participate in the conversations and reflections that she attempts to facilitate. Norwegian-Pakistani Raheela outlines her reasons for non-participation:

> Breastfeeding seems to be a hobby horse [*kjepphest*] for the midwives and public health nurses. I don't even dare to mention to them that I use NAN

[baby formula]. It is the same with solids ... but I don't talk to them about this, because I know they want people to breastfeed exclusively until the baby is 6 months old.

In interviews, many migrant mothers explain to me that although public health nurses often open up for multiple *correct* answers in the groups, they simultaneously suspect that PHNs have a clear idea of what the correct answer is, but that they choose to under-communicate this. In other words, migrant mothers may have clear ideas about which knowledge *counts*, but sense that PHNs to some extent facilitate a pretend dialogue. Raheela is acutely aware of the hierarchical mechanisms through which knowledge is transmitted, and knows very well which kind of knowledge counts in the clinical context. This causes Raheela to withdraw into her own reflective processes rather than share and reflect together with others in the group consultations. In this sense, both migrant mothers and PHNs may, in line with Gullestad's perspective, engage in an interaction style that plays down differences and where a sameness-oriented ideology is prominent (2002). Yet at the same time there is also another form of equality that emerges in clinical interactions and that may extend beyond this: a more multifaceted and inclusive outlook that includes greater room for diverse opinions and practices.

PUBLIC HEALTH NURSES MEETING MIGRANT MOTHERS "WHERE THEY ARE"

At a 6-month-old group consultation I attended, Elin spoke to parents about the importance of "allowing for some crying" and to "*stå i det*" ("to keep it up", lit. to stand in it) when introducing "good sleeping habits", because although "it can be exhausting, a few nights will give results". In an interview, she explains to me why routines for sleeping are important:

"People need structure. Children must go to bed in order to get up in the morning." Another public health nurse, Linda, shrugs off the seeming necessity of children having to go to bed early in the evening and to get up early in the morning.—"It is just as fine", she tells parents at a 6-month-old group consultation, if parents and children go to bed at the same time, late in the evening, in the same room, even in the same bed, if this "suits the family" (*hvis det passer seg i familien*) She explains to me after the consultation:— "Treating everyone the same .. we have moved away from that, we meet them where they are."

Elin is concerned with parents and children having correct daily routines, such as not merely getting up, but getting up *in the morning*, in time for a regular working day. Linda's approach to the governing of intimate practices is more flexible, taking into account the different family constellations and nature of relations. Elin is of the opinion that even though mothers do not work *now*, they should aim at formal employment at some stage if not for themselves then for their children, and considers the introduction of routines for children a necessary measure for women to achieve employment. With a strong dominant family model in Norway, entailing symmetrical gender relationships and female employment,[7] mothers who live in complementary relationships and choose not to combine care work and paid employment as a dimension of their motherhood, fail to meet these ideals. As Aarset's and Jacobsen's chapters in this book discuss, (Chaps. 13 and 14, in this volume), complementary gender roles are considered central to the sameness-oriented Nordic egalitarianism with the implication that the scope of moral action becomes limited.

Danielsen and colleagues write about public health nurses in Alna that their "understanding of themselves is that they adapt to the reality which they are set to manage" (Danielsen et al. 2011, 8, my translation), and further that PHNs recognize that the migrant population can have other needs than the majority population (Danielsen et al. 2011, 30). Accordingly, if PHNs understand the reality to be changing, for instance, through a population diversification, in their own perspective, their approach to managing the population changes too. Linda, for instance, explained that with regards to a recently-arrived refugee family, she departed from what normally is very tangible and strict advice, namely never to give children juice in their bottles:—"They just fled from a war ... Imagine what this family has been through ... a little juice in the bottle is not going to be the end of the world, is it?"

Other times, migrant mothers are marked as *different*, and singled out as a "special needs group" (Nordberg and Wrede 2015, 55), requiring special measures in order to move them toward equality. While migrant mothers are seen as both competent and capable of personal reflection and motivated to adapt mothering ideals and practices which are different to those of their own mothers, many PHNs, such as Linda, are aware of the limitations and constraints in migrant mothers' everyday lives that influence their abilities to turn guidance and advice into practice. The adjustment in governing strategy Linda does when she decides that she will be less strict on the usually very specific advice that children should not have juice in their bottle is a way to meet people *where they are*, as opposed to *treating everyone the same*. Thus, to empower women in their private spheres, where stratified relationships are more accepted, and influence what kind of knowledge counts, migrant mother/public health nurse relationships call for an egalitarianism in institutional spheres that shifts from sameness toward encompassing diversity in relational orientation and background. However, the flipside of under-emphasizing sameness can be the establishment of more essentialized social interactions.

Does Meeting Migrant Mothers "Where They Are" Take on Racialized Connotations?

Like other professional training, such as that for social workers and teachers, public health nurse training does not prepare PHNs for the increasing population diversity in Norway.[8] Meeting mothers *where they are* is a skill or a competence developed from the dual legitimacy of the profession, individual PHNs' general outlook on migrants, and experience of working in the borough. I understand this practice-developed understanding of how to meet, manage, and govern *cultural difference* as a capacity or *diversity competence*. This is not a competence that directs practice in a specific direction. Rather, it may lead professionals' approaches to migrant mothers to become both more essentializing and regulative, and more flexible and open to differences. One implication of the dual mandate and the discrepancy between training and practice is that professional discretion takes on a greater role in their professionalism because it can bridge the gap between how the *reality* was presented to them through their training and how they experience it in practice.

There is a flipside to the governing strategy of PHNs aiming to meet mothers *where they are* if the criterion for defining where or what people are is based on preconceived and essentialized assumptions about what kind of information minorities want, need, and are able to understand. While allowing for diversity in practices, the way the refugee family was met may also have the effect that families are not given the information they need to be included as the *same*. During my fieldwork I often noted that PHNs were so concerned with countering the perceived implications of culture that they sometimes missed out on markers such as educational status or language skills that could potentially have changed the nature of the parent-professional interaction to become less concerned with race or *cultural difference*.

One example is Sonia, a second-generation Norwegian Pakistani, a biochemist, who came with baby Amir to his 4-month check-up. She was surprised that PHN Astrid started talking about the vaccination she was about to give little Amir, because Sonia could not remember being told anything about a vaccination the last time she was there:

Sonia: What kind of vaccination is this?
Astrid: It is a part of the vaccination program.[9]
Sonia: Yes, but what kind of vaccination is it?
Astrid: Let's just get this over and done with.

The conversation goes on without Sonia getting the information she is requesting. Astrid attempts to meet a migrant mother *where she is* by not explaining in detail and assuming that the fact that the injection was part of the vaccination program was answer good enough for Sonia. I speculate that this is because Astrid does not want to confuse Sonia with knowledge that she senses may influence Sonia to make the *wrong* decision—not to inoculate her son. In my perspective, Astrid's governing strategy was a kind of racial marking of Sonia, where she gave her the information she thought a Norwegian-Pakistani woman, living in Alna might be able to take in. Meanwhile Sonia, who herself has gone through the Norwegian vaccination program and holds a master's degree in biochemistry, is perfectly capable of understanding which injections are for what diseases, but wanted some more detail on the risk of side-effects.

As Aarset shows (Chap. 13, in this volume), "becoming" middle class is central to being seen as integrated, "same" as equal and Norwegian. There is a middle-class ideology inherent in the PHN profession and treating everyone the same has strong undercurrents of a middleclass-ness as an ideal. Also Neumann, referring to Gullestad's writings about the regulation of children identifies the middleclass-ness of the nursing profession (2009, 60, 196). Although some PHNs in Alna explained to me that they find migrant mothers "problematic", most of them simultaneously emphasized that they find working with a diverse population to be "professionally exciting" and as a way to extend the reach of their professionalism through getting deeper into people's lives or the private sphere, and to adapt their governing strategies accordingly. In allowing for some juice in the bottle, changing the advice given on children's sleep, and extending their own involvement before reporting families to the child welfare services, they may allow for more diversity in practices and orientations, and may serve to broaden the community of disagreement (*uenighetsfelleskap*).

Mothers' Strategies to Be Met "Where They Are"

Less than a month after Sunita (28) gave birth to her first child, a healthy baby girl that she breastfed exclusively, Sunita's maternal uncle told her to introduce baby formula, arguing that this would make the baby "grow faster and become healthier". Sunita, however, wanted to breastfeed exclusively for the first 6 months as this was in line with public health nurses' and World Health Organization recommendations. When the uncle listened neither to Sunita nor to her husband Ismail, who supported her, Sunita brought her uncle along to a consultation so that he was given "the facts", as Sunita termed it, directly from the professional. With the uncle present, she asked the PHN if there was a good reason for her not to breastfeed exclusively for 6 months, and if baby formula would be better for her daughter. As Sunita hoped for, the professional explained her line of reasoning using biomedical knowledge, directing her attention at both Sunita and her uncle. Sure enough, the PHN's arguments in the form of tangible advice convinced the uncle and he did not bring the topic up again with the young couple.

Migrant mothers adapt a variety of strategies to gain approval for their view on the home front, such as bringing authoritative family members along to the clinic so that they can get information directly from other persons of authority, the PHNs. Mothers alone do not have the authority to transmit biomedical knowledge from the clinic to the home due to the stratified and complementary social relations that characterize their private spheres. Strategies such as that of Sunita work well for mothers when there is agreement among professionals, migrant mothers and their family as to what knowledge *counts*. Most situations are not as straightforward as this, as is evident in the case of Amna. Both Amna and her husband Said are born in Norway, have tertiary education, and stable well-paid jobs. Living with Said's mother, Mrs. Raja means that they can save money to invest in their own apartment, but it also means that Mrs. Raja is involved in certain aspects of Amna and Said's private lives. Amna brought Mrs. Raja to consultations with the midwife during her pregnancy, but later went alone, choosing to limit the involvement of her mother-in-law:

> My mother-in-law ... I don't mind listening to information or advice, but I will still do it my own way. When it comes from her, I certainly don't want to do it. I know that it's wrong, but I still won't do it. Besides, the midwife told me "Don't listen to the family!" She did say that! She said that often there is so much different advice out there, it gets confusing, so seek professional advice instead.

The midwife assumed that Amna was subject to cross-pressure between two different knowledge systems, needing support in standing up against her mother-in-law. Telling Amna, in front of Mrs. Raja, not to listen to her family, the midwife may have sought to give Amna a tool she could use in strengthening her own view within this family context, similar to the context that Sunita staged. Amna appreciated the midwife telling her this while Mrs. Raja was present, as she did not have to offend Mrs. Raja later at home when not taking her advice. At home, Amna encountered a similar strategy to that from the midwife from her mother-in-law who told Amna that what the PHN had said "is not good advice—this [Amna points at herself, pretending to be her mother-in-law] is how you do it". In families with stratified relationships, the older generation may try to proclaim the legitimacy of traditional experience over scientific knowledge from professionals as Mrs. Raja attempted, rhetorically asking Amna: "I've had six children, does that not count?"

Living with parents-in-law may limit mothers' ability to implement advice they get at the Parent and Child Health Services (see Danielsen et al. 2011). Yet, a number of migrant mothers in my study express the need for tangible advice precisely because they are entangled in these stratified relations at home. When migrant mothers such as Amna and Sunita expect tangible advice or a quick fix from the professional, this is not necessarily because they are not willing to or capable of engaging reflexively with knowledge. Rather, they have already reflected upon different kinds of knowledge and made up their mind, they just need an authority to confirm this so that their choice becomes legitimate in others' eyes. In other words, they are self-reflexive and have ambitions of transformation—similar to the aims PHNs have for them. They have, in Gullestad's terms, shifted from a perspective of obedience to one of negotiation, entailing "the ability to live with tensions and paradoxes and to find solutions not in terms of either one or the other poles of an opposition, but in terms of their integration" (Gullestad 2006, 71).

Conclusion: Moving Beyond Equality as Sameness

Migrant diversity is written into health care systems through the ways in which institutional practices deal with diversity, and the ways in which migrant groups articulate their needs (Falge et al. 2012, 3). In this chapter, I have challenged the often taken-for-granted Nordic sameness-oriented form of egalitarianism. Andreas Pihl Kjærsgård argues that attitudes—such as egalitarianism—"need to be reproduced, and in the process of reproduction, individuals have a reflexive potential allowing [for] change" (2015, 2). For Pihl Kjærsgård, changed perceptions may pose a threat to Scandinavian egalitarianism (2015, 5). In my understanding of the relationships of care and control, of public and private, and of treating everyone *the same* and meeting people *where they are*, egalitarianism emerges as two-sided. This is in line with Bruce Kapferer's argument that egalitarianism is "deeply contradictory and perpetually locked in struggle with itself" because inegalitarianism is "the enduring potential of egalitarianism's other side" (Kapferer 2015, 106). The dilemmas that I identify in PHNs' different perspectives on empowerment seem to be part of their governing strategies. Clinic interactions between (mainly) majority professionals and a diversifying population do not necessarily threaten egalitarianism. Rather, I find that egalitarianism shifts and broadens through the reflexivity of social actors. This, I argue, indicates that PHNs do not understand difference as temporary, but rather translate it into diversity, incorporating it into their governing techniques.

I identify an under-communication of difference in the interactions between migrant mothers and professionals, and an egalitarian perspective that leads to an essentialized outlook on migrant mothers where cultural difference is understood as unwanted variation. This is evident, for instance, in the ways in which PHNs reflect upon when and how to share the knowledge that counts with migrant mothers. Yet, I also argue that there is a tendency, both through the organization of consultations into groups and through parent/professional interactions, toward the establishment of a broader discursive space that allows for and facilitates difference understood as diversity as integral to egalitarianism. In this sense, the sameness-dimension of equality and egalitarianism becomes less pronounced.

Based on the national guidelines, local PHNs are concerned with the development of self-reflective subjects who desire self-realization and autonomy. Some migrant mothers yearn for clear instructions and unambiguous professionals in order to strengthen their arguments and negotiations with other kinds of knowledge from other sources, primarily the older generation. Both groups agree on the value of empowerment, but the path to reach this is different from the perspectives of the migrant mothers and the professionals. Migrant mothers self-reflexively work toward becoming more independent. PHNs try to facilitate this, but their techniques may actually prevent mothers from reaching the goals that they share, namely, migrant mothers' independence-oriented egalitarianism.

This has led me to question the fairly rigid opposition between public and private spheres that Gullestad proposed. Exploring both migrant mothers' and public health nurses' efforts in transmitting information between clinical and private spheres, it emerges that these are connected in more intricate ways than Gullestad observed.

Gullestad argued that "it has long been a central value in Norway that people who live close to each other should have something more in common than the mere materiality of the place" (2006, 109–10). In a place like Alna, where what people have in common is difference, many PHNs take on a broader mandate that goes beyond facilitating an egalitarianism based on similarity, and work toward creating a sense of community of difference. PHNs may adjust their ideals and practices when meeting a diverse population, building and using their diversity competence, de- and re-naturalizing difference and to some extent encouraging a community of disagreement. What is at stake is an understanding of equality based on sameness in which migrant mothers, through being categorized as "others", are expected to adapt to the majority standards, and one in which migrant mothers are not subjected to paternalistic ideals (see also Neumann 2009, 205).

Taking a closer look at her writings, it emerges that Gullestad also made the point—albeit less forcefully—that increased interactions (presumably across lines of difference), might lead to both increased conviviality and heterogeneity as well as to increased cultural stereotyping (Gullestad 2006, 30). It is this dual picture that I have sought to present in this chapter. If we as social scientists adapt preconceived theories of how we think about and categorize difference, we might end up missing out on the kind of work that takes place in diverse contexts, through which egalitarianism becomes re-worked. Although ethnicity comes to matter in shaping governing techniques, PHNs also adjust their own governing ideals and practices in their meetings with a diverse population. Although I view PHNs' work toward establishing commonalities as concerned with the quest for sameness that Gullestad has argued for, I also find that public health nurses allow for, even encourage, differences through the organization of consultations into groups, by working toward meeting migrant mothers where they are, and by arguing that a little juice in a bottle is not the end of the world.

Notes

1. Persons with a migration background, or Norwegian-born to immigrant parents are born in Norway with two foreign-born parents and four foreign-born grandparents. https://www.ssb.no/en/befolkning/artikler-og-publikasjoner/oversikt-over-personer-med-ulik-grad-av-innvandringsbakgrunn (accessed 7 August 2016).
2. As Aarset writes in Chap. 13 (this volume), several of her South Asian middle-class informants have moved from the Grorud Valley to typically white middle-class suburbs in Oslo West. This does not free them from having to deal with a sameness-oriented ideology that also my informants are met with in Oslo East, although these segments of the ethnic minority population may do so differently.
3. For a discussion on diversity and super-diversity, see Erstad (2015).
4. For a discussion of the term *ghetto* in the Grorud Valley, see Rosten (2015) and Andersen (2014).
5. See http://ssb.no/helse/statistikker/helsetjko/aar/2016-06-28?fane=tabell&sort=nummer&tabell=271489 (accessed 7 July 2016).
6. See https://helsedirektoratet.no/horinger/nasjonal-faglig-retningslinje-for-helsestasjons-og-skolehelsetjenesten (accessed 11 November 2016).
7. *Arbeidslinja*, a directive prioritizing employment among both men and women, is a strong ideal in the welfare state. Female employment is relatively high in Norway at 68 percent among 15–74-year-olds, https://www.ssb.no/arbeid-og-lonn/statistikker/aku/kvartal/2016-04-28 (accessed 22 July 2016).
8. Some books have been written on diversity and social work (e.g., Eide et al. 2009; Otterstad 2008), but these perspectives are not an integral aspect of the training.
9. *Barnevaksinasjonsprogrammet*, administered by the Parent and Child Health Services.

References

Andersen, Bengt. 2014. *Westbound and eastbound. Managing sameness and the making of separations in Oslo* Unpublished PhD thesis, Department of Social Anthropology, University of Oslo.

Andrews, Therese. 2002. Grenseløse krav i helsestasjonstjenesten – Dilemmaer og mestringsstrategier. *Sosiologisk Tidsskrift* 10 (1): 27–47.

Andrews, Therese, and Kari Wærness. 2011. Deprofessonalization of a female occupation: Challenges for the sociology of professions. *Current Sociology* 59 (1): 42–58.

Bråten, Stein. 2000. *Modellmakt og altersentriske spedbarn. Essays on dialogue in infant and adult.* Oslo: Sigma.

Dahl, Berit Misund, and Anne Clancy. 2015. Meanings of knowledge and identity in public health nursing in a time of transition: Interpretations of public health nurses' narratives. *Scandinavian Journal of Caring Sciences* 29 (4): 679–687.

Danielsen, Kirsten, Ada I. Engebrigtsen, and Jon Erik Finnvold. 2011. *For å jobbe her, må en være interessert i folka som bor her. Helsesøstre og brukere på tre helsestasjoner i Alna bydel.* Oslo: Norsk institutt for forskning om oppvekst, velferd og aldring.

Eastmond, Marita. 2011. Egalitarian ambitions, constructions of difference: The paradoxes of refugee integration in Sweden. *Journal of Ethnic and Racial Studies* 37 (2): 277–295.

Eide, Ketil, Naushad A. Qureshi, Marianne Rugkåsa, and Halvard Vike, eds. 2009. *Over profesjonelle barrierer. Et minoritetsperspektiv i psykososialt arbeid med barn og unge.* Oslo: Gyldendal Akademisk.

Erstad, Ida. 2015. *Here, now and into the future: Child-rearing among Norwegian-Pakistani mothers in Oslo, Norway.* Unpublished PhD thesis, Department of Social Anthropology, University of Oslo.

Falge, Christiane, Carlo Ruzza, and Oliver Schmidke. 2012. Introduction: The political fight over the accomodation of cultural diversity. In *Migrants and health. Political and institutional responses to cultural diversity in health systems*, ed. Christiane Falge, Carlo Ruzza, and Oliver Schmidke, 1–18. Farnham: Ashgate.

Gidley, Ben. 2013. Landscapes of belonging, portraits of life: Researching everyday multiculture in an inner city estate. *Identities: Global Studies in Culture and Power* 20 (4): 361–376.

Gullestad, Marianne. 1992. *The art of social relations: Essays on culture, social action and everyday life in modern Norway.* Oslo: Scandinavian University Press.

———. 1997. A passion for boundaries: Reflections on connections between the everyday lives of children and the discourses on the nation in Norway. *Childhood* 4 (1): 19–42.

———. 2002. Invisible fences: Egalitarianism, nationalism and racism. *Journal of Royal Anthropological Institute* 8: 45–63.

———. 2006. *Plausible prejudice. Everyday experiences and social images of nation, culture and race.* Oslo: Universitetsforlaget.

Høydahl, Even. 2014. *Innvandrere og norskfødte med innvandrerforeldre i 13 kommuner.* Oslo: Statistics Norway.

Iversen, Lars Laird. 2014. *Uenighetsfellesskap. Blikk på demokratisk samhandling.* Oslo: Universitetsforlaget.

Jordan, Brigitte. 1997. Authoritative knowledge and its construction. In *Childbirth and authoritative knowledge*, ed. Robbie E. Davis-Floyd and Carolyn F. Sargent, 55–79. Berkeley: University of California Press.

Kapferer, Bruce. 2015. Afterword: When is a joke not a joke? The paradox of egalitarianism. In *The event of Charlie Hebro. Imaginaries of freedom and control*, ed. Alessandro Zagato, 93–114. New York: Berghahn Books.

Kjærsgård, Andreas Pihl. 2015. *Scandinavian egalitarianism. Understanding attitudes towards the level of wage inequality in Scandinavia*. Unpublished PhD thesis, Aalborg Universitet.
Larsen, Birgitte Romme. 2013. Becoming part of welfare Scandinavia: Integration through the spatial dispersal of newly arrived refugees in Denmark. In *Migration, family and the welfare state. Integrating migrants and refugees in Scandinavia*, ed. Karen Fog Olwig, Birgitte Romme Larsen, and Mikkel Rytter, 153–170. London: Routledge.
Linnet, Jeppe Trolle. 2011. Money can't buy me hygge. Danish middle-classness consumption, egalitarianism, and the sanctity of inner space. *Social Analysis* 55 (2): 21–44.
Lipsky, Michael. 2010 [1980]. *Street-level bureaucracy: Dilemmas of the individual in public service*. New York: Russell Sage Foundation.
Neumann, Cecilie Basberg. 2009. *Det bekymrede blikket: En studie av helsesøstres handlingsbetingelser*. Oslo: Novus Forlag.
Nordberg, Camilla, and Sirpa Wrede. 2015. Street-level engagements: Migrated families encountering the local welfare state. *Nordic Journal of Migration Research* 5 (2): 54–57.
Norman, Karin. 2004. Equality and exclusion: "Racism" in a Swedish town. *Ethnos* 69 (2): 204–228.
Otterstad, Ann Merete, ed. 2008. *Profesjonsutøvelse og kulturelt mangfold – fra utsikt til innsikt*. Oslo: Universitetsforlaget.
Rhys-Taylor, Alex. 2013. The essences of multiculture: A sensory exploration of an inner-city street market. *Identities: Global Studies in Culture and Power* 20 (4): 393–406.
Robbins, Joel. 1994. Equality as a value: Ideology in Dumont, Melanesia and the West. *Social Analysis: The International Journal of Social and Cultural Practice* 36: 21–70.
Rosten, Monika. 2015. *"Nest siste stasjon, linje 2" – Sted, tilhørighet og unge voksne i Groruddalen*. Unpublished PhD thesis, Department of Social Anthropology, University of Oslo.
Rugkåsa, Marianne. 2011. Velferdsambisiøsitet – sivilisering og normalisering. Statlig velferdspolitikks betydning for forming av borgeres subjektivitet. *Norsk Antropologisk Tidsskrift* 22 (3–4): 245–256.
SHdir. 2004. Kommunenes helsefremmende of forebyggende arbeid i helsestasjons- og skolehelsetjenesten. In *IS-1154*. Oslo: Sosial og helsedirektoratet.
Vertovec, Steven. 2007. Super-diversity and its implications. *Ethnic and Racial Studies* 30 (6): 1024–1054.
Vike, Halvard. 2013. Egalitarianisme og byråkratisk individualisme. *Norsk Antropologisk Tidsskrift* 24 (2–3): 181–193.
———. 2015. Likhetens natur. *Norsk Antropologisk Tidsskrift* 26 (1): 6–21.

CHAPTER 10

The Limits of Egalitarianism: Irregular Migration and the Norwegian Welfare State

Marry-Anne Karlsen

INTRODUCTION

Egalitarianism in the Nordic context is frequently related to the strong and positive value placed on equality within these societies, which again is seen as institutionalized in and through the structures of the welfare state. Several anthropologists, however, have problematized exclusivist aspects of Nordic egalitarianism evident in the way these countries have dealt with cultural difference, suggesting that equality comes with a demand for "sameness" or cultural conformity (Eastmond 2011; Gullestad 2002; Olwig 2011). Accordingly, Nordic egalitarianism produces its own "in-egalitarianism" or hierarchy based on the ability to conform to social norms and cultural values defined in dominant discourse on proper citizenship (Bendixsen et al., Chap. 1, in this book).

In this chapter, I explore another exclusivist side of Nordic egalitarianism, namely how the assumed egalitarian nature of these societies has been premised on the nation state and thus a conception of a community that is territorially bounded. I also explore how the territorial premise of egalitarianism has been challenged by so-called irregular migration and what

M.-A. Karlsen (✉)
Centre for Women and Gender Studies, University of Bergen.
Bergen, Norway

implications this has for understanding egalitarianism in the Nordic context. More specifically, I investigate what norms and values govern irregular migrants' access to basic services such as food, shelter, and health care. The central question for this chapter is: How is the exclusion, or differential treatment, of irregular migrants in terms of social rights justified within a welfare state supposedly based on egalitarian notions of justice?

Irregular migrants are migrants who enter or dwell on state territory without proper authorization. They are as such a product of immigration law (De Genova 2002), and expose the limits of border policing strategies. What makes the question of irregular migrants' access to social protection a particularly tricky problem for policy-makers, and an interesting lens through which to explore questions of egalitarian norms and welfare distribution, is precisely the fact that they are legally excluded, but still physically present within state borders.

In the following, I will begin by discussing what the egalitarian welfare approach entails in relation to migration, before I investigate what norms and values govern irregular migrants' (lack of) access to welfare. A central part of the analysis is focused on the legal and discursive construction of the outsider and insider. The reflections offered are based on analysis of public texts (laws and regulations, consultation papers and guidelines, government press releases), but also draw on ethnographic fieldwork conducted in Norway (Oslo and Bergen) between 2011 and 2014. In the course of this fieldwork I interviewed a wide range of health care providers, NGOs, and irregular migrants. I also followed some irregular migrants over time, in the sense of having multiple encounters and conversations with them, as well as accompanying them in their various daily activities.[1]

Egalitarianism and the Nordic Approach to Welfare

Norway, along with its Nordic neighbors, has received significant interest and admiration both academically and in international political circles for what is considered a comparatively egalitarian and generous approach to welfare distribution. Egalitarianism, as a European Enlightenment idea, emphasizes, as noted by Bendixsen, Bringslid and Vike (Chap. 1, in this book), each individual's equal moral worth. As a political project, egalitarianism can be said to form principles for the allocation and distribution of goods, and shapes the form and practices of welfare delivery. So, while all welfare states to various degrees and in various forms entail a commitment to securing people's basic security, they vary in terms of to what extent egalitarian principles guide the distribution of rights, duties, and social goods.

In the welfare state literature, the "egalitarian nature" of the Nordic welfare state is related both to how it redistributes wealth through progressive taxation and the way the welfare services are organized (Kuhnle and Kildal 2005). A key feature in regard to the organization of welfare is the (relative) absence of a connection between the financing of provisions and one's right to them. A basic premise behind the Nordic welfare state model is that the right to receive welfare should not be based on previous occupation, income, and contributions, nor should it be limited to the poor through means testing. The commitment to social and economic equality, rather than simply poverty alleviation or income maintenance, is considered a particular feature of the Nordic welfare model (Esping-Andersen and Korpi 1986).

The Nordic experiences, though, also show how the relationship between egalitarian principles and institutions of welfare is complex. For instance, while the Nordic welfare states are typified by universalism (that is inclusive welfare schemes targeting the entire population), very few welfare schemes are universal in the sense that there are no admission criteria. An example is social assistance that can be considered universal in the sense that the circle of people who can apply for such support is very broad, but it is not so universal in the sense that it is awarded on assessment and the sums conferred can vary. The welfare schemes can thus be said to be characterized by "universalism" to varying extents (Brochmann and Hagelund 2012). Furthermore, the Nordic welfare states contain a combination of universal schemes with entitlements based on citizenship or residence and work-related benefits (Kildal and Kuhnle 2014).

In the past decades, Nordic welfare state researchers have also cautioned against what they see as welfare policy trends that modify the basic principles of the welfare state (Kuhnle and Kildal 2005). One example is the increased linking of contributions and benefits represented by workfare schemes introduced in the social services. Nilssen and Kildal (2009) argue that the movement from a policy of "social rights" to a policy of "rights and duties" implies that the traditional resource-based egalitarian notion of justice, including ideas of redistribution, equal opportunity, and equal respect, is being replaced by an idea of "justice as reciprocity".

Despite these reservations, though, egalitarian norms are still generally considered as relevant markers of the Nordic welfare states (Dahl 2012; Vike 2015). Moreover, the "egalitarian welfare state" can be seen to constitute a core part of the national self-understanding, and as something of a brand by which to position the Nordic countries in the world

(Browning 2007; Fuglerud 2005). As such, egalitarianism in the Nordic context can be understood and approached as what Cox (2004) calls a "logic of appropriateness" for the consideration of policy options. By "logic of appropriateness", Cox refers to values that are so highly regarded that "scholars and policy-makers are compelled to justify their observations and proposals for reform by making reference to those values" (Cox 2004, 216). Hence, while egalitarian welfare values such as universalism and equality are not necessarily achieved or expressed in all policies, they can be understood as possessing a strong degree of shared attachment.

Soft Inside, Hard Outside?

In relation to migration policies, the egalitarian welfare approach has, in theory, implied that migrants should have the same formal rights to welfare as every other citizen and that access should mainly be organized through regular welfare state institutions (Brochmann and Hagelund 2012). The adherence to egalitarian norms from within have, at the same time, been linked to restrictive admission policies, thus following what Bosniak (2006) has called "the hard on the outside and soft on the inside" model of citizenship. This model is based on the assumption that there is an inherent contradiction between egalitarian welfare policies and widespread international migration. As famously argued by Walzer; "[t]he idea of distributive justice presupposes a bounded world within which distribution takes place" (1983, 31).

According to Brochmann and Hagelund (2012), the duality between inclusive welfare policies (soft inside) and restrictive admission policies (hard outside) has, in Norway, been seen as necessary to ensure the economic sustainability of the welfare state and to avoid huge social differences that would delegitimize it. As they state: "Good welfare states do not want to have large numbers of people or groups that fall through the net, disturb regulated working life, overload social budgets, or eventually undermine solidarity" (2012, 13). In this sense, immigrants who are legally present ought to be included in the welfare arrangements on equal grounds for their own good and for that of society.

What the societal considerations are in regard to irregular migrants, however, is less agreed upon. As I contend here, irregular migrants pose a considerable challenge to the "hard outside—soft inside" model, as they expose the unsustainability of a notion of a territorially bounded space within which egalitarian distribution can take place. The presence of irregular migrants on state territory exposes how states cannot completely control admission at its outer geographical borders, thus rupturing any neat connection between territorial presence and membership. The challenge facing policy-makers thus becomes: Should the welfare state approach to territorially present, but unwanted, migrants be guided by the "hard" threshold norms or the "soft" interior ones?

It should briefly be noted here that the Nordic countries are also known for having a sort of "soft outside". Scholars of international relations have, for instance, suggested that a distinctive Nordic brand of "normative internationalism" is a central part of the "Nordic model" (Bergman 2007; Ingebritsen 2002). Normative internationalism refers in this literature to a foreign policy driven by the countries' domestic values, including equality. In the Swedish case, normative internationalism has also, at least until recently, been seen to influence their comparatively welcoming approach to refugees and asylum seekers. I would suggest here though, that the normative internationalism of the Nordic countries rests rather heavily on a humanitarian rather than egalitarian foreign policy agenda. The main emphasis has been on comparatively generous provisions of overseas development aid rather than a commitment to a more equitable distribution of global income. The Nordic countries, though, tend to be seen, and see themselves, as both egalitarian *and* humanitarian. and Norway has promoted an image of itself as a "humanitarian super-power" (Fuglerud 2005). Nonetheless, humanitarianism and egalitarianism represent different commitments and projects.

Humanitarianism, like egalitarianism, can be seen as a product of European Enlightenment's commitment to a shared humanity. But rather than emphasizing equality, humanitarianism is oriented towards alleviating human suffering (Feldman and Ticktin 2010). Actions are based on compassion and benevolence, and oriented towards "victims" rather than bearers of rights (Fassin 2012). As such, humanitarian discourse and practice rest on a distinction between "us" and "them" and are grounded in a specific type of difference created by material inequality (Dauvergne 2005).

Humanitarianism has, like egalitarianism, also been seen as a moral principle guiding welfare policy, but in a different way. While egalitarianism is associated with support for social rights and an active government that intervenes in economic processes to rectify existing inequalities in society, humanitarianism is associated with support for more modest welfare policies directed at poverty relief (Feldman and Steenbergen 2001). Whereas the Nordic countries are seen as an example of egalitarian approach to welfare, humanitarianism is, for instance, seen as a value underpinning US welfare policy.

In the Nordic context, though, humanitarianism is first and foremost associated with a particular moral and political project concerned with international aid and intervention in crisis and conflict situation abroad either by non-governmental organizations or the state (Ticktin 2014). Hence, the tension between an egalitarian and humanitarian project has rarely been problematized in the literature on "Nordic normative internationalism". However, as I will return to later, the normative tensions and differences between egalitarian notions of justice committed to social leveling and a humanitarian policy based on benevolence and compassion are intensified when the principles of humanitarianism are not only applied to distant strangers, but applied in the domestic field in regard to irregular migrants. First, though, I will turn to how the demarcation of an inside and an outside on state territory is legally and discursively constructed, drawing the limits for when egalitarian principles should apply in regard to welfare distribution.

Legally Demarcating the Outsider

One of the intriguing traits that emerged when I was doing fieldwork among irregular migrants in Norway was the state's ambiguous and inconsistent approach when it came to the provision of welfare. Zeki's case can serve as one example. Zeki came to Norway as an unaccompanied minor in the mid 1990s, but years later lost his residence permit due to drug-related offences. When I met him, he was trying, with the assistance of a community outreach worker, to get a place in a drug rehabilitation centre and housing and economic assistance from a local Labour and Welfare Administration office. He was initially denied both, but after a year he was granted so-called emergency aid. This included a room in a hospice and approximately 60 percent of what state guidelines for social benefits stipulated. Although this was only meant to be short term, Zeki continued to live on this emergency support for years, yet remained unable to access any form of treatment for drug addiction due to his status as illegal.

A different example is provided by Aster. Aster, at the time we met, had been living illegally in Norway for 12 years. For most of that time, she had managed to support herself by working, having received a temporary work permit in 2001. At that time, it was not unusual for rejected asylum seekers to be granted temporary work permits so that they could provide for themselves until a departure could be effected. This policy changed in 2003, but Aster kept receiving a tax card, worked and paid taxes until

2011, when a clean-up in the Norwegian Tax Administration revealed that tax cards had by error been sent out automatically to rejected asylum seekers like Aster. After the tax card stopped coming, Aster lost her job, and she came to depend on friends' support. Ironically, for Aster, paying tax, and thus contributing to financing welfare, did not open formal possibilities for claiming welfare benefits. She was also not entitled to the emergency aid granted to Zeki. However, as a rejected asylum seeker, she was offered accommodation in an asylum reception centre.

As these two examples show, irregular migrants are not completely excluded from access to welfare, yet they are not included on equal grounds nor are they receiving the same standard of welfare. One of my suggestions in this chapter, is that in the past decade there has been a dual process in Norway whereby irregular migrants increasingly are legally demarcated outside the scope of welfare legislation, while at the same time humanitarian exceptions are built into the system to relieve some of the tension between the welfare state's commitment to basic security and immigration law enforcement

In Norway, the legal changes that have taken place in response to irregular migrants' presence, have primarily taken the shape of administrative reinterpretation concerning *the scope* of existing laws to restrict irregular migrants' access, thus making it explicit that they are excluded from an initially inclusive entitlement. Norwegian welfare law, including the Social Services Act (2010) and the Patients' Rights Act (1999), generally defines the scope of the law as "everyone residing in the Realm" in line with egalitarian principles of everyone's equal moral worth. There is no mention of legality as a requirement. However, in the past decade, as the issue of irregular migration has gained increased attention, there has been an ongoing discussion concerning who should be included in "everyone". While irregular migrants are still included in a few cases (i.e., the Child Welfare Act (1992), the Education Act (1998) and the Act on Crisis Shelters (2009), see Søvig 2013), their access to services has increasingly been circumvented by various regulations and circulars issued by state departments that define the scope of the law to mean legal residents. Access to health care is a prime example.

In 2010, the Ministry initiated a review of existing laws due to what they called "continuing doubt and varying practices" regarding irregular migrants' access to health care. One of the major challenges, according to a consultation paper issued by the Ministry of Health and Care Services (2010), was precisely how to interpret "all" ("*alle*") in the Patients' Rights

Act (1999), "reside or temporally reside" ("*bor eller midlertidig oppholder seg*") in the Municipal Health Services Act (1982) and "permanent domicile or residence" ("*fast bopel eller oppholdssted*") in the Specialized Health Services Act (1999). Although, the Ministry conceded that the wording seemed to imply that the scope of the Acts covered people residing illegally, they concluded that it would be reasonable "to interpret into the law" a legality requirement so that "one cannot be considered to be 'a resident' when unlawfully staying in the country". This formed the basis for a new health care regulation that came into force in July 2011, restricting irregular migrants' access to health care to emergency care and health care that cannot wait "without danger of imminent death, permanent and seriously reduced functionality, serious injury, or severe pain" (Healthcare Regulation 2011). Children, pregnant women, prisoners, and persons with communicable diseases, however, were still granted some additional rights.

Policies concerning irregular migrants' access to public accommodation and economic support have also been changed several times during the past decade. The first major change occurred in 2002 when rejected asylum seekers' access to shelter and financial support was revised. Up to that point, they had generally been accorded the same services as asylum seekers through the asylum reception system. However, from 2002 rejected asylum seekers gradually lost the economic support granted by the state, the possibility of a work permit and eventually, from January 2004, access to accommodation in asylum reception centres.

The "loss of accommodation" policy, though, was highly controversial and received considerable opposition from municipalities, as the municipalities now had to face the dilemma of how to deal with rejected asylum seekers' social needs (Brekke and Søholt 2005). Furthermore, the regulations and political signals regarding municipalities' responsibilities for irregular migrants were unclear. Circulars and letters from various state departments stated that while individuals without legal residence were not entitled to financial support under the Social Services Act, "no one should starve or freeze to death in Norway" (Ministry of Labor and Social Affairs 2004). As such they were entitled to emergency aid based on what was considered an "unwritten Act of Necessity". The application of this "unwritten Act" was left to the discretion of each municipality, which varied significantly (Brekke and Søholt 2005).

In 2006, in response to local criticism, the government established two "waiting centres" to house rejected asylum seekers. However, these centres soon became controversial due to low standards of care. In June 2010, riots erupted among residents of both centres, and they were subsequently closed due to extensive fire damage (Valenta et al. 2010). In September 2011, the government announced that rejected asylum seekers would again be offered accommodation in ordinary reception centres. They would also receive economic support, though at a lower level than asylum seekers awaiting a decision. Rejected asylum seekers (single adults) would receive just above one-third of what the state guidelines stipulated for those receiving social benefits, and approximately 60 per cent of the support granted to asylum seekers (Karlsen 2015). Furthermore, while the Immigration Act states that asylum seekers "shall" be offered accommodation, rejected asylum seekers only "can" be offered accommodation pending departure.

Still, not all irregular migrants are rejected asylum seekers and eligible for accommodation in asylum reception centres.[2] Zeki, for instance, was denied accommodation through the asylum reception system because he had previously had a residence permit. Irregular migrants such as Zeki continued, in theory, to be eligible for support from municipal social services through the "unwritten Act of Necessity". In January 2012, this Act was formalized through the Social Services Regulation (2011), which made it obligatory for municipalities to help people in "dire need" with financial support and assistance in finding temporary accommodation until the person could leave the country.

Irregular migrants' access to welfare is, as my account above illustrates, mainly governed through regulations, circulars, and letters issued by state departments. As such, the restrictions have been implemented without any comprehensive parliamentary debate (Søvig 2013). Legal scholars have thus questioned the legal basis for the restrictions both in relation to due process and human rights obligations (Andersen 2014; Süssmann 2015). Here, I wish to draw attention to another problematic aspect, namely, how, through the decrees, access to social services becomes meted out through benevolence rather than as rights, as illustrated by the "can" in regard to shelter in the Immigration Act. I will return to the implication of this later, but first I will look at the discursive demarcation of irregular migrants as "the outsider".

DISCURSIVELY DEMARCATING THE OUTSIDER

In February 2013, just a year after the emergency provision in the Social Services Regulation was implemented, Norwegian newspapers reported that a man from the Middle East, convicted of attempted rape in Sweden and expelled from Schengen, had been granted social assistance from the Norwegian Welfare Administration. The man had initially come to Norway as an unaccompanied minor, before moving to Sweden in 2010. On his return, as the media account displayed, the local office in the city of Skien granted him emergency aid for ten days. However, when he applied for regular social support, he was denied this. The man complained to the county governor, who concluded that he indeed was entitled to financial support and temporary accommodation "until he in practice could leave the country", a phrase used in the emergency clause.

In response to the media coverage, several prominent politicians reacted with condemning statements. Torbjørn Røe Isaksen, a conservative Member of Parliament, exclaimed that this gave anyone with illegal residency a "carte blanche" to get money from the welfare administration, while the Progress Party's Robert Eriksson claimed that "we now find ourselves in the insane situation that we have become the social welfare office for the entire world" (Hegvik et al. 2013). The Minister of Labour at the time, Anniken Huitfeldt (the Labour Party), was also quick to declare that granting benefits to this man contradicted her opinion of who should receive welfare benefits. However, while the opposition seemed to protest giving support to people with "illegal residency" in general, the Minister focused on the man's criminal behaviour. In a statement she wrote, "If the current emergency provision has such unreasonable effects, I will change it. I want to make sure that it is not abused by persons who have committed crimes and who have been expelled from the country" (Hegvik 2013a). Five months later, the Minister, on the basis of this particular case, initiated a consultation on changing the regulation. As the regulation was only a year old, it became the second consultation on the emergency provision in less than two years (Ministry of Labour and Social Affairs 2011, 2013).

This case, and the changing system of welfare support described above, draw attention to how access to welfare services also reflects wider societal values regarding the legitimate and illegitimate, and not only the legal and illegal. How irregular migrants are increasingly cast as "undeserving", and not merely "illegal", in public discourse is widely commented upon within the migration literature (Anderson 2013; Watters 2007). In particular, the "culture of disbelief" surrounding the category of asylum seekers in Europe, and the distinction increasingly made between legitimate and deserving refugees and bogus asylum seekers, have been seen to justify harsher policies, including restricting access to basic services for those deemed illegitimate. Constructed as undeserving and denied political voice, irregular migrants are not only excluded from the political community, but also, Willen suggests, from "the moral community of people whose lives, bodies, illnesses, and injuries are deemed worthy of attention, investment, or concern" (2012, 806). The question of deservingness thus becomes central to the way migrants' civic value is defined and measured, and translated into care.

Also in Norway, alongside state efforts to define irregular migrants outside of the scope of welfare laws, there has been an attempt to discursively distinguish more tightly between whose lives are worthy of care and whose are not. This however, is not straightforward. A central question, as illustrated in the introductory case, is whether all irregular migrants are viewed as undeserving, or are there some that are more or less worthy of compassion?

In recent years, research has shown how humanitarian discourse portrays irregular migrants as human beings variously in need, and deserving, of care (Ticktin 2006; Aradau 2004). This introduces an ambivalence in regard to how irregular migrants are perceived and managed by states, and contributes to an increased differentiation and hierarchy as certain categories of irregular migrants evoke more or less compassion. Which suffering becomes recognized in the public domain, Ticktin (2011) notes, is a question of struggle and construction and not of inherent "merit". Labels are in this regard central to the struggle and construction of deservingness. Is the migrant illegal, irregular, undocumented, or something else?

The central contested issue that is expressed in the various labels used to describe irregular migrants in Norway, I suggest, is who is to be held morally responsible for their precarious situation—the migrants themselves or the state that fails to deport them? At stake in the labels is thus the question of innocence and individual versus social responsibility for suffering. In 2004, the term "unreturnable" (*"ureturnerbar"*) was a prominent label used in the discussion concerning rejected asylum seekers' loss of state accommodation. The term gained acceptance academically, politically, and within the bureaucracy, and contributed to public sympathy (see, e.g., Aarø and Wyller 2005; Brekke and Søholt 2005). Many of those who lost access to state accommodation at that time were people who were difficult to deport, either because the country of origin did not accept deportees or because their identity was not established. However, in 2011, the official view became that no one was "unreturnable"; there were only "return refusers" (*"returnektere"*). The term was first used by

State Secretary Pål K. Lønseth at the Ministry of Justice and Police in a widely published newspaper comment in October 2011 (Lønseth 2011). Lønseth acted as the government spokesperson on asylum issues between 2009 and 2013.

The labelling of irregular migrants as "return refusers" can be seen as an active attempt by the authorities to contradict the more established terms of "unreturnable" and "undocumented" ("*papirløs*", a term adapted by NGOs), and also the victim-position these terms imply. Several scholars have commented upon how morally blaming individuals for their own predicament, of which the term "return refuser" is an example, is a trend within neoliberal governmentality (Pratt 2005; Mitchell 2006). Also, in the dominant Western European model of personhood, the individual is generally characterized as rational and autonomous, and the author of their own experience of the world. In this model, notions of agency become central to attributing responsibility and accountability (Jacobsen and Skilbrei 2010). Hence, whereas "unreturnable" give the migrant a passive subject-position and signals a failure on the part of the state to act, "return refuser" puts the agency and the moral responsibility of not returning clearly on the migrant. It also makes the migrant, and not the state, responsible for their and their children's living conditions while they are irregular. As State Secretary Lønseth (2011) put it, "They are themselves responsible for putting their own and their children's lives on hold by refusing to return."

Still, throughout the past decade of changing policies, certain groups were continuously singled out for special care. For instance, families with children and individuals with health problems were allowed to remain in ordinary asylum reception centres when other rejected asylums seekers were to be evicted. This draws attention to how recognition of vulnerability and perceived responsibility are used to distinguish *between* irregular migrants. As illustrated in the opening passage, a distinction between the "good" and "bad" illegal is also used to some extent to distinguish between irregular migrants. Here, the Minister singled out "convicted criminals" as those who should be excluded from services. These are lives that are "extra mismanaged" as they are perceived to have failed in some important moral way. In this way, the deservingness discourse can be seen to construct particular subject-positions for the irregular migrant. For instance, while the focus on irregular migrants as "bogus refugees" or "criminals" has helped construct the category of the "bad illegal", irregular migrants are also encouraged to make themselves "good illegals" to counter these associations in an attempt to gain acceptance both morally and legally (Coutin 2003). According to Chauvin and Garcés-Mascareñas (2012), the good character of irregular migrants has in several European countries and the USA been increasingly defined in terms of noncriminal conduct, economic reliability, fiscal contribution, identity stability, and bureaucratic traceability. As such, irregular migrants can make themselves "less illegal" and more deserving by working and avoiding crime.

Also in Norway, irregular migrants have attempted to present themselves as "good workers" and "contributing members of society" in an attempt to become "less illegal". For instance, in February 2011, a group of Ethiopians who by default had received a tax card for years launched a hunger strike in Oslo Cathedral when this practice was discovered. Examining their political mobilization, Bendixsen (2013) points out how, during the protests, the Ethiopians emphasized their deservingness as taxpayers, and as such attempted to inscribe themselves into what Anderson (2013) calls "the community of values". However, in the Norwegian context, being good workers and taxpayers does not create formal possibilities of gaining access to welfare, nor does it lead to regularization, as it does, for instance, in France and Spain. Thus, working and paying tax, rather than translating into rights, work to document a lengthy breach of immigration law, making it a more serious offence in the view of the immigration authorities. Still, not committing crimes, or not actively hiding from authorities by staying in asylum reception centres, are ways that irregular migrants can construct themselves as "less illegal" in the Norwegian context (Karlsen 2015).

While casting irregular migrants as "undeserving", and not merely illegal, in public discourse has been part of justifying harsher policies, including restricting access to basic services, there is no straightforward or automatic translation between how migrants are perceived and welfare policies. For instance, neither the centre left government, nor the right-wing government that succeeded it, has removed the emergency clause, despite their criticism of it. Why the construction of irregular migrants as illegitimate welfare recipients does not necessarily translate into policies that restrict "undeserving" migrants access to welfare completely, I suggest, is related to how access to welfare is not only a question of how the "Other" is perceived, but also how "We" understand ourselves in relation to the "Other". It is to this issue, I will now turn.

Humanitarianism and the Nation as a Moral Community

By returning to the debates surrounding the emergency aid provision in February 2013, it is possible to see from the way it developed that it did not only become a question of migrants' deservingness, but also about the nature and moral limits of the welfare state. For instance, the consultation paper issued by the Ministry of Labour and Social Affairs (2013) clearly shows a tension between immigration control and more traditional social policy concerns. Whereas the Minister stated to the media that the changes she initiated were to prevent the system from "being abused to enable illegal stay" (Hegvik 2013b), particularly by perceived criminals, the consultation paper sent out by her department directly contradicted this objective. Moreover, it underlined that it was "important that the welfare services were not attempted to be used as a tool for solving problems related to illegal immigration" (Ministry of Labour and Social Affairs 2013). In the public debates, the Minister further specified, as the Ministry also had done in relation to the "loss of accommodation" policy in 2004, that "no one should starve or freeze to death in Norway". In this sense, it became very unclear what the suggested amendments were meant to achieve. In the end, the changes implemented only stressed the temporary nature of the support and that NAV "may" demand that the person contribute to her/his own departure (Regulation amending the social services regulation 2014).

The idea that "no one should starve or freeze to death" highlights, I suggest, a particular part of the Norwegian self-perception that made it difficult to remove all support to irregular migrants. Norway, in addition to its self-perception as egalitarian, also fosters an understanding of the nation as good and caring. Vike (2004), exploring how the Norwegian welfare state embodies a form of community that is emotional and moral, has suggested that there is a particular sort of "welfare state nationalism", where suffering is rarely considered to be solely the sufferer's own problem, but is a kind of stain that testifies to an incomplete and somewhat immoral society.[3] Thus, safeguarding and providing care to groups defined as weak are important to maintain the welfare state's legitimacy, and, as Rugkåsa (2010) suggests, citizens' identity as citizens in an inclusive society. This creates a strong normative pressure or expectation on the state to address suffering of different kinds and to ensure that no one lives under conditions defined as undignified.

There is of course a big question of how far such welfare nationalism goes in terms of including those who are not deemed to belong, morally or politically, in the state or the nation. Still, the argument that suffering testifies to a somewhat immoral society, has been present within debates about irregular migrants and welfare. During my fieldwork, prominent voices supporting a more "humane" approach, including bishops, politicians from different political parties, and humanitarian organizations, frequently referred to irregular migrants' dismal situation as a "disgrace to the welfare state", or even characterized the policies as "un-Norwegian". Brekke, who conducted the commissioned evaluation of the loss of state accommodation policy in 2004, has also linked irregular migrants' continued access to food and shelter, despite political efforts to remove it, to core values underpinning the welfare system. As he argues in relation to the unwritten Act of Necessity:

> [T]he debate over the rights of these people showed that at rock-bottom there is a limit to what people can be allowed to suffer, which is frost and starvation … The norm that provides emergency aid in such extreme cases is not a formal obligation of the welfare state, and was not based on any formal entitlement. These softer norms that call for provision of help can possibly be seen *as a side effect of a long-term tradition of provision of welfare*, or even more possibly as the result of *basic humanitarian concerns and ideas of equality, which have served as the basis for the establishment of the welfare state*. (Brekke 2008, 21, my emphasis)

Brekke suggests in this quote that the values and norms of the welfare state, including "ideas of equality", create a "logic of appropriateness" also for policies aimed at the politically excluded, to use Cox's (2004) term. While I agree with Brekke that the discussions concerning the rights of rejected asylum seekers showed that there is a limit to what people can be allowed to suffer in the Norwegian welfare state, I suggest their inclusion is based on humanitarian concerns regarding the survivability of the body, while contradicting ideas of equality. Accordingly, there is a tension between "humanitarian concerns" and "ideas of equality".

Irregular migrants' limited access to welfare services departs in many ways from the normal frame through which the Norwegian welfare state traditionally frames and addresses suffering. Nilssen and Kildal have described this frame as a "social right" policy that satisfies basic needs and expresses "a resource-based egalitarian notion of justice, including ideas of redistribution, equal opportunity and equal respect" (Nilssen and Kildal 2009, 313). Kuhnle and Kildal (2005, 23) note that an essential historic reason for adopting the twin concepts of social rights and universalism in Norwegian welfare politics was to remove the humiliating loss of status, dignity, and self-respect that goes along with exclusion from programmes and entitlements. Human dignity, they argue, was a salient theme in the Norwegian socio-political debates, expressing first and foremost a deep dissatisfaction with the pre-WWII poor relief system. As I have argued above, the basic safety net granted to irregular migrants is based on compassion and benevolence, distributing services as "sovereign gifts" rather than as rights, and with an increased emphasis on deservingness and moral worth. As such, the very modest and substandard services given could be seen as reintroducing poor relief and charity into the Norwegian welfare state. At the same time, these services can be said to protect the integrity of the welfare state by hiding poverty and social suffering. Dauvergne has argued that "[t]he need that is met by humanitarianism is the need to define and understand the nation as compassionate and caring" (Dauvergne 2005, 75). Equally, I suggest here, that humanitarian assistance to irregular migrants allows the welfare state to maintain an idea of itself as compassionate and caring without granting access to the welfare system on egalitarian grounds.

Conclusion

In this chapter, exploring how the Norwegian state addresses the question of irregular migrants' welfare needs, I have drawn attention to how the idea of the Nordic countries as comparatively egalitarian is premised on a conception of a community that is bounded and exclusive. This idea could be sustained because there was for a long time a close match between the polity and territory, with the nation-state understood as a natural container of social relations. This notion has become increasingly unsustainable in light of the growing gap between the declared intent of immigration law to exclude (certain) migrants and the excluded migrants' continuing presence on state territory. This, I suggest, exposes an exclusivist side to Nordic egalitarianism.

Immigration has resulted not only in growing cultural complexity, but also legal complexity, with differentiated forms of citizenship and non-citizenship emerging due to increasingly stricter immigration laws. The premise of legality as the basis for identification as equals makes, I suggest in this chapter, certain kinds of difference more acceptable within the Nordic context. Even though these hierarchies result in socio-economic inequality within state borders, they are not always seen to contradict the "egalitarian nature" of Nordic countries. The irregular migrants that I followed in my fieldwork had lived in Norway for years. They had to various degrees become informally incorporated in society, and could as such be said to be part of Norwegian society. Aster and Zeki, for instance, had lived in Norway for 12 and 17 years when I met them and could more precisely be labelled irregular residents than migrants. Yet, they were not included in the structures of the welfare state and were dependent on various forms of charity. Hence, the egalitarian welfare approach in Norway could still be said to rely on the "hard on the outside and soft on the inside" model of citizenship where the egalitarian "We" is still very much bounded, although not so much in territorial terms.

In this chapter, I have also suggested that, as the "hard" threshold norms have come to occupy the same (internal) terrain as the "soft" interior ones, humanitarian assistance has become a way of alleviating the tension between migration control and a normative commitment to people's basic security found in the ethos of the welfare state. The humanitarian approach to irregular migrants is not unique to Norway and has been seen as a premise for irregular migrants' access to health care in various European countries, including France (Ticktin 2011) and Germany (Castañeda 2010). Yet in the Norwegian context, I suggest that this approach contradicts and undermines the egalitarian notions of justice hailed as a central characteristic of the Nordic model of welfare as it indicates a growing willingness to distinguish between people based on a hierarchy of moral worth. In this sense, the treatment of irregular migrants is both moulded by and helps mould wider transformations of the welfare state related to the introduction of neoliberal policies (Bendixsen et al., Chap. 1, in this book). Still, one of the main achievements of the parallel regime of care to irregular migrants is that it reproduces the migrants' formal exclusion in everyday life while at the same time confirms and reifies the identity of the nation as decent and caring.

Notes

1. The material was collected for my PhD, which was part of the umbrella project "Provision of welfare to irregular migrants". This project used anthropological and legal approaches to explore the complex relationship between law, institutional practice, and migrants' experience (see Karlsen 2015).
2. The term irregular migrant comprises, in addition to rejected asylum seekers, those who remain on state territory after having overstayed their visa, having had their residency revoked, or never having applied for residency.
3. Welfare nationalism should not be confused with welfare chauvinism, i.e., that only national citizens should receive welfare.

References

Aarø, Ann Helen, and Heidi Wyller. 2005. *Mat, tak over hodet og helsetjenester. Statens forpliktelser overfor personer uten lovlig opphold.* SMED: Oslo.

Andersen, Njål W. 2014. Den nasjonale reguleringen av retten og plikten til å yte nødhjelp til personer med ulovlig opphold i Norge – analysert ut fra et rettssikkerhetsperspektiv. *Nordisk socialrättslig tidskrift* 9 (10): 31–77.

Anderson, Bridget. 2013. *Us and them?: The dangerous politics of immigration control.* Oxford: Oxford University Press.

Aradau, Claudia. 2004. The perverse politics of four-letter words: Risk and pity in the securitisation of human trafficking. *Millennium-Journal of International Studies* 33 (2): 251–277.

Bendixsen, Synnøve. 2013. Becoming members in the community of value: Ethiopian irregular migrants enacting citizenship in Norway. In *Migration matters*, ed. Arnon Edelstein and Mahni Dugan, 3–22. Oxfordshire: Inter-Disciplinary Press.

Bergman, Annika. 2007. Co-constitution of domestic and international welfare obligations. The case of Sweden's social democratically inspired internationalism. *Cooperation and Conflict* 42 (1): 73–99.

Bosniak, Linda. 2006. *The citizen and the alien: Dilemmas of contemporary membership.* Princeton: Princeton University Press.

Brekke, Jan-Paul. 2008. Making the unreturnable return. The role of the welfare state in promoting return for rejected asylum seekers in Norway. *IAFSM Conference.* Cairo: ISF Paper.

Brekke, Jan-Paul, and Susanne Søholt. 2005. *I velferdsstatens grenseland. En evaluering av ordningen med bortfall av botilbud i mottak for personer med endelig avslag på asylsøknaden*, Rapport 2005: 005. Oslo: Institutt for samfunnsforskning

Brochmann, Grete, and Anniken Hagelund. 2012. *Immigration policy and the Scandinavian welfare state 1945–2010.* London: Palgrave Macmillan.

Browning, Christopher S. 2007. Branding nordicity models, identity and the decline of exceptionalism. *Cooperation and Conflict: Journal of the Nordic International Studies Association* 42 (1): 27–51.

Castañeda, Heide. 2010. Deportation deferred: "Illegality", visibility, and recognition in contemporary Germany. In *The deportation regime: Sovereignty, space, and the freedom of movement*, ed. Nicholas De Genova and Nathalie Peutz, 245–261. Durham: Duke University Press.

Chauvin, Sébastien, and Blanca Garcés-Mascareñas. 2012. Beyond informal citizenship: The new moral economy of migrant illegality. *International Political Sociology* 6 (3): 241–259.

Coutin, Susan B. 2003. *Legalizing moves: Salvadoran immigrants' struggle for U.S. residency.* Ann Arbor: University of Michigan Press.

Cox, Robert. 2004. The path-dependency of an idea: Why Scandinavian welfare states remain distinct. *Social Policy and Administration* 38 (2): 204–219.

Dahl, Hanne Marlene. 2012. Neo-liberalism meets the Nordic welfare state – Gaps and silences. *NORA – Nordic Journal of Feminist and Gender Research* 20 (4): 283–288.

Dauvergne, Catherine. 2005. *Humanitarianism, identity, and nation: Migration laws in Canada and Australia*. Vancouver: University of British Columbia Press.

De Genova, Nicholas. 2002. Migrant "illegality" and deportability in everyday life. *Annual Review of Anthropology* 31 (1): 419–447.

Eastmond, Marita. 2011. Egalitarian ambitions, constructions of difference: The paradoxes of refugee integration in Sweden. *Journal of Ethnic and Migration Studies* 37 (2): 277–295.

Esping-Andersen, Gøsta, and Walter Korpi. 1986. From poor relief to institutional welfare states: The development of Scandinavian social policy. *International Journal of sociology* 16 (3/4): 39–74.

Fassin, Didier. 2012. *Humanitarian reason: A moral history of the present times*. Berkeley: University of California Press.

Feldman, Stanley, and Marco R. Steenbergen. 2001. The humanitarian foundation of public support for social welfare. *American Journal of Political Science* 45 (3): 658–677.

Feldman, Ilana, and Miriam Ticktin. 2010. *In the name of humanity: The government of threat and care*. Durham/London: Duke University Press.

Fuglerud, Øivind. 2005. Inside out: The re-organisation of national identity in Norway. In *Sovereign bodies. Citizens, migrants, and states in the postcolonial world*, ed. Thomas Blom Hansen and Finn Stepputat, 291–311. New Jersey: Princeton University Press.

Gullestad, Marianne. 2002. Invisible fences: Egalitarianism, nationalism and racism. *Journal of the Royal Anthropological Institute* 8 (1): 45–63.

Healthcare Regulation. 2011. *Forskrift om rett til helse- og omsorgstjenester til personer uten fast opphold i riket*, December 16, no. 1255.

Hegvik, Gunn Kari. 2013a. Huitfeldt: Utvist mann burde ikke fått sosialhjelp. *VG*, February 25.

———. 2013b. Huitfeldt strammer inn Nav-hjelp. *VG*, July 25.

Hegvik, Gunn Kari, Lars Joakim Skarvøy, and Audun Beyer-Olsen. 2013. Dømt for voldtektsforsøk, utvist fra Norge, får sosialhjelp og bolig av Nav. *VG*, February 25.

Ingebritsen, Christine. 2002. Norm entrepreneurs. Scandinavia's role in world politics. *Cooperation and Conflict* 37 (1): 11–23.

Jacobsen, Christine, and May-Linn Skilbrei. 2010. "Reproachable victims"? Representations and self-representations of Russian women involved in transnational prostitution. *Ethnos* 75 (2): 190–212.

Karlsen, Marry-Anne. 2015. *Precarious inclusion: Irregular migration, practices of care, and state b/ordering in Norway.* PhD thesis, University of Bergen.

Kildal, Nanna, and Stein Kuhnle. 2014. The principle of universalism challenged: Towards an ideational shift in the Norwegian welfare state? In *Reshaping welfare institutions in China and the Nordic countries*, ed. Pauli Kettunen, Stein Kuhnle, and Yuan Ren, 122–138. Helsinki: Nordic Centre of Excellence NordWel.

Kuhnle, Stein, and Nanna Kildal. 2005. *Normative foundations of the welfare state: The Nordic experience.* Florence: Routledge.

Lønseth, Pål K. 2011. Returnekternes ansvar. *Aftenposten, kronikk*, October 24.

Ministry of Health and Care Services. 2010. *Høringsnotat. Endring av prioriteringsforskriften – Helsehjelp til personer som oppholder seg ulovlig i landet.* Oslo: Helse- og omsorgsdepartementet.

Ministry of Labor and Social Affairs. 2004. *Nødhjelp til personer uten lovlig opphold.* Press release.

———. 2011. *Høringsnotat. Utkast til forskrift til lov om sosiale tjenester i arbeids- og velferdsforvaltningen.* Oslo: Arbeids- og sosialdepartementet.

———. 2013. *Høringsnotat. Utkast til endring i forskrift om sosiale tjenester til personer uten fast bopel i Norge – kortvarig akutthjelp.* Oslo: Arbeids- og sosialdepartementet.

Mitchell, Katharyne. 2006. Geographies of identity: The new exceptionalism. *Progress in Human Geography* 30 (1): 95–106.

Nilssen, Even, and Nanna Kildal. 2009. New contractualism in social policy and the Norwegian fight against poverty and social exclusion. *Ethics and Social Welfare* 3 (3): 303–321.

Olwig, Karen F. 2011. "Integration": Migrants and refugees between Scandinavian welfare societies and family relations. *Journal of Ethnic and Migration Studies* 37 (2): 179–196.

Pratt, Geraldine. 2005. Abandoned women and spaces of the exception. *Antipode* 37 (5): 1052–1078.

Regulation amending the social services regulation. 2014. Forskrift om endring i forskrift 16. desember 2011 nr. 1251 om rett til sosiale tjenester for personer uten fast bopel i Norge.

Rugkåsa, Marianne. 2010. *Transformasjon og integrasjon: Kvalifisering av minoritetsetniske kvinner til arbeid og deltakelse i den norske velferdsstaten.* PhD thesis, University of Oslo.

Social Services Regulation. 2011. Forskrift om sosiale tjenester for personer uten fast bopel i Norge 16. desember 2011 nr. 1251.

Søvig, Karl Harald. 2013. Hvorfor nekte, eller gi, irregulære immigranter tilgang til velferdsytelser? In *Undring og erkjennelse*, ed. Ørnulf Rasmussen, Sigrid Eskeland Schütz, and Karl Harald Søvig, 705–717. Bergen: Fagbokforlaget.

Süssmann, Andrea. 2015. Dronning i grenseland? Et menneskerettslig perspektiv på forskrift om rett til helse og omsorgstjenester til personer uten fast opphold i riket. In *Eksepsjonell velferd? Irregulære migranter i det norske velferdssamfunnet*, ed. Synnøve K. Bendixsen, Christine M. Jacobsen, and Karl Harald Søvig, 66–87. Oslo: Gyldendal Norsk Forlag.

Ticktin, Miriam. 2006. Where ethics and politics meet: The violence of humanitarianism in France. *American Ethnologist* 33 (1): 33–49.

———. 2011. *Casualties of care: Immigration and the politics of humanitarianism in France*. Berkeley: University of California Press.

———. 2014. Transnational humanitarianism. *Annual Review of Anthropology* 43: 273–289.

Valenta, Marko, Kristin Thorshaug, Thomas H. Molden, Berit Berg, and Halvar Kjærre. 2010. *Avviste asylsøkere og ventemottaksordningen Mellom passiv tvang og aktiv returassistanse*. Trondheim: NTNU Samfunnsforskning.

Vike, Halvard. 2004. *Velferd uten grenser: Den norske velferdsstaten ved veiskillet.* Oslo: Akribe.

———. 2015. Likhetens natur. *Norsk antropologisk tidsskrift* 25 (01): 7–21.

Walzer, Michael. 1983. *Spheres of justice: A defense of pluralism and equality.* New York: Basic Books.

Watters, Charles. 2007. Refugees at Europe's borders: The moral economy of care. *Transcultural Psychiatry* 44 (3): 394–417.

Willen, Sarah S. 2012. Migration,"illegality," and health: Mapping embodied vulnerability and debating health-related deservingness. *Social Science & Medicine* 74 (6): 805–811.

PART IV

Egalitarianism, Inequality, and Difference

CHAPTER 11

Riding Along in the Name of Equality: Everyday Demands on Refugee Children to Conform to Local Bodily Practices of Danish Egalitarianism

Birgitte Romme Larsen

INTRODUCTION

In 2011, I ended an anthropological study based on ethnographic fieldwork carried out among newly recognized refugees who had been subjected to mandatory placement in small communities in rural Denmark. Over a period of 12 months, I followed four refugee families in their everyday lives, motivated by a curiosity to know what happens when a larger, national integration strategy of dispersing new refugees to ethnically homogeneous Danish local communities concretizes itself locally, as this policy transforms into everyday interpersonal practice and face-to-face encounters. Thus, I investigated how these refugee families experienced moving to and becoming part of their new environments, with a particular focus on interactions with the local population. The families, who have

---

B.R. Larsen (✉)
Centre for Advanced Migration Studies, The Saxo Institute, University of Copenhagen, København, Denmark

© The Author(s) 2018
S. Bendixsen et al. (eds.), *Egalitarianism in Scandinavia*, Approaches to Social Inequality and Difference, DOI 10.1007/978-3-319-59791-1_11

Burmese, Sudanese, Palestinian and Iranian-Kurdish backgrounds, had been resettled in villages and small towns between six and 12 months prior to the beginning of the fieldwork. In this chapter, I specifically focus on the refugee children and adolescents amidst their settlement process within the local communities.

I spent time with the families' children and youths in their homes and residential areas, at leisure time activities, and at school, exploring the various negotiations over inclusion, exclusion, and belonging that took place within these different social spaces. This chapter particularly analyzes the implicit norms and expectations imposed on the refugee children and youngsters by the surrounding society, and the ways in which they have to act and maneuver in sharp relation to these expectations when it comes to their everyday efforts toward inclusion and belonging. These norms and expectations, I show, largely center around inherent local understandings of, on the one hand, what it means to be *an independent individual*, and, on the other hand, what it means to be *a member of society*.

Commonly perceived by their local social surroundings as "having" less independence than their Danish peers, the analysis shows how refugee children and adolescents are being exposed to an encroachment on their individual free will while seeking to maneuver within this local schema for child development and its dual emphasis on individuality and collectivity. This schema, I argue, amounts to what could be termed an *everyday schooling in Danish egalitarianism*. Seen through the eyes of the local population, this implicit schooling process is about an emancipatory undoing of the discipline, obedience, and social constraint that the refugee children are largely understood to be exposed to in their homes and families. This perspective, however, obscures the fact that this culturally informed effort is in itself strongly bound by social norms. The analysis thus especially relates to what in the Introduction, Chap. 1 in this book, is stressed as *the dynamics of egalitarianism*: I explore how, within an everyday Scandinavian context, individuality is conceptualized, and how at the same time this conceptualization is played out and reproduced collectively; and I explore the fundamental tension between equality and freedom that seems inherent to "egalitarian individualism" (Gullestad 1992). In which ways, I ask, do these dynamics concretize and materialize in everyday interfacial encounters involving refugee children and their local Danish surroundings?

I discuss how Danish norms tied to everyday bodily practices, techniques, and routines prove crucial to the refugee children's local inclusion and acceptance. An example of this is how—to the surrounding local communities—the bodily technique of cycling simultaneously comes to represent: (1) an ideal of the refugee child's individual autonomy; and (2) a marker of his/her belonging to "the Danish collective". Thus, the analysis illuminates the ways in which macro-political, *explicit* expectations of refugees becoming attached to local Danish *people* constantly—when seen at the everyday micro-level—come to intertwine with a range of much more unpredictable, *implicit* expectations of becoming attached to local Danish *practices*, in the form of tacit material and bodily routines (see also Larsen 2011a, b).

On this ground, two main arguments run through the chapter. First, it is shown how the refugee children's mastering of locally taken-for-granted everyday practices and routines commonly proves to be the voucher for social inclusion and acceptance. This means, I would argue, that the local mechanisms of "integration" generally prove to be working the other way round than politically projected (that is, if refugees live among largely ethnic Danish co-residents, they will automatically be included, and then, eventually, pick up on central "Danish" ways of doing). Second, and following from this, it is shown how, paradoxically, refugee children and youths are expected to be "individualized" and made "autonomous" in exactly the same way as everyone else, which in daily life—I argue—turns the envisioned *emancipation from discipline* into an actual *disciplining in emancipation*. In carrying out this overall analysis, the chapter's first section will focus on the refugee schoolchildren, while in the second section the focus expands to include their older, sometimes adult siblings.

The Scattering of Refugee Families and the Role of the Local Primary School

In 1999, Denmark saw its first Integration Law (*Integrationsloven*). This included regulations concerning how best to incorporate recognized refugees into Danish society. Among other measures, it stipulated a three-year period of mandatory placement outside the country's urban areas. Dissatisfied with the emergence of enclaves of largely unemployed refugees living in council housing in the larger cities, the dispersal policy intended to prompt social relations with the local ethnically Danish population, thus giving them better opportunities to become "integrated" into mainstream Danish society. Today's Danish Integration Law still calls for a three-year, mandatory placement of recognized refugees across the country.[1]

Three of the families in the study had resided in international United Nations (UN) refugee camps for years before having been accepted by Denmark as UN-quota refugees.[2] Upon their arrival, these families, who have Burmese, Sudanese, and Iranian-Kurdish backgrounds, had been taken straight from the airport to their homes-to-be in the Danish countryside. The fourth family, which has a Palestinian background, had arrived in Denmark as asylum seekers and had thus stayed in Danish asylum centers for an extended period prior to their resettlement. The fieldwork was carried out in two municipalities in the Northern part of the Danish peninsula of Jutland. In "Næsdal Municipality", two families were respectively located in the town of *Næsdal* (4,300 inhabitants) and the village of *Fuglestrup* (500 inhabitants), and in "Maglelund Municipality", two families were residing respectively in the villages of *Maglelund* (3,500 inhabitants) and *Askbjerg* (2,000 inhabitants).[3]

The decentralization of newly arrived refugee families in Denmark stands in contrast to an increasing urban centralization of various institutional, economic and social resources that refugees (along with everyone else) need in daily life, for example, shopping facilities, work opportunities, language schools, and so on. Together with kindergartens and nurseries, the public primary school is often one of the few remaining institutions left in smaller Danish communities. This makes it an important (if not the most important) local institution that policy-makers refer to when suggesting that placement in a small community will promote refugees' social incorporation with a view to the successful integration of the next generation. During fieldwork, I had the opportunity to spend time with all four families' children in their respective local public schools—a total of seven children between 3rd and 9th grade at three different schools.

According to anthropologist Sally Anderson (2000), in the Danish public school, children of refugees and immigrants often hold peripheral and marginalized positions in relation to both their teachers and classmates, and this she links to a particular social and cultural attribute of the Danish school system that renders it difficult to contain "the immigrant" (Anderson 2000, 253). This attribute, Anderson states, relates to the value of "sameness" as the fundamental premise of Danish school class practice. My material suggests that two opposite ideals simultaneously prove vital to the refugee children's social inclusion and acceptance within their schools: collective "sameness" and personal "autonomy". The following section, which is based on ethnographic field note excerpts, illustrates a typical day at school with two of the children and serves as a background for developing the analysis.

A Day at Askbjerg School

I am going to Askbjerg School together with the Iranian-Kurdish family's two youngest children: their daughter, Sirwa, 13 years old, and their son, Merdem, 11 years old. The school has around 250 pupils from 0 to 9th grade. Maria greets me. She is the "receiving-teacher" [*modtagerlærer*] for the school's so-called "bilingual pupils" [*tosprogede elever*]. She says that both Sirwa and Merdem are very shy and that she had spent three months just to get to know them. Now that they have been here for 12 months, they have opened up. I follow Maria to Sirwa's group of 6th graders, who are about to have history class. I tell her that some time ago I had given Sirwa a disposable camera, asking her to photograph her daily life. Later, when we talked about the pictures, Sirwa had pointed to a girl in one of the photos, saying that this was her best friend, Martha, from class. Maria points out Martha for me in the room, and then says: "Ugh, we're not happy about that.". A bit surprised, I ask her why. She responds:

> In a way, Martha herself is bilingual. Her mother is English, and Martha is very strictly brought up. If she just raises one eyebrow, she's scolded, and she's not allowed to walk up to Sirwa's house on her own, for instance. We have tried to separate them a little bit—and actually, they *did* have a little quarrel a while ago, but obviously, it has all turned good again. Sirwa needs a friend where she gets the opportunity to visit a Danish home—where it's not so strict.

Later, during the break, Maria and I watch over the schoolyard together. We see Martha and Sirwa walking together, laughing. Maria says: "She needs to get out of that twosome. Sirwa is a tremendous resource for the group of 6th graders. She's actually very social, and she often serves as a unifying force to the class group."

Next, Sirwa and Merdem are going with Maria to the "receiving class unit" [*modtagerklasse*]: the unit where the school's bilingual pupils start out until they can fully participate in their ordinary class groups, and where at the moment only Sirwa and Merdem are enrolled, now down to eight hours per week. The other three children at school with refugee backgrounds "are already fully integrated", Maria explains. It is just the four of us in the room. When Sirwa enters, Maria says to her: "You're wearing your new boots today!" Sirwa smiles and Maria explains: "I gave some boots to Sirwa yesterday, as last week she had been playing in the snow with Martha and Sidsel, not wearing any winter boots—so she was completely soaked. And you were *so* happy about the boots, isn't it true, Sirwa?" Sirwa confirms with a shy smile.

Today they are doing math. Maria praises them and tells them repeatedly that they are very clever. She tells me that she sometimes uses SMS as spelling instruction when she teaches Danish to Sirwa. She sends Sirwa a text message that she needs to answer. In addition to spelling training, Maria says, the point is that in this way Sirwa becomes familiar with the use of a cell-phone so that in her leisure time she can participate in the general SMS communication between her classmates. I ask Merdem if he also has a mobile phone, which he does not. Maria says that she has promised him her old phone as soon as she gets a new one.

In the following lesson, Sirwa is the only participant in the receiving class unit, where she sits together with Emmy, the head coordinator of the receiving class unit. Emmy mentions to me that the local municipal authorities had been refusing Sirwa's family's application for financial support for the purchase of a bike for Sirwa. So, Emmy had now handed in a formal request to the municipality's Department of Integration on behalf of the family, but she had not heard back from them yet. "Sirwa's class group is going to have their cycling tests in May, so she will have to learn how to cycle before then", Emmy says, continuing in an encouraging voice to Sirwa: "Then the two of us will be cycling together, right? Because me too, I cycle". Sirwa laughs and says that she hopes they will succeed in finding a bike in due time for the bicycling test.

The school-bell rings and Emmy asks: "So, what are you up to now, Sirwa—will you be looking for Martha?" Sirwa says yes, and Emmy mumbles with a wry smile: "Yeah, I thought so." Once more, I watch Sirwa and Martha walking the schoolyard closely together, and I ask them whether they have been visiting each other's homes. "Yes, and she has seen my room!", Sirwa responds eagerly and kind of proud. At the end of the school day, Emmy says to me that she finds that Sirwa and Merdem are doing very well in school: "They're two such lovely children—and so competent. I think that Sirwa is such a clever girl—and it also amazes me that she's able to make these beautiful Kurdish rings from beads." She points to her finger, showing me a ring that Sirwa had made for her.

The school day described above is in many ways illustrative of the refugee children's daily life in the local public schools that I visited. Characteristic of the children was that they expressed joy about their school attendance. In addition to quickly learning the Danish language, they seemed to flourish and feel comfortable within their class groups, and they made friends relatively easily. Overall, it appeared that they had been well received and welcomed by classmates as well as by teachers. The majority of the refugee children had a best friend from class with whom they often spent time in each other's homes or in local sports clubs, and none of them had been exposed to teasing or social exclusion at school. In other words, and unlike a number of anthropological studies conducted in other Danish public school settings, I did not find that the refugee children occupied a marginalized position in class among their ethnic Danish peers (see, e.g., Anderson 2000; Gilliam 2009). On the contrary, I observed the refugee children as popular classmates, who were both generally liked and included. While there may be several reasons for this successful social position, the following suggests two particular explanations, which are connected to the issues of "proximity" and "sameness".

Matters of Proximity and Sameness

At each of the three public schools, the number of pupils from families with a refugee or immigrant background could be counted on one hand. I observed how this small number of students generally allowed the teachers to invest extra time in each refugee child. In general, this meant that the teachers accumulated a broad knowledge concerning the individual refugee child's background and family situation and, through this, an awareness of eventual problems to be solved. Hence, in their daily work the teachers approached each refugee child in a rather holistic manner, which—as illustrated—contributed to a general situation of proximity between the child and its teachers, especially the receiving teachers.

However, the closeness between the children and their teachers cannot be explained by the small number of refugee pupils itself. Rather, this minority led to the situation of each refugee pupil in fact becoming an important project for the involved class groups and teachers, and to the entire school as such. When, in general, I witnessed teachers taking great pride in successfully incorporating refugee pupils into the school setting, I did not immediately link their efforts to a strong awareness of serving within a small local community where "everyone knows everyone". The teachers not only hinted at their individual pride in relation to their colleagues, but potentially also in relation to their neighbors (who might also happen to be the refugee child's football teacher), or their local medical practitioner (whose daughter might also happen to be the refugee child's best friend). Thus, the successful incorporation of the individual refugee child into the school collective constituted more than an internal school project, but also an external affair, which the entire surrounding community could follow and evaluate. As I will show, a prerequisite for the teachers in accomplishing their personal and professional goal of inclusion was that their relationships with the refugee children were characterized by proximity and confidentiality.

Anderson (2000) has pointed out that the fundamental premise of Danish school class practice relates to the value of "sameness". She argues how, in Denmark, school teachers' understanding of "the good class" is that it is "smooth" and "even", without too many children "standing out":

> In relation to the school class, the troublesome children are those who are too stupid, too smart or too different in other ways (too obedient, destructive, self-important or too foreign). *The ideal is evenness.* A lot of time and energy is allotted to the control, regulation and forming of such smoothing. *Lack of sameness is seen as a problem.* (Anderson 2000, 209, my translation, my added emphasis)

Thus, to successfully become a non-marginalized child within the Danish school class, Anderson (2000, 216) points out that "the important thing is to convince the desired others that you are exactly 'like them' and therefore also 'naturally' should be included" [my translation]. It is in this situation, she argues, that pupils with refugee or immigrant backgrounds often come to be seen as not "alike" and therefore are not "naturally" included. Hereby, a peripheral social position within the school class, and among its teachers, is imposed on the child.

In my own study, rather, it was social inclusion, trust, and friendship that characterized the relationship between refugee children and their classmates/teachers. As we saw, it could even be the case that the children were regarded as "a tremendous resource and a unifying force to the class group". The point here is that an interacting and dialectically reinforcing relationship existed between the aspects of (1) the refugee children's close relationships with their teachers, and (2) their ability to become part of the egalitarian, sameness-based community among their Danish school peers. For example, when Sirwa got a pair of winter boots, she could join in playing in the snow during breaks "just like" her classmates. Similarly, her acquisition of a cell-phone meant that she could participate in the SMS communication, "just like" the others. Similarly, Sirwa hoped that soon, if only the receiving teacher's application for financial support went through, she would, "just like" her peers, be cycling the streets of Askbjerg. Thus, the teachers' steady attendance and personal commitment to the refugee children's (school)life had the effect of opening up for them a number of equal opportunities, in terms of their ability to participate in a community of peers. As Anderson (2000) states, the individual child's successful positioning as socially included within the Danish school class is about convincing the others that you are "just like" them, and hence belong with them. However, this somehow necessitates an equal access to the various material things that this sameness-based community might center around, and the teachers invested themselves in helping to secure these items.

Hence, the refugee children were themselves co-actors in this everyday similarity-based inclusion project, along with their teachers. They displayed a great desire to *be* and *do* "like" their peers in many areas of daily life: Sirwa was eager to learn SMS texting and riding a bicycle, just as she was focused on having small dishwasher and newspaper distribution jobs after school, "just like" many of her classmates. Likewise, most of the refugee children in the study were keen to be enrolled in local sports clubs, along with their Danish peers. In much the same manner, many of the children expressed a desire to eat the same food as their Danish friends. Through the children's own strong aspirations and wishes to become and do "just like" the others, they came to be socially liked and included among their peers, both inside and outside school hours. However, this inclusion did not take place automatically, but was conditional on the ability and desire to take part in a range of bodily practices and routines that were taken-for-granted locally. In the second part of this chapter, this everyday entanglement of local social acceptance and individual maneuvering within tacit bodily expectations is analyzed in more depth.

The Everyday Schooling in Danish Egalitarianism: Negotiations of Individuality and Collectivity

Since the mid-twentieth century, in what are called the Western parts of the world, the process of individualization increasingly has reached society's youngest—a development reflected in the induction of the UN Convention on the Rights of the Child in 1989. The increased focus on children's individualization has led to significant changes in the perception of the upbringing of children and adolescents. Norwegian anthropologist, Marianne Gullestad (2002), has discussed how, just a few generations ago, children were expected to be obedient and dutiful, whereas today it is believed that children need to "find themselves" and build a self-identity. More than transferring specific ideas and values, parents' responsibility today is to transfer the ability to "find", "develop", and "create" oneself (Gullestad 2002, 255f.). Although, today, ideals of individual equality and free will generally apply across Europe, Swedish historian, Lars Trägårdh (1997), among other scholars, stresses that, in the Nordic welfare states, including Denmark, the way that values of individualization play out in daily life differ from elsewhere in Europe. This, he argues, relates to the individualist aspect of reciprocity that underlies the Scandinavian welfare societies, which is unheard of in other national welfare programs, and in which benefits are tied to the individual person instead of, for example, to the family or the job as elsewhere in Europe. Thus, the central, organizing principle of the Nordic welfare state is the alliance between the state and the individual, bringing a strong individualist dimension to "the Nordic social contract" (Trägårdh 1997). Hence, scholars have argued that in Scandinavian countries the broader "Western" ideals of individual equality and solidarity combine with a remarkably strong desire for personal *autonomy* and *independence* (e.g., Bruun et al. 2015; Gullestad 2002; Trägårdh 1997). Based on empirical cases, in the following I break down the ways in which these larger values of autonomy and independence are concretized and materialized in the everyday encounters between refugee children/adolescents and the local Danish communities.

One evening, I attended a community dinner event for local refugees and Danes, organized by *Live Together,* the local voluntary refugee association in Maglelund and Askbjerg, which is run by ethnically Danish local residents. At the event, I sat down with Lisa, the association's coordinator of local volunteers. Elsa, the Iranian-Kurdish family's volunteer contact person, joined us, wanting to discuss a specific situation. Elsa, who had been the family's volunteer contact person for a few months now, showed great involvement in the family members' general well-being. Elsa told us with frustration, though, that she was mostly doing things together with the parents and that she would like to spend more time with the family's adolescents as well, but she did not know how to go about it:

> With the two eldest, Gulbîn and Jino [24 and 25 years old], it's very difficult to come up with things to do with them. They cannot even ride a bike, while the younger siblings [Merdem and Sirwa] are already learning it. But it is as if Gulbîn and Jino are completely out of the race—and just have to stay at home with Mom and Dad. Couldn't they just get a bicycle? Then I could teach them how to ride! Indeed, it gives you a bit more individuality to have a bike—then you can just get out more quickly and get away from the home a little bit.

I mentioned to Elsa that both the son, Jino, and the daughter, Gulbîn, had, on their own initiatives, begun playing football in Askbjerg's local sports club, and that this would give them a little more diversion from the daily routine of moving between the home and the local language school. "Oh, I didn't know, that's great", Lisa said. "Yes, but still they cannot ride a bike or swim, and they do need that individuality," Elsa emphasized.

One month later, I sat on the living room floor in the home of the Iranian-Kurdish family, where Sirwa was teaching me how to make Kurdish rings of beads. We were interrupted when Elsa passed by to give the family a message. The mother, Gulan, smilingly shook Elsa's hand and offered her tea. Elsa asked Sirwa to translate for the rest of the family that she would pass by on Saturday to bring some food for them to eat together—and a bicycle. She said: "After eating, we will load the bike into my car, and then drive somewhere where there's no traffic, so that Gulbîn can learn how to ride". Sirwa translated. Everyone looked at Gulbîn. Judging from her eyes wide open, she was not keen on the idea. Elsa insisted: "Of course, you can learn how to ride a bike, Gulbîn! If Sirwa has learned it in Denmark, so can you!" A few days later, I went for an evening walk with Sirwa. A group of boys from school passed by on their bikes, which led us on to the issue of whether Elsa had succeeded in getting Gulbîn to learn to ride a bike. She had, Sirwa told me, but it had not gone well. Gulbîn could not keep her balance, so she had felt very unsafe.

Later that spring, I attended the general assembly in *Live Together*. The participants, ten volunteer contact persons for refugee families living in the area, started the meeting by telling the others what they each had been up to with "their family". When it became Elsa's turn, she said:

> This Sunday, I took the family on a picnic, and it was simply *such* a success! We sat on a blanket in the woods, and it was really nice. Then, I tried having Gulbîn and Jino to come with me a bit, alone, as they shouldn't just be with their parents all the time. Because … in a way it is as if the four of them are just inseparable. But they *need* to able to do something on their own too, right? And Gulbîn was the braver of the two. I got her all the way into a creek, barefooted, fishing with a net! And she laughed and enjoyed it so much. It is so important that she can do things like this on her own, without her mother.

The above examples point to how Elsa sought to rectify what she saw as a lack of "individuality" concerning 24-year-old Gulbîn. This manifested in Elsa's presentation of various physical activities, such as cycling and fishing in a creek. Her aim was to promote more personal independence and autonomy for Gulbîn through the physical and figurative separation from her parents implied by these activities.

Regarding today's general expectation in Denmark that children and adolescents are to "find themselves", the relationship between children/adolescents and their parents is of central social significance, as the individual child/youngster largely develops his/her own values and preferences precisely by relating to and transforming the influence of their parents (Gullestad 2002, 255). However, I argue that in the context of the reception of refugees, the central importance of "the family" as institutional space is often given intensified attention by the surrounding society. My material suggests how, in that context, "the home" is often seen as a social space that hinders (versus secures) the children/adolescents in "finding", "creating", and "developing" themselves. Hence, they are encouraged to emancipate themselves from the home in various ways. As illustrated in the example of Gulbîn and Elsa, the goal of "finding oneself" is often sought by means of *physical* emancipation. This confluence of physical and personal independence was also reflected one day while following 13-year-old Burmese Thaung in his class group at Maglelund School. At the end of the school day, Thaung's teacher told me in a low voice:

> I don't know if you have heard … and I don't know if this is still so, but Thaung has had a very hard time sleeping without his mother next to him. It might very well be that they sleep together with their children a little bit longer than we do. But I mean… not *that* long! It's about time that he starts to separate a bit from his mother.

That the refugee children and youths had to "find" and "create" themselves by way of physical emancipation was not only a common expectation among volunteer refugee helpers and schoolteachers. This phenomenon also proved recurrent among the families' municipal integration caseworkers, which the following example illustrates.

Before my first encounter with the Palestinian refugee family who lives in Næsdal Municipality, I had a meeting with the local integration caseworker, Lone. The aim of the meeting was to brief me on the family and its members before I was to visit them for the first time a few hours later. Among other things, Lone told me:

At one point, I had arranged things so that Hadia [the family's eldest daughter, 24 years old] could move into a youth apartment here in Næsdal. But her mother wouldn't let her move, I think. So, to me Hadia pretended that she lived in the apartment and received money for setting-up [furniture, and so on]. When I discovered that she actually didn't live there, obviously, I got angry—and asked them to pay the money back.

One day, several months later, I had a talk with Hadia about her family's time at various Danish asylum centers and how it had all ended back then. Here, for the first time Hadia touched upon the incident with Lone, and how she had planned to make her move away from home:

When, after six years at Danish asylum centers, we were granted permission to stay, we were *too* happy! But I hadn't been given the same kind of residence permit as the rest of the family. Why, I don't know. Unlike the others, mine depended on whether Libya and Lebanon, the two countries we had lived in before, denied receiving me after being asked a total of three times, half a year apart. Only if both said no all three times—which they did— could I finally get permission to stay here with my family [parents and four younger siblings]. The last inquiry was just last month. Each time, I have had stomach pain and headaches for months, and sometimes I cried for days and had to stay home from language school. Only *now*, I know for sure that I can continue staying here with my family! Lone from the municipality has tried to make me move away from home. She had already found the youth apartment and everything! But I did *not* want to live by myself, so I moved back home immediately. But I didn't dare tell her, as I was afraid that she would be angry. So, it took a while before she found out. Now, for more than seven years, I have been fighting for permission to live here in freedom together with my family—and for not being sent back without them. Why on Earth would I suddenly wish to live alone, *without* my family? That is the last thing that I want.

The examples concerning Gulbîn, Thaung and Hadia all demonstrate how the local social surroundings sought to support them in attaining "more" independence through various forms of emancipation from the parents and the home. The cultural norm in Danish society that young people at a certain age move away from home in order to become *independent* individuals by "taking care of themselves" [*klare sig selv*] and "standing on their own two feet" [*stå på egne ben*], is not necessarily a practice that is taken for granted in other societies. In the Danish context, the understanding of the child's development of personal independence and autonomy—or, as Elsa put it, "individuality"—is largely tied to "freedom" in the sense of separation from one's parents. However, while the integration caseworker's attempt to have 24-year-old Hadia move away from home was linked to the intention of *providing* Hadia with freedom (understood as independence and autonomy), Hadia herself connected the attempt with a *deprivation* of freedom. After several years of struggling to be granted asylum in Denmark, Hadia finally experienced having obtained the individual freedom to live in peace *with* her family.

While Scandinavian welfare societies largely have been characterized as individualistically oriented, they are simultaneously marked by strong collective values. This makes it difficult to speak of Scandinavian individuality without also focusing on sociality. Thus, as we have seen, it is not a question of children and youths like Sirwa, Gulbîn, Thaung and Hadia having to become individualized *at the expense* of collectivity. On the contrary, they are intended to be individualized *into* a collective—that of "Danish society". Regarding this process of social incorporation, in what follows I discuss the particular ways in which tacit everyday bodily practices, techniques, and routines come to play a decisive role.

FROM MEMBERS OF FAMILIES TO MEMBERS OF SOCIETY: THE ROLE OF BODILY ROUTINES AND TECHNIQUES

In her studies of sociality and civilizing processes among children and youth in Denmark, Anderson (2008) shows the general perception that in order for children to develop not only into independent individuals, but also into members of society, they must gradually increase community activities on their own, hereby learning to "stand on their own two feet" outside the safe walls of the home. Anderson argues that this training in maneuvering on their own in society typically takes place by way of children being enrolled in leisure-time associations, such as sports clubs. Generally, such participation is seen as important in order for the child to become an integrated member of society—besides being a member of a family. However, when it came to the refugee children and adolescents, I found that it was generally not seen as sufficient that they actively participated on their own in Danish association life along with their Danish peers. For the refugee children, there was more at stake. As Elsa put it when I informed her that Gulbîn and Jino, on their own initiatives, had both started playing football in Askbjerg's local sports club: "Yes, but still they cannot ride a bike or swim, and they do need that individuality."

Seen from the perspective of the surrounding Danish community, it was not solely about the refugee children and youths being present in public space through an active association life. It was just as much about being able to master some very specific individual bodily practices *within* this public space (in this situation, swimming and cycling). Thus, when Elsa insisted on teaching Gulbîn how to ride a bike, the mastery of this bodily technique served as more than just *a means* to get Gulbîn moving around on her own in public space, away from the home and her parents. The everyday routine of cycling, I argue, also manifested *an end* in itself, namely, that of Gulbîn developing into a member of the surrounding Danish society. Hence, the idea of "Danish society" as a sort of social collective does not relate to an *imagined* community alone, but, in line with Koefoed and Simonsen (2009), also to a *practiced* community that rests on everyday face-to-face encounters, through which other people's bodies—and bodily practices—are continuously recognized as either familiar or unfamiliar, and, from this, as belonging or not belonging. My material shows how this does not necessarily depend on ethnic or physical appearances, but on bodily participation and involvement (or lack thereof) in various situational practices and routines deemed significant to belong. Indeed, in some ways Scandinavian nationalism seems "less ethnically essentialist than performatively orthodox" (Bendixsen et al., Chap. 1, in this book).

In his article "Techniques of the Body" (1992 [1934]), Marcel Mauss discusses, among other things, how the individual is considered a member of a given social group through certain ways of eating, washing, digging, carrying, sitting, sleeping, dancing, walking, standing, running, and so on. With these come a number of bodily techniques, which are only commonly practiced within some societies and not others. As an example of this, he mentions swimming (Mauss 1992 [1934], 455f.). In short, to be considered a member within a particular social community, the individual must "inhabit" his or her body in a certain way, in the sense of mastering particular tacit bodily practices, techniques and routines—and this mastery, Mauss argues, is important both in creating and sustaining the social affiliation.

In Danish society, swimming and cycling form two specific bodily techniques that children are expected to pick up and master as they grow up. The significance of, for example, being able to cycle is something implicit and taken for granted. In Danish society, it is simply that children are expected to have learned to ride a bike before they reach a certain age. Looking at two of the most popular family handbooks in Denmark on children's health, upbringing, and general well-being, one reads that "children at the age of 5–6 should be able to ride a bike without support wheels" (Manniche 2005 [1995], 209). Furthermore, in order to be seen as ready for school, the child "is required to have advanced its balance and muscular activity, meaning, among other things, that the child must be capable of cycling" (Hansen 2008 [1998], 186). Few children raised in Denmark actually do start school without being able to ride a bike. Thus, for refugee children and youths, this bodily technique suddenly becomes of great importance. While their surroundings both understand cycling as *significant of* and *a necessity for* social affiliation to the Danish community, this practice comes to be viewed as both *a means* to—and *a goal* for—the individual refugee's integration. This idea of the routine of cycling as such a "national thing" (Žižek 1990) was further illustrated recently, by the previous Danish Minister of Culture, Bertel Haarder. As part of his formulation of a so-called "Canon of Denmark" (*Danmarkskanon*) in the Danish newspaper *Berlingske* (Kamil 2016), he distilled five of the most central cultural values, which in his belief concretize what "Danishness" is, and which are therefore the most important values for foreigners to adopt, he stressed, if they were to call themselves Danes. The five key cultural values were: gender equality, freedom of speech, the Danish Folk High School culture (*Højskolekulturen*), the importance of having a job, and the Danish bicycling culture (*den danske cykelkultur*).

The "Right" and "Wrong" Kinds of Personal Autonomy

The centrality of the cases presented of course does not lie in the simple question of whether one can cycle or not, or if one has moved away from home or not, as much as it lies in a realization and comprehension of the individual will and personal autonomy to be found in these examples. Gulbîn did not wish to ride a bike; her little sister, Sirwa, had a great desire to learn to ride a bike (but did not have a bike). Hadia did not wish to leave home; others dreamt of moving away from home and getting their own place (but usually could not find a flat). The point here is this: when refugee children and adolescents showed a wish to leave home or to learn how to ride a bike, this was seen by their social surroundings as expressions of seeking individual independence and autonomy. Wishes of *not* wanting to leave home, or *not* wanting to learn how to ride a bike, were not understood as such. Hence, only the autonomous intentions pointing *away* from the home and *toward* the public space (that is, wanting to ride a bike or leave home) were understood as expressions of individual independence and self-determination. The kind of personal autonomy that pointed back toward the domestic space (that is, *not* wanting to ride a bike or leave home) was not acknowledged—if at all noticed—as expressions of independence and self-determination. Yet, the "wrong" directionality of this form of autonomy is not the only explanation for the lack of acknowledgment these actions received. The case of newly arrived refugees in Denmark reveals an additional complexity, which I will elaborate on in the following.

As shown, in Danish society, children's general societal incorporation is seen as contingent on two diverse, simultaneous processes tied to individuality and collectivity. While refugees should foster an *individual autonomous body* (through gradual emancipation from the home/parents), they should also develop a collectively embedded and *socially bounded body* (through presence in public space by way of specific bodily practices, routines, and techniques). Thus, in Denmark, as in any society, tension exists between individual independence and collective dependence (rather than predominantly the one over the other). The essence here is that in the refugee families' everyday Danish surroundings, there seems to be a prominent idea of "a Western self" as primarily individually autonomous, as opposed to "a non-Western self" as primarily socially bound (e.g., by "family", "gender", or "tribe")—an understanding of personhood within "the West" and "the Rest" (Sahlins 1976) that formerly was emphasized in anthropology (e.g., Dumont 1985) and later criticized for being exaggerated and oversimplified (e.g., Spiro 1993). From such discursive understandings follow real consequences. As illustrated, this understanding means that when it comes to our "non-Western" co-citizens, in Danish society there is a tendency to see "the home" as *the* social space, which hinders (as against secures) their children and youths from developing into fully independent individuals.

When, in the empirical situations illustrated above, some of the independence and personal autonomy that the refugee children and adolescents displayed were understood by their surroundings as expressions of the opposite (that is, obedience and social boundedness), this cannot alone be explained by their autonomy's "wrong" directionality (pointing back toward the home and not out toward society). More precisely, the personal autonomy displayed did not point back toward just any home, but a "non-Danish" home, and thus a home where discipline and obedience are understood as characteristic of the relation between parents and children. This is perceived as a problem, since obedience is seen as an obstacle to the individual child's ability to "find" and "create" him or herself. When, for instance, Palestinian Hadia would not leave home, it was automatically understood by her local integration caseworker as an expression of obedience to the family ("Her mother didn't want her to move, I think"); hence, as a lack of personal autonomy. That Hadia herself did *not* wish to move away from home and that in fact what she therefore showed was rather disobedience in the face of the municipal authorities, and thereby a considerable degree of personal autonomy, was not understood, let alone considered a possibility. Just as Hadia "found" herself in the company of her family, Sirwa "found" herself with Martha. However, Sirwa's teachers perceived this friendship as a wrong companionship for her to be a part of (a "bilingual" companionship including "a strict English mother" seen as unrepresentative of Danish family life). In this situation, however, what Sirwa displayed, in insisting on her togetherness and inseparability with Martha, could be considered very independent and autonomous in the face of her professional surroundings.

Danish Egalitarianism: Emancipation from Discipline and Disciplining in Emancipation

In this chapter, I have examined the negotiations over social inclusion, exclusion, and belonging, which take place in everyday encounters between newly arrived refugee children/adolescents and their local social surroundings in rural areas of Denmark. Concerning the study's schoolchildren, the chapter's first half showed how they were socially included as well-liked, popular peers in their class groups. Overall, the local public schools in the small communities proved rewarding in terms of the refugee children's general experiences of feeling locally included and accepted. The main background to this positive outcome seems to be found in a combination of the children's own strivings for "sameness" and for being "just like" their Danish peers, and their close relationships with teachers who showed a strong commitment in supporting them in this everyday sameness-based inclusion project. For the surrounding person involved (e.g., the schoolteacher, volunteer helper, or municipal caseworker), it is, however, a delicate balance between being supportive and helping—or demanding, if not even patronizing. In their strivings for local social inclusion and belonging, the analysis has shown how refugee children must often, in great measure, act and maneuver within a very specific and culturally defined set of norms and expectations, not least tied to everyday bodily techniques and routines. As discussed, these norms and expectations, which they face daily, are largely linked to tacit understandings of what it takes to be, on the one hand, an independent individual, and, on the other hand, a member of Danish collective society.

I have argued how this schema for childhood development, with its dual emphasis on individuality and collectivity, locally becomes synonymous with an "everyday schooling in Danish egalitarianism", based on which the social surroundings both understand and act in relation to the refugee children/adolescents in daily life. Essentially, this implicit project of egalitarianism and "Danishness" feeds into a specific emancipation project, where refugee children are expected to free themselves from the discipline, obedience, and social boundedness that—locally and within society at large—is often understood to be characteristic of their refugee homes. Thus, the local project of emancipation amounts to a specific culturally defined project, which is itself strongly bound by social norms: while refugee children and youths have to become emancipated, individualized, and made autonomous, this should take place in exactly the same manner as "everyone else". Hence, during everyday life, the *emancipation from discipline* often translates into a *disciplining in emancipation*— a disciplining in which the acquisition and mastering of specific bodily techniques and practices proved crucial, such as cycling. In the local communities, the bodily routine of cycling was equally taken for granted as respectively *a bearer* of Danish cultural and national significance; *a qualifier* for social membership into the Danish society; and *a marker* of an envisioned "integration" process in due forward motion.

As stated in the opening of this chapter, one of the macro-political thoughts behind the policy of scattering recognized refugees to non-urban areas around the country is that if the refugees just get to live "out there"—among largely ethnic Danish co-residents—they will automatically become included, and *then*, eventually, adopt central Danish everyday norms and ways of doing As my analysis has shown, in practice this process works the other way around: the voucher for inclusion and acceptance proves to be the refugee families' successful maneuvering within local tacit understandings of how to culturally inhabit and orchestrate one's body, its activities and routines in Danish everyday life. Similarly, in Gullestad's (1992) well-known argument, in the Scandinavian societies, everyday identifications of "equality" tend to be conflated with "sameness". However, what is perhaps more important to stress here, are precisely the strong "value-mastering hierarchies" (Bruun et al. 2011) encapsulated in the daily process of refugees becoming socially included in the Danish egalitarian society—*through* the mastery of tacit ways of doing, not the other way around.

In Denmark, as in other places, contemporary understandings of children's personal development are tied to an unmistakable tension between individualism and collectivism. This tension seems to have a particular Scandinavian flavor, characterized by the widespread understanding of (1) "individuality" as personal autonomy and independence, and (2) "equality" as sameness or alikeness. On the one hand, children and adolescents are encouraged to develop individual independence and personal autonomy by way of gradual physical separation from the home and their parents, in favor of increased movement on their own within the public social space. On the other hand, the maturing of this independence and autonomy requires a significant encroachment on children's free will, as they are expected to occupy this public space in exactly the same way as "everyone else"—in a certain prescribed pace, and by way of specific bodily techniques and routines. In a Scandinavian and rural context, this chapter has shown how the scope and nature of this general encroachment on children's free will often only intensify further when it comes to "non-Western" refugee children and youths, who are commonly assumed by the surrounding society *a priori* to possess less individuality than their ethnic Danish peers.

Notes

1. For an extensive analysis of the Danish refugee dispersal practice and its local outcomes, see Larsen (2011b).
2. Since 1989, each year Denmark has been resettling 500 "UN-quota refugees" from around the world, selected annually by a Danish ministerial delegation. In 2016, the Danish government announced a pause for an indefinite period.
3. All names of places and personal names are pseudonyms.

References

Anderson, Sally. 2000. *I en klasse for sig*. Copenhagen: Gyldendal Uddannelse.
———. 2008. *Civil sociality: Children, sport, and cultural policy in Denmark*. Charlotte: IAP-Information Age Publishing.
Bruun, Maja H., Gry S. Jakobsen, and Stine Krøijer. 2011. Introduction: The concern for sociality—Practicing equality and hierarchy in Denmark. *Social Analysis* 55 (2): 1–19.

Bruun, Maja H., Stine Krøijer, and Mikkel Rytter. 2015. Indledende perspektiver: forandringsstaten og selvstændighedsstaten. *Tidskriftet Antropologi* 72: 11–37.

Dumont, Louis. 1985. A modified view of our origins: The Christian beginnings of modern individualism. In *The category of the person: Anthropology, philosophy, history*, ed. Michael Carrithers, Steven Collins, and Steven Lukes, 93–122. Cambridge, MA: Cambridge University Press.

Gilliam, Laura. 2009. *De umulige børn og det ordentlige menneske: Identitet, ballade og muslimske fællesskaber blandt etniske minoritetsbørn*. Aarhus: Aarhus University Press.

Gullestad, Marianne. 1992. *The art of social relations: Essays on culture, social action and everyday life in modern Norway*. Oslo: Scandinavian University Press.

———. 2002. *Det norske sett med nye øyne*. Oslo: Scandinavian University Press.

Hansen, Margrethe B. 2008 [1998]. *Rød stue kalder: Familiehåndbog i institutionsliv*. Copenhagen: Gyldendal.

Kamil, Carolina. 2016. Bertel Haarders fem forventninger til indvandrere: "Jamen, så lær dem at cykle!" *Berlingske*, 29 June. http://www.b.dk/nationalt/bertel-haarders-fem-forventninger-til-indvandrere-jamen-saa-laer-dem-at-cykle. Accessed 17 Jan 2017.

Koefoed, Lasse, and Kirsten Simonsen. 2009. *"Den fremmede", byen og nationen*. Roskilde: University Press of Southern Denmark.

Larsen, Birgitte R. 2011a. Drawing back the curtains: The role of domestic space in the social inclusion and exclusion of refugees in rural Denmark. *Social Analysis* 55 (2): 142–158.

———. 2011b. Becoming part of welfare Scandinavia: Integration through the spatial dispersal of newly arrived refugees. *Journal of Ethnic and Migration Studies* 37 (2): 333–350.

Manniche, Vibeke. 2005 [1995]. *Bogen om barnet*. Copenhagen: Politikens Forlag.

Mauss, Marcel. 1992 [1934]. Techniques of the body. In *Incorporations*, ed. Jonathan Crary and Sanford Kwinter, 455–477. Brooklyn/New York: Zone Books (Urzone Inc.).

Sahlins, Marshall D. 1976. *Culture and practical reason*. Chicago: Chicago University Press.

Spiro, Melford E. 1993. Is the Western conception of the self "peculiar" within the context of the world cultures? *Ethos: Journal of the Society for Psychological Anthropology* 21 (2): 107–153.

Trägårdh, Lars. 1997. Statist individualism: On the culturality of the Nordic welfare state. In *The cultural construction of Norden*, ed. Øystein Sørensen and Bo Stråth, 253–285. Oslo: Scandinavian University Press.

Žižek, Slavoj. 1990. Eastern Europe's Republics of Gilead. *New Left Review I* 183: 50–62.

CHAPTER 12

Egalitarianism Under Siege? Swedish Refugee Reception and Social Trust

Kjell Hansen

INTRODUCTION

The large influx of refugees arriving in Sweden in late 2015 and its aftermath, revealed a number of potential and actual tensions in the welfare state and the egalitarian ideas on which it had been built. In order to reach a better understanding of how local governments and civil societies managed the large influx of refugees, we conducted fieldwork in three rural municipalities in central Sweden (Falun, Hedemora, and Leksand). The chapter is based on interviews with about 60 informants. Some worked in the municipal administration, as teachers, social workers, etc., others were local representatives of the Swedish Migration Board and the county board and a final group were regional representatives, local managers of refugee accommodation, and volunteers in a number of civil society organizations.[1] It was clear that the large influx of refugees did lead to increased pressure on the public and civil sectors but it did not create a crisis. However, civil society felt let down by the way the state acted over the processes of integration.

K. Hansen (✉)
Department of Urban and Rural Development, Saint Louis University (SLU), Uppsala, Sweden

The chapter will discuss the reception process and its transformation, showing how what was feared would grow into a crisis for the welfare system, created increasing tensions between civil society and the state over the integration process.

During the autumn and early winter of 2015 more than 160,000 refugees arrived in Sweden. People were fleeing wars and poverty in Syria, Afghanistan, Iraq, Somalia and some came from other countries. The situation was somewhat chaotic as the pressure on the authorities to register everyone and to provide housing was extremely high. The media coverage focused on crowded train stations and overworked civil servants. Politicians were worried about the strain on the welfare system, and some went as far as to warn of its collapse. We were given dramatic accounts of how some of the refugees had to sleep out in the open or in corridors and the reception areas of offices.

As in most other European countries, migration had become a major and charged political issue in Sweden but the opposition to migration in its early phases was notably absent in the political institutions. The question of refugee reception seemed to have been turned into a practical matter of handling a difficult situation. Egalitarian ideals seemed to rule.

Officials at the Swedish Migration Board (SMB), the agency responsible for receiving and registering all refugees, worked day and night to find accommodation. The SMB had no facilities themselves, neither could municipalities solve the acute problems of housing. This opened a market for private entrepreneurs, in keeping with the dominant political ideology of market solutions. A large number of often run-down or unused hotels, schools and leisure facilities were hired and sublet to the SMB. Particularly at the local level, egalitarian ideas seemed to rule the public debate with strong elements of compassion and a will to help and do good. Locals helped in collecting clothes, shoes and toys in ways that surpassed all expectations and which, we were told in interviews, even included people who had formerly been against immigration. But at the same time, in different places across the country, groups started to set fire to facilities intended for refugee housing. Quickly county boards started to classify information on where new accommodation should open. For different reasons, mainly because burning down asylum centers was illegal but also because expressing xenophobic ideas in public was not acceptable, these arsonists maintained contact on a face-to-face basis or through closed communities on social media. But they revealed the cracks in the egalitarian ideology.

Most of the refugee centres opened in rural areas, many of which had for a long time experienced shrinking and ageing populations. In interviews, local politicians and officials stressed that the new arrivals were an opportunity to reverse this trend: new inhabitants would work, pay taxes and use local services, which was exactly what was needed. Little attention was paid to the fact that the asylum seekers' background differed from a traditional Swedish one. When discussed, these differences were seen not as issues of ethnicity or culture but as a series of practical problems that had to be solved: language, education, child care and job training. This is consistent with the claims that integration in the Nordic welfare states is based upon "work, education, local government and the production and dissemination of practical knowledge" (Stenius 2010, 3; see Vike, Chap. 5 in this book). Even the breaches in the rules of behaviour, e.g., boys and young men groping girls in swimming baths, were transformed into a practical matter of education. Everyone that we encountered during fieldwork presented what they were doing as taking care of practical matters. As leading local politicians in all three municipalities stressed, there was a broad political consensus on how to deal with reception and integration, and, as they claimed, there was no need to discuss the process in ideological terms.

After the first turbulent months in early 2016, all the refugees had a place in a refugee facility where they were supposed to wait for their asylum application to be dealt with. Before the end of 2015 this was a process that normally would take three to four months, but now the SMB calculated it would take approximately two years. The accommodation became more permanent than had originally been planned. As a government agency, the SMB did not have any formal responsibility to promote integration mainly because their efforts were supposed to end after the four months of asylum reviewing. For a while the facilities became places where nothing but waiting took place.

As the refugees arrived, volunteer groups gathered in railway stations and other entry points, and in the villages where receptions centers were opened, to welcome refugees and to hand out food, drink, and clothes. Many of these groups displayed the banner of *Refugees Welcome!*, and were formed in places where refugees were placed, often in small rural neighbourhoods at a distance from the local centre. These groups took on a clear responsibility for starting integration measures, such as cafés, language education, and general social events, as well as undertaking all the activities that developed around the distribution of clothes, shoes and toys.

In the interviews, representatives of such groups were the ones who most clearly conceptualized what was going on in terms of egalitarian ideas. A recurring theme was that the asylum seekers were people just like you and me and therefore needed social support.

In the local communities the reception of the asylum seekers soon became yet one part of everyday life. Some found this to be a rewarding way to use one's time and efforts, others were more neutral and simply acknowledged the presence of the asylum seekers. At the national political level, the issue was different and the large numbers of refugees were recognized as a threat to the welfare system. It became a political dilemma to manoeuvre between the basic egalitarian values of international solidarity, as expressed in the Universal Declaration of Human Rights, on the one hand, and not threatening the funding base of the national egalitarian welfare system, on the other. This led to a broad political settlement that resulted in the Swedish government's decision to "close"[2] the borders in early 2016. The reception and early integration measures also raised the question of whether or not the welfare state as such has retreated in a way that it no longer will fulfil its primary tasks. The reception of refugees was in that sense a test of the endurance of the state. Whereas the state, through legislation and other political decisions, established control over the influx, and also supported municipalities and civil society organizations (CSOs) financially in their work with the integration, the practice of creating egalitarian communities took place locally and without much discussion.

The Actors

Apart from the refugees, there were three types of actors or institutions involved: (1) the Swedish Migration Board; (2) the municipalities; and (3) civil society. The state and government were making the decisions about the refugees and working through the Migration Board on the reception, placement, and review of asylum applications. Whereas the liberal politics on refugee reception was motivated and legitimated by references to humanism and solidarity, the SMB dealt with its tasks through a more instrumental rationality, sticking to the formal regulations of the process. However, these regulations do not address the process of the integration of refugees, which normally follows from the issuing of a permanent residence permit. This may be reasonable when the asylum process lasts three months, but less so when the process is extended to a year or more. One of the consequences of the SMB sticking strictly to its own bureaucratic rules was that there was almost no cooperation between the SMB and the municipalities and civil society. The SMB stood out as a bureaucratic apparatus characterized by an instrumental rationality in which ideals such as equality and cooperation were subordinated to strict legal judgements of asylum reasons.

The second main actor, the municipalities, had no influence over the number of refugees to be cared for, where they stayed, or when they would arrive. Most local politicians and civil servants reported how they had received a phone call from the SMB informing them that early next morning a couple of hundred refugees would arrive at a specific facility in the municipality. However, the municipal tasks in relation to the refugees' reception were restricted: the social services were responsible for all children under the age of 18 who arrived without parents. The municipality was responsible for offering all children a place in an ordinary school. The practical pressures on social services and on teachers and headmasters were severe, but our interviews indicated a common view that "Yes, there was pressure, but we managed." There was also pressure on municipal politicians and officials to take advantage of what generally was seen as an opportunity. For about 50 years most rural Swedish communities had been facing declining and ageing populations as a result of urbanization. Now, quite suddenly, these small municipalities had an influx of mostly young people and the realization was that if only they could be persuaded to stay, schools and other kinds of local services could be placed on a more secure footing. This, rather than worries about cultural differences, was the dominant discourse at the time.

The third main actors were made up of civil society, i.e., associations of different kinds that became engaged in the reception and early integration of the asylum seekers. There was a range of different ways of engagement. Groups like *Siljansnäs Hjälper*[3] were formed the night before the unexpected arrival of 150 refugees, to help out with clothes and shoes. Local branches of the Red Cross, IOGT, or Free Churches adjusted their ordinary activities to accommodate the refugees. Local football clubs and other sports associations welcomed new participants but otherwise did not really modify their activities. By and large, the newly arrived refugees revitalized civil society throughout rural Sweden. Young and old took part in teaching Swedish, arranging children's activities, social gatherings ("language cafés") and collecting clothes, shoes and toys that often were distributed in specific premises that also became meeting places. In these ways social relations were created, not only between asylum seekers and locals, but also between locals who previously had had very little to do with each other.

A Shrinking Public Sector?

In social theory there is a dominant discourse that claims that government is transformed from being regulated by clear rules from a distinct centre to a process where government is achieved through networks that "conduct" (Dean 1999). Often the argument is linked to an idea that the state has retreated. The withdrawal of the state might, however, be better understood as a slimming down of functions, mainly apparent through the closure of public offices such as those of the National Insurance Office or employment bureaus. In rural areas the transformation has been experienced as a reduced public presence of institutions such as schools, social insurance offices or police patrols. There has also during the past decades been a marked decrease in public investment in infrastructure in areas with "negative economic development". There is thus plenty of consistent proof that the public sector has lost interest in rural areas.

But when tensions became acute, the public sector still seemed to be there. Formal organizations were proof of great flexibility in spite of the regulations rather than because of them. At the SMB offices, everyone worked on registration and finding accommodation, no matter which section they belonged to. In schools, assistants were hired to help with pupils who did not know any Swedish, and ordinary teachers took on larger workloads. Municipal organizations started working on integration and new positions with responsibility for integration were established.

At the local level, the traditional and clear division of tasks between civil society and the public did not change. Both spheres worked within their rationalities: the municipal organizations with a base in legislation and civil society organizations with a base in their individual engagements and ideological claims. Our study concluded that in terms of demographic composition and size, it does matter what kind of local community was involved. Generally, what we could see from our interviews and observations, was that mobilization through already existing or newly founded associations seemed to be easier to achieve in smaller rural areas than in the more urban areas. Even though we seemed to meet a "smaller" public sector, the division of roles between the public sector and civil society were undisturbed. Judging from our fieldwork, there was in fact no sign of a public sector that had shrunk to the degree that it could not fulfil its primary tasks. It did, however, happily receive contributions from civil society within the spheres that were not explicitly a public sector responsibility.

The Social Contract

It has been claimed (Hort 2014) that the so-called Swedish Model for the welfare state to a large part was built upon the wage settlement between the unions and the employers in the 1930s. This guaranteed higher wages for workers in return for a restricted use of walk-outs. A strong alliance between the government, the unions, and the employees' organizations was established and made possible a high level of income redistribution. A high tax level was combined with ambitions to provide social security to all households in all the country. However, the welfare model also implied that the state and the municipalities, negotiated and collaborated with organizations rather than with individuals even when the aim was to secure the welfare of individuals (cf. Berggren and Trägårdh 2006). The establishment of the welfare state thus strengthened the position of civil society in Swedish government. Locally, public institutions such as sports centres, schools and community halls became resources for local associations. A social contract was established where the state guaranteed a fair distribution of the country's wealth while receiving support from CSOs in terms of political stability. The social contract thus during the post-war period was based upon strong social trust between practically all social actors (cf. Berggren and Trägårdh 2006; see also Vike's Chap. 5 in this book).

With the decline in welfare expansion, and the retreat of public engagement, civil society has become more of a solitary player in the maintenance of social cohesion in rural areas. People living in rural areas have learnt to take initiatives to replace or complement functions they find missing. These included services that previously were provided by the public sphere or through the market, as well as new needs that were not met by state or market actors. In such processes CSOs provide a model for organizing as well as maintaining organizations through which even new tasks may be introduced. Here a long Scandinavian tradition of organizing joint tasks through associations has turned out to be a model in the sense that people know how to organize themselves and are also aware that in order to gain access to municipal or other authorities and their resources, they must form an association with a board, a charter, and minutes of annual meeting.

The retreat of the state has been a more severe problem under conditions of poor economic growth and in sparsely populated rural areas in contrast to expanding urban centres. The policy has tended to leave greater responsibility to the market to deliver services but it is a market that does not work satisfactory in sparsely populated rural areas. In this sense the withdrawal of the state in terms of service provision can also be regarded as a step back from the state's egalitarian responsibilities, which the market, for obvious reasons, is not willing to take on. Whereas the retreat of the state has weakened its ambitions to de-commodify necessary services (Esping-Andersen 1990), in most rural areas this gap has not been filled by market measures, but rather by the state offering economic means to CSOs that are willing to take on the task.

Even though there has not been much research on rural CSOs, the evidence points to the fact that local initiatives are often crucial for the development and survival of rural communities and small towns. Previous research has demonstrated that CSOs that are active in rural areas often have different objectives and repertoires of activities than have urban CSOs (Berglund 1998; Forsberg 2010; Westlund 2001). The issue here is not so much that local associations actively replace former public functions, but rather that they represent a form that is used to fulfil goals and ambitions which are seen as important to local populations. The role of the state has changed from actively taking part in establishing welfare to being a provider of funding when and if there exists a local group willing to organize and realize a project. The social contract has thus been renegotiated and the terms for local populations have deteriorated.

It is disputed whether or not this is a new phenomenon. In socio-geographical terms urbanization has led to a thinning out of rural inhabitants' access to welfare services, such as schools, health services and elderly care. This thinning out was based on an instrumental-economic rationality (Horkheimer 2012), i.e., the supply of services was centralized due to economic reasons which then outweighed ideas of equality, independent of where you lived. In Norway, a strong critique in this vein was launched by Ottar Brox (1966, 1971, 1984, 1988) pointing to how a capitalist instrumental rationality tended to replace egalitarian values, leading to geographically unbalanced development. The rural-urban imbalance has escalated during the past decades, partly due to continued centralization of public services, partly due to increased dependence on private markets, and partly due to declining rural populations.

In the reception of refugees we can see a clear division of roles between public authorities, on the one hand, and civil society, on the other. The state and municipalities act according to what they legally are obliged to do, and CSOs tend to fill in the gaps that arise. In the municipalities where we conducted fieldwork, local associations receive economic support from the municipalities[4] for their activities with asylum seekers, but the driving force for the volunteers is not the grants but rather idealism. Likewise the boundaries between CSOs and public activities are not always strict. In Falun, the public library came up with the idea of letting refugees/immigrants *borrow a Swede*: creating an opportunity for people to meet, in much the same way that CSOs work. Many of the municipal staffs and some politicians have personally engaged in activities organized by local associations working with the asylum seekers.

The Role of the CSOs

The most active civil society groups in relation to the refugees emerged as a response to SMB opening accommodation in their neighbourhood. In interviews with representatives of such groups two reasons stood out. One was compassion: the refugees needed help. One of the informants explained it like this: "I heard that the refugees were going to come the next day, and I had learnt from pictures on TV that they were not dressed for the winter that we have here. So I sent out a message on Facebook asking people in my network to help out with shoes and clothes." Compassion is not an abstract sentiment but strongly linked to practical measures, and its relationship to ideas of egalitarianism is somewhat complex, not least because egalitarianism in the local context is produced through practices rather than through ideological statements (Bruun et al. 2011). On the one hand, compassion can be seen as the practice of solidarity, on the other, it clearly reflects uneven positions of social power. By regarding the asylum seekers more as fellow human beings rather than as categories for bureaucratic handling, the CSO activists are making a political statement in relation to questions of integration. The friendly smiles, the use of names, the small talk, and showing curiosity about the refugees' backgrounds and lives are primarily ways of making contact but can also be seen as demonstrating a will to be equal.

The second motive was political in a more straightforward sense. One of the informants told us: "People in the big cities believe that we out here in the countryside are narrow-minded and xenophobic, and we just felt we had to show them that they are wrong." The background for this comment has to be seen in the light of the growth of the right-wing political party. The Swedish Democrats (*Sverigedemokraterna*) aim to stop immigration and restore a traditional welfare state. However, the statement also refers to the increasing gap between rural and urban populations. Leaving a plastic bag with clothes for the CSO in this sense became a political manifestation, both against anti-immigration politics and against urban prejudices.

Most of the groups that started as a spontaneous reaction to the provision of accommodation, and there seems to have been one with every new refugee housing, dealt with practical tasks relating to the distribution of clothes and shoes. The emergence of large numbers of participants was striking. Word got around and locals lined up with bags and boxes with clothes, shoes and even toys. Volunteers had to be recruited to organize the reception of goods and their distribution to the refugees. Premises for sorting and storing had to be found, and more volunteers had to be recruited to exercise these tasks. Without any formal decisions, organizations were established with informal boards consisting of the founding members and the most active participants. Premises were found either with someone who had an empty suitable building or in a more public building owned either by a local organization or by the municipality. These groups were *practising* care rather than ideology and discussions within them focused on practical matters of the distribution of clothes and toys rather than the values themselves. Instead of pointing to the need for integration in an abstract sense, in interviews, CSO activists tended to point to how they developed personal relationships with refugees, and could speak of how they had "adopted" specific refugees whom they brought into their own everyday lives.

All our informants confirmed that these first few weeks were quite chaotic and groups were occupied with the practicalities of collecting and distributing clothes. In the local communities these activities functioned in a mobilizing manner in a sense that gave people an assignment that was broader than the everyday routines but which did not claim much of money or time if one did not want to spend that. One of the informants told us: "I knew from social media that some of the villagers actually did not want to welcome any refugees in our village, but when we opened the reception of clothes and shoes and just everyone were there, even they came with plastic bags and contributed."

Through these practices the CSOs implicitly stated that equal citizenship included everyone. Soon practice took a step further in the direction of establishing social relations with the asylum seekers. Most groups developed routines in the premises where clothes and other things were distributed that included establishing personal relations through small talk and practical information about how things work in Sweden. Many groups also, like many other local associations, started cafés where refugees could start to learn Swedish and just socialize. Within the villages, a pressure to act in certain ways in relation to the refugees, including other immigrants, evolved not least because the small scale made everyone's actions visible to all others. Practice was clearly based on the personal relationships of the local lifeworld. In the practices linked to taking care of the asylum seekers, an image of the local culture was chiselled out, based on values such as openness, solidarity and capacity to deal with problems. On the one hand, the engagement of CSOs made the "refugee question" visible on a local level and as something that concerned all inhabitants, not just the asylum seekers and the authorities. On the other hand, the activities also served as a way to empower rural communities in a way that can be said to mimic Angela Merkel's famous "*Wir schaffen das*", when she positioned German refugee policies. The pride we met among civil servants and volunteers echoed a will to prove the capacities of local rural communities.

Teaching the language proved to be the most popular way for CSOs to work with the asylum seekers and this was also a first step on the way to a broader integration process. In a positive sense, most local groups regarded the inhabitants of the nearest refugee accommodation as "their" refugees. Obviously the relationships between volunteers and asylum seekers were not equal, neither in the sense of legal rights nor in terms of material resources. One could therefore see the actions of the CSOs as an attempt to mediate this specific breach through a deep-rooted idea of what egalitarian society is about. By working to establish personal relationships with the refugees, CSOs established a sense of equality that not only went beyond inequalities of legal and material kinds, but actually *used* these inequalities to establish personal relationships between individuals. In interviews, volunteers stressed that establishing personal friendships was a concrete and direct way of making the refugees part of the local community. Equality thus in this context was not seen by the volunteers as a formal trait but rather as the individualization of members of a large group called "the refugees". One of the main differences between official authorities and CSOs is that whereas the former always work from and within formal positions, CSO volunteers tended to establish personal relations and friendships with the refugees. Cultural differences were a driving force in the efforts to establish equal relationships. In the so-called language cafés that we observed, there was very little formal education going on; rather they were social events in which conversations were used to teach Swedish. Even the more formal sessions held by adult educational associations tended to be turned into coffee parties.

Towering Problems

It turned out that receiving almost 160,000 refugees over a few months did not create a crisis for the welfare system. The system was put under strain but representatives of the migration board, of the municipalities and civil society volunteers claimed they managed to cope. But the national political level was worried that if immigration did not come under stricter control, continued large-scale immigration would create unmanageable problems for the welfare state. This led to an immediate "stop" for further "uncontrolled" immigration, including border controls, and this was followed by a number of political decisions affecting also the fate of those asylum seekers who had already arrived.

Municipal representatives and even more so CSO volunteers were challenged by the sudden change in conditions and requirements introduced by the national parliament. At the local level there was for the most part close and trusting cooperation between the authorities and the associations working with the early integration processes. For the leadership in rural municipalities as well as among CSO volunteers, the will to integrate immigrants was fuelled not only by moral obligations but maybe primarily by the hope of changing the demographic conditions for development. Most strongly this was evident in the CSOs, whose engagement created strong personal ties to the asylum seekers and promoted a discourse based on compassion, friendship, and humanity.

The SMB, on the other hand, had as its mission to realize a refugee politics decided by the parliament. This promoted a strict formal and bureaucratic view of the refugees which anonymized them in order to treat them according to political decisions and rules and regulations, i.e., to see to it that they were moved into some accommodation that had vacant beds so that other housing could be closed down, and that their asylum applications were handled as correctly as possible.

Analytically speaking, what we find in the closing down of accommodation can be regarded as a classical clash between two kinds of rationality: one based in the everyday lifeworld and its strivings for consensus, and one based on the instrumental rationality of the ruling system (cf. Habermas 1984a, b; Horkheimer 2012). In the process of integrating new arrivals, the conflicts had another twist: which rationality, or logic, should apply: the one emanating from common social relations or the one coming from the state?

After the introduction of restrictions on immigration and as some refugees were granted residence permits and others chose to go back home or were deported, the SMB had an excess supply of housing. The board was also required to cut costs by the government, and the process of closing down facilities started in the summer of 2016. The logic of the process was governed by the contracts SMB had with the private operators. These turned out to be practices of an extremely instrumental rationality in relation to the emerging integration processes that communities and refugees had been engaging in.

Just as municipalities and CSOs were surprised by the sudden arrival of asylum seekers, they were now, less than a year later, just as surprised by the sudden moving of refugees and the closure of their housing. Reactions were strong. State policies were seen as counterproductive in relation to the ongoing efforts toward integration. Reactions from the refugees themselves and from the volunteer organizations working with them were particularly strong. Teachers and nursing staff were sad and regretted the work they had put in and the relations they had built. Municipal politicians were more diplomatic in their expressions but, in the local context, very few defended what was taking place.

In most places this was as far as it went: disappointment and sadness and incomprehension over how the government chose to deal with local processes of integration. However, our study reveals two more dramatic examples. In housing on the outskirts of Falun, a fairly large town, a number of refugees simply refused to move. They said: "We thrive here, have friends and are learning the language. Some of us even have trainee posts." Instead of measures based on force, such as bringing in the police, the government, through the SMB, simply withdrew their allowances and said that you are free to live wherever you want, "it is not our responsibility."

When we visited the place a few weeks after the accommodation had formally been closed down, about 20 asylum seekers still lived there. The staff, hired by the private operator, was worried since every day the refugees stayed meant a loss to the owner's business, and the owner did whatever s/he could to let the premises to someone who could pay now that the SMB no longer wanted them. The representative of the CSO working with this specific group of refugees was upset and angry. She had tried to negotiate with the municipality to convince them to take it over, but they had shown no interest. In connection with the decision to close down the accommodation, several volunteer associations of different kinds had arranged a large demonstration in support of the asylum seekers. But now she was discouraged saying, "I don't know what to do." In contrast to most other CSO representatives that we talked to, this one was disappointed in and critical of the way the municipality had acted.

The other example is from Siljansnäs where the original loose group, *Siljansnäs Hjälper*, had merged with an association formally connected to the local parish hall. This group now worked with social gatherings and had a small house where refugees could come and get clothes and meet representatives of the parish hall association. The accommodation scheduled to close down was a cabin village usually rented to tourists during summer. When the decision to close came from the SMB, this group sought an alternative. Their argument went as follows: "If the problem SMB has to solve is linked to the costs of accommodation, maybe we can find a solution that takes on the costs from SMB." They started negotiations with the owner of the cabin village, who agreed to let the cabins for cost price. The next step was to start fundraising by appealing to locals and this succeeded as well. The deal became that the parish hall association rents the cabins and pays half the rent, while the asylum seekers themselves pay the other half, using their allowances. When we visited, we encountered 70 or so refugees, many children among them, who were living what seemed to be relatively calm and content everyday lives. Twice a week a car with a trailer comes by, organized by a few of the refugees, with foodstuff imported to Sweden from the Middle East, where the other asylum seekers can shop. Here the relationship between the CSO running the accommodation and the municipality is extremely good and supportive.

Whereas the protests against the SMB's relocations may be understood as a disappointment in how the possibilities for integration were destroyed, and thus the possibilities of increasing the local rural population vanished, the tensions created when refugees receive residence permits is of a different kind.

Within the Swedish system of immigration, official integration measures start when the refugee is granted a residence permit and this consists primarily of three steps: (1) to learn the language; (2) to get a job; and (3) to have housing. Of the three, learning the language was what most CSOs devoted their energies to. The possibilities of finding a job or a trainee post for refugees vary considerably between communities, whereas finding housing is difficult in almost all villages. This links the refugee question directly to the failed Swedish housing policies during the past decades. Currently more than eight out of ten municipalities in Sweden have shortages in housing and this is not solely a problem linked to big cities; even small rural towns and villages lack sufficient housing.

Housing as a Contested Resource

The housing shortage problem emerged in the media in the autumn and early winter of 2016 as a result of new legislation passed by parliament. This distributed responsibility for receiving new arrivals[5] among all the municipalities throughout the country. According to the new laws, a municipality is given the responsibility for receiving and starting the integration process for a specific number of new arrivals. Especially in big city areas this was not only criticized but was deemed impossible because of the lack of housing facilities. In the news during the early autumn of 2016 representatives, particularly of well-off suburban municipalities argued along the lines that refugees now appear as competitors for scarce resources that *should* be given first to young Swedes.

Quite independent of political party affiliations, we here see something that points to the strain on the welfare system itself in terms of its ability to deal with fundamental needs, such as housing. It is no longer evident that all persons granted residence should also have the same rights. Naturally there is a competition over scarce housing resources but what is new now is those who are termed as "young Swedes" are being contrasted to refugees and immigrants. The "Swedes" are considered to have more legitimate rights than "the immigrants", and in relation to basic public ideas on equality, this is something that previously used to be restricted to political groups explicitly against immigration. In this way competition over scarce resources has uncovered conflicting ideas on equal rights, one of the cornerstones of egalitarianism. The tensions become even stronger because of the additional ethnic dimensions.

In the smaller rural communities where we did fieldwork, the housing situation was also under pressure but representatives of the municipal housing companies approached the problem by saying: "Yes, there is a lack of housing, but somehow we will be able to solve it." There seems to be something about scale that allows civil servants to get a sort of grip on the situation. It might be tempting to go from this to claim that rural people are more egalitarian than representatives of a well-off, urban middle class, but a more fruitful approach might be to initiate a discussion on the importance of scale in shaping social relations. Small-scale communities tend to be characterized by personal relationships between inhabitants, and in rural communities that for decades have experienced being ignored by the government, personal relationships favour working to find consensual solutions to problems rather than blaming the political system.

Gambling with Social Trust

Lack of housing is obviously a massive problem. However, in the rural municipalities where we did fieldwork, it is considered a problem that is amenable to solution through practical means. The consequences of how the state deals with housing seem to be of a different and more severe kind, i.e., the municipalities work to find consensual solutions whereas the SMB works through already-made unquestionable decisions.

When volunteer associations got engaged with asylum seekers and helped them not only with clothes but generally to adjust to their new circumstances of life, they followed a long tradition. This tradition has seen CSOs as an important bridge between the state and its citizens and has been characterized by a sense of reciprocal trust. This can be seen as the driving force behind the involvement of the volunteers in the refugee reception process: the state and other public authorities will do what they are expected to and "we" will be the web that makes it work on a human and practical level.

This is an approach that is based upon a fundamental trust between citizens and the state, which has been strong in the Scandinavian welfare states. According to World Value Study, approximately 65% of the population in countries like Sweden, Norway and Denmark claim that *one can trust other people in general* (Delhey and Newton 2005) and the general welfare state has built up a strong sense of trust. Basically this goes back to a government that has kept its promises in terms of delivering welfare and building institutions that are considered democratic, i.e., that not only give citizens influence over them but that actually reflect their values (Beugelsdijk et al. 2004; Putnam et al. 1993; Zak and Knack 2001).

Social trust depends upon social actors to maintain it. If it is broken, it will be hard to restore (Hardin 1968), and the fact that trust will make it possible to achieve things that otherwise would be unattainable is what turns trust into social capital (Coleman 1990). The logic of social trust is based on a principle of reciprocity: *I trust you because you trust me* (Aumann and Dreze 2005). When SMB closed down a series of accommodations without anchoring the decisions and the processes among those who had taken an active part in the reception and integration processes, this implied more than simply the decisions to close down. On the one hand, there is a strong and overarching political rhetoric about integration and a will to make the new arrivals part of Swedish society. On the other, it is felt that the state undermines and destroys the local measures already undertaken to achieve this.

In the long-term perspective, the acts of the SMB may prove to be counterproductive in terms of society's social trust, and lead to a reluctance by CSOs to engage in common tasks initiated by the government. Since trust is a reciprocal phenomenon, all parties involved need to fulfil promises and expectations. As has been claimed, the basis of the Swedish welfare state was that it actually kept its promises and provided welfare for taxes (Rothstein 1996). And if this is regarded as the kernel of the Swedish social contract, the breaking up of relationships between refugees and volunteers for what the CSOs see as economic and bureaucratic reasons, this is seen as an attack on the social contract itself.

When talking to disappointed volunteers, we encountered an understanding of the problems that SMB has in terms of keeping to its budget and not spending tax money unnecessarily. The objections are rather directed against how the process has been run and the lack of communication between volunteers and the SMB. The sense created due to the lack of dialogue concerning the closure of the refugee premises is that the volunteers and their efforts do not matter. In a longer perspective, this may be a fundamental break with how the state usually manages its relationships with citizens. Even though the state has always had the power of implementation, it has rarely done so without negotiations with the CSOs. This has been central to the Swedish welfare state.

It is still an open question what will happen the next time the Swedish society faces a crisis in which civil society's efforts not only are expected and needed but also are necessary to smooth the process. All those who during this period have exerted themselves more than they had to—volunteers, teachers, social welfare secretaries, nursing staff—presently express doubts that they will be as engaged in the future. The same actually goes for the municipalities that in many cases have lost the opportunity of working with new arrivals in such a way that they would choose to stay in the municipality.

Conclusion

The large number of refugees arriving in Sweden in the latter part of 2015 placed a certain strain on the welfare system. Initially the reception showed that the idea about the withdrawal of the welfare state was an exaggeration. State, regional, municipal and civil society organizations all showed an ability and willingness to expand and work in a flexible manner in order to deal with the new challenges.

In the early phase, the main part of integration was carried out by volunteers within the framework of CSOs that did not make any distinction between reception and integration, whereas the authorities due to legislative rules had to make this distinction. This was most obvious in the SMB, whereas municipal actors tended to work also with early integration measures. It seems useful to discuss this as a difference in rationalities (Horkheimer 2012), where the different positions and tasks of authorities and rural CSOs respectively have created a deep communication gap between them. More concretely this means that whereas the SMB works as a bureaucratic large-scale organization, the CSO volunteers, when acting as such, strive to establish relationships with the refugees, based on common ground.

Permanent housing and probably in the next phase even labour market issues have proved to be a field in which ideas about equal rights have been focused. Linked to these are also questions about how restrictive Swedish policies on migration and refugee reception are now, while the needs of the world's refugees to find shelter have not decreased. What we saw in the early phase was thus not a crisis but rather an ability to quickly adjust to a new situation.

But during the year that passed after the large numbers of refugees started to arrive, the highest political level, the government and the parliament, changed the preconditions. This has chiefly been challenging to the civil society. In practice, most of the integrative measures were taken by CSOs. But if civil society is run over by the government, is it then reasonable to imagine that it will readily help in the next crisis? This is possibly the real challenge to the system, since Swedish egalitarian ideas are based upon social trust between civil society and the government. The reception of refugees has brought moral questions into the political debate from the personal commitments that exist among the volunteers who worked with such questions for a long time and the groups that have arisen more spontaneously.

The real crisis emerging from the great influx of migrants thus seems not to be the one linked to the refugees themselves, but rather to the changes in the relationships that build social trust in Swedish society or the egalitarian base itself. The profound differences in Sweden between the urban and the rural play an important role in the understanding of the problem: whereas urban areas have had increasing populations and economic growth for a long time, rural areas have faced ageing and shrinking populations and economic decline. For small rural municipalities and communities, the influx of refugees represented an opportunity to turn the demographic development around and to start a process of economic growth, whereas the influx of refugees from a political point of view based on an urban perspective mostly represented problems and difficulties. Differences in scale also promoted two different ways of approaching refugee reception. In large-scale settings, the national level and in larger urban areas, the process was dealt with according to an instrumental understanding of rules, regulations and numbers. In contrast, in small-scale rural settings opportunities opened for not only to establish but even to use personalized relationships as a tool for integration. When the instrumental rationality of the state in fact leads to the break-up of the relationships between local and newly arrived inhabitants, this can be interpreted as yet another example of how the state has abandoned rural areas. The state thus is not only shrinking in terms of its physical presence, it has also given up its position as a trustworthy partner.

Notes

1. The fieldwork was part of a research project, "Turmoil in the Welfare State", financed by the Swedish research council Formas and run by the Swedish University for Agricultural Sciences. Field work was primarily executed by Arvid Stiernström, Cecilia Waldenström and Kjell Hansen.

2. Closing is an exaggeration since Sweden still receives refugees although on a much smaller scale.
3. Siljansnäs is a small village in Leksand municipality and the name of the organization translates into *Siljansnäs Helps*.
4. Funding for this comes to the municipalities from the state.
5. In formal language a person moves from being an asylum seeker to a new arrival when s/he receives a resident permit.

REFERENCES

Aumann, Robert J., and Jacques Dreze. 2005. *Assessing strategic risk*. CORE discussion paper no. 2005/20.
Berggren, Henrik, and Lars Trägårdh. 2006. *Är svensken människa: gemenskap och oberoende i det moderna Sverige* [Is the Swede Human: Autonomy and Community in Modern Sweden]. Stockholm: Norstedts.
Berglund, Anna-Karin. 1998. Lokala utvecklingsgrupper på landsbygden. Uppsala Universitet, Geografiska regionstudier nr 38.
Beugelsdijk, Sjoerd, Henn L. F. de Groot, and Ton van Scaik. 2004. *Trust and economic growth*. Tinbergen Institute working paper no. 2002-049/3.
Brox, Ottar. 1966. *Hva skjer i Nord-Norge? Studier i norsk utkantpolitikk*. Oslo: Pax Forlag.
———. 1971. *Avfolking og lokalsamfunnsutvikling i Nord-Norge*. Bergen: Sosialantropologisk Institutt, Universitetet i Bergen. Stencil.
———. 1984. *Nord-Norge: Fra allmenning til koloni*. Tromsø/Oslo/Bergen/Stavanger: Universitetsforlaget.
———. 1988. *Ta vare på Norge! Sosialdemokratiet under høyrebølgen*. Oslo: Gyldendal Norsk Forlag.
Bruun, Maja Hojer, Gry Skrædderdal Jakobsen, and Stine Krøijer. 2011. Introduction: The concern for sociality. Practicing equality and hierarchy in Denmark. *Social Analysis* 55 (2): 1–19.
Coleman, James S. 1990. *Foundations of social theory*. Cambridge: Harvard University Press.
Dean, Mitchell. 1999. *Governmentality. Power and rule in modern society*. London: Sage Publications.
Delhey, Jan, and Kenneth Newton. 2005. Predicting cross-national levels of social trust: Global pattern or Nordic exceptionalism? *European Sociological Review* 21 (4): 311–327.
Esping-Andersen, Gösta. 1990. *The three worlds of welfare capitalism*. Cambridge: Polity Press.
Forsberg, A. 2010. Kamp för bygden. En etnologisk studie av lokalt uvecklingsarbete. Umeå universitet, Institutionen för kultur- och medievetenskaper.

Habermas, Jürgen. 1984a. *The theory of communicative action.* Cambridge: Polity Press.

———. 1984b. Legitimation problems in the modern state. In *Communication and the evolution of society*, ed. Jürgen Habermas. Cambridge: Polity Press.

Hardin, Garrett. 1968. The tragedy of the commons. *Science* 162 (3859): 1243–1248.

Horkheimer, Max. 2012 [1967]. Critique of instrumental reason. London/New York: Verso.

Hort, Sven E.O. 2014. *Social policy, welfare state, and civil society in Sweden. Vol. 1, History, policies, and institutions 1884–1988.* Lund: Arkiv förlag.

Putnam, Robert D., Robert Leonardi, and Rafaella Y. Nanetti. 1993. *Making democracy work: Civic traditions in modern Italy.* Princeton: Princeton University Press.

Rothstein, Bo. 1996. *The social democratic state. bureaucracy and social reforms in Swedish labor market and school policy.* Pittsburgh: University of Pittsburgh Press.

Stenius, Henrik. 2010. Nordic associational life in a European and an inter-Nordic perspective. In *Nordic associations in a European perspective*, ed. Risto Alapuro and Henrik Stenius. European Civil Society. bd. 8. Baden-Baden: Nomos.

Westlund, Hans. (red). 2001. *Social ekonomi i Sverige.* Stockholm: Nordstedts tryckeri.

Zak, P., and P. Knack. 2001. Trust and growth. *The Economic Journal* 111: 295–321.

CHAPTER 13

Conditional Belonging: Middle-Class Ethnic Minorities in Norway

Monica Five Aarset

Introduction

Being immigrants, or we're not immigrants—but you understand what I mean—being dark or Muslim, or whatever—it is burdened with so many extra things we have to pay attention to, that others don't have to. Let me give you an example: Let's say you go into a doctor's office, and you get in and it smells [like] curry, oil, and bad, and the doctor has dark skin. That's disgusting, isn't it? I have to pay attention to that sort of things. Not because I smell bad, but if I've had a foreign patient in my office that smelled of all those things, and then that patient leaves and the smell stays in the room... And then the next patient that comes in is Norwegian, and you can just imagine what that patient will think of me. And it has come to ... and it's extremely stupid, sad and stupid and racist of me, but it has come to that when I see that the next patient has got dark skin I place that patient in another office. It's ... I'm a bit ashamed for doing it, but I do not want that connected to me when the next guy comes in. (Maiwand, doctor)

M.F. Aarset (✉)
NOVA – Norwegian Social Research, Centre for Welfare and Labour, Oslo and Akershus University College for Applied Sciences,
Oslo, Norway

© The Author(s) 2018
S. Bendixsen et al. (eds.), *Egalitarianism in Scandinavia*,
Approaches to Social Inequality and Difference,
DOI 10.1007/978-3-319-59791-1_13

Maiwand belongs to an emerging generation of adult children of labor migrants that came to Norway in the late 1960s and early 1970s. This so-called second generation is now entering the labor market, marrying and having children of their own. They are spoken of as a litmus test of the integration of migrants into Norwegian society (Henriksen and Østby 2007; see also Hermansen 2015). How they perform, not only in education, the job market and housing, but also in their family lives is understood as defining how successful the integration process is. It is to a large degree the mainstream middle class and their ideals and practices that migrants and their children are compared to (cf. Skilbrei 2010)—not only education and work life, but also in their family life and gender relations. In the context of the Norwegian ideology of gender equality, which emphasizes both genders' full participation in the work force as well as at home, migrants' (and their descendants') views on gender equality become indicators of successful integration. However, the Norwegian gender equality project has a class dimension, as it is the middle class that traditionally has been in the carriers of the gender-equal ideals (Aarseth 2008; Skilbrei 2010).[1] To become successfully integrated thus implies to become more like the Norwegian educated middle class.

According to Ghassan Hage, capitalist societies, like Norway, produce and distribute societal hope through mechanisms of national identification and through their ability to maintain a belief in the possibility of upward social mobility (2004, 13). For immigrants and their children there is an implicit intimate connection between these two; a promise that upward social mobility will grant them a place in "the Norwegian We".[2] The societal hope thus refers not only to a hope for economic security but also for inclusion and belonging.

Based on their educational and occupational achievements, many children of migrants, like Maiwand, can be seen as living the trope of the successfully-integrated second generation. They have done well in the eyes of their parents' generation in the sense that they have pursued higher education and entered prestigious and well-paid occupations. They can also be said to be examples of successful integration in the eyes of Norwegian authorities. Still, Maiwand talked about the extra things they, as "dark, or Muslim, or whatever" have to pay attention to, and he distinguished between immigrants/dark/Muslims/foreigners and an unmarked category of "Norwegians". Maiwand placed himself in-between these two categories; he is not an immigrant as he was born in Norway, he does not smell of "curry, oil and bad", he is a doctor not a patient, *but* he is "dark" and Muslim and his parents immigrated to Norway from Pakistan. Positioned in-between, he has to do extra work to distance himself from the negative charged non-Norwegianness of the "immigrant patient" to be acknowledged as a doctor and as a part of the "Norwegian We". This indicates that the promise of the societal hope may be deceiving; Norwegianness operates as *an unequal resource*. Speaking with Bourdieusian concepts, the resources needed to pass as Norwegian, as middle class, and as free, modern, mobile individuals are not democratically distributed.

In general, Norway has been characterized by low unemployment, high-income equality, and universal and inclusive welfare arrangements. Gender equality is ideologically held high, and the welfare state provides a context that supports women's employment, for instance through childcare services (Nadim 2014). Furthermore, the Norwegian educational system consists of free higher education and of institutions with relatively even standards of education (Reisel 2012), which makes the possibility for equality more likely than in, for instance, countries like the United States or the United Kingdom.[3] This has given Norway a reputation as an egalitarian country. Norway is, however, commonly associated with a specific type of *sameness-oriented* egalitarianism where difference is avoided and down-played and sameness has to be felt in order to see each other as equal (Gullestad 1997, 2002).

This chapter will discuss how Norwegian egalitarianism is played out in specific ways in relation to highly-educated descendants of migrants from Pakistan and how they work on their social habitus to become accepted as middle class in Norway. The discussion will concern the making and maintaining of social boundaries and their impact on experiences of belonging in a Norwegian context. Maiwand and many others of the second generation are socially upwardly mobile; they are making what in Scandinavian languages has been termed *en klassereise* (a class-journey) (see for instance Seljestad 2010). Simultaneously, as children of immigrants from Pakistan, the differences and boundaries in question are not only based on social class but also on ethnicity and racialization. As such this chapter deals with the intricate relationship between ethnicity and class in a Norwegian context. Through empirical cases, I will discuss the in-between position of being *middle class* and an *ethnic minority* in Norway, and the extra work and investments ethnic minorities do to transgress boundaries, to fit in and be acknowledged as equal, so that their sense of belonging can be confirmed. Furthermore, the chapter discusses how this continuous work and how being categorized as "successfully integrated" may be experienced as not being enough when facing critical events such as what was for some hours believed to be an Islamic terrorist attack on Norway on 22 July 2011. I argue that the significance of sameness-oriented egalitarianism must be studied empirically in relation to particular contexts and segments of society, as social boundaries are classed in specific ways and as class defines the ideals of equality. I further argue that for this specific segment of ethnic minorities—an emerging middle class—the need to conform in order to be seen as equal and to achieve belonging becomes precarious in specific ways. I describe their belonging as conditional. By using the term *conditional belonging*, I do not mean that their belonging is at stake all the time, every day, for everyone. It does not mean that they never feel at home nor that they never find acceptance. They do. Rather, it is precisely because they do and because they invest so much in doing so, that the question of belonging becomes precarious and the conditionality salient in particular moments in time. The term *conditional belonging* is used to underline how feelings of belonging co-exists with awareness of the conditionality of this belonging and of not being in control of these conditions.

Studying an Emerging Middle Class

The discussion is based on a study in which I investigated the possibilities and dilemmas that descendants of immigrants sometimes face when establishing families of their own, and the negotiations and the social processes these generate (Aarset 2015). The fieldwork was conducted over 24 months from 2010 to 2012, with 20 couples and families of Pakistani and Indian descent. Here I will draw mainly on the material based on the ones of Pakistani descent. At the time of research, the couples were between the ages of 30 and 40, and most had been married for several years and had children in kindergarten or at primary school. The families lived in Oslo and neighboring municipalities. Furthermore, I focused on couples where at least one spouse has higher education. Following a pragmatic approach to class, where class position or class aspiration is based on the level of education and work (Stefansen and Farstad 2008), they may be seen as part of a new, emerging Norwegian middle class.

Being between 30 and 40 years old, they were among the oldest in the second-generation and thus the first to enter adulthood, get higher education and enter work life in Norway. They can be seen as forerunners for the processes of change among descendants, described later in this chapter (see also Nadim 2014). Some explicitly referred to themselves as "pioneers moving in unploughed ground", maneuvering between different and often conflicting understandings and practices in the intersections between the parental generation, Norwegian society and transnational social fields. Their experiences of growing up in Norway and their educational backgrounds have led them to more individualized life projects than their parents had and to place more emphasis on their nuclear family than their extended family. They were conscious of how their life choices, successes and failures could impact their younger siblings, cousins and future generations. Furthermore, many carried with them experiences of what Paul Gilroy terms *double consciousness*; the double position as minority and citizen characterized by a feeling of being both inside and outside the nation (Gilroy 1993; see also Andersson 2010).

The pioneering aspect of the couples in my study can be seen, for instance, in where they take up residence. Oslo is a class-divided city with an upper and middle-class dominated western side and a more working-class dominated Eastern side (Andersen 2014). Immigrants and their descendants from non-Western countries generally live in the largely working-class parts of the city (Søholt and Astrup 2009). There is also a tendency to move out of the inner and eastern parts of the city when they can afford a larger apartment or house in eastern or southern satellite towns. Several of the couples in my study departed from this general pattern by moving to more typical white middle/upper middle-class suburbs on the western side of the city. Some did this because they thought that they would fit in better in a middle class neighborhood than in working-class areas, others because they wanted their children to go to particular schools in those areas, and others again because they wanted to establish a distance from their parents.

Background: Pakistani Immigrants and Their Descendants

Labor migrants who came to Norway in the late 1960s and early 1970s represented the first substantial immigration to Norway from outside the Nordic countries. This migration started relatively late compared to other Western European countries, but increased after other European countries began to restrict immigration. The immigrants came predominantly from Pakistan, but also from Morocco, Turkey, Yugoslavia, and India. These initial immigrants were young men who came in search of work when Norway was in demand of cheap labor in the unskilled labor market (Brochmann and Kjeldstadli 2008). The education and skills that the immigrants brought with them were generally undervalued and did not easily translate into cultural capital. Similar to that of other countries in Western Europe, the general picture was that labor immigrants came from the middle layer in their countries of origin and moved downwards into Norway's working-class (Brochmann and Kjeldstadli 2008). By the second half of the 1970s, more restrictive immigration policies were introduced, and in 1975 Norway enforced a temporary ban on immigration. This put a stop to the previous unskilled labor migration from Asia, Africa, and Southern Europe, but migration, in particular from Pakistan, continued in the form of family immigration; women and children came either to join their husbands or fathers after years of separation, or as newlywed marriage migrants. From the 1990s onwards the immigration pattern changed from family reunification to family formation as children of immigrants reached marrying age and predominantly married spouses from their parents' country of origin.

Today Pakistanis are considered to be among the old immigrant groups in Norway. Pakistani migrants and their descendants are the third largest immigrant group in Norway (36 000), and children of immigrants from Pakistan constitute the largest group of descendants (16 500).[4] The dominant story of the Norwegian-Pakistani population is that of intergenerational change and social mobility. Descendants of migrants in general, and Norwegian-Pakistanis of both genders in particular, are much more likely to attain higher education levels than both their parents and the majority Norwegian population (within specific age groups) (Dzamarija 2010; Olsen 2016).[5] Income inequalities between descendants and the majority population are smaller than those for the parental generation; in fact, the income levels of the second generation are close to that of the majority population (Hermansen 2015). Significant changes are also taking place in gender relations and family formations. The large gender differences found in labor market participation among Pakistani immigrants seem to be reduced in the next generation; women in the second generation participate in work-life to a larger degree than their mothers (Olsen 2013; Nadim 2014).[6] During the last 15 years we find a marked increase in marriage age and a decrease in transnational marriages (Sandnes 2013). Furthermore, second generation women have children at an older age and have fewer children than their mothers (Sandnes 2013). In other words, descendants of immigrants can be said to settle into family patterns found in the population at large.

Norwegian Integration Discourse

Despite having a history of ethnic diversity and of complying with colonialism (Keskinen et al 2009), Norway in in the 1960s and 70s viewed itself as a small country without an internal elite or an oppressive or imperial history (Gullestad 2006; McIntosh 2013). The idea of Norway as originally ethnically, culturally and socially homogenous is still widespread and influences ideas of what is "natural" (Gullestad 2006). Understandings of what is "natural" in relation to belonging and the nation-state have placed "the immigrant" as a conceptual opposite to "Norwegian", and "Norwegianness" has been constituted as the undefined normative centre (Gullestad 2003, 91). Several studies document experiences of racism and discrimination among ethnic minorities (see Andersson 2010; Midtbøen 2014; Tronstad 2009). Although the patterns of immigration have changed with increasing labor migration from European countries, "Muslims" to a large degree still represent the prototype of "the immigrant". Through such stereotypical images of immigrants and their descendants as working-class and the conflation of middle-class, whiteness and Norwegianness, little room has been left for middle-class ethnic minorities, as there has been no collectively recognized scripts or representations for them (see also Orupabo 2010). Further, as in other Western countries, Islam and Muslims are increasingly associated with security threats and terrorism.

At the same time, important changes are taking place. In the last 10–15 years, ethnic minorities, and youth in particular, have become increasingly visible as participants in public debates, speaking from broad range of political and social positions (see also Midtbøen forthcoming). Media representations of ethnic minorities are also becoming more complex (Figenschou and Beyer 2014). More so, today people of immigrant backgrounds occupy a wider range of positions in Norwegian society, including high-status occupations like doctors, lawyers and politicians. As an increasing number of descendants of migrants enter public debates and hold various positions in society—and in so doing claim Norwegianness—established understandings of Norwegianness as based on ethnicity and descent are challenged (Vassenden 2010). The situation today appears complex, with forces moving in different directions; everyday diversity and renegotiations of what it means to be Norwegian are taking place alongside naturalized and ethnicized understandings of Norwegianness. Furthermore, we find both a broadened *and* a sharpened, politicized debate climate, in particular in relation to issues dealing with Islam and Muslims.

Social Boundaries and the Logic of Equality

The making and maintenance of social boundaries are significant in discussions of processes of inclusion and exclusion, and of feelings of belonging in the national state. In his now-classic introduction to *Ethnic Groups and Boundaries,* Fredrik Barth (1969) urged researchers to observe the making and maintenance of *boundaries* between ethnic groups, and he discussed ethnicity as a product of a *social process* rather than as culturally given. He emphasized that ethnicity and ethnic groups are created through an interaction of internal and external boundary makings, making ethnicity situational and malleable—at least to some degree. An important aspect of Barth's theoretical perspective is that the ethnic boundary can be maintained as a social boundary marker despite being crossed by persons *and* despite changes in the cultural content, or what Barth called the "cultural stuff". Barth's perspective has had an enormous influence on studies not only of ethnic identity and ethnic boundaries, but also other forms of social identity, and in the process it has been challenged, criticized and renewed. One main critique is that Barth passed over the role of the "cultural stuff" too easily (cf. Eriksen 2002). When concerned with the question of belonging and what hinders or enables feelings of belonging, the "cultural stuff" may play a significant role. Identity and social and ethnic boundaries are not only strategic and organizational concerns, but are matters to which people give huge value, and the cultural differences invoked in social boundary-making may have a profound bearing on how ethnic or social relations are experienced (Cohen 2000; Eriksen 2002).

In her discussions of the Norwegian immigrant and integration discourse, Gullestad (2002) places more explicit emphasis on the importance of the cultural content for the making and maintaining of social boundaries than does Barth. Gullestad argues that "the process of ethnification needs to be understood in terms of *cultural content* as well as in terms of boundaries and relationships" and that in the Norwegian debates on immigration and ethnic minorities, "the boundary is not only organizational, but also *cultural*" (2002, 45–46, my emphasis). The cultural content Gullestad refers to is the significant role that the concept of equality as sameness plays in Norwegian society. Gullestad argues that the idea of equality—that people have to feel more or less the same in order to be of equal value—is particularly strong in Norway. According to Gullestad (2002), this notion of equality as sameness exists together with a distinct individualism that emphasizes self-reliance and independence, giving egalitarianism a specific meaning in the Norwegian context.

She holds that the Norwegian egalitarian tradition and the *logic of equality* lead people to emphasize commonalities and down-play difference in social encounters and underline the importance of "fitting in together" and "sharing the same ideas". This often implies that being "too different" and "sticking out" is seen as problematic and negative. She points out that the logic of equality creates an *imagined sameness* which is used to draw a line, *an invisible fence*, between "us" and "them", contributing to a racialization of difference (Gullestad 2002). Gullestad further argues that "the dividing-lines between people in terms of social class have become blurred" and that "the differences between 'Norwegians' and 'immigrants' have become discursively salient" (2006, 171). The significance of social class has not diminished, but there is a tendency in society to explain social differences by pointing to ethnicity and culture instead of socioeconomic factors.

Gullestad's perspective may be criticized for being too *all-encompassing* and for placing a too unified significance on the logic of equality. For instance, as Marianne Lien notes, Gullestad's empirical material is mostly from the southern Norway (Lien 2001; see also Abram 2008). Lien argues that the situation in Northern Norway diverges from what Gullestad describes in that in the North difference is more taken for granted. Furthermore, as Ida Erstad points out in her Chap. 9 in this volume, Gullestad primarily bases her analytical discussion on media discourse and to a lesser degree on everyday social encounters. The situation in Norway today, presented earlier in this chapter, is more complex and diverse than Gullestad's analysis gives the impression of. The social boundaries are complex, and as Barth emphasized, situational and relational. Anders Vassenden (2010) thus argues that there is a need to untangle the different components of Norwegianness, as being Norwegian in some contexts refers to having a Norwegian citizenship, in others to ethnicity, descent or religion, and in others again to sharing cultural codes (for instance middle-class culture and/or the logic of equality).

Here Richard Alba's (2005) distinction between *bright* and *blurry* social boundaries can prove fruitful. Alba discusses how, in contexts where the boundaries are bright, the distinction involved is unambiguous, so that individuals know at all times which side of the boundary they are on. Citizenship is an example of a bright boundary. Blurry boundaries on the other hand, are "zones of self-presentation and social representation that allow for ambiguous locations with respect to the boundary" (Alba 2005, 20). Individuals can be seen "as simultaneously members of the groups of both sides of the boundary or that sometimes they appear to be members of the one and at other times members of the other" (Alba 2005, 25). Like Barth, Alba points to how boundaries are complex, plural and contextual and also to how boundaries may persist despite the crossing of persons and despite immense cultural change. The boundaries of Norwegianness are both blurry and bright depending on context.

Drawing on this discussion of theoretical perspectives on the making and maintenance of social boundaries, I now turn to the experiences and strategies of middle-class ethnic minorities and their efforts to fit in and confirm their belonging to Norway.

MIDDLE-CLASS ETHNIC MINORITY FAMILIES: FITTING IN AND STICKING OUT

Maiwand described his strategy of down-playing his association with negative difference by placing "immigrant" and "Norwegian" patients in different rooms. Others described different types of extra-work and ways of down-playing difference and of trying fit in. Several of those who lived in areas dominated by ethnic majority Norwegians described feelings of sticking out. Kubra and Karim, a married couple, had moved to a majority dominated middle-class area in the outskirts of Oslo. They wanted their children to grow up "as part of Norwegian society, not in a minority dominated enclave". They knew, however, that their ethnic and religious background made them stick out in the neighborhood, and they made great efforts to down-play what they perceived as a negatively charged otherness. They were active and engaged parents and took part in school and after-school activities in ways which can be described as typical middle-class parenting strategies (Bach 2012; Vincent and Ball 2007). They also wanted to be a positive factor in their neighborhood. When asked if they felt that having a minority background made it extra important for them to make a good impression, they nodded. Kubra said:

> We think like that a lot. We sometimes think that we have to. Sometimes it's almost like being forced—we have to join in otherwise we'll become the Pakistani family that doesn't bother, that doesn't do anything. And particularly here, where we're the only ones…

Karim declared:

> I feel… that in everything I do I represent all the others.

Kubra continued:

> It's like with the lawn. Karim has had… this summer Karim had an alarm clock to remember to mow the lawn once a week. Because the summer before that I was like: Ah, we have to mow the lawn or we become "those who do not mow the lawn". So he got an alarm clock.

Becoming "those who do not mow the lawn" meant, in this particular context, to fulfill stereotypes of Pakistani or immigrant families as backwards: they have "too many" children, do not contribute to the common good, do not understand or care about how a garden should look in a nice, middle class neighborhood and thus they lower the general standard of the neighborhood. Kubra and Karim, and the other couples in my study, were well aware of the existence of such stereotypes and several of them had encountered them during their childhood but also as grown-ups. Having an un-mown lawn may be seen to signal a lack of *respectability*, in the words of Beverly Skeggs (1997). Drawing on Bourdieu, Skeggs, discusses how British working class women suffer from the stigma of not being respectable because they have "the wrong femininity". To *pass* as middle class and become respectable they have to make an extra effort. They must over-achieve and downplay their otherness. I am not suggesting that mowing the lawn is necessarily a middle-class practice, but in this context knowing when it is time to mow the lawn and remembering to do it, is presented as symbol of being *an insider* with an embodied white middle-class habitus or Norwegianness. An insider just knows when it is needed. Writing about the emotional politics of class, Skeggs points out that people of working class background who are trying to move into the middle class "…can never have the certainty that they are doing it right which is one of the signifiers of middle-class dispositions… [t]hey feel they have to prove themselves through every object, every aesthetic display, every appearance" (1997, 90). Being the only visible ethnic minority family in the neighborhood, Kubra and Karim felt they had to prove themselves through their appearance, to not stand out in a negative way or to feed into the negative stereotypes.

The area that Kubra and Karim lived in is a typical move-in-area, where people belonging to the middle class of various social and regional backgrounds settle down. Even though Karim and Kubra were the only couple of ethnic minority background, others in their neighborhood may be people that have climbed the social ladder and may also be concerned about keeping up appearances, trying to pass and to fit in. The point here is that Kubra and Karim felt that *they* are the ones that stick out. Maiwand's fear that white Norwegian patients will associate the smells of a dark/foreign/Muslim patient with him and Kubra's and Karim's fear of how they will be judged if they have an unmown lawn can be understood as fears of imagined reactions as a result of *imagined boundaries*. This does not mean that they are not real; they are based on embodied experiences incorporated throughout life.

In the case of Kubra and Karim, and others in my material, their desire to not be seen as typical immigrants, working class, backwards, traditional, and so on are *lived through* their bodies, their clothes, and their homes (see also Skeggs 2004). To mow the lawn, to be a good neighbor, to not eat food that makes you "smell", to place "foreign" patients and "Norwegian" patients in different rooms, to excel in studies and work life; all these activities are invisible work ethnic minorities do to down-play negative difference so that they can fit in and pass as Norwegian middle class. Socially mobile persons may bear traces of their class origin in their bodily hexis, that is, in their accent, taste, posture, and so on (Bourdieu 1977). For socially mobile ethnic minorities, such as descendants of Pakistani migrants, their origins are marked in and on their body in an even more fundamental way; it is in the color of their skin, hair and eyes.

Future Horizons

Kubra, Karim, and the others in my study grew up with feelings of not quite belonging or of *not being acknowledged* as belonging in Norway. They spoke of their role as bridge-builders between the minority and the majority population, and between their parents' and their children's generations. As parents, they wanted their children to feel an entitlement in and belonging to Norway, and not to question their identity and their right to belong like they themselves had. They wanted their children to be proud of their backgrounds and of their cultural traditions and religious identities. At the same time, they did not want them to suffer for sticking out. They were working to find a balance between *difference* and *sameness,* and to both challenge and comply with the logic of equality. There were, however, variations in what they saw as the right way to go about this. For some, it meant down-playing their differences in the public and keeping religious and cultural practices within the four walls of their home, for others it meant trying to push social boundaries to carve out a space where being both Muslim and Norwegian could be seen as a "natural" and public category. Other still sought a mix of both, depending on the context. In their efforts to equip their children for a future in Norway they sometimes face reactions from others of the same ethnic background as themselves and from relatives in the country of origin. For instance, they might be scolded for not visiting Pakistan enough, for prioritizing the Norwegian language, or for becoming "too Norwegian". In other words, the *boundaries of Norwegianness* were guarded from several sides.

Despite their different efforts to find a balance, they all emphasized the importance of education and of being fluent in Norwegian. One father said he feared that his kids would be classified as foreigners if they did not speak Norwegian fluently. Having a good education was particularly important, many said, because they knew their children would have to work extra hard to reach their goals and to be accepted. Karim:

> I think that we place high demands on our children, and that we have influenced them a lot... to pursue higher education, an academic education. We tell them almost daily that education is important. And there is a reason for that. The motivation behind it is... it's a little bit sad saying it, but it is not exactly a good environment in Norway for Muslims these days. And perhaps it'll get even worse in the future.

The couples hoped for a better future for their children, at the same time as they prepared them for the extra work they would have to do to pass and fit in as middle class and Norwegians, and to achieve a sense of belonging. They knew, however, that it was not only up to them, and that forces beyond their control would impact the situation and the future.

One day as Kubra and I were sitting in her kitchen, she talked about the challenges of growing up with parents that knew little about Norwegian society and spoke little of the Norwegian language. I asked if she thought it would be easier for her children's generation. She said it would be both easier and more difficult: Easier because they had parents that were familiar with Norwegian society and spoke Norwegian fluently, but more difficult because the younger generation would expect to be recognized and acknowledged *as Norwegians*. She continued:

> They have no other group to belong to. And if they're not accepted, they don't have any explanation or apology to protect themselves with. They can't say to themselves that it is because they're really Pakistanis, because they're not. Our parental generation never thought of themselves as Norwegians.

> It was never important for them. Our generation is more like fifty-fifty, or not fifty-fifty, but we were also Pakistanis [in addition to being Norwegian] and we had belonging and a community there. The third generation does not have that.

In her book on Caribbean transnational family networks, Karen Fog Olwig discusses how a personal link to a place of origin in the form of "concrete family relations and family history provide[s] a means whereby they could give the externally imposed social identity personal meaning and form" (2007, 245). Olwig points out that these personal links to a place of origin make migrants and their children more robust and better equipped when the majority society categorizes them as "other".[7] What Kubra pointed out was that her children and their generation have lost that link, and without it they will be more vulnerable when categorized as belonging to something other than the mainstream society. Hage (2010) elaborates this type of vulnerability in his discussion of a form of racialization he calls *mis-interpellation*. He describes mis-interpellation as "a drama set in two acts" (2010, 122). In the first act, the racialized person is treated as if they belong to the collectivity like "everyone else". Then in the second act, he/she is particularized and excluded from the "we":

> S/he is hailed by the cultural group or the nation, or even by modernity, which claims to be addressing "everyone". And the yet-to-be-racialized person believes that the hailing is for "everyone" and answers the call thinking that there is a place for him or her awaiting to be occupied. Yet, no sooner do they answer the call and claim their spot than the symbolic order brutally reminds them that they are not part of everyone: "No, I wasn't talking to you. Piss off. You are not part of us". (Hage 2010, 122)

This *mis-interpellation* is what Kubra feared her children would be subjected to. She hoped that they would believe that they are the "'normal' universal subjects of modernity" (Hage 2010, 125) and that they would be acknowledged as belonging to Norway in similar ways as other Norwegians—but at the same time she feared that they would be told that they are not.

22 July 2011: From Blurry to Bright Boundaries

A couple of weeks after the conversation in Kubra's kitchen took place, Norway experienced its worst terror attack since World War II. On the 22nd of July, 2011, a bomb went off in the center of Oslo, killing eight people, and later the same day 69 people, most of them children, were massacred at the small island of Utøya. In the hours before the perpetrator's identity was known, it was widely believed that Islamic terrorists were behind the attacks. Stories of ethnic minorities receiving threats, and being harassed and attacked were spread on social media almost immediately after the bomb went off (see also Andersson 2012; McIntosh 2013). Boundaries that previously seemed blurry suddenly appeared to be shining bright. My interlocutors described how, in the hours after the bomb went off, and before the terrorist's identity was known, continuing to live in Norway as a Muslim—or as someone that could be mistaken for a Muslim—seemed almost impossible.[8] The potential future Kubra had feared seemed suddenly to have become the present. Many believed they had to pack up their things and leave Norway. Ghalib, who had thought that he and his family had to move away from Norway and said:

> I was frustrated because I have lived here all my life, and like all my friends who are ethnic Norwegians I have gone to school and worked here. But feeling that what had happened might change that… "You are maybe not one of us after all". It felt like a knife through my heart.

He was "successfully integrated", he had done like his majority Norwegian friends, but still felt (or feared) that majority Norwegians' reactions would not only excluded him from the imagined community of the "Norwegian We", but also make it impossible for him to live in Norway.

Like so many others, minority and majority Norwegians alike, the couples in my study described a feeling of enormous relief when, late on the evening of July 22nd, it became known that the perpetrator was a Christian, white Norwegian.[9] In the following days torch and rose marches were held in several Norwegian cities, politicians spoke of tolerance, inclusion, and openness as important Norwegian values, religious leaders of different beliefs stood together in grief, and inter-religious funerals were held. Several of my interlocutors spoke of how they felt an increased love for and belonging to Norway and Oslo in the aftermath—but underlined at the same time that they felt a sense of precarity. Karim said he sometimes feared that all the talk of tolerance and inclusion after July 22nd might only be hype and that there would be a backlash. Ikhlaq, another of my interlocutors, spoke about how his (white, majority) work colleagues had described to him how they, in the hours before the perpetrator's identity was known, had felt a hatred towards all Muslims and an urge to "kick those bastards out of the country". The fact that his colleagues whom he had known for a long time had reacted this way, frightened Ikhlaq.

He said that July 22nd had made him think of how humanity is covered by a thin layer of civilization with something darker, more dangerous lurking beneath the surface. July 22nd had opened the door to a possible future and given them a glimpse of the potential consequences of a terror attack by Muslims in Norway.

The terror attack and its aftermath seemed both to strengthen their feeling of belonging to Norway *and* to underline that this belonging is conditional– and that they do not control those conditions themselves. In other words, July 22nd, 2011, seemed to trigger and actualize—in different stages of the event—complex feelings that were already there.

Conditional Belonging

In this chapter I have discussed how ethnic minority families work on their social habitus to become accepted as middle class, but also how, for this particular segment, becoming a part of the middle class is seen as necessary for being acknowledged as belonging in Norway.

The empirical cases discussed can be said to illustrate the complex and conflicting trends we find in Norwegian society as described earlier in this chapter. On the one hand, the stories of Maiwand, Kubra, Karim and the others, point to social mobility, to crossings and challenges of boundaries, and to central processes of change in Norwegian society. The emergence of a new Norwegian middle class made up of doctors, engineers and academics with ethnic minority background, and the fact that some of these also move into previously white residential areas, point to increasing diversity and to renegotiations of existing social boundaries. The Norwegian education system and welfare services such as childcare play important roles in the educational achievements and work participation among descendants of both genders (in addition to other aspects such as individual ambition, immigrant drive, cultural values and strategies and so on). As such Norwegian egalitarianism, understood as an aspect of institutional structures and forms of redistributive policy (see Introduction, this volume) are an important resource for immigrants and their children.

At the same time, the amount of work that Maiwand, Kubra, Karim and the others do to fit in and to be acknowledged as middle class and as Norwegians, points to the forces of *the logic of equality* and to how the *imagined sameness* may contribute to create invisible fences between "us" and "them" based on naturalized understandings of social class and

Norwegianness. We may say that Norwegian egalitarianism contributes to enabling *structural* integration but at the same time, in some contexts and on some levels, it may be an obstacle for *social* integration.

As Erstad points out (Chap. 9, this volume), if we take the notion of equality as sameness as an empirical fact *a priori* we might miss important contextual differences. The making and maintaining of social boundaries, as well as the significance of the logic of equality and how it is played out, have to be investigated empirically in specific contexts and groups. For the particular segment discussed here, the forerunners of a new Norwegian middle class, the question of belonging becomes salient in particular ways. These people are part of the narrative of successful integration and are on many levels included and feel that they belong in Norway. Positioning themselves in the middle class, in what can be said is *center of Norwegianness* as defined in the integration discourse, they live their lives "close" to the social and ethnic boundaries and are constantly crossing and challenging them. They see themselves as bridge-builders and pioneers and they place huge investments in being accepted as belonging to the mainstream, middle-class "Norwegian We". In doing so they are viewed as more integrated and as more Norwegian—as more same/equal—than other ethnic minorities. At the same time, they may also be more exposed to experiences of *mis-interpellation* (Hage 2010).

Norwegian society and understandings of Norwegianness move in different directions at the same time. There are simultaneous processes that make blurry and bright boundaries, of both hybridization and fixed, naturalized understandings of middle-classness and Norwegianness (see also Erstad, Chap. 9, this volume). Aspiring ethnic minority families can be seen as both challenging and complying with the social boundaries and with the logic of equality. They are continuously negotiating how much difference—and perhaps more importantly what *types* of difference—there are room for while still being accepted and acknowledged as equal and as belonging. However, because of the imbalance in power-relations between ethnic majority and minorities, minorities are seldom in the position to define when, where, and how the social boundaries are drawn. In many ways Maiwand and the others are incorporating, as well as expanding, the "cultural stuff" of the Norwegian middle class. Sometimes this may be enough to be seen as same/equal. At other times, they know that whether or not they share the "cultural stuff" and manage the cultural codes, does not matter, underlining the conditionality of their belonging.

Notes

1. There has for instance traditionally been a tendency for low participation in employment and low-status jobs to overlap to some degree with higher valuation of a traditional gender based family form (Stefansen and Farstad 2008).
2. The "Norwegian We" is of course an imagined community and perhaps a *fata morgana* dissolving in to thin air when one is trying to capture and deconstruct it. That does however not make the experience of being excluded or the wish to be included less real or significant.
3. Nevertheless, socioeconomic background and parent's level of education still play an important role in the level and type of education people have.
4. From Statistics Norway, the numbers are per 1 January 2016. Here descendants are defined as Norwegian born to two parents who migrated from Pakistan.
5. Researchers point to a tendency for a polarization among descendants of immigrants; at the same time as more enroll in higher education, there are also a substantial share who do not complete upper secondary (Støren 2010).
6. But still to a lesser degree than women in the majority population (Olsen 2013, 31).
7. This resembles experiences and feelings described in writings on *klassereiser*; a fear of who you will become and what you must leave behind, the anticipation (and fear) that once you have made that journey it is impossible to return to what was before (Seljestad 2010; Trondman 1994).
8. This was not only experienced by Muslims, but also by the Sikhs and Hindus in my material. They feared that the hatred would be turned towards all visible minorities and immigrants (Aarset 2015; for similar experiences see also McIntosh 2013).
9. However, most majority Norwegians had not feared that theirs or their children's right to live in Norway would be questioned by their fellow citizens because of their skin color or religious background, in the way Kubra, Karim and several others with ethnic and religious minority backgrounds did in the hours before the terrorist's identity became known.

References

Aarset, Monica F. 2015. *Hearts and roofs. Family, belonging and (un)settledness among descendants of immigrants in Norway.* PhD thesis, University of Oslo.

Aarseth, Helene. 2008. *Hjemskapingens moderne magi.* Dr. polit. thesis, University of Oslo.

Abram, Simone. 2008. Reproducing the Norwegian: Egalitarianism and the normal. *CTCC Research Papers. Current research in critical tourism studies.*

Alba, Richard. 2005. Bright vs. blurred boundaries: Second-generation assimilation and exclusion in France, Germany, and the United States. *Ethnic and Racial Studies* 28 (1): 20–49

Andersen, Bengt. 2014. *Westbound and eastbound. Managing sameness and the making of separations in Norway*. PhD thesis, University of Oslo.

Andersson, Mette. 2010. The social imaginary of first generation Europeans. *Social Identities* 16 (1): 3–21.

———. 2012. The debate about multicultural Norway before and after 22 July 2011. *Identities: Global Studies in Culture and Power* 19 (4): 418–427.

Bach, Dil. 2012. Det civiliserede familieliv: Opdragelse i velstående familier. *Antropologiske Studier* 1: 211–249.

Barth, Fredrik, ed. 1969. Introduction. In *Ethnic groups and boundaries. The social organization of cultural difference*. Oslo: Universitetsforlaget.

Bourdieu, Pierre. 1977. *Outline of a theory of practice*. Cambridge: Cambridge University Press.

Brochmann, Grete, and Knut Kjeldstadli. 2008. *A history of immigration: The case of Norway 900–2000*. Oslo: Universitetsforlaget.

Cohen, Anthony, ed. 2000. Introduction. In *Signifying identitites: Anthropological perspectives on boundaries and contested identities*. London/New York: Routledge.

Dzamarija, Minja T. 2010. *Barn og unge med innvandrerforeldre – demografi, utdanning, inntekt og arbeidsmarked*. Rapporter (12). Oslo/Kongsvinger: Statistics Norway.

Eriksen, Thomas Hylland. 2002. *Ethnicity and nationalims: Anthropological perspectives*. London: Pluto Press

Figenschou, Tine U., and Audun Beyer. 2014. Elitene, minoritetene og mediene. Definisjonsmakt i norsk innvandringsdebatt. *Tidsskrift for Samfunnsforskning* 01: 24–50.

Gilroy, Paul. 1993. *The black Atlantic. Modernity and double-consciousness*. Cambridge, MA: Harvard University Press.

Gullestad, Marianne. 1997. A passion for boundaries: Reflections on connections between the everyday lives of children and the discourses on the nation in Norway. *Childhood* 4 (1): 19–42.

———. 2002. Invisible fences: Egalitarianism, nationalism and racism. *Journal of Royal Anthropological Institute* 8: 45–63.

———. 2003. *Det norske sett med nye øyne: Kritisk analyse av norsk innvandringsdebatt*. Oslo: Universitetsforlaget.

———. 2006. *Plausible prejudice. Everyday experiences and social images of nation, culture and race*. Oslo: Universitetsforlaget.

Hage, Ghassan. 2004. Migration, hope and the making of subjectivity in transnational capitalism. *International journal of critical Psychology* 12: 107–121.

———. 2010. The affective politics of racial mis-interpellation. *Theory, Culture & Society* 27 (7–8): 112–129.

Henriksen, Kristin, and Lars Østby. 2007. Etterkommerne – integreringens lakmustest. *Plan* 5: 30–37.

Hermansen, Are S. 2015. *Coming of age, getting ahead? Assessing socioeconomic assimilation among children of immigrants in Norway*. PhD thesis, University of Oslo.

Keskinen, Suvi, Salla Tuori, Sari Irni, and Diana Mulinari. 2009. *Complying with colonialism: Gender, race and ethnicity in the Nordic region*. Surry: Ashgate Publishing.

Lien, Marianne. 2001. Likhet og verdighet. Gavebytter og integrasjon i Båtsfjord. In *Likhetens paradokser. Antropologiske undersøkelser i det moderne Norge*, ed. Hilde Lidén, Marianne Lien, and Halvard Vike. Oslo: Universitetsforlaget.

McIntosh, Laurie. 2013. Before and after: Terror, extremism and the not-so-new Norway. *African and Black Diaspora: An International Journal* 7 (1): 70–80.

Midtbøen, Arnfinn H. 2014. Discrimination of the second generation: Evidence from a field experiment in Norway. *Journal of International Migration and Integration* 17 (1): 253–272.

———. 2016. The making and unmaking of ethnic boundaries in the public sphere: The case of Norway. *Ethnicities*. doi: 10.1177/1468796816684149.

Nadim, Marjan. 2014. *Forrunners for change. Work and motherhood among second generation immigrants in Norway*. PhD thesis, University of Oslo.

Olsen, Bjørn. 2013. *Unge med innvandrerbakgrunn i arbeid og utdanning 2013*. Reports (Vol. 36). Oslo/Kongsvinger: Statistics Norway.

———. 2016. Norskfødte med innvandrerforeldre er mye mer likestilt enn innvandrere. *Statistics Norway*.

Olwig, Karen F. 2007. *Caribbean journeys. An ethnography of migration and home in three family networks*. Durham: Duke University Press.

Orupabo, Julia. 2010. En klassereise nedover. In *Klassebilder*, ed. Kenneth Dahlgren and Jørn Ljunggren. Oslo: Universitetsforlaget.

Reisel, Liza. 2012. Is more always better? Early career returns to education in the United States and Norway. *Research in Social Stratification and Mobility* 31: 49–68.

Sandnes, Toril. 2013. Ekteskap og skilsmisser blant innvandrere og deres norskfødte barn. Kjenner kjærligheten ingen grenser? *Samfunnsspeilet* 5.

Seljestad, Lars O. 2010. I begynnelsen var klassereisa. In *Klassebilder*, ed. Kenneth Dahlgren and Jørn Ljunggren. Oslo: Universitetsforlaget.

Skeggs, Beverley. 1997. *Formations of class and gender: Becoming respectable*. London: Sage.

———. 2004. *Class, self, culture*. London/New York: Routledge.

Skilbrei, May-Len. 2010. Middelklassen som ideal. *Dagbladet*. Retrieved from http://www.dagbladet.no/2010/05/29/kultur/debatt/debattinnlegg/innvandring/integrering/11901955/

Søholt, Susanne, and Kim Astrup. 2009. *Etterkommere av innvandrere: Bolig og bostedsmønster*. NIBR-rapport 2009: 3. Oslo: NIBR.

Stefansen, Kari, and Gunhild Farstad. 2008. Småbarnsforeldres omsorgsprosjekter. Betydningen av klasse. *Tidsskrift for Samfunnsforskning* 49 (3): 343–374.
Støren, Liv A. 2010. Unge innvandrere i utdanning og overgang til arbeid. *Rapport 45.*
Trondman, Mats. 1994. *Bilden av en klassresa: sexton arbetarklassbarn på väg till och i högskolan.* Stockholm: Carlsson.
Tronstad, Kristian R. 2009. *Opplevd diskriminering blant innvandrere fra ti ulike land.* Rapport 2009/47. Oslo/Kongsvinger: Statistisk sentralbyrå.
Vassenden, Anders. 2010. Untangling the different components of Norwegianness. *Nations and Nationalism* 16 (4): 734–752.
Vincent, Carol, and Stephen J. Ball. 2007. Making up the middle-class child: Families, activities and class dispositions. *Sociology* 41 (6): 1061–1077.

CHAPTER 14

The (In)egalitarian Dynamics of Gender Equality and Homotolerance in Contemporary Norway

Christine M. Jacobsen

INTRODUCTION

Gender equality features prominently in both national and international accounts of egalitarianism in the Scandinavian context. The implementation of the Gender Equality Act (*Likestillingsloven*) in Norway in 1978 and the development in the 1980s of what Hernes (1987) coined as "state feminism" promoted and institutionalized egalitarian policies simultaneously from below through grassroots women's movements and from above through state institutions and party politics. Gender equality was pursued through arrangements meant to promote equal participation in paid work and unpaid domestic work for women and men, and women's economic independence through wage labor and public welfare services was encouraged. Gro Harlem Brundtland's 1986 "women's government", in which eight of the 18 ministers were women, became a symbol of a new era of gender equality in the political arena, and a starting point for the global marketing of Norwegian gender equality policies (Danielsen and Larsen 2013).

C.M. Jacobsen (✉)
Centre for Women's and Gender Research, University of Bergen, Bergen, Norway

In the literature on democracy, the welfare state, and state feminism, the "Nordic model" came to represent a dominant analytical paradigm and was held up as a "possible utopia" for gender equality (Lister 2009). In 2009, Norway outranked Sweden for the first time in the *Global Gender Gap Report* released by the World Economic Forum, and newspapers confirmed what had already become part of the public's self-understanding: Norway was the world champion of gender equality (Barstad 2008).[1] The then Minister of Children and Equality, Anniken Huitfeldt stated that gender equality, in Norwegian, called "*likestilling*", is a Norwegian export article, and that the ranking would strengthen opportunities to promote gender equality internationally. By that point, the political promotion of equality had been extended to the field of sexuality, and rights and tolerance for non-heteronormative sexuality was promoted abroad alongside gender equality. The political platform for cooperation between the Labor Party (Ap), the Centre Party (Sp) and the Socialist Party (SV) (Soria Moria declaration 2005–9) defined equality for homosexuals as a strategic area in foreign politics. During the same period, Norway also became involved in supporting sexual minorities in numerous countries across the Global South and supported European and UN efforts in the area (Danielsen and Larsen 2013).

Rather than reiterating Norway's success story as an exceptionally egalitarian society, this chapter critically examines some functions of contemporary discursive articulations of gender and sexual equality. In a comparative perspective, the Scandinavian welfare states stand out for their achievements in promoting gender and sexual equality. Recent critical scholarship has, however, started problematizing some of the functions of what Martinsson et al. (2016) call the "myth of gender equality". My concern in this chapter is with a particular function of contemporary equality discourses, namely, the process of bordering the national community and citizenship. To investigate equality discourses and their functions, I analyze policy documents and media debates related to gender equality, homosexuality, and integration and citizenship policies. I also draw on analyses I have made in a series of ethnographic works on gender and migration in Oslo (Andersson et al. 2012; Jacobsen 2011; Jacobsen and Stenvoll 2010). My approach is inspired by anthropological, feminist, and post-colonial appropriations of Foucauldian discourse analysis. This means that I am not so much concerned with identifying the opinions, motivations, and intentions of various actors, as with unpacking dominant discursive articulations of egalitarianism and examining their functions. To analyze the process of bordering the national community and normativizing citizenship, I draw on recent work from Bridget Anderson (2013) on the mutual constitution of the figures of the citizen and the migrant.

Anderson (2013, 2) notes that modern states portray themselves not as an arbitrary collection of people held together by a common legal status, but as communities of value, comprised of people who share common ideals and (exemplary) patterns of behavior expressed through ethnicity, culture and/or language—that is, its members have shared values. The "community of value" consisting of "Good Citizens" is defined from the outside by the Non-Citizen (the external Other) and from the inside by the "Failed Citizen" (the internal Other who is imagined as incapable of, or failing to, live up to the ideals or values in question). I argue that gender and sexual equality have become crucial to the understanding of Norwegian society as a "community of value". The idea of the good citizen is anchored in ideas about the individual, autonomy, and equality and defined by the outside by the non-citizen and the failed citizen. Gender and sexual equality have become crucial to the production of Norway as a particular kind of national imagined community (Anderson 1983); patrolling the borders of the national community and its citizenry and entrenching gendered and racialized differences between "us" and "them". The enduring in-egalitarian potential of egalitarianism, "the many-headed Hydra that continually springs up against egalitarianism in the moment of egalitarianism itself " (Kapferer 2015, 106), is thus unleashed. By this I do not mean to suggest that bordering is the only or even the most important function of contemporary discourses on gender and sexual equality, only that we should carefully unpack the multiple and sometimes contradictory functions of such discourses in particular socio-cultural contexts.

GENDER EQUALITY AS A NATIONAL VALUE

The idea of Norway as the world champion of gender equality (*likestilling*) took form in Norway during a period marked by post-colonial migration and by the nationalist and ethnicist sentiment that spread across Europe partly as a response to globalizing forces that were perceived as threatening to the autonomy and integrity of the nation-state.[2]

In public debate and policy documents, gender equality was claimed as a national trait that distinguished Norwegians from post-colonial immigrants as well as from foreign countries (cf. Danielsen and Larsen 2013). The concern to promote gender equality among immigrants was an explicit part of Norwegian efforts to carve out a politics for an increasingly diverse society—the "multicultural Norway" that became the object of governance in the 1990s. Gressgård (2010) argues that in both White Paper No. 17 (1996–7) on "Immigration and Multicultural Norway" and White Paper No. 49 (2003–4) on "Diversity through Inclusion, Responsibility and Freedom", respect for cultural distinctiveness was restricted to practices that reaffirm prevailing norms and values grounded in the ideal of equality. The recognition of cultural distinctiveness was subsumed under the ideal of equality, which was equated with the liberation of individuals from cultural constraints. The good citizen who appears in the White Papers is firmly anchored in ideas about the individual, autonomy, and equality. As several authors have noted, these values figure prominently alongside sameness and solidarity in Scandinavian versions of egalitarianism (see, e.g., Gullestad 2002, 2006; Longva 2003; Trägårdh 1997).

The policies devised to promote gender equality among immigrants by securing women's independence from cultural constraints associated with the family and cultural and religious groups can be read as an expression of what Trägårdh (1997) calls the "statist individualism" of the Nordic welfare states. Statist individualism refers to the state being conceived as the liberator of the individual from ties of dependency within civil society—to the family, the church, or private charity organizations. The state is not seen as opposed to individual freedom, but rather as guaranteeing it against social, cultural, and religious power structures and dependencies. According to Trägårdh, statist individualism has led to a tendency in the Nordic countries to imagine gender equality as first and foremost a matter of granting individual rights and autonomy. Women's liberation has been subsumed within the broader agenda of promoting individual dignity-as-autonomy (Trägårdh 1997, 272).

White Papers No. 17 (1996–7) and No. 49 (2003–4) reflect a concern for the possibility of autonomy, choice, and self-creation for immigrant and Muslim women in particular, a concern that has also been very present in the public debate. Through a sustained focus on themes such as forced marriage, female circumcision, and female seclusion, public debate from the 1990s onwards constructed Muslim women as passive victims of foreign patriarchal cultures and religion (Jacobsen and Stenvoll 2010; Thorbjørnsrud 2003). While great weight was put in the White Papers on enabling immigrant women and children to create their own identities and futures, only certain choices were considered to be properly autonomous within the majority discourse (Gressgård and Jacobsen 2003). The modern freedom to choose applies only within certain confines and these only come clearly into view when they are transgressed (Gullestad 2002, 35). One example is the recurrent debates over whether adapting oneself to a religious context, for instance, by wearing a hijab can be a free choice. The refusal to accept a religious lifestyle as a choice seems to rest on a particular vision of gender equality that assumes that if immigrant women were properly free, they would choose a lifestyle similar to that of white majority women—e.g., to live in "love" marriages rather than arranged marriages, monogamous rather than polygamous marriages, and to uncover rather than cover their bodies. The hijab in particular is often problematized as a hindrance to the bodily routines and techniques that Romme Larsen describes, Chap. 11, in this book as crucial to the production of free individuals in the Nordic context, such as bicycling, swimming, and being present in the public space.

A particular feature of the Nordic context is the extent to which the state has been seen as having a legitimate and decisive role in eradicating inequalities and promoting women's independence from a social order based on the patriarchal family and its extensions in society at large (Trägårdh 1997). As discussed in the Introduction, Chap. 1, in this book, although the population's dependence on the state is paramount, this dependency is not generally viewed as deeply problematic. What this conception of the state hides is arguably how policies and practices geared at empowering migrant women themselves naturalize particular gendered and (hetero)sexual cultural and social norms and embodied practices. Romme Larsen (Chap. 11, in this book) shows how emancipation projects directed at refugees in order for them to free themselves from the discipline and obedience associated with their homes amount to specific culturally defined projects, which are themselves strongly bound by social norms. By construing such social norms as expressions of "freedom", the governmental power of gender equality policies is obscured. In promoting the right of individuals to "autonomy" and their freedom to make individual choices as the basis for "equality", the state in practice contributes to naturalizing a particular gendered and (hetero)sexual order.

More recent policy documents continue the tendency of identifying patriarchal cultural traditions and practices in the home as the main obstacle to equality for immigrant women. For instance, the White Paper "Action Plan to Further Equality and Prevent Ethnic Discrimination" (2009–12, 4) declares that it is unacceptable if women are bereft of the right to education or work, are prevented from making their own choices or in other ways are oppressed "on the basis of culture-based explanations that are not in accordance with the Norwegian Equality Act or human rights". The challenges are thus presented as ones of cultural integration or assimilation, which blur the structural challenges of a labor market that is segregated along gendered as well as ethnic lines (Annfelt and Gullikstad 2013). In their analysis of public documents on labor, welfare, and equality politics, Midtbøen and Teigen (2013) also show how low participation in working life is mainly addressed as a problem when it concerns immigrant women. While the decision of women belonging to the majority to work part-time is understood as a choice based on individual preferences, minority women's low participation in paid work is understood as a consequence of traditional gender roles among immigrants rather than as an individual choice. Minority women thus appear as failed—unproductive and dependent—citizens.

Gender equality as constitutive element of national identity and as defining of Norwegian society as a community of value is more explicitly asserted in recent documents. White Paper No. 7: 7 (2015–16) "Gender Equality in Practice: Equal Opportunities for Women and Men", for instance, declares gender equality (*likestilling*) to be part of Norway's identity and a societal value. It states in the Introduction that Norwegian society is built on gender equality and dignity (*likestilling og likeverd*) between women and men. These formulations are indicative of the ways in which gender equality is closely connected to the state and the nation. Presenting gender equality as a consensual ground for society, they obscure the fact that social life in Norway is characterized by ongoing controversies and conflicts over what gender equality means, whether it should be based on sameness or difference, whether we now have too little or too much equality, and the role the state should have in promoting it. They also overlook the continued proliferation of unequal relationships between women and men. This national self-identity and representation of society based on equality are contrasted both to an internal Other (immigrants) and external Other identified as the large parts of the world in which gender roles are said to strongly limit individual rights and opportunities.

The incorporation of gender equality into the national identity and its presentation as a collective and undisputed value are also structured by a temporal othering. Gender equality is discursively constructed as a linear process of evolvement, so that Norway appears as temporally "ahead" of countries that are less gender-equal and thus appear to be "lagging behind" or "living in the past"—temporal locations that are often attributed, in public debate, to internal and external Others.

A growing discourse of urgency around integration, fueled by the post-9/11 discourse on Islam as opposed to the West, and the growth of the anti-immigration populist right—in 2013, a part of the government in Norway for the first time—has led to an attack on so-called multiculturalist policies and a growth in neo-assimilationist policies. Despite strongly normative assessments of equality and freedom of choice and the problematization of immigrant cultures, White Paper No. 17 (1996–97) on "Immigration and Multicultural Norway" presented gender equality as an offer that was (at least partly) up to immigrant women to accept or refuse:

> The aim is also to give women of immigrant backgrounds the opportunity to choose the extent to which they want to make use of the possibilities given by the policy of gender equality. For this it is necessary to give them and their families and networks sufficient insight into what gender equality between men and women in Norway means in daily life. (White Paper No. 17 1996–97, my translation)

This is in line with Brochmann's (2002, 36–37) analysis of how policy formulations in the 1990s underscored the importance of facilitating real choices and protecting immigrants against forced assimilation. This approach started to change in the late 1990s and, as we will see below, gender equality has since been changing from being a possibility offered to immigrants into a precondition for entry and membership into the national community.

Homotolerance as a National Value

After the horrific massacre at a gay nightclub in Orlando committed by an Afghan-American, who declared sympathies for extremist Islamist networks, an editorial in the Norwegian tabloid newspaper *VG* (14 June 2016) declared that "Gay bars are civilization. That humans can love whom they want and live out their sexuality in mutual understanding with others is today the most important characteristic [*fremste kjennetegnet*] of a liberal and free society." The editorial invoked a "we" who were encouraged to join the upcoming gay parades to stand up for "our values" and the "freedom of our societies". Religious groups and their leaders, Muslims in particular, were demanded to stand behind everyone's right to love and make love to whomever they want in "our societies". This incorporation of gayness and sexual freedom as not only one value among many, but even as society's most important value can be understood in light of Puar's concept of "homonationalism". Puar (2007) developed the conceptual frame of homonationalism to understand the complexities of how acceptance and tolerance for gay and lesbian subjects have become a barometer by which the right to and capacity for national sovereignty are evaluated. As Gressgård and I have argued (2008, 2014), tolerance for gay and lesbian subjects also functions as a barometer by which the right and capacity for individual autonomy and the capability of being a good, self-governing citizen are assessed. Homonationalism is an understanding and enactment of homosexual acts, identities, and relationships that incorporates them as not only compatible with, but even exemplary of, neo-liberal democratic ethics and citizenships (Külick 2009).

With the expanding notion of equality covering not only gender but also other "differences", such as ethnicity and sexuality, homosexuality gained importance in the discursive and practical articulation of equality (*likestilling*). Policy measures were put in place in order to establish particular provisions based on the assumed differences and special needs of homosexuals (i.e., the Registered Partnership Act from 1993) and subsequently to include homosexuals in general provisions (e.g., in the Marriage Act in 2009). Parallel to this rights-based and legal approach to the equality of individuals regardless of their ethnic background or sexual orientation, there was also a resurgence of tolerance discourses.[3] In Norway, as in other contemporary Western contexts, this resurgence was associated mainly with the political left's calls for "tolerating" (as opposed to assimilating) the differences associated with minority cultures and religions. With the nationalist and ethnicist resurgence of the 1990s and the post-9/11 civilizational discourse on Islam, tolerance increasingly came to be identified as a virtue associated with the West, producing an opposition between the free, tolerant, and civilized, on one side, and the fundamentalist, intolerant, and barbaric on the other (cf. Brown 2006). Tolerance as a civilizational discourse has come to central importance regarding homosexuality. It positions the good citizen in relation to the non-citizen (the external Other) and the failed citizen (the internal Other), and is used to identify threats to the nation and to Western civilization (Gressgård and Jacobsen 2008, 2014).

VG is a tabloid newspaper, and that it should use this occasion to entrench a split between "us" and "them" is not unexpected. The presuppositions on which this articulation of homotolerance as a national and civilized value rests, however, reoccur across a number of sources, for instance, in White Paper No. 25 (2000–1) on the "Living Conditions and Quality of Life for Lesbians and Gays in Norway". The White Paper situates its problematic from the beginning in the context of a diverse society. The Introduction states that diversity in ways of living and lifestyle is a positive value for society. There is a thorough discussion of the challenges and discrimination that homosexuals face in society and a chapter is devoted to the challenges associated with the Church of Norway's reluctance to grant equal rights to homosexuals. A separate section identifies attitudes toward homosexuality in minority groups as particularly problematic. While the overall White Paper paints a nuanced portrait of the (sometimes contradictory) norms and practices that shape the quality of life of lesbians and gays in Norway, the section on minority groups establishes a dichotomy between a modern, Western, individualistic point of view and a traditional, collectivist view associated with minority groups. In the modern Western view, the individual chooses his or her sexual and love relationships, the White Paper states, whereas from a traditionalist point of view, the family is seen as the bedrock of society.[4] Moreover, the White Paper claims that the traditionalist view limits sexuality to heterosexual relationships between man and woman. "Islamic culture" is pointed out as particularly bound to tradition and it is stated—without any textual reference—that the Koran is explicit in its condemnation of homosexuality. What is interesting here is that the White Paper inadvertently enters the domain of a theological dispute in authorizing the dominant interpretation of the Koran as condemning homosexuality.[5] In the section on homosexuals and the Church of Norway, reference is, in contrast, not made to the Bible but to the many controversies over the position of homosexuals in the Church and a general liberal turn in "Christian opinion".

Concern with those who grow up in a traditionalist, collectivist "Islamic culture" received renewed attention in the spring of 2006 when the Labor Party's gay network sent out an invitation to a public meeting called "Gay at the Bar, Straight in the Mosque". They claimed that the Social Democrats and other political parties were ignorant and cowardly concerning the problem of homosexuality and Islam (Meek and Hegtun 2006). When the trustee (*mutawalli*) of a central mosque in Oslo told the papers that homosexuality is a non-issue among Muslims, the Minister of Equality declared that she wanted a dialogue with Muslim leaders and wanted to make sure that "the Norwegian view of homosexuality" was made known to immigrants through the mandatory introduction courses organized by the government. Homotolerance was thus hailed by politicians in a way that erased traces of the historical and ongoing controversies over homosexuality in Norway, which was presented as being unified with a shared "Norwegian view" that Muslims, who were identified as "immigrants" and hence not Norwegian, needed to be taught. This unified picture was presented, despite the widespread use of "homo" as an abusive term in Norway, that discrimination and violence are a part of everyday life for homosexuals, and controversies regarding the rights of homosexuals to marriage and adoption are still commonplace. Just as in the above-mentioned White Paper, the contrast with an immigrant Other made it possible to claim homotolerance as *the* Norwegian view and made homotolerance available to patrol the distinction between "us" and "them" and Norwegians and immigrants.

After a second debate meeting in November 2007, national newspapers reported that two prominent representatives of the Muslim community had failed to publicly condemn the death penalty for homosexuality in Iran. One was a member of the Social Democratic Party and the Vice President of the Islamic Council of Norway.[6] The other was the former leader of the Muslim Student Society. At the time, the question of which attitude to adopt on the topic of homosexuality was the subject of controversy both within the Muslim Student Society and the Islamic Council of Norway (see Jacobsen 2011). As demands for Muslims to publicly condemn (*ta avstand fra*) acts committed by Muslims or Muslim politicians in other parts of the world increased, some Muslims had also started resisting the demand by insisting on their position as "Norwegian Muslims". The debate took a new turn when Rana, the above-mentioned former leader of the Muslim Student Society, won a young writers' competition in a leading Norwegian newspaper with an op-ed entitled "Secular extremism". In the op-ed, he argued that Norwegian society is marked by a secular hegemony that threatens pluralism and degrades religious believers. The tolerance advocated in moral questions, he argued, does not extend to people who base their personal and political choices on their religious faith (Rana 2008). Rana also included Christians who "want to hold on to the principles of the Bible" in his argument for greater tolerance toward religious expression in public. The op-ed spurred a heated debate in the Norwegian media, and Rana's call for greater societal religious tolerance was immediately flipped in order to accuse Rana of being intolerant himself. According to a controversial NGO named Human Rights Service (until recently financed by the state budget to work with the emancipation of immigrant women), his previous refusal to publicly condemn the death penalty for homosexuality in Iran represented a development "away from hundreds of years of the Norwegian fight for freedom". Others accused Rana of defending a religious practice that allows stoning and bodily mutilation (see Bangstad 2009, for a discussion of the Rana debate).

While Rana positioned religious believers as objects of secular tolerance toward religion (cf. Brown 2006), his critics responded by designating Rana and other Muslims as failed "tolerant subjects". The limits of liberal tolerance are usually said to be tested when a subject must be tolerant of intolerance. In this case, (the idea of) Muslim intolerance toward homosexuals functioned to patrol the boundary between the modern and individualist good citizen, and the traditional collectivist, failed citizen. Framed within a tolerance discourse rather than within a discourse of law, equality and rights, the question was not so much whether Rana and others had broken laws against discriminating against homosexuals, but whether they harbored the right kind of liberal and tolerant attitudes. This was made explicit by the trustee of a major mosque in Oslo, Basim Ghozlan, when responding to a suggestion from a conservative politician that the mosque should lose its government subsidies and that Ghozlan should be dismissed from his position due to his claims that homosexual practice is a "sin" and an "aberration" and that Muslim homosexuals should be healed—a controversial position also defended publicly by some Christians. Ghozlan responded by stressing that he had not broken the law. By this, he questioned the governmental and regulating functions of tolerance discourse as a supplement to the law. He drew on (liberal) distinctions between law/norms and theology/politics to question the demand that Muslims publicly demonstrate their tolerance toward homosexuality, but did not challenge the opposition that contemporary tolerance discourse draws between liberal culture, premised on moral autonomy, neutrality and tolerance, on the one hand, and non-liberal, intolerant and ultimately barbaric cultures on the other.

A more recent example concerns the controversy that occurred over the prospect of a Muslim being elected mayor of Oslo after the Green Party's success during the local elections in 2015. Speculating that Shoaib Sultan may become Oslo's new mayor, *Dagbladet* (Malm and Thorenfeldt 2015) ran a feature article on Sultan's "most controversial statements". These had been made during his time as General Secretary of the Islamic Council of Norway between 2007 and 2010, and one of the highlights, according to *Dagbladet,* was a statement given to the magazine *Fri Tanke* [Free Thought] in 2007: "In my opinion homosexuality is a sin since the Koran forbids it. But of course I do not think there should be a death penalty" (my translation). When questioned again as a mayoral candidate in 2015, Sultan replied that the question of sin was a theological question that was not his to answer as a politician: "Being a homosexual is totally OK. I do not see any problem with people being homosexual. But it [whether homosexuality is a sin] is a theological question. I am not a theologian, but a politician, and should therefore be concerned with people's rights. And I am" (Malm and Thorenfeldt 2015, my translation). Sultan's insistence on upholding "people's rights" rather than harboring particular attitudes, makes visible the split between tolerance and contemporary standards of egalitarianism that often disappear when Muslims are interpellated as intolerant subjects. As Brown (2006) notes, tolerance historically functioned not merely to protect, but simultaneously stigmatized and overtly regulated the targeted group (Brown 2006). Both the question of whether the majority should tolerate religious minorities deemed intolerant and whether Muslims should tolerate homosexuals indicate a "conditional" acceptance on the part of a dominant "us" rather than an egalitarian principle of equality and universal rights. The "tolerated citizen" must work hard to remain in the zone of toleration and not slip into failure, and his or her assertion of deservingness can play an important role in upholding the virtues of "good citizenship" (Anderson 2013).

What these various cases show is how sexual politics have come to be crucial to the production of Norwegian identity as modern and egalitarian, defined in opposition to an intolerant Muslim Other. The demand that Muslims be tolerant toward homosexuals implies an incitement to discourse—to speak of one's religion and to reveal one's inner religious selves, motivations, and intentions, making "the private" thus more governable and able to be judged not only by the law but also in relation to what is cast as "Norwegian values" (cf. Fernando 2014). Butler (2009, 143) argues that the framework of tolerance orders identity according to its requirements and effaces the complex cultural realities of gay and religious lives. The framework assumes that religion and sexuality are both singly and exhaustively determining of identity. Significantly, the normative framework of tolerance discourse produces two opposing subjects, gay versus Muslim, where the Muslim comes to be defined by his or her ostensible homophobia, and the homosexual becomes defined as either anti-Muslim or fearful of Muslim homophobia.[7] This polarization hides the complex navigation and negotiation that those who identify themselves as both gay and Muslim in Norway experience and the ways in which norms intersect to produce minoritized subjects as deviant both in terms of their sexuality and religion (Narvesen 2010). The production of "gays" and "Muslims" as opposing subjects is further entrenched by the ways in which homotolerance has been mobilized in recent attempts to regulate access to citizenship on the basis of knowledge and moral attitudes through the so-called citizenship test. As the examples above have suggested, in order to be considered a "good citizen", it is not sufficient that one respects the law. One also has to harbor the sentiments and attitudes that society deems fit for citizens of the egalitarian Norwegian nation state.

Gender and Sexual Equality as Thresholds for Citizenship

The rearticulation of gender equality and sexual equality as "Norwegian values" in opposition to an ethnicized and religious Other is evident in the debate about whether Norway should introduce a test for those who wish to become Norwegian citizens.[8] In 2009, the Conservative Party (*Høyre*) suggested that a mandatory citizenship test be introduced for all new citizens, a suggestion that did not obtain sufficient support from the government coalition in power (Labor Party, Socialist Party and Centre Party). It was evident from the suggested questions for the test that citizenship was conceived of as something much "thicker" than membership in a polity in liberal terms. Among them was a question related to skiing, which a member of the Conservative Party said was crucial to becoming Norwegian.[9] Out of 19 questions, two concerned gender equality and sexuality, showing its centrality to conceptions of Norwegianness. Familiarity with the fact that the general right to marriage includes homosexuals and that women have full rights to divorce were included as preconditions for being granted status as a Norwegian citizen. The former is particularly interesting since the changes in The Marriage Act giving equal rights to homosexual couples were made the same year as the citizenship test was suggested. A legal transition that was very recent and highly controversial could thus be presented as required "knowledge of society" and as defining of what it means to be Norwegian. Some critical voices argued that a citizenship test focused on national values and belonging could in fact be experienced as exclusive. Among the defenders of the test, Morten Tjessem, at the time the head of the Norwegian Organization for Asylum Seekers (NOAS), argued that the test might stimulate integration for women who were not allowed by their men to leave the house to attend Norwegian classes.[10] Tjessem's articulation exemplifies what Trägardh (1997) calls "statist individualism", namely, the view that the state provides freedom for the individual woman from dependency upon and control by the patriarchal family. The possibility that women would choose to stay in the house rather than attend Norwegian classes was not considered, demonstrating again that choices are only considered properly free when they align with the dominant understanding of freedom and equality—what Romme Larsen (Chap. 11, in this book) refers to as the "right" and "wrong" kinds of personal autonomy.

In 2014–2015, the government, at the time a coalition between the Conservative Party and the populist right-wing Progress Party (FrP), suggested that the Norwegian Nationality Act of 2005 should be amended, making a language and "knowledge of society" test mandatory for applicants aged 18–67. The law of 2005 was, as Midtbøen (2015) argues, highly ambiguous, maintaining the principle of unitary citizenship, conditioning naturalization on requirements of language proficiency and reintroducing an oath of allegiance in citizenship ceremonies. On the other hand, the power of the authorities to exercise discretionary power was curtailed by the fact that all those who fulfil the conditions for naturalization are entitled to Norwegian citizenship. The consultation paper for the amendments to the Norwegian Nationality Act (White Paper 2014) states that "citizenship symbolizes belonging and loyalty to the Norwegian community and the principles that it is based on" (my translation). The language and "knowledge of society" test is thus explicitly envisaged as a normative delineation of citizenship made through assessing particular affective attachments (in the form of belonging and loyalty) that bind one to the national community and the principles seen as foundational to it. The testing of future citizens thus serves to mark a symbolic boundary between those who live in Norway—but without the proper affective attachments—and those who belong in a more fundamental sense to the imagined national community.[11] By questioning the belonging and loyalty of non-citizens, the test thus simultaneously produces the good citizen as someone whose belonging and loyalty to the national community are beyond questioning. Those who are affectively attached to other communities and citizenries can accordingly be questioned as bad or less-than-good citizens (cf. Anderson 2013).

Gender equality, and increasingly also sexual equality, function as crucial symbolic elements in the delineation of the "Norwegian community and the principles that ground it". Thus, the political debate around the need for a citizenship test has focused on the assumed lack of value in the estimation of gender equality and homotolerance among immigrants—Muslims in particular—through a repetitive invocation of Muslim women's sartorial practices, forced marriages, circumcision, and more. Programs that aim to prepare immigrants to become Norwegian citizens—such as the mandatory[12] cultural orientation programs provided by the Directorate of Integration and Diversity (IMDi) for recently arrived refugees—teach dialogue between spouses, gender equity, and women's independence as elements that define "Norwegian culture".[13] In fact, the distinction between gender equality as a value and as a reality is effectively blurred by presenting it simply as "how things are in Norway" or "Norwegian culture". This culturalization of gender equality as a property of the national culture is supplemented in the cultural orientation program by teaching migrants about the rights of homosexuals in Norway to marry and adopt children—accompanied by an image of two men kissing (Stokke 2014). While the rights of homosexuals are very recently acquired and still controversial questions for the Norwegian public, acceptance and tolerance of gay and lesbian subjects have come to symbolize a national community whose unity is reiterated against internal and external racialized Others.

Citizenship tests can be understood as part of what Anderson (2013) identifies as a broader tendency toward understanding the nation state as a community of value that is comprised of good citizens and defined from the outside by the non-citizen and from the inside by the failed citizen. As Kerry Ryan and Tim McNamara (2011) note, citizenship tests have been introduced in several European countries largely in response to worries related to immigration. The rhetoric around testing is usually related to a perceived crisis of cultural difference and to "multiculturalism" as a way of dealing with such difference. The fear is that the non-citizen will fail to integrate and live up to the ideals that are seen to define the "community of value", and that she or he will thus fail to become a good citizen (Anderson 2013). When a country is worried about immigration and difference, the response is often to affirm a national identity through making citizenship into a normative category. Testing immigrants thus becomes a political instrument to that end in an age when national sovereignty seems to be faltering. Such a normativization of citizenship is apparent in the Norwegian suggestion to introduce a citizenship test in a form that combines language and knowledge of society. The "knowledge of society" demanded is highly normative and defines what is required of the "good citizen".

Both gender equality and tolerance of homosexuality have traditionally been associated with the left of the political spectrum, although liberal feminist arguments have also to some extent been articulated from the right. The right side of politics has traditionally been more critical of state intervention in furthering a feminist agenda, criticizing it for curtailing individual freedom. The incorporation of gender equality and tolerance of homosexuality as defining traits of national identity and societal values has made new political subject positions possible that paradoxically combine an endorsement of gender equality and homotolerance as Western and Norwegian values, on the one hand, and nostalgia for a heteronormative and patriarchal society, on the other. Such a paradoxical discourse is found in the anti-Islamic movement described by Berntzen (2011). Here, as well as on the populist right, with the Progress Party as its main political representative, the endorsement of gender equality and homotolerance may be read as a form of political rhetoric instrumentalized as a part of an anti-immigration and nationalist discourse (Akkerman and Hagelund 2007). And yet it also signals the extent to which gender equality and homotolerance have become crucial in defining the "good citizen" and in drawing boundaries around membership to a national "community of value". The normativization of citizenship not only defines who is excluded, but also establishes rules for those who are included, for example, in establishing particular virtues as the foundation for the "community of value" as such (Anderson 2013).

The centrality of immigrant and Muslim Others to the definition of a "community of value" defined through gender equality and sexual freedom is not unique to Norway. According to Sarah Bracke (2011), in the past two decades Dutch identity and citizenship have been profoundly rearticulated and the framing of Islam as the Other is crucial to this rearticulation. Western Enlightenment values are asserted as distinct from—and under threat from—Islam. What is striking in the Dutch context, Bracke argues, is the way in which sexual politics became the preferred trope (more than, for instance, freedom of speech, which has recently played quite an important role in the Norwegian debate, cf. Bangstad 2014). Like the Norwegian cultural orientation programs, in the Dutch citizenship test, immigrants who apply for citizenship are asked to look at photos of two men kissing and asked to report their reactions to these photos. Critically discussing the Dutch test, Judith Butler (2009, 106–7) suggests that freedom is instrumentalized to establish a specific cultural grounding— presumably secular—that functions as a prerequisite for admission of the acceptable immigrant. The paradox is that the adoption of certain cultural norms becomes a prerequisite for entry into a polity that defines itself as the avatar of freedom (Butler 2009, 107). Butler (2009, 32) also notes more generally that an ostensibly secular politics simultaneously mobilizes sexual progressives against new immigrants in the name of a spurious conception of freedom and deploys gender and sexual minorities in the rationalization of recent and current wars.

Conclusion

In this chapter I have argued that gender equality and homotolerance have been shaped as "Norwegian values" and incorporated into the national identity in opposition to a racialized and religious internal and external Other. To be a Norwegian is, in the dominant discourse, to be gender equal and homotolerant. The construction of gender equality and homotolerance as "Norwegian values" has been facilitated by the conjunction between egalitarianism and increased nationalist and ethnicist sentiments. Constructed as a part of the national identity and as communal values, gender equality and sexual freedom have become crucial to patrolling the borders of the national community and its citizenry. Gender equality and sexual freedom have come to be perceived as "embattled" values that must be defended in the name of liberal democracy and national citizenship. Promoting gender equality and sexual freedom thus becomes a technique for restoring the idea of the unified nation at a moment when it is being challenged by processes of globalization and neo-liberal governance.

Under circumstances of a revitalization of nationalist and ethnicist sentiments, egalitarianism's in-egalitarian potential is released in the form of racialized boundaries between "us" and "them". The fact that the value of gender equality and sexual freedom is mobilized for boundary production and maintenance does not mean, however, that its egalitarian potency is necessarily exhausted. Indeed, many immigrant women and homosexuals find the discourse of "*likestilling*" to be an important tool in challenging power relationships in their own religious and ethnic communities. In order to release this potency, however, we must carefully unpack the inegalitarian functions of gender and sexual equality discourses in contemporary Norway. Defending equality as a value against internal and external Others serves to mold and deepen the affective attachments of citizens to the nation-state as an exclusionary community of value. It not only excludes non-citizens, but also disciplines citizens by making visible the normative borders of citizenship, thus restricting the space for political contestation and egalitarian projects that are unaligned with the dominant discourse of nation, gender, and sexual equality.

Notes

1. One of the first such gender equality ranking lists was the UNDP gender-related development index, where the Scandinavian countries already figured at the top of the first report in 1995. Developments in making gender equality a part of national identity similar to the ones described in this chapter have occurred in Sweden in particular, and in Denmark.
2. Eriksen's *Typisk norsk* (1993) and Klausen's (1995, 1996) work on the Olympic Games in Norway were contemporary attempts to grasp these nationalist rearticulations of identity and community.
3. My discussion here is based on Gressgård and Jacobsen (2008, 2014).
4. Christian fundamentalism and traditionalism are not discussed with respect to this dichotomization between a modern, Western, individualistic point of view and a traditional, collectivist view.
5. The Koran includes the narrative of Sodom and Gomorrah, which were destroyed by the wrath of God because the inhabitants engaged in lustful carnal acts between men, a story that is also found in the Christian Bible. The dominant interpretation of this narrative is that it is a condemnation of homosexuality, although some have challenged this by arguing that it could be interpreted as condemning lust (see, e.g., Kugle 2010). In addition, there are sayings (*hadith*) from the Prophet Muhammad on how to deal with homosexual violators, of which there is some disagreement regarding their reliability. Punishment for homosexuality has historically been related to public sexual penetrative acts witnessed by four adults.
6. An umbrella organization that by 2016 had gathered 42 member organizations spread across the country.

7. "The gay Muslim" does figure in the public debate in Norway, but primarily as a potential victim of Muslim intolerance. Some voices try to escape this discursive framework by challenging both racialization and anti-Muslim sentiment and homophobia.
8. As the Introduction, Chap. 1, in this book notes, the understanding of the citizenry as being comprised of women as well as men came as a result of the political struggle for women's rights, including to suffrage.
9. "That sport [skiing] is crucial. It was important to Norwegians to see King Olav learn how to ski. That's when he became Norwegian" (Lode and Glomnes 2009, my translation). See Romme Larsen, Chap. 11, in this book for a discussion of bicycling as a "national thing" and its centrality to the production of autonomous individuals and integration of refugees in Danish discourses.
10. "Unfortunately, there are women who are not allowed to participate because their husbands want them to stay at home. Mandatory Norwegian courses could thus be positive" (Lode and Glomnes 2009).
11. What Unni Wikan (1995) refers to as "*norsk i navnet heller enn i gavnet*" [Norwegian in name rather than in deed].
12. In the sense of being a requirement for receiving the economic support given to refugees and asylum seekers in reception centers.
13. *The Guardian* recently reported on this teaching program (Kleeman et al. 2016).

REFERENCES

Akkerman, Tjitske, and Anniken Hagelund. 2007. "Women and children first!" Anti-immigration parties and gender in Norway and the Netherlands. *Patterns of Prejudice* 41 (2): 197–214. doi:10.1080/00313220701265569.

Anderson, Benedict. 1983. *Imagined communities: Reflections on the origin and spread of nationalism*. London: Verso.

Anderson, Bridget. 2013. *Us & them? The dangerous politics of immigration control*. Oxford: Oxford University Press.

Andersson, Mette, Christine M. Jacobsen, Jon Rogstad, and Viggo Vestel. 2012. *Kritiske hendelser—nye stemmer. Politisk engasjement og transnasjonal orientering i det nye Norge [Critical events–New voices. Political engagement and transnational orientation in the new Norway]*. Oslo: Universitetsforlaget.

Annfelt, Trine, and Berit Gullikstad. 2013. Kjønnslikestilling i inkluderingens tjeneste? *Tidsskrift for Kjønnsforskning* 37 (03–04): 309–328.

Bangstad, Sindre. 2009. *Sekularismens ansikter*. Oslo: Universitetsforlaget.

———. 2014. *Anders Breivik and the rise of islamophobia*. London/New York: Zed Books.

Barstad, Stine. 2008. Norge er verdensmester i likestilling. *Aftenposten*, November 12. http://www.aftenposten.no/norge/Norge-er-verdensmestere-i-likestilling-273856b.html. Accessed 7 Dec 2016.

Berntzen, Lars Erik. 2011. *Den eksistensielle trusselen: En sosiologisk studie av politisk motstand mot islam, muslimsk kultur og innvandring til Norge*. Master thesis, Department of Sociology, University of Bergen.

Bracke, Sarah. 2011. Subjects of debate: Secular and sexual exceptionalism, and Muslim women in the Netherlands. *Feminist Review* 98: 28–46.

Brochmann, Grete. 2002. Velferdsstat, integrasjon og majoritetens legitimitet. In *Sand i maskineriet. Makt og demokrati i det flerkulturelle Norge*, ed. Grete Brochmann, Tordis Borchgrevink, and Jon Rogstad. Oslo: Gyldendal Akademisk.

Brown, Wendy. 2006. *Regulating aversion. Tolerance in the age of identity and empire*. Princeton: Princeton University Press.

Butler, Judith. 2009. *Frames of war: When is life grievable?* London: Verso.

Danielsen, Hilde, and Eirinn Larsen. 2013. Likestillingslandet Norge 1990–2013. In *Norsk likestillingshistorie 1814–2013*, ed. Hilde Danielsen, Eirinn Larsen, and Ingeborg W. Owesen, 186–223. Oslo: Fagbokforlaget.

Eriksen, Thomas Hylland. 1993. *Typisk norsk—Essays om kulturen i Norge*. Oslo: Huitfelt.

Et angrep på homofile er et angrep på våre grunnleggende verdier. 2016. *Verdens Gang (VG)*, June 14. http://www.vg.no/nyheter/meninger/orlando-massakren/et-angrep-paa-homofile-er-et-angrep-paa-vaare-grunnleggende-verdier/a/23711192/. Accessed 7 Dec 2016.

Fernando, Mayanthi L. 2014. Intimacy surveilled: Religion, sex, and secular cunning. *Signs* 39 (3): 685–708. doi:10.1086/674207.

Gressgård, Randi E. 2010. *Multicultural dialogue: Dilemmas, paradoxes, conflicts*. Oxford/New York: Berghahn Books.

Gressgård, Randi E., and Christine M. Jacobsen. 2003. Questions of gender in a multicultural society. *NORA—Nordic Journal of Feminist and Gender Research* 11 (2): 69–77. doi:10.1080/08038740310002923.

———. 2008. Krevende toleranse. Islam og homoseksualitet. *Tidsskrift for Kjønnsforskning* 32 (2): 22–40.

———. 2014. Citoyens intolérables: Tolérance, Islam et homosexualité. *Nordiques* 28: 41–49.

Gullestad, Marianne. 2002. *Det norske sett med nye øyne. Kristisk analyse av norsk innvandringsdebatt*. Oslo: Universitetsforlaget.

———. 2006. *Plausible prejudice: Everyday practices and social images of nation, culture and race*. Oslo: Universitetsforlaget.

Hernes, Helga. 1987. *Welfare state and woman power: Essays in state feminism*. Oslo: Norwegian University Press.

Jacobsen, Christine M. 2011. *Islamic traditions and Muslim youth in Norway*. Leiden: Brill.

Jacobsen, Christine M., and Dag Stenvoll. 2010. Muslim women and foreign prostitutes. Victim discourse, subjectivity and governance. *Social Politics* 17 (3): 270–294. doi:10.1093/sp/jxq011.

Kapferer, Bruce. 2015. When a joke is not a joke? The paradox of egalitarianism. In *The event of Charlie Hebdo—Imaginaries of freedom and control*, ed. Alessandro Zagato, 93–112. New York: Berghahn Books

Klausen, Arne-Martin. 1995. *Fakkelstafetten: En olympisk overtyre*. Oslo: Ad Notam Gyldendal.

———. 1996. *Lillehammer-OL og olympismen*. Oslo: Ad Notam Gyldendal.

Kleeman, Jenny, Tom Silverstone, and Mustafa Khalili. 2016. Norway's Muslim immigrants attend classes on western attitudes to women—Video. *The Guardian*, August 1. https://www.theguardian.com/world/video/2016/aug/01/norway-muslim-immigrants-classes-western-attitudes-women-video. Accessed 3 Aug 2016.

Kugle, Scott Sir ajal-Haqq. 2010. *Homosexuality in Islam: Critical reflection on gay, lesbian, and transgender Muslims*. Oxford: Oneworld Publications.

Külick, Don. 2009. Can there be an anthropology of homophobia? In *Homophobias: Lust and loathing across time and space*, ed. David A.B. Murray, 19–33. Durham: Duke University Press.

Lister, Ruth. 2009. A Nordic Nirvana? Gender, citizenship, and social justice in the Nordic welfare states. *Social Politics* 16 (2): 242–278. doi:10.1093/sp/jxp007.

Lode, Veslemøy, and Lars Molteberg Glomnes. 2009. "Fortjener" du å være norsk? Ta testen her. *Dagbladet*, June 5. http://www.dagbladet.no/2009/06/05/nyheter/politikk/statsborgerskap/test/morten_tjessem/6545981/. Accessed 3 Aug 2016.

Longva, Anh Nga. 2003. The trouble with difference: Gender, ethnicity, and Norwegian social democracy. In *Multicultural challenge (Comparative social research, volume 22)*, ed. Grete Brochmann, 153–175. Bingley: Emerald Group Publishing Limited.

Malm, Mari Sand, and Gunnar Thorenfeldt. 2015. Kan bli Oslos nye ordfører: Her er Sultans mest kontroversielle uttalelser. Og dette mener han i dag. *Dagbladet*, September 14. http://www.dagbladet.no/2015/09/14/nyheter/shoaib_sultan/valg15/mdg/politikk/41090281/. Accessed 3 Aug 2016.

Martinsson, Lena, Gabriele Griffin, and Katarina Giritli Nygren, eds. 2016. *Challenging the myth of gender equality in Sweden*. University of Bristol: Policy Press.

Meek, Kristine, and Halvor Hegtun. 2006. Homo på kafé—Hetero i moské. *Aftenposten*, March 2. http://www.aftenposten.no/norge/Homo-pa-kaf---hetero-i-mosk-416355b.html. Accessed 3 Aug 2016.

Midtbøen, Arnfinn H. 2015. Citizenship, integration and the quest for social cohesion: Nationality reform in the Scandinavian countries. *Comparative Migration Studies* 3 (3): unpaginated.

Midtbøen, Arnfinn H., and Mari Teigen. 2013. Sosial investering i kjønnslikestilling? Flerdimensjonale perspektiver på norsk aktiveringspolitikk. *Tidsskrift for Kjønnsforskning* 37 (03–04): 294–308.

Narvesen, Richard Ruben. 2010. Bestem deg, er du homo eller muslim?—Jeg er et menneske!: En kvalitativ studie av livshistoriene til åtte lesbiske, homofile og bifile med muslimsk bakgrunn. Master thesis, Avdeling for samfunnsfag, Høgskolen i Oslo.

Puar, Jasbir. 2007. *Terrorist assemblages: Homonationalism in queer times*. Durham: Duke University Press.

Rana, Muhammad Usman. 2008. Den sekulære ekstremismen. *Aftenposten*, February 25. http://www.aftenposten.no/meninger/kronikk/Den-sekulare-ekstremismen-310699b.html. Accessed 3 Aug 2016.

Ryan, Kerry, and Tim McNamara. 2011. Testing identities: Language tests and Australian citizenship. In *Uniformity and diversity in language policy: Global perspectives*, ed. Catrin Norrby and John Hajek, 180–195. Bristol: Multilingual Matters.

Stokke, Olga. 2014. Her blir syriske kvoteflyktninger forberedt på norsk kultursjokk. *Aftenposten*, September 14. http://www.aftenposten.no/norge/Her-blir-syriske-kvoteflyktninger-forberedt-pa-norsk-kultursjokk-70024b.html. Accessed 7 Dec 2016.

Thorbjørnsrud, Berit. 2003. Weeping for the Muslim Cinderellas. A lament of tears shed though not shared. *Tidsskrift for Migrasjonsforskning* 4 (2): 133–145.

Trägårdh, Lars. 1997. Statist individualism: On the culturality of the Nordic welfare state. In *The cultural construction of Norden*, ed. Bo Stråth and Øystein Sørensen. Oslo: Universitetsforlaget.

White Paper. 1996–1997. Om innvandring og det flerkulturelle Norge, No. 17 (1996–1997). Stortingsmelding, Kommunal- og arbeidsdepartementet, Norwegian Government. https://www.regjeringen.no/no/dokumenter/stmeld-nr-17-1996-1997-/id191037/. Accessed 7 Dec 2016.

———. 2000–2001. Levevilkår og livskvalitet for lesbiske og homofile i Noreg, No. 25 (2000–2001). Stortingsmelding, Barne- og likestillingsdepartementet, Norwegian Government. https://www.regjeringen.no/no/dokumenter/stmeld-nr-25-2000-2001-/id470716/. Accessed 7 Dec 2016.

———. 2003–2004. Mangfold gjennom inkludering og deltakelse, No. 49 (2003–2004). Stortingsmelding, Arbeids- og sosialdepatementet, Norwegian Government. https://www.regjeringen.no/no/dokumenter/stmeld-nr-49-2003-2004-/id405180/. Accessed 7 Dec 2016.

———. 2009–2012. Handlingsplan for å fremme likestilling og hindre etnisk diskriminering (2009–2012). Handlingsplan, Barne- og likestillingsdepartementet, Norwegian Government, April 16. https://www.regjeringen.no/no/dokumenter/handlingsplan-for-a-fremme-likestilling-/id555077/. Accessed 7 Dec 2016.

———. 2014. Høring—forslag til endring i statsborgerloven krav om at søkere mellom 18 og 67 år skal beherske et minimum av norsk muntlig og bestå en test i samfunnskunnskap. Høringsnotat, Barne- og likestillingsdepartementet. Norwegian Government, October 24. https://www.regjeringen.no/contentassets/7ad9bc8bf8524a5c8a8f1ad33f7bbba7/horingsnotat.pdf. Accessed 14 Dec 2016.

———. 2015–2016. Likestilling i praksis –Like muligheter for kvinner og menn No. 7 (2015–2016). Stortingsmelding, Barne- og likestillingsdepartementet. Norwegian Government. https://www.regjeringen.no/no/dokumenter/meld.-st.-7-20152016/id2456562/sec1. Accessed 7 Dec 2016.

Wikan, Unni. 1995. *Mot en ny norsk underklasse*. Oslo: Gyldendal.

CHAPTER 15

Postscript

Jonathan Friedman

NOTES ON SWEDISH EGALITARIANISM AND ITS DECLINE

The issue of egalitarianism in Scandinavia is part of a larger issue that has become strongly linked to the welfare state itself being seen by many as a formidable equalizing mechanism. The redistributive aspect of the welfare state has been held to be the capitalist alternative to socialism. Scandinavia, along with the United Kingdom, the Netherlands and New Zealand are paradigms of this development. In order to understand this phenomenon as well as what appears to be its demise, it is important to analyze the different domains of equality as they are connected to political power and governance. The importance of this collection is that it takes on the issues from an anthropological perspective that might enable us to see how a culture of equality can be articulated with a political practice of egalitarianism. The following remarks are primarily some notes on egalitarianism from my point of view as a long-time resident of Sweden. I do suggest that the variations on the Scandinavian model are quite significant but I cannot and will not do justice to the matter here.

J. Friedman (✉)
EHESS and University of California, Berkeley, CA, USA

© The Author(s) 2018
S. Bendixsen et al. (eds.), *Egalitarianism in Scandinavia*, Approaches to Social Inequality and Difference, DOI 10.1007/978-3-319-59791-1_15

Equality

Equality has to be one of the most loaded words in current political discourse, part of a panoply of sacred terms clustering around the familiar terms: democracy, human rights, basic human values, which are part of superpower rhetoric. In anthropology, it is related to various discussions concerning "egalitarian" societies, sometimes linked to the term segmentary societies and in neo-evolutionary models to the earliest forms of human social organization associated with hunter-gatherer modes of subsistence. The equality attributed to a number of hunter-gatherer societies and their defining characteristics is not so much one of active social strategy but a result of individual equality, not the existence of something shared. It is often assumed that primitive equality is simply the absence of hierarchy, which had not yet developed in such societies. Of course this is somewhat absurd, given the fact that such societies belong to the ethnographic present. Equal in such anthropological descriptions refers to equal-in-status, an *absence* of class relations or even ranking, as it is known in the neo-evolutionary literature. The egalitarianism specific to the European historical experience is something quite different, even if many have likened it as an ideology to primitive social orders, not least Marx (on primitive communism).

The egalitarianism specific to Scandinavia is one that I have experienced since the 1970s and it is related to well-known and widely discussed notions of forms of sociality and social control. It is, I suggest, related to a mode of social being that stresses collective belonging in which equality is about being part of the same social field, a social project in which all members are equal in their situation with respect to others. This is expressed in the term *likhet*, which stresses sameness as opposed to difference. A very different story than American egalitarianism where freedom is central and where equality is equality before the law, equality of opportunity but not sameness. On the contrary, it is very much about the equivalent treatment of difference. And of course *likhet* is a concept that is not reducible to cloning of individuals, although it is a sometimes used possibility, as when nationality becomes ethnicized. The shared features in *likhet* are rather shared relations to a larger whole, whether a project, a set of values but most generally a set of implicit assumptions, not often articulated explicitly, about interaction itself. The sociality is strongly contradictory since it locks autonomous individuals into a field of mutual dependence. This might account for the very strong desire to "be alone", i.e., to be free of the social gaze of the other. The famous song (1982), "Jag trivs bäst i öppna landskap" by Ulf Lundell was suggested by some as a candidate for a new national anthem. In translation, "I feel best in open landscapes" where I can make my own alcohol and where it is far enough away from the nearest neighbor, but close enough that on a summer night I can hear voices in the distance. A lot of Swedish literature is about the contradictions of strong sociality and the yearning to escape, just as American cultural production is about loneliness and the yearning for community. In Dumont's conceptual framework, the Swedish model is not quite as individualist as that of the liberal European tradition or the more extreme version found in the USA.

The equality among men in Australia, i.e., mateship (Kapferer 1988) is an activity, a practice of being equal. It is not generated by an egalitarian ideology but rather is the resonance base for such ideology. It is an expression of the individual subjects' participation in a collectivity of individuals. The Declaration of Human Rights is not the source of egalitarian practice in this interpretation. It is rather a statement of a relation between an instance of power, like a state, and a population over which it presides. It is notable that while Australian and American forms of popular identity are pitted against the state, the Scandinavian model, with variations, is one in which the state is the mere extension of the people, i.e., closer to Rousseau's ideal of the will of the people expressed in governance.

Equality and liberty, the odd couple of political theory, are better represented in terms of equality and autonomy. The autonomous individual, *homo aequalis* in Dumont's terms, is equal to other individuals only in their mutual autonomy. What they do with that autonomy specifies significant variations in egalitarian regimes as outlined above. From a French perspective, liberal individualism is quite the opposite of real equality which is a collective project. Sweden represents, or represented, one pole of that collective egalitarian project. Autonomy and collectivity do not mix well. This is illustrated in Alberoni's classic work, *Movement and Institution* (1982). The *nascent state*, in his work, the formation of a social movement, is one in which individual subjects offer themselves for a larger collective project. The power of a movement lies in this collectivization process. It works as long as the project of the movement can be kept alive. As the latter weakens, for whatever reason, individuals abandon the collective project and retreat into their autonomous lives. The movement can either dissolve or transform itself into an institutionalized structure, most commonly totalitarian. In macro-political terms, one might use this scheme to characterize political orders in terms of their degree of movement characteristics, project orientation, and the willing sacrifice of the self to the collective project. The difference between liberal egalitarian regimes and the Swedish regime lies in the degree to which the self is assimilated into the larger project.

A Simplified Scheme of Egalitarian Practice

Equality in practice contains several components that are crucial to understanding the way it is reproduced and maintained. The latter are primarily mechanisms of control. These are not statements about equality as such but specific practices of control. As Clastres (1973) understood, equality in so-called primitive societies is not a mere absence but a very strong and even violent presence of equality-in-practice that is maintained by totalitarian methods. In his examples the role of ritual is crucial and the latter is marked by violence. Children are initiated into equality and have it beaten into them. The "society against the state" is a society at war with a potential state, a war that it lost in world historical terms. Clastres's (1978) analysis offers a penetrating critique of the image of the happy-go-lucky primitive. His model is, rather, the torture machine of Kafka. While Clastres was indeed an excellent ethnographer, his theoretical anarchism was probably misplaced. The tightly controlled equality that he discusses is more likely a general phenomenon, a form of sociality rather than a historical institutional form.

An important aspect of this control is shame and the fear of being exposed as "not fitting in". This is not a sociality of independent individuals but one of individuals dependent on one another. While it is not a question of clinical narcissism, it might be hypothesized that on a scale from the totally autonomous individual to the totally dependent subject, the equality-in-practice lies closer to the narcissistic pole, at least in the social sense. This is related to the socialization of subjects into a kind of mutual dependency. In joking terms, it is all for one and one for all, i.e., the practice of collectivity by individuals in concert. This is not a simple situation that is self-perpetuating, but one that is full of potential and sometimes real conflict. Competition always leads to differentiation and in order to avoid its institutionalization, there must be equalizing mechanisms. The "limited good" is one type of equalizer made famous by Foster's work on peasant society (Foster 1965). *Jantelagen* is a Scandinavian variant of this, even if the term is a late nineteenth-century product. The "Who do you think you are?" leveler is clearly an act of, at least, symbolic violence.

There is no necessary, even if potential, contradiction with the existence of the state here. If governance is understood as an extension of the "will of the people", then we have the equality principle introduced into the political order. The classical Greek notion of democracy was *demo-kratos*, i.e., the *power* of the people and the notion of *kratos* is a notion of violent power, not merely formal control. There has been much discussion of the Scandinavian welfare state from the point of view of the individual vs the state, but, of course, in the strong egalitarian model, the state is not an independent entity but a mere extension of the people, and in fact welfare is really just tax money that is used for the redistribution of existing wealth. It is not the state that is "generous" but the people who are the source of this generosity. And it should not be forgotten that it is not the rich who pay for the poor. It is the working class or the middle class that accounts for the majority of tax monies. However, the state does tend to take on an authoritarian form since it has a crucially instrumental function to perform. The issue here is the real or imagined autonomization of the state. I had a neighbor in Paris, who told me how Prime Minister Ingvar Carlsson had rented a room with his mother in Chicago, when he studied there. The neighbor once visited Sweden and got in touch with the PM who invited him to his summer house on Gotland. He was amazed at the total lack of security that allowed him to simply show up at his house. My wife who did fieldwork in Madagascar had difficulty in getting permission to work in a specific area and after several attempts wrote to PM Palme, who not only received her mail but intervened on her behalf. All this has changed substantially since Palme was assassinated. Most prime ministers previous to Social Democrat Göran Persson lived in their personal abodes instead of the official palatial housing that they were offered. And ministers and staff ate lunch in a government cafeteria and had relatively limited salaries. In the past three decades, the political representatives of the people have become increasingly like a class, i.e., a political class, as known in other parts of Europe. A female minister from this period exclaimed after being criticized for having bought a $5000 hat, "I need to be well dressed as representative of the people." And PM Persson himself made his soon-to-be wife head of the state wine and liquor monopoly, one of the highest-paid positions in the government, between them they built/renovated a large manor house which was also something that did not happen previously. When questioned about it, he replied: "I think that people should be happy that it's possible to create something that is both beautiful and lasting" (*Svenska Dagbladet* 2005). What is interesting in this transformation is the way in which the same terms are used to mean something quite different. This is the Orwellian principle in all its glory. It is also the source of the growing issue of *populism* that has plagued the new elites during the past few years. This transition is not a specifically Scandinavian phenomenon but an aspect of a more general transformation that has affected the various forms of egalitarian political orders in the West (Kapferer 2017).

There are several key aspects to the way this transformation has occurred in Sweden:

1. Shame: People who shop for wine and spirits at the wine monopoly used to hide their bottles in leather or cloth bags, and in interviews some said that they felt "the others" staring at them from behind burning holes in their heads. Not being part of the larger society or group is ambivalent, depending on which society. The laws against drinking in Sweden were part of the alliance between teetotalers and the working-class movement. But they are translated into a question of being part of a larger entity, and not to belong is shameful behavior. This appears to be an extension of the sociality of equality in small communities, a sociality captured by the state. The fact that this has more or less disappeared is an index of the decline of that form of sociality that was instrumental in state-church control. Alcohol has had a strong symbolic meaning in Sweden, representing both freedom and social marginalization, and the two are closely related. Drinking is a signal to its participants that anything can be said, if not done. It is therefore that it punctuates the temporal scheme so markedly. On weekends one can drink and do bad things but definitely not during the week.
2. Scandinavia has been marked by very strong local society, i.e., the *byalag* in Sweden, an organization of equals, armed against the larger world, including neighbors. This organization was obliterated with the emergence of the absolutist state under King Wasa but the struggle against local communities continued until quite recently. This is not the case in Denmark or Norway where local identities and local political power still exist. Sweden succeeded in massive population displacements in its industrialization (*strukturationalisering*) which did not occur to the same extent in the rest of Scandinavia, where local and regional political power was able to resist centralized politics. One might suggest that the difference between Sweden, and

Denmark and Norway lies in both the strength of local politics against the state but is based on historically weaker centralized power in those countries. Egalitarianism in Sweden was not opposed to the state but imposed upon it from within. This is based on the identification of the people with their state-as-instrument.
3. The increasing penetration of the state into the local and even individual spheres has created a new situation. The ultimate development is what has been called "state individualism" (Trägårdh and Berggren 2006), an investment in freeing the individual from all social bonds except that to the state itself. But this has not led to a strengthening of individual egos, but to their increasing dependency on the welfare state. This is a continuation of state intervention and expansion into new domains, the family being the most recent. The typical characterization of this transformation is the shift of sociality of equality onto a relation with the state since the latter is assumed to be an extension of the people.

Equality in practice is restricted to the domains of interpersonal interaction. It does not eliminate class structures but it does alter the way in which they are practiced. Class was not marked in interrelations although there were spheres of interaction that were clearly segregated, at least for the elites. But there has never, in my experience, been a legitimate respect for elite status.

The sociality of equality has been seriously eroded since the 1980s. This is the period that has been characterized as the decline in the Swedish economy, increasing debt, and a gradual move toward neo-liberal solutions. This is not a Scandinavian phenomenon but one that characterizes the transformation of Western political orders and is, I would suggest, related to the decline of Western hegemony. In this process there has been a decline of industrialism and a rise of financial capital, including a new class of financially-based elites in the financial markets as such but also in the media, entertainment, sports. And, of course, political elites have been intimately connected to this upward mobility of the few, just as the great majority of "the people" have seen their life chances decline. This is also a period of massive immigration, more in Sweden, less in other Scandinavian countries that has fueled a new rhetoric of equality based on multiculturalism. But the older equality was very much based on being part of the same project, and this is no longer the case. In the abandonment of assimilation lies a multiplication of cultural and even political projects that overturns the premises of the previous equality. The right to difference is not the same project as that of a particular collective future. The erosion of equality in practice and the emergence of state-based multiculturalism are closely linked in historical if not logical terms. It is not absurd that a political class that distances itself from its own people might tend to embrace a population containing several peoples. This has led to the new identification of political and other elites with the global and opposed to the local and especially the national, redefined as a dangerous enemy. Egalitarian practice as a strongly cultural phenomenon can only articulate with multiculturalism if the latter is symbolic and not real, i.e., if assimilation is dominant so that individual subjects come to live in the same forms of sociality, even if they maintain some aspect of their particular cultures in the private sphere. Several works have documented the process in the Social Democratic Party, in which a tendency for family relations to encroach on political positioning is clearly marked, including party endogamy and inheritance of position (Isaksson 2002) and kinship linking media and politics.

The ideal-type of Swedish egalitarianism is one that links the individual to the collective project that is instrumentalized in the state. This has been "dialectically" orchestrated by the reverse historical process of state penetration that began with King Wasa and ended with state individualism. It has failed insofar as it has not completely succeeded in producing state subjects. Throughout this process there have been popular movements and the egalitarian culture has elicited a strong sense of representativity in the state which might account for the particular aspects of egalitarian behavior described above including the lack of clientelism and the strong bureaucratic morality that in Sweden is associated with Axel Oxenstierna who is seen as the founder, in the early seventeenth century, of an autonomous bureaucracy. But all that has been rapidly changing since the 1980s as partially detailed above. The decline of collective egalitarian morality is reflected in the growing number of scandals which have become increasingly rampant. Much of the latter involves what might be called the privatization of the state apparatus, an expression used in Africa but not in Europe until recently. It is not "the people" who have abandoned the state, but the increasing elitism of the state and the associated elites that expresses their abandonment of the people. As I say above, this is not a Swedish phenomenon but it might be all the more radical, given the former egalitarian relation between elites and "the people". It is why populist movements are such a shock to Swedish elites and why their political strategies are so focused on eliminating such movements, a strong contrast with what is sometimes called the accessibility of ordinary people to government officials. The inequality expressed in this politics is the inequality of Orwell's *Animal Farm* (1945) and *1984* (1948), in which some people "are more equal than others" and where non-conforming political agendas are categorized as racism and dangerous for "the people". The recent discussion of the control of non-official news sites or sites of "disinformation" is a project of elimination, like Orwell's Ministry of Truth. Equality, then, can indeed be transformed into its opposite but the transition requires that all opposing voices be eliminated, by fiat and even by force. We should expect an increase in clientelism, corruption, elitism, and even absolutist politics as well as an increasing rise in populist movements, which, however one might think of them, do represent an "egalitarian" reaction to this historical development.

References

Alberoni, Francesco. 1982. *Movement and institution*. New York: Columbia University Press.
Clastres, Pierre. 1973. De la torture dans les sociétés primitives. *L'homme* 13 (3): 114–120.
———. 1978. *Society against the state*. Cambridge, MA: MIT.
Foster, George M. 1965. Peasant society and the image of the limited good. *American Anthropologist* 67 (2): 293–315.
Isaksson, Anders. 2002. *Den politiska adeln*. Stockholm: Wahlström & Widstrand.
Kapferer, Bruce. 1988. *Legends of people, myths of state*. Washington, DC: Smithsonian Inst.
———. 2017. Ideas on populism. *Arena Magazine* 146: 31–34.
Orwell, George. 1945. *Animal farm*. London: Secker and Warburg.
———. 1948. *1984*. London: Secker and Warburg.
Svenska Dagbladet, September 10 2005.
Trägårdh, Lars, and Henrik Berggren. 2006. *Är svensken människa: Gemenskap och oberoende i det moderna Sverige*. Stockholm: Norstedts.

Index

A
Aarset, Monica, 36, 196n5, 212, 214
Abram, Simone, 34, 128
Ågotnes, Hans-Jacob, 68, 69
Åland Islands, 37n1
Alba, Richard, 299
Alberoni, Francesco, 339
Andersen, Rikke S., 196n14
Anderson, Benedict, 103
Anderson, Bridget, 235, 315, 324, 327, 328
Anderson, Sally, 250, 254, 260
annorlundaskap (difference), 24
Anthias, Floya, 25
Arbeidslinjen (directive prioritizing employment), 22
Archetti, Eduardo, 167
Aschehoug, Torkel Halvorsen, 69, 71
Association for Social Politics (Verein für Sozialpolitik), 51–2
asylum centers
  Danish, 250, 259
  Norwegian, 228–31, 235
  Swedish, 270

asylum seekers
  bogus, 232
  Danish reception of, 250, 258, 259
  Norwegian Organisation for Asylum Seekers (NOAS), 326
  Norwegian reception of, 229–31, 233–5, 237
  rejected, 228–31, 233, 234, 237
  Swedish reception of, 36, 227, 277, 279–82, 287, (*see also* refugees)
austerity, 10, 15
authoritarianism, 12, 20, 54, 61, 63, 99, 123, 130, 341
autonomy, vii, viii, 10, 31, 32, 113, 125, 339
  and citizenship, 37, 315–17, 320
  and civil society, 12–13
  and farmers/peasants, 93, 175
  and homotolerance, 323, 327
  and migrants, 217
  municipal, 171
  and refugees, 249, 250, 256, 258, 260, 262, 266

autonomy (*cont.*)
  right and wrong, 262–4, 326
  and the state, 13, 23, 141, 176, 184, 256

B
Bailey, F. G., 34, 158, 174
Banting, Keith, 22
Barnes, John, vi, 1–5, 115, 116, 159
Barth, Erling, 92, 93, 97, 98, 104
Barth, Fredrik, 4, 127, 298, 299
Bendixsen, Synnøve, 224, 235
Bergen School, 4, 206
Berlin, Isaiah, 50, 51, 60
Berntzen, Lars Erik, 328
bildning education and schooling, 57
  dannelse/bildning, 58
Billig, Michael, 94
Bismarck, Otto von, 51–3
bønder/bönder (farmers, peasants), 48, 49. *See also* peasants and farmers
Borchgrenvik, Tordis, 24
Bourdieu, Pierre, 187, 293, 301
bourgeoisie, 16, 54, 58, 60, 112, 118, 159
Bracke, Sarah, 328, 329
Brandes, Georg, 56
Bråten, Stein, 209
Brekke, Jean-Paul, 24, 237
Bringslid, Mary Bente, 224
Britain. *See* Great Britain
Britan, Gerald M., 165
Brochmann, Grete, 28, 29, 226, 319
Brown, Wendy, 324
Brox, Ottar, 100–2, 276
Brundtland, Gro Harlem, 313
Bruun, Maja Hojer, 17, 34, 102, 103, 127, 182, 196n13, 265
bureaucracy, 12, 14, 16, 27, 74, 75, 78, 82
  bureaucratic individualism, 175
  and clientelism, 344
  and municipal governments, 160, 165, 174, 175
  and political mobilization, 120, 121
  and refugees, 272, 277, 280, 285, 286
  street-level bureaucrats, 202, 207
Butler, Judith, 324, 329

C
cancer, 191–4
capitalism, 2, 8, 10, 16, 17, 49, 50, 59, 60, 62, 63, 68, 82, 92, 97, 103, 112, 115, 276, 337
Charlie Hebdou shooting, 9
Chauvin, Sébastien, 235
Chief Municipal Executive (CME), 161–6, 169–74
Christiansen, Niels F., 181
citizenship, 36, 71, 94, 96, 223, 225, 226, 238, 239, 279, 299, 314, 315, 325, 329, 330
civil society, 124, 138, 150, 151, 316
  and refugees, 270, 273–7, 280, 285–7
  and schooling, 80–2
  and welfare state, 12, 34, 127, 128, 130, 138
civil society organizations (CSOs), 269, 272, 274–87
Civilsamhället (civil society), 61
Clastres, Pierre, 340
Cohen, Ronald, 165, 172
collective bargaining, 9
collectivity, 248, 255, 263, 265, 339, 340
committees, vi, 1, 2, 126, 159, 176, 177n1
conservatism, 12, 16, 21, 53–61, 73, 99, 121, 129, 323, 326
Cox, Robert, 226, 237
creative destruction, 10

D

Dahl, Hans Fredrik, 19, 20, 68, 90
Danielsen, 212
Danishness, 26, 28, 103, 262, 265
dannelse/bildning (education), 56–8, 60. *See also* education and schooling
Dauvergne, Catherine, 227, 238
de-commodification, 11, 139, 141, 142
democracy, 7, 20, 21, 28, 50, 54, 55, 59–62, 69, 72–4, 79, 81, 82, 87–95, 112, 115, 117, 118, 159, 314, 338, 341
democratic capitalism, 92
democratization, 17, 21, 26, 91, 113, 118, 123
Denmark
    Cooperative Housing Act, 137, 140, 145
    danishness, 26, 28, 103, 262, 265
    education, 21, 57, 81, 146–8, 185, 187, 193–5, 195n3, 265
    Fukuyama on, 111, 112
    and health, 35
    history, v, 1, 16, 17, 20, 21, 54, 55, 70, 73, 74
    housing cooperatives, 34, 103, 151
    hygge (togetherness, coziness), 103, 183
    and immigration, 22, 24
    Integration Law (*Integrationsloven*), 249
    language, 28
    and neoliberalism, 146–8
    passion for equality, 68, 103
    politics, 74, 111–14, 118, 127, 131
    and refugees, 247–66
    religion, 55
    social differences in health, 181
    social movements and, 59, 60, 102, 103
    Social Reform Act (1933), 139, 140, 150, 185
Disraeli, Benjamin, 52
diversity, vii, viii, 22, 24, 27–9, 35, 92, 103, 189, 203, 204, 213, 214, 216, 218, 297, 306, 316, 321
dugnad (work parties), 25
Dumont, Louis, 4, 339
Durkheim, Émile, 53
Dyrvik, Ståle, 116, 117

E

Eastmond, Marita, 31, 205
education and schooling, vii, 30, 62, 137
    dannelse/bildning, 57, 60
    in Denmark, 21, 57, 81, 147, 185–7, 190, 191, 193, 194, 195n3, 265
    and ethnic minorities, 291–4
    folkehøjskolen (folk high school), 57
    in Norway, 66, 74, 77, 80, 82, 292–4, 296, 303, 306, 318
    and peasants, 49
    and people's movements, 55–8
    and refugees, 248–65, 271–5, 280
    in Sweden, 270–5
egalitarian individualism, 4, 182
egalitarianism
    and cultural and social values, 17–19
    denaturalizing, 47
    and discipline, 264–6
    and diverse populations, 201–18
    and humanitarianism, 227–9, 233, 236–9
    inegalitarian egalitarianism, 27–9
    and irregular migration, 223–39
    institutionalization of, 19–21, 29
    interpretations of, 87, 106
    and logic of equality, 298, 302, 307
    and natural individual, 7, 297, 303, 306
    and neoliberalism, 146–8
    as political project in era of migration, 22–3

egalitarianism (*cont.*)
  political roots of, 111
  of public and privates spheres, 206–7
  and racialization, 204–6
  as social construct, 47
  and social equality, 65–82
  and sociality of equality, 342–3
  as theoretical possibility, 7–9
  as unintended effect, 15–17
  and welfare state, 9
Ekman, Ann-Kristin, 136
employment, 20, 22, 24, 26, 29, 98, 138, 212, 274, 293, 308n1.
  See also labor markets
England. *See* Great Britain
enlightenment, 7, 8, 11, 15, 21, 30, 32, 75, 82, 328
equality. *See* egalitarianism
Eriksen, Thomas Hylland, 100, 102, 330n2
Eriksson, Robert, 232
Erstad, Ida, 35, 299, 307
Esping-Andersen, Gøsta, 10, 11, 30, 141, 142
European Union (EU), 20, 89

F
Faber, Stine, 183, 187
Faist, Thomas, 23
family organization, vi, vii.
  See also kinship
Faroe Islands, 37n1
fascism, 16, 123
Fassin, Didier, 188, 189
feminism, 18, 314, 328
Finland, v, 15, 37n1, 54–6, 58–61, 72, 73
fishing industry, vi, 2, 76, 79, 80, 82, 93, 101, 102, 116–18, 121
flexicurity, 10
folk/volk (people), 58, 59
folkhem (nation as home for the people), 53, 54

Forest Finns, 38n6
Foster, George M., 340
Foucault, Michel, 3
France, 20, 56, 60, 235, 239, 339
  French Revolution, 7, 12, 18, 32, 48, 49, 55
  Paris Commune, 51, 75
freedom, 56–8, 60–3
  of assembly, 121
  and autonomy, 141, 165, 175
  egalitarianism, 8, 12, 13, 15, 34, 48, 49, 51, 248, 338, (*see also* liberty)
  of expression, 81, 82, 262
  and gender relations, 19
  and individualism, 316
  and individuality, 260
  and nationalism, 20
  and Norway, 67–71, 79, 316, 317, 319, 320, 323, 326, 328, 329
  of political participation, 94
  positive and negative, 50, 51, 60
  and the state, 16
  and Sweden, 17, 24
  and welfare state, 20
French Revolution, 7, 12, 18, 32, 48, 49, 55
Frykman, Jonas, 3, 4, 20
Fukuyama, Francis, 111, 112, 115

G
Garcés-Mascareñas, Blanca, 235
gay tolerance, 25
gender, 18
gender equality, vii, 6, 18, 28, 29
  and citizenship, 325–9
  in Denmark, 261, 262
  and diversity, 27
  and homotolerance, 313
  myth of, 314
  national value, 315–19
  in Norway, 292, 293, 313
  as political ambition, 25–6

Germany, 3, 15, 20, 21, 51, 52, 56, 59, 122, 239, 279
  Association of the Tax and Economy Reformers (Vereinigung der Steuer- und Wirtschaftsreformer), 53
  Bildungsbürgertum (educated bourgeoisie), 57, 58
  Central Federation of German Industrialists (Centralverband deutscher Industrieller), 53
Gershon, Ilana, 147
Ghozlan, Basim, 323
Gilroy, Paul, 295
globalization, 18, 138, 315, 329. *See also* neoliberalism
Graubard, Stephen, 68, 90, 114
Great Britain, 16, 17, 97
  and gender equality, 301
  civil servants, 189
  Employers and Workmen Act (1875), 52
  government, 113
  modernity, 59
  NHS, 104 (*see also* United Kingdom)
Great Depression, 53
Greece, 38n2, 341
Greenland, 37n1
Gressgård, Randi, 24, 25, 316, 320
Grundtvig, N.F.S., 21, 57, 58
Gullestad, Marianne, 17, 96, 102, 105, 136, 194
  on children, 255, 256, 258
  on egalitarian individualism, 4, 99, 100, 141, 157, 248
  on equality as sameness, 4, 26–8, 99, 100, 135, 181–4, 187, 188, 205, 218, 265, 293, 298
  on ethnification, 298, 299
  Family and Kinship in Europe (with Segalen), vi
  on integration discourse, 216, 297, 298
  on public/private spheres, 158, 207, 218

H
Haarder, Bertel, 262
Habermas, Jürgen, 12, 60
Hage, Ghassan, 292, 304, 307
Hagelund, Anniken, 38n5, 226
Hamsun, Knut, vi, 98
Hansen, Kjell, 36
Hauge, Hans Nielsen, 79, 80, 121, 122
health and healthcare, 30, 35, 52, 104, 126, 139, 141
  and migrants, 224, 229, 230, 234, 239
  and social differences, 181
  municipal, 164, 166, 168, 169
  public health nurses, 202–4, 206–11
Hegel, Georg Wilhelm Friedrich, 12, 61
Heiret, Jan, 68, 69
Hernes, Helga, 18, 29, 38n3, 313
Hilferding, Rudolf, 53
Højrup, Thomas, 195n4
housing cooperatives, 138
Howell, Signe, 97
Huitfeldt, Anniken, 232, 314
humanitarianism, 227–9, 236
Humboldt, Wilhelm von, 57, 58

I
Ibsen, Henrik, 56
Iceland, 37n1
immigration and migration, vi, 9, 18, 22, 32, 96, 270, 278, 280, 281, 283
  and conditional belonging, 36, 294, 306–11

immigration and migration (*cont.*)
  and double consciousness, 295
  and integration discourse, 297
  irregular migration, 223
  law, 224, 229, 231, 235, 238
  middle-class ethnic minorities, 291
  migrant mothers and public health nurses, 203, 218
  return refusers, 234 (*see also* refugees)
  and social boundaries, 298–300
  and societal hope, 292, 293
inclusion
  performative criteria for, 20, 28
  social inclusion, 249, 250, 254, 264
individualism, egalitarian, 4, 158, 182
individuality, 8, 32, 100, 112, 248, 255–60, 263, 265, 266
Isaksen, Torbjørn Røe, 232
Islam, 9, 19, 291–3, 297, 302, 303, 305, 306, 316, 319, 320, 322, 323, 327–9, 331n7
Islamic terrorism, 294, 305

J
Jacobsen, Christine M., 37, 212
Jakobsen, Gry Skrædderdal, 102, 136, 182
Jämlikhet (equality), 27, 135
Jenkins, Richard, 21, 138
Jöhncke, Steffen, 28, 29, 31, 136, 147, 182–4
Jordan, Brigitte, 209

K
Kagan, Jerome, 79
Kapferer, Bruce, 7–9, 188, 217, 315
Karlsen, Marry-Anne, 35, 36
Keynes, John Maynard, 61
Kielland, Alexander, 98
Kildal, Nanna, 225, 237
kinship, vi–viii, 96, 97, 103

Kjærsgård, Andreas Pihl, 195n1, 204, 216
Kjeldstadli, Knut, 122
Kjellén, Rudolf, 53, 54
Knudsen, Tim, 115, 116
Krøijer, Stine, 102, 136, 182, 196n13
Kven people, 38n6, 96
Kymlicka, Will, 22

L
labor markets, 9, 10, 19, 22, 23, 26, 27, 29, 61, 62, 138, 142, 286, 295, 296, 318. *See also* employment
labor movement, 11, 15, 17, 55, 56, 58, 69, 70, 93, 112, 122, 123, 129, 137, 140
Lafferty, William M., 94, 104
Landsorganisasjonen, The National Union(LO), 122
language, 21, 22, 34, 70, 88
  and citizenship, 326, 328
  class language, 51, 54, 56, 187
  English, 34, 92, 102–5
  and immigration, 213, 279–81, 283
  Norwegian, 34, 91, 97, 102, 103, 303
  and refugees, 250, 252, 257, 271–3
  and understanding of welfare state, 34, 87–92, 97, 99–105
Laville, Jean-Louis, 150
liberalism, 24, 49, 55, 57, 60, 81, 116. *See also* neoliberalism
liberty, 50, 59, 112, 339. *See also* freedom
Lidén, Hilde, 135
Lien, Marianne, 135
likestillingskamp (gender struggle), 18
likhet (sameness), 27, 34, 69, 91, 99, 103, 135, 204, 205, 338
Linnet, Jeppe Trolle, 103, 182, 183, 205
Lo, Christian, 34, 127
Löfgren, Orvar, 3, 4, 20, 136

Lønseth, Pål K., 234
Lower working class (LWC), 186, 187, 192
Lutheranism, 19, 21, 55, 56, 72, 76, 116, 121
LWC. *See* lower working class (LWC)

M

Markkola, Pirjo, 181
Martinsson, Lena, 314
Martinussen, Willy, 94, 104
Marx, Karl, 58, 60, 338
Mauss, Marcel, 261
McDonald, Maryon, 88
McNamara, Tim, 327
Merkel, Angela, 279
Merrild, Camilla Hoffmann, 35
middle class, 17, 30, 194, 196n14
　entrepreneurial, 60
　ethnic minorities, 291–307
　higher middle class (HMC), 184, 187
　in-between, 183, 187
　lower working class (LWC), 184, 186, 187, 192
　and social mobility, 3
　urban, 56
　and welfare state, 11, 136
Midtbøen, Arnfinn H., 318, 326
migration, 22–5, 28, 203, 219n1, 223–39, 269, 270, 280, 286, 295, 296, 314, 315. *See also* immigration and migration
mobility, 66, 67, 77, 78, 292, 296, 306, 343. *See also* social mobility
modernization, 3, 15–17, 19, 58, 112, 114, 128, 136, 175
Moene, Karl Ove, 93
Mouritsen, Per, 28
multiculturalism, 23–5, 30, 316, 319, 327, 343, 344
Muslims. *See* Islam
Myhre, Jan Eivind, 33, 93, 96, 98

N

nationalism, 20, 21, 27–9, 34, 53, 60, 63, 91–7, 102, 103, 105, 236, 237, 261, 315, 320, 328, 329
neoliberalism, 95, 96, 125, 127, 184, 185, 190, 195n13, 343
　and gender equality, 329
　and homotolerance, 319–25
　housing policy, 34
　influence of on egalitarianism, 8, 10, 29, 31–3, 59, 61, 63, 135–52
　and migrants/immigrants, 31, 234, 239
　and social imaginaries, 136, 152
neo-Nazism, 99
network structure, vi
Neumann, Cecilie Basberg, 203, 209, 214
Nilssen, Even, 225, 237
Njåstad, Magne, 117
Norden, v, 33
　cultural construction of equality, 47–63
　defined, 37n1
　and people's movements, 55–60
　and Sonderweg (special path), 15, 47, 56, 59, 61
Norman, Karin, 27, 205
Norway
　abolition of nobility, 71
　Assosiationsaanden
　　(spirit of association), 81
　and asylum seekers, 229, 233, 237
　and nationalism, 91–7, 102, 103, 105
　Centre Party, 314, 325
　citizenship, 97, 223, 225, 226, 238, 239, 299, 314, 326–30
　Conservative Party, 325–7
　constitution, 69–76, 82
　contemporary local politics, 124–8
　economics, 78–80
　education and literacy, 66, 74, 75, 77–85, 292–6, 300, 306, 318

Norway (*cont.*)
  enlightenment, 75, 82
  Fra mangfold til enhet (From pluralism to unity), 69
  freedom of expression, 79
  and gender equality, 292, 293, 313–30
  Gender Equality Act (1978), 313
  geopolitical features of, 89, 90
  Green Party, 324
  Haugians, 121–2
  integration thesis, 68
  interpretations of egalitarianism, 87–106
  introduction of parliamentarianism, 73
  irregular migration, 223
  knowledge-promise/improvement (kunnskapsløftet) programme, 30
  Labor Party, 91, 92, 126, 232, 314, 321, 325
  law, 71–2
  and *likhet* (sameness), 91, 99–103
  Lofthus rebellion, 120–1
  Menstad battle, 122–3
  middle-class ethnic minorities, 291
  municipal policy, 157–76
  19th century, 82
  Norwegian Model of social equality, 65–82
  Parent and Child Health Services (PCHS), 202, 218
  Patients' Rights Act (1999), 229
  peasants and farmers, 68–71, 73, 75–80, 82
  political mobilization, 120–4, 130, 131
  politics, 72–6, 88–106
  Progress Party, 232, 328
  rettferd (justice), 90
  schooling and civil society, 80–2
  Social Democratic Party, 322
  Socialist Party, 314, 325
  Social Services Act (2010), 229, 230
  social structure, 66, 76–8
  Stortinget (parliament), 70
  Thrane movement, 71, 73, 74
  22 July 2011 attacks, 304–6
  urmyten (primordial myth), 68
  voting rights, 72, 91
  welfare state, 223
Norwegian We, 292, 293, 299, 300, 305, 307, 308n2
Norwegianization, 23, 96, 100, 293, 297, 302, 303, 306, 307, 325, 326
Norwegianness, 26, 100, 293, 297, 299–301

O
Offersen, Sarah, M. H., 196n14
Olwig, Karen Fog, 26, 304
one-norm society, 17, 25, 26, 32, 118
Orlando nightclub shooting, 319
Orwell, George, 342, 345
Østerud, Øyvind, 88–92, 94–100
Others and Otherness, 24, 235, 315, 318, 319, 321–30
Oxenstierna, Axel, 344

P
Pakistan, 36, 96, 203, 206, 210, 214, 292–6, 300, 301, 303, 304, 308n4
Palme, Olof, 61, 341
Papakostas, Apostolis, 14, 137
Pausewang, Elin, 196n10
peasants and farmers, v, 2, 11, 17, 32, 33, 48, 49, 51, 54, 56–8
  and enlightenment, 112
  and municipal policy development, 159, 160
  and 19th century Norway, 69–71, 73, 76–82

part-time, 2, 115, 119, 159
and political resistance, 114–21
and state capitalism, 115–17
and welfare state, 92, 94, 102
Pedersen, Ove K, 138, 139, 146–8
Pickett, Kate, 87, 106
Protestant Reformation, 19, 112, 118
Prøysen, Alf, v–vi
Puar, Jasbir, 320
public health nurses, 202–4, 206–13, 215, 218
puritanism, 59, 98

Q
Quisling, Vidkun, 122
Qvam, Ole Anton, 18

R
racialization, 28, 35, 37, 204–6, 213, 214, 293, 299, 304, 315, 327, 329, 331n7
Rana, Muhammad Usman, 322–3
Reay, Diane, 187
rechtstaat (legal state), 14, 112
redistribution, viii, 6, 9, 10, 62, 92–4, 184, 225, 237, 275, 306, 337, 341
refugees, 29, 63, 213, 317, 327, 331n9, 331n12
  and assimilation, 318
  bogus, 232, 234
  children, 247
  and civil society organizations (CSOs), 270, 272–87
  Danish reception of, 36, 247
  and education, 247–65, 271–5, 280
  and housing, 249, 270, 278, 280–4, 286
  and normative internationalism, 227
  and schooling, 249–59, 262, 264, 265, 273–5 (*see also* asylum centers; asylum seekers)
  Swedish reception of, 269–87
  UN-quota refugees, 250
resistance movements, 5, 6, 9, 20, 32, 111–31
Robbins, Joel, 205
Rokkan, Stein, 14, 68, 91, 92
romanticism, 57–9
Romme Larsen, Birgitte, 36, 317, 331n9
Rousseau, Jean-Jacques, 339
Rugkåsa, Marianne, 23, 30, 202, 236
Ryan, Kerry, 327
Rytter, Mikkel, 196n13

S
Sami people, 3, 21, 38n6, 95–7, 104
Sandemose, Aksel, 102, 195n2
Schmidt, Garbi, 24, 26
schooling. *See* education and schooling
Segalen, Martine, vi
segregation, 23, 194, 318
Sejersted, Francis, 11, 20, 59, 68, 69, 80, 119
Selle, Per, 95
Semmingsen, Ingrid, 68
sexuality, 25, 37, 314, 328. *See also* homotolerance
Simmel, Georg, 8
Skeggs, Beverly, 301, 302
social class, 1–3, 31, 35, 116, 123, 124, 136, 181–8, 191, 192, 194, 195, 195n3, 293, 299, 306
  higher middle class (HMC), 184, 187
  lower working class (LWC), 184, 186–8, 192
  middle class, 3, 11, 17, 30, 36, 55, 56, 60, 77, 78, 103, 136, 183, 187, 194, 196n14, 214, 291, 292, 306, 307, 341
  upper class, 81, 195n3
  working class, 3, 51, 52, 54–6, 59, 67, 144, 295–7, 301, 341, 342

social constructs, 6, 9, 25, 28, 33, 47
social democracy, 21, 60, 69, 93
social democrats, 11, 16, 54, 60, 123, 321
social equality, 31, 33, 65, 79, 80, 150
social imaginaries, 136, 138, 148
social inclusion, 264
social mobility, 66, 67, 77, 78, 292, 296, 306, 343
social structure, 7, 66, 69, 76, 185
social trust, 65, 67, 74, 269
socialism, 13, 15, 49, 51–3, 73, 104, 337
Socialist Party (SV), 314, 325
Solway, Jacqueline, 5, 6
Sonderweg (special path), 15, 33, 47–50, 56, 59, 61, 68, 80
Sontag, Susan, 192
Sørensen, Øystein, 7, 15, 93, 116
Sørhaug, Hans Christian, 159, 160, 174, 177n1
Sozialstaat (welfare state), 52. *See also* Welfare state
state feminism, 18, 29, 38n4, 94, 313
statist individualism, 316, 326
Stenius, Henrik, 19, 20, 115, 116
stereotypes, v, 56, 57, 88, 90, 95, 97, 104–6, 301
Stråth, Bo, 7, 15, 33, 93, 94, 114, 116
suffrage, 18, 72, 91, 98
Sultan, Shoaib, 324
Sverdrup, Johan, 70
Sweden, v, 1, 13, 14, 16, 17, 20–5, 91, 98, 99
and asylum seekers, 205, 227, 270–4, 277, 279–82, 288n5
declining egalitarianism, 337, 339–45
and Norden cultural construction of equality, 48, 52–5, 59, 60
politics, 70, 73, 118
and refugees, 36, 205, 269

Riksdagen (parliament), 70
social structure, 76
Swedish Democrats, 278
Swedish Migration Board (SMB), 269–72, 274, 277, 280–6
Swedish, 205

T
Taylor, Charles, 136, 138
Teigen, Håvard, 117
Teigen, Mari, 318
temperance movement, 13, 16, 58
Ticktin, Miriam, 233
Tilly, Charles, 14, 112, 113, 118, 127, 131, 137
timber industry, 2, 79, 116–20
Tocqueville, Alexis de, 50, 90
Todd, Emmanuel, vii
Trägårdh, Lars, 7, 12, 13, 94, 97–9, 159, 192, 256, 315–17, 326, 343

U
uenighetsfellesskap (community of disagreement), 205, 206, 214, 218
United Kingdom (UK), 87, 104, 106, 189, 204, 293, 337
United Nations (UN), 92, 250, 314
Convention on the Rights of the Child, 255
Universal Declaration of Human Rights, 272, 339
United States (US), 50, 89, 227, 293, 339
universalism, 11, 19, 28, 30, 92, 113, 124, 125, 128–30, 135, 137, 138, 141, 149–52, 160, 181, 184, 207, 210, 225, 226, 238
urbanization, 273, 276
utanförskap (outsiders), 24

V

væreieren (village owner), vi
Vassenden, Anders, 297, 299
Vedsted, Peter, 196n14
Venezuela, 67
Vike, Halvard, 34, 135, 138, 141, 158, 174–6, 192, 196n12, 204, 207, 209, 236
villages, 159, 168, 174, 176, 177n1, 248, 250, 271, 279, 282, 233
Volkskunde (folklore), 3

W

wage bargaining, 97–8
wage compression, 9
wage equality, 98
Walzer, Michael, 226
Weber, Max, 35, 98, 158, 161, 165, 167
welfare state, vii, 5
  and civil society, 12, 130
  and egalitarianism, 9–12
  and fear of institutionalization, 29–31
  history of, 51–63
  and homogeneity, 28
  and inclusion, 20
  and irregular migration, 223
  and language as means of understanding, 87–8
  and local governments, 13–15
  and migration, 22–5
  and refugees, 269
  and social differences in health, 181–95
  Swedish Model, 275, 339 (*see also* universalism)
  woman-friendly, 18, 29, 38n4
Wergeland, Henrik, 72
Wikan, Unni, 26, 331n11
Wilkinson, Richard, 87, 106
working class, 95–7, 302
World War I, 60, 66, 139
World War II, 99, 135, 304

X

xenophobia, 63, 270, 278

Y

Yuval-Davis, Nira, 25